MUSLIM AND CATHOLIC PILGRIMAGE PRACTICES

Exploring the distinctive nature and role of local pilgrimage traditions among Muslims and Catholics, *Muslim and Catholic Pilgrimage Practices* draws particularly on south central Java, Indonesia. In this area, the hybrid local Muslim pilgrimage culture is shaped by traditional Islam, the Javano-Islamic sultanates, and the Javanese culture with its strong Hindu-Buddhist heritage. This region is also home to a vibrant Catholic community whose identity formation has occurred in a way that involves complex engagements with Islam as well as Javanese culture. In this respect, local pilgrimage tradition presents itself as a rich milieu in which these complex engagements have been taking place between Islam, Catholicism, and Javanese culture.

Employing a comparative theological and phenomenological analysis, this book reveals the deeper religio-cultural and theological import of pilgrimage practice in the identity formation and interaction among Muslims and Catholics in south central Java. In a wider context, it also sheds light on the larger dynamics of the complex encounter between Islam, Christianity, and local cultures.

Ashgate Studies in Pilgrimage

Series Editors:

Simon Coleman, University of Toronto, Canada
Dee Dyas, University of York, UK
John Eade, University of Roehampton, UK and University College London, UK
Jas' Elsner, University of Oxford and University of Chicago

Once relatively neglected, pilgrimage has become an increasingly prominent topic of study over the last few decades. Its study is inevitably inter-disciplinary, and extends across a growing range of scholarly fields, including religion, anthropology, geography, history, literary studies, art history, archaeology, sociology, heritage and tourism studies. This process shows no sign of abating – indeed, it looks set to continue to expand.

This series seeks to place itself at the forefront of these conversations. Covering new work from both established and emerging scholars it encompasses themes as diverse as pilgrimage within national and post-national frames, pilgrimage-writing, materialities of pilgrimage, digi-pilgrimage and secular pilgrimage.

Also in the series

Pilgrimage, Politics and Place-Making in Eastern Europe
Crossing the Borders
Edited by John Eade and Mario Katić

Muslim and Catholic Pilgrimage Practices
Explorations Through Java

ALBERTUS BAGUS LAKSANA
Sanata Dharma University, Indonesia

ASHGATE

© Albertus Bagus Laksana 2014

All rights reserved. No part of this publication may be reproduced, stored in a retrieval system or transmitted in any form or by any means, electronic, mechanical, photocopying, recording or otherwise without the prior permission of the publisher.

Albertus Bagus Laksana has asserted his right under the Copyright, Designs and Patents Act, 1988, to be identified as the author of this work.

Published by
Ashgate Publishing Limited
Wey Court East
Union Road
Farnham
Surrey, GU9 7PT
England

Ashgate Publishing Company
110 Cherry Street
Suite 3-1
Burlington, VT 05401-3818
USA

www.ashgate.com

British Library Cataloguing in Publication Data
A catalogue record for this book is available from the British Library

The Library of Congress has cataloged the printed edition as follows:
Laksana, Albertus Bagus.
  Muslim and Catholic pilgrimage practices : explorations through Java / by Albertus Bagus Laksana.
     pages cm.—(Ashgate studies in pilgrimage)
  Includes bibliographical references and index.
  ISBN 978-1-4094-6396-2 (hardcover)—ISBN 978-1-4094-6397-9 (ebook)—ISBN 978-1-4094-6398-6 (epub) 1. Java (Indonesia)—Religious life and customs. 2. Muslims—Indonesia—Java. 3. Catholics—Indonesia—Java. 4. Islam—Relations—Catholic Church. 5. Catholic Church—Relations—Islam. I. Title.
  BL2120.J3L35 2014
  203'.5095982—dc23

2013042227

ISBN 9781409463962 (hbk)
ISBN 9781409463979 (ebk – PDF)
ISBN 9781409463986 (ebk – ePUB)

Printed in the United Kingdom by Henry Ling Limited,
at the Dorset Press, Dorchester, DT1 1HD

Dedicated to the loving memory of my grandmother, Aloysia Darmasuwita, who first introduced me to the beauty of pilgrimage and accompanies me with her presence during my own pilgrimage journeys.

Contents

List of Maps and Figures	*ix*
Acknowledgments	*xi*
Notes on Spelling, Transliteration, and Sources	*xiii*
List of Abbreviations	*xv*
Introduction: Pilgrimage, Hybridity, and Identity Making	1

PART I   JAVANO-MUSLIM CASE

1	Formation of Javano-Islamic Identity: Saints, Shrines, and Sacred History	23
2	Muslim Self and Hindu-Javanese Other: Spatial, Architectural, and Ritual Symbolisms	51
3	The Richness of Pilgrimage Experience: Devotion, Memory, and Blessings	77

PART II   JAVANO-CATHOLIC CASE

4	Identity as Memory: Sacred Space and the Formation of Javano-Catholic Identity	105
5	The Trace of the Other in the Javano-Catholic Identity	135
6	Immersed in the Web of Blessings and Communion	163

PART III   COMPARATIVE PERSPECTIVE

7	A Double Visiting: Comparative Insights on Muslim and Catholic Pilgrimage Practices in Java	191
	Conclusion: Going Home and Setting Off Again	219

Glossary	*227*
Bibliography	*231*
Index	*245*

List of Maps and Figures

Maps

1	Indonesia and Southeast Asia	*xvi*
2	Java	*xvii*
3	Muslim, Catholic, and other shrines in South Central Java (research area)	*xviii*

Figures

1.1	Pilgrims at the grave of Sunan Pandanarang, Tembayat, 2009	26
1.2	Pilgrims reading the Qurʾān at Gunungpring shrine, Muntilan, 2009	27
1.3	Mawlana Maghribi Shrine, Parangtritis, Yogyakarta, 2009	27
1.4	Popular depiction of Kalijaga (in the center with Javanese head dress) and other *wali*s of Java on a rug sold at shrines	33
4.1	Pilgrims at the Sendangsono Marian Shrine, 2009	110
4.2	The Sacred Heart Shrine at Ganjuran with the Sacred Heart Statue in the Inner Sanctum, 2009	111
4.3	Pilgrims at the grave of Father Sanjaya in the Mausoleum of Muntilan, 2009	112
5.1	Statue of Christ the King and the Sacred Heart in the Hindu-Javanese style, Ganjuran	148
5.2	Statue of Madonna with child in a Hindu-Javanese style, Ganjuran	149

Acknowledgments

The writing of every book is a journey. In many ways, this saying holds even truer in the case of this one. For this book is a study on pilgrimage, a special kind of journey. Like doing a real pilgrimage, the research for and the writing of this book have taken me to various places, near and far. As a pilgrim, I encountered so much help from many generous people—a clear manifestation of God's blessings (Ar. *baraka*)—along this journey. In Boston, my deepest gratitude goes to James Winston Morris, my Ph.D. supervisor, whose presence at Boston College has truly been a gift and blessing to me on many levels. Francis X. Clooney of Harvard University has also been a wonderful mentor in comparative theology over the years. My heartfelt thanks also go to Roberto Goizueta and Catherine Cornille at Boston College.

My language studies, library research, and fieldworks in the Netherlands, Syria, Turkey, and Indonesia (Java, Bali, and Sumatra) in 2007 and 2008–2009 were made possible by funding from the New York Province of the Jesuits and the Comparative Theology Area at Boston College, while the Ernest Fortin Foundation helped me with my summer Arabic studies at Harvard in 2006. I also enjoyed throughout the years of study and research the hospitality of various Jesuit communities in Cambridge, Boston (St. Mary's Hall), Washington D.C., The Hague, Yogyakarta, Damascus, and Los Angeles. The final part of this project took shape during my postdoctoral fellowship at Loyola Marymount University, Los Angeles (2011–12).

Furthermore, the at times formidable challenge of doing this kind of interdisciplinary project has been made so much easier by many librarians and archivists at the following institutions who have responded with such remarkable expertise and generosity to my various requests: Boston College, Harvard University, Cornell University, the Dutch Jesuit Archives in Nijmegen, the KITLV (Royal Netherlands Institute of Southeast Asian and Caribbean Studies) and Leiden University, the IFPO (*Institut français du Proche-Orient*) in Damascus, St. Ignatius College in Yogyakarta, and the Indonesia Province Archives of the Jesuits in Semarang.

I am especially grateful that this project that touches on the theme of saints and friends of God has also been marked by a lot of collaboration and friendships. Here I should mention Tom Michel, James Fredericks, Fr. Gregorius Utomo, Karel Steenbrink, James Spillane, Christian Krokus, Karen Enriquez, Bede Bidlack, Tracy Tiemeier, Julian Millie, Thomas Tjaya, Kuntoro Adi, Casey Beaumier, Sukidi, Dadi Darmadi, Hari Tjahyono, Niko Setiaputra, Elisabet Esti R., Kinda Ahmed, Lyly Lukman, Riesa and Rudi Suparman, Rose and Ling Ho, the Hadinoto family, Sophie Toligi, F. Purnawijayanti, and many others. My colleagues at Sanata Dharma University and Jesuit brothers at Kolese St. Ignatius, Yogyakarta, have been wonderful companions along my journey as well. I also thank Sarah Lloyd, my editor at Ashgate, and two anonymous reviewers for their generous and helpful advice and suggestions.

Finally, my heartfelt gratitude goes to my parents (Agustinus Wahadi and Cecilia Sugihartati) and my whole family for being a constant source of strength and comfort throughout these years. If my years away from them have taught me anything, it is that this bond of love and affection gets even stronger. It is to my grandmother, whose loving memory is ever present to me, that I dedicate this work.

Yogyakarta
ABL

Notes on Spelling, Transliteration, and Sources

In dealing with the variations in Javanese, Indonesian, and Dutch spelling, I decide to maintain the original spelling in the respective sources for words in quotations. For Javanese toponyms and words not in quotations, I use the Indonesianized system especially with regard to the letter "o" (spelling it as "a"), except for certain names that have been widely known in its original Javanese system such as Sendangsono (rather than Sendangsana). Also, with regard to Javanese proper names, I opt for the one that has been more widely used in this scholarship, such as Tembayat (not Bayat), Kalijaga (not Kalijogo), Walisongo (not Walisanga), Yogyakarta (not Jogjakarta), and Soegijapranata (not Sugiyapranata). For Javanese words in general, I employ the simplest transliteration system, doing away with diacritical marks (such as è and é), except for very few cases of proper names.

In cases when Javanese words derived from Arabic are used, I provide the Arabic root to make the semantic field clearer for readers with knowledge of Arabic. The same principle applies to Javanese words derived from the Sanskrit, mostly in the context of Javanese Hinduism and Buddhism.

For Indonesian words not in quotations, I use the most recent spelling rule, that is, the EYD system (*Ejaan Yang Disempurnakan*). For the transliteration of Arabic words I follow the *International Journal of Middle East Studies*. As for the Dutch, I employ the spelling of the original text that in some cases can be different from the present Dutch spelling system.

The names of persons interviewed in this study are pseudonyms, except for the names of well-known figures. However, all names of places, including the places from which these persons come from, are real and true. All translations from Javanese, Indonesian, Dutch, and French sources are mine, unless otherwise noted.

List of Abbreviations

Ar.	Arabic
b.	born
BKI	*Bijdragen tot de Taal-, Land- en Volkenkunde*
D.	Dutch
d.	died
I.	Indonesian
Jv.	Javanese
L.	Latin
r.	reigned
S.	Sanskrit
ST	*Swara-Tama*

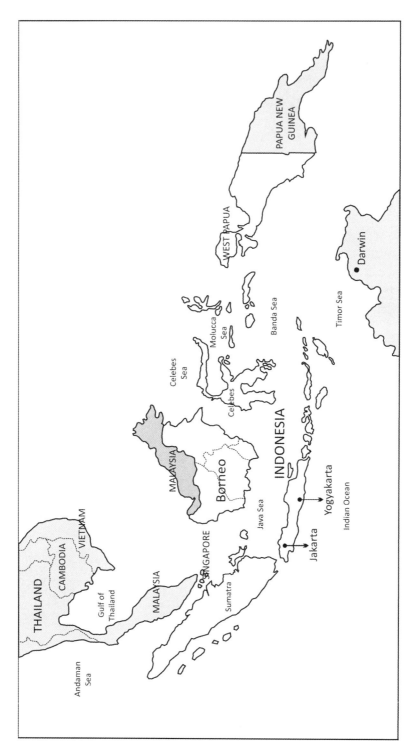

Map 1 Indonesia and Southeast Asia

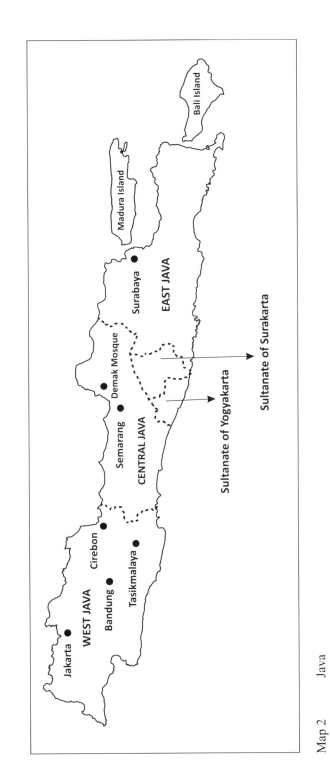

Map 2   Java

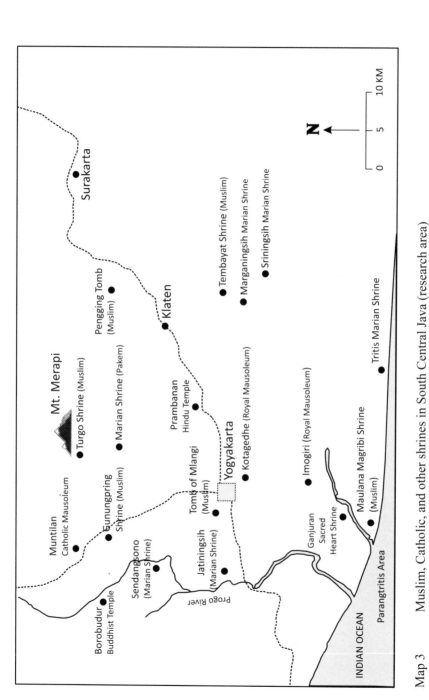

Map 3   Muslim, Catholic, and other shrines in South Central Java (research area)

Introduction
Pilgrimage, Hybridity, and Identity Making

> I'm drawn to the idea that the pilgrimage will help me find my way to God and thus to myself.
>
> Hape Kerkeling[1]

> I roam the lands east and west; to many a wanderer and hermit was I a companion.
> I saw every strange and marvelous wonder, and experienced terror in comfort and misery.
> I have come to be buried alone beneath the earth; I hope that my Lord will be my companion.
>
> ʾAlī ibn Abī Bakr al-Harawī (d. 1215)[2]

Pilgrimage is indeed a very ancient practice. And it continues to be done in countless ways in which the various facets of human life intersect with one another. Pilgrimage is also an extremely rich and complex practice where a deep religious and spiritual search for God and self exists along side the more mundane need for the therapeutic effects of travels and tourism, and where a strictly pious activity for obtaining God's blessings intersects with a complex framework of cultural or ethnic identity formation. A great many Christian and Muslim saints and mystics have been among its most ardent and prominent participants and promoters, such as Ignatius Loyola and Ibn al-ʿArabī. For al-Harawī (d. 1215), an avid Muslim pilgrim whose words I quoted above, pilgrimage was an extremely rich and complex experience that afforded him in sometimes dramatic fashion an intimate understanding of the profound meanings of existence—as he said, "I saw every strange and marvelous wonder, and experienced terror in comfort and misery"—and put him in an intimate relationship with God. It is remarkable that al-Harawī's pilgrimage itineraries included many Christian and Jewish sites, while he counted among his companions a number of Christian monks as well. And, while understanding himself as a "non-religious" person, the German comedian Hape Kerkeling somehow conceived his life-changing pilgrimage along the traditional Christian route to Santiago de Compostella in terms of searching for God and self.

---

[1] Hape Kerkeling, *I'm Off Then* (New York, 2009), p. 4.
[2] Josef W. Meri's introduction to al-Harawī's *A Lonely Wayfarer's Guide to Pilgrimage* (Princeton, 2004), p. xxv.

In contemporary Java, pilgrimage is highly popular across religious boundaries as well, although this book focuses mainly on the Muslim and Catholic contexts.[3] Among Javanese Muslims, pilgrimage has attracted the whole gamut of persons, from monarchs and princes to Sufi mystics and countless ordinary persons seeking the blessings (Ar. *baraka*) of God and His righteous Friends (Ar. *awliyā'*).[4] Hundreds of thousands of pilgrims flock to the famous Nine Saints (Jv. *Wali Songo*) pilgrimage sites in Java annually. Compared to the Muslims, Catholics are newcomers in Java (from late nineteenth and early twentieth centuries), but local pilgrimage culture quickly took deep root among Javanese Catholics during their formative years.

This wider pilgrimage culture in Java has resulted in the proliferation of countless pilgrimage sites. Over time the tradition of pilgrimage also becomes much more complex. Among others, it intersects with the whole process of identity formation for the respective religious communities in interaction with local realities and with one another. In the context of Java, the relationship between pilgrimage and Javanese identity formation is quite crucial. In fact, the famous Javanese text *Serat Centhini* (nineteenth century) imagines the collective identity of "Java" in terms of journeying to all of its sacred and potent places of all kinds, while being attentive to various local customs, natural wonders, and so forth. In this text, this journeying also corresponds to the various stages in the personal growth of the human person. This encyclopedic work on the collective understanding of "Java" thus argues that pilgrimage is crucial both in terms of personal and collective identity formation.

Taking into account the richness and complexity of the pilgrimage tradition mentioned above, this book is a comparative phenomenological and theological discourse focused on Catholic and Muslim traditions of pilgrimage to tombs and shrines (Jv. *ziarah*, Ar. *ziyāra*) in south central Java. My basic argument runs as follows. Both in the Muslim and Christian traditions, pilgrimage is a rich and complex religious practice that has served as a privileged milieu in which pilgrims and their communities attempt to foster diverse kinds of communion with God and His spiritual company of saints and paradigmatic figures, including founders and ancestors of the community. Precisely due to its richness and complexity as a spiritual and religio-cultural practice driven by the deeper dynamics of communion, pilgrimage also becomes a crucial practice in which a distinctive religious identity is forged and negotiated in creative and fruitful ways, among others through the process of engaging various forms of otherness including other religious traditions and cultures, in the context of a long historical continuum that is also marked by tensions and ambiguities.

---

[3] Cf. George Quinn, "Local Pilgrimage in Java and Madura: Why is it booming?" *IIAS Newsletter*, 35 (2004): p. 16; also Mark Woodward, *Java, Indonesia and Islam* (New York, 2010), p. 6 and *passim*.

[4] See Nelly van Dorn-Harder and Kees de Jong, "The Pilgrimage to Tembayat: Tradition and Revival in Indonesian Islam," *The Muslim World*, 91 (2001): pp. 325–54.

Guided by the method of the new comparative theology, I attempt to offer a comparative phenomenological overview of the Javanese Muslim and Catholic pilgrimage traditions in south central Java, focusing on the major ways in which one can make sense of their deeper shared features and intimate encounters, as well as certain particularities (to a lesser degree) that exist between these two pilgrimage traditions. The principal category of communion with God, the self, and the other will serve as a guiding hermeneutic principle for this comparative study.

Case Study of Pilgrimage in South Central Java

As has been mentioned, this book focuses on the particular context of the practices of pilgrimage among the Muslim and Catholic communities in south central Java, Indonesia (Maps 1–3). This area is historically very crucial in the construction of Javanese identity, particularly in terms of its long and distinctive engagement with both the Hindu-Buddhist heritage and later Islamic elements. This area roughly covers the former Javanese principalities (D. *Vorstenlanden*) during the Dutch colonial era, now represented by the sultanates of Yogyakarta and Surakarta that descended from the Javano-Islamic kingdom of Mataram that was founded in the late sixteenth century. In the early history of the Republic of Indonesia (1940s), Yogyakarta and its sultan (Sri Sultan Hamengkubuwono IX) played a significant role. This sultan was a major supporter of the independence movement against the Dutch colonial power and the city served as Indonesia's capital from 1946 to 1949, an extremely crucial time when the country tried to secure its newly declared independence against all odds. Based on this history and its cultural legacy, Yogyakarta was granted a special territory status. In the recent controversy over the special status of Yogyakarta, this historical fact was employed by its supporters as one of the legitimate reasons for the special status of this royal city.

The distinctive cultural identity of Yogyakarta within Indonesia has a long history. During the New Order regime (1966–98), as part of the central government's project to construct a distinctively "Indonesian" identity, Yogyakarta was imagined as a national symbol of unity in diversity, a beacon of the so-called *Pancasila* tourism.[5] On this point, Heidi Dahles writes:

---

[5] The New Order regime under the late President Suharto began with a political upheaval associated with the abortive communist rebellion in 1965. In the realm of national identity formation, this regime's project was to firmly root the Indonesian identity in the principle of unity in plurality in terms of ethnicities, local cultures, religions and so forth, as expressed in the state philosophy of *Pancasila* consisting of five principles: belief in one supreme God, just and civilized humanitarianism, nationalism based on the unity of Indonesia, representative democracy through consensus, and social justice for all. The cultural maxim of the regime was that the Indonesian culture is the sum total of all its ethnic and local cultures. That regime ended in 1998 following political chaos triggered by the worsening of the Southeast Asian economic crisis.

Representing the common history, revolutionary spirit, national pride, and the defeat of the colonial power, Yogyakarta had been designed as an obligatory place to visit for Indonesians to experience both "Indonesianess" and "Javaneseness" and for foreign tourists to be lectured about Indonesian national identity. Therefore it is argued here that Yogyakarta had been created as the centre of "Pancasila tourism." A visit to Yogyakarta, particularly for domestic tourists, bears elements of a national pilgrimage, with an emphasis on cultural continuity.[6]

In general, Yogyakarta and Surakarta's distinctiveness always lies in the realm of culture and cultural imagination, both in the specific context of what comes to be understood as "Javanese" and the more general notion of "Indonesia." Since the colonial era, Yogyakarta and Surakarta have been identified as the repositories of the most authentic and highest of Javanese cultural traditions.[7] With regard to Surakarta, John Pemberton observed: "For many New Order Javanese, it is a city of origins, a siting of the past in place, a privileged locus for much that is recalled as 'Javanese.'"[8] Indeed both the courts of Yogyakarta and Surakarta understand themselves as distinctive religio-cultural entities in many ways, but particularly in the manner in which the Islamic dimension is integrated within a rich religio-cultural framework that incorporates Java's older legacies, such as Javanese Hinduism and indigenous religious systems, manifested among others in the distinctive ritual, art and cultural style of the court (Jv. *kraton*).[9]

For the most part, local residents of Yogyakarta and Surakarta share this view, identifying the sultan's palace in particular as the center of the preservation of the Javanese tradition and culture.[10] The recent controversy on the special status of Yogyakarta within the Republic of Indonesia has only highlighted this strong collective sense of distinctive identity among the people of Yogyakarta. For them, the central government's attempt to "democratize" Yogyakarta by removing the Sultan from his status as the *ex officio* governor of the province without election was an insult to the time-honored distinctive cultural and political identity of Yogyakarta.[11] In response, Yogyakartanese mounted an organized response that finally succeeded in securing the special status of this region in 2012.

This distinctively hybrid self-understanding, however, begs the question of hegemony, particularly with regard to the nature and exact role of Islam in it. There is a certain sentiment among Indonesian Muslims that the Islamic contribution to

---

[6] Dahles, *Tourism, Heritage and National Culture in Java* (New York, 2001), p. 220.
[7] Suzanne Brenner, *The Domestication of Desire* (Princeton, 1998), pp. 24–9, 60.
[8] John Pemberton, *On the Subject of "Java"* (Ithaca, 1994), p. 25.
[9] Hamengkubuwono X, *Kraton Jogja* (Yogyakarta, 2002), p. 25. On the Surakarta court, see Pakubuwana XII, *Karaton Surakarta* (Singapore, 2006).
[10] Timothy Daniels, *Islamic Spectrum in Java* (Aldershot, 2009), p. 19.
[11] Mark Woodward, "Resisting Wahhabi Colonialism in Yogyakarta," *COMPS Journal: Analysis, Commentary and News from the World of Strategic Communications* (2008): pp. 1–8; see also his *Java, Indonesia and Islam*, pp. 2–3.

this local identity is either truly lacking or not deservedly recognized. Nurcholish Madjid (d. 2005), one of the most influential Muslim scholars that Indonesia has ever had, compared the role of Islam in Indonesia and India this way: "In the Hindu India, Islam has a glorious past (showing its deep cultural influence), while in the Muslim Indonesia, Islam only has a future (since it did not influence the local culture in the past)."[12]

This sentiment should be understood within the background of a cultural vision that took the Majapahit kingdom (1294–1478) and the Hindu and Buddhist cultures as the real backbone of Java and Indonesia's glorious past. In this regard, the New Order did not really initiate the glorification of the Hindu-Javanese culture and polity in the make-up of modern Indonesian statehood and national identity. This tendency had been firmly in place since the colonial era among the earliest generation of Dutch orientalist scholars who fell in love, personally and professionally, with the cultural legacy of pre-Islamic classical Java.[13] Many Dutch Jesuit missionaries who worked in south central Java, including Father Franciscus van Lith (1863–1926), adopted this colonial view. To a large extent, the view that Islam was an "other" and that there was a significant degree of incompatibility between the Hindu-Javanese legacy and Islamic tradition was indeed part of the colonial orientalist mode of scholarship of this period.

In light of this background, I will show that Islam has actually played an important role in the religio-cultural shaping of the local Muslim communities in Indonesia, more particularly in Java. An authentic vision of Islam is preserved and expressed in the pilgrimage tradition in south central Java, in a highly creative and complex religio-cultural framework that includes genuine appropriation of the older Hindu-Javanese religio-cultural legacy as well.[14] In this regard, this book explores the role of Javanese culture as a complex positive force that has been deeply influenced by Islam and other religio-cultural traditions. Certainly, the Javanese culture in its complexity has served as a common bond among diverse religious groups in south central Java.

What is also distinctive about south central Java is that this role has become stronger and more pervasive due to the support of the courts of Yogyakarta and Surakarta as the contemporary heirs to the legacy of the Javano-Islamic kingdom of Mataram. It is in this religio-cultural setting that a rich and diverse tradition of pilgrimage flourishes today. All the major Muslim shrines in this area are officially under the patronage of either one of these courts, or both. In recent years, the unifying role of Javanese culture and its specific relation to the pilgrimage traditions has become more apparent in many forms and levels. On the popular

---

[12] Nurcholish Madjid, *Islam Doktrin and Peradaban* (Jakarta, 1992), p. lxvii.

[13] Pemberton, *On the Subject of "Java"* and Nancy Florida, "Reading the Unread in Traditional Javanese Literature," *Indonesia*, 44 (1987): pp. 1–15; also her *Javanese Literature*, vol. 1 (Ithaca, 1993), p. 11ff.

[14] M.C. Ricklefs, *Mystic Synthesis in Java* (Norwalk, 2006); also his *Polarizing Javanese Society* (Honolulu, 2007). See also Mark Woodward, *Islam in Java* (Tucson, 1989).

level, this revival of Javanese culture is observable in the retrieval of various communal rituals and festivals among many local communities in this area. In various ways this book will showcase the prevalence of certain elements of this court culture, both among Muslims and Catholics.

Within the larger context of Java or Indonesia, south central Java is quite unique due to the significant presence of Catholic Christianity and its distinctive dynamics of encounters with the Javanese culture and Islam. The presence of Catholics in this area dates back to the earliest period of the Catholic mission under the Dutch Jesuit missionaries in the late nineteenth and early twentieth centuries.

Before dealing with the particular significance of south central Java in the history of the Dutch Jesuit mission in Java, a general overview of the Protestant and Catholic missions in what is now the Indonesian archipelago is in order. Historically the Catholic presence among native Indonesians dates back to the Francis Xavier era in the sixteenth century, with the formation of small Catholic communities in the Moluccas. In the period after Francis Xavier, Portuguese missionaries also worked in other outer islands of Indonesia. However, with the arrival of Dutch colonialism in the early seventeenth century, the progress of Catholic missions in the Moluccas was practically halted, while in the outer islands that were still under the Portuguese it continued to grow until the second half of the eighteenth century. The island of Flores, where Catholicism still constitutes the majority religion now, remained under Portuguese rule until 1859. In general Protestant missions began in a very modest way, mostly in the outer islands of the archipelago, starting circa the seventeenth century. Since the second half of the eighteenth century, however, Protestant missions were becoming more intensive in many parts of Indonesia, with the exception of Java, with the active role of various missionary societies, while Catholics were being discriminated against during most of this period, both in the Netherlands and the Indies. This discrimination was lifted only in 1808, allowing some Jesuit priests to work for the European Catholics in the Indies. However, the Jesuit mission among native Javanese only started in 1859.[15]

It is in the context of the early Jesuit mission in Java that the small town of Muntilan, located some twenty miles to the north of Yogyakarta (Map 3), played a crucial role. It was the center of the Catholic mission in Java for the first two or three decades of the twentieth century, largely due to the pioneering work of Father Franciscus van Lith (1863–1926), a remarkable figure whose memory and legacy have become an important pillar in the identity formation of Javanese Catholics, as I will show later. Based on the foundation laid by Father van Lith, the Catholic mission in south central Java can be considered a success, especially compared to other areas in Java. As a result, south central Java still has the largest percentage of Catholics in the whole of Java. Catholicism has a visible public presence in this area. This college town houses two major Catholic universities as well as numerous higher education institutions and schools that draw thousands of

---

[15] See Aritonang and Steenbrink (eds), *A History of Christianity in Indonesia* (Leiden 2008).

students from all over the country. The area is also dotted with numerous Catholic hospitals, orphanages, convents and seminaries, as well as historic churches and shrines. The Christian presence in this area becomes even more remarkable if one takes into account the local Protestant churches with their vast networks of educational institutions, health care systems, and so on. In general, both Catholic and Protestant missions have had an amicable relationship with the sultans since the beginning; at times during the colonial period this relationship was considered too cozy by certain elements in the Muslim population.[16]

In short, south central Java presents itself as a fascinating region marked by rich and distinctive religio-cultural dynamics among four elements: the presence of Islam, the centrality of the Javanese culture (with various elements from earlier local Hinduism, Buddhism, and indigenous religious beliefs and practices), the crucial role of the sultanates, and the significant presence of Christianity and Catholicism. In this area almost all the Islamic shrines and the indigenous Javanist ones are historically and spiritually connected in one way or another to either or both of the sultanates. On the Catholic side, this area houses the most foundational and important Catholic shrines in Java. Furthermore, in this area these Muslim and Catholic shrines share spatial and cultural proximity to one another, thus forming a more intense and concentrated milieu of devotion. Even within the wider context of Java, this area has the rare concentration of diverse important shrines and holy sites, not only Muslim and Catholic, but also Hindu, Buddhist, and Javanist.[17]

Given the fact that this area has so many Muslim and Catholic pilgrimage sites (Map 3) and for the sake of focus and clarity, the backbone of this book will be primarily based on three shrines of each tradition. On the Islamic side, these sites include the shrines of Tembayat, Gunungpring, and Mawlana Maghribi. A major shrine with some hundred thousand pilgrims per year, the shrine of Tembayat houses the tomb of Sunan Pandanarang, the famous disciple of Sunan Kalijaga (late fifteenth and early sixteenth century) who is one of the most important early saints of Islam in Java (Jv. *Wali Songo*) and the one who is considered to be the patron and paradigmatic embodiment of a Javano-Islamic identity. The second site, the shrine of Gunungpring, is located in the outskirts of the town of Muntilan. Attracting up to 250,000 pilgrims per year, this site houses the tomb of Raden Santri (ca. late sixteenth and early seventeenth century), a Javanese Muslim saint who was also a rather important royal ancestor of the Sultanate of Yogyakarta; it also houses the tombs of local Muslim saints from the more recent times, such as Mbah Dalhar (d. 1959) and his son, Gus Jogorekso.

The shrine of Mawlana Maghribi, the third Muslim shrine under study, contains a tomb believed to be the grave of Mawlana Maghribi. In the Javanese

---

[16] Cf. Alwi Shihab, *The Muhammadiyah Movement and Its Controversy with Christian Mission in Indonesia* (Ph.D. Dissertation, Temple University, 1995), p. 252.

[17] Important ancient Hindu and Buddhist sites in this area include the Hindu temple of Prambanan and the Buddhist temple of Borobudur; while many popular Javanist sites are found in the Parangtritis, Mount Merapi, and Mount Merbabu areas. See Map 3.

folklore, Mawlana Maghribi (ca. fifteenth century) is related to Najmuddin al-Kubra, a rather well-known Sufi mystic who is considered to be the ancestor of the founders of Islam in Java.[18] This shrine is located on a hilltop on the southern coast of Yogyakarta (Parangtritis), which according to local Javanist beliefs, is a sacred and potent place due to the presence of the goddess of the Southern Sea, a pre-Islamic mythical figure whose romantic alliance with Panembahan Senapati (r. 1582–1601), the founder of the Mataram dynasty, is traditionally considered a crucial support for the legitimacy and spiritual power of the Javano-Islamic sultanates of Yogyakarta and Surakarta.[19]

On the Catholic side, the three shrines include the Sendangsono Marian grotto, the Sacred Heart shrine at Ganjuran, and the Mausoleum of Muntilan. Modeled on the famous shrine at Lourdes, the Sendangsono grotto is perhaps the most important as well as the oldest Marian shrine in Indonesia. Its foundation in 1929 commemorated the birth of the indigenous Catholic community in Java. For it was on this very site that in 1904 the first large group of the Javanese people (173 persons) received their baptisms into the faith through the hands of the Jesuit Father Franciscus van Lith. The second site, the Sacred Heart Shrine at Ganjuran, is considered to be the sister shrine of the Sendangsono grotto. Founded in 1930 by a pious Dutch Catholic family, the Schmutzers, this shrine has from the very beginning been known to be a model for an inculturation of the Catholic faith in Javanese culture due to the predominant employment of local Hindu-Buddhist symbolisms and architectures. In recent years this shrine has attracted a significant number of non-Catholic (mainly Muslim) pilgrims. The third Catholic site, the Mausoleum of Muntilan, is an historic mausoleum that houses the tombs of some of the most prominent figures in the history of the Catholic church in Java, such as Father van Lith, the founder of the local Catholic community, and Father Sanjaya, the community's "first martyr." Located in the town of Muntilan (Map 3), it shares a geographical proximity with the world famous Borobudur temple, as well as the Muslim pilgrimage site of Gunungpring.

The use of the term "Javanese" in this book needs an explanation since not all the pilgrims and members of the local communities, both Muslim and Catholic, belong to the ethnic Javanese. It is largely in relation to the cultural and geographical location (not primarily the ethnic identities) of the shrines, their pilgrims, and their communities that I understand the term "Javanese" in both the Muslim and Catholic contexts, although it is still true that the overwhelming majority of the Muslim and Catholic pilgrims to these shrines are ethnically Javanese. However, it has to be noted that a significant number of the Catholic pilgrims are of Chinese descent, while the presence of non-Javanese Muslim

---

[18] Martin van Bruinessen, "Najmuddin al-Kubra, Jumadil Kubra and Jamaluddin al-Akbar: Traces of Kubrawiyya influence in early Indonesian Islam," *BKI*, 150 (1994): pp. 305–29.

[19] H.J. de Graaf, *Awal Kebangkitan Mataram* (Jakarta, 1985), p. 74ff; Ricklefs, "Dipanagara's Early Inspirational Experience," *BKI*, 130 (1974): pp. 227–58.

pilgrims, especially in the Tembayat and Gunungpring shrines, is also remarkable. In most cases, interestingly, these Chinese Catholics embrace features of Javanese culture as well, due to their upbringing. Perhaps more importantly, Javanese culture is overwhelmingly preserved in these shrines in many different ways such as in the forms of the rituals, architectures, festivals, and so on. And this has become their distinctive feature that is generally appreciated by pilgrims from all ethnic backgrounds. In this book, then, the terms "Javano-Islamic" and "Javano-Catholic" identities correspond to this hybrid religio-cultural framework that is shared around these shrines by the local communities and by pilgrims across ethnic backgrounds. These shrines have developed a pan-Indonesian character as well. Many pilgrims and shrines officials formulate this character in terms of the inclusive principles of *Pancasila*, the official and foundational principles of the Republic of Indonesia that, among others, includes the respect for all religions.

Pilgrimage and Saint Veneration in Christianity and Islam

Even to casual observers, the contemporary popularity of the tradition of making pilgrimage to local shrines and sacred tombs among Catholics and Muslims is self-evident. However this now widespread practice has a quite dramatic and contentious history in both traditions. On the Christian side, it is true that the metaphor of pilgrimage has been a favorite collective image for the Church since the earliest time—namely, the Church and the Christians as pilgrims on earth on the journey to God.[20] However, when it comes to the question of real pilgrimage to sacred places, the picture is quite complex. For the propriety of the practice of pilgrimage was hotly debated in early Christianity. The Christian debate on the propriety of pilgrimage in late antiquity revolved around the tension between local sites of pilgrimage on the one hand and Jerusalem on the other; as well as around the dilemma of earthly sacred journeying to encounter God versus interior journeying through an inner and spiritual space.[21] Among others, the main concern also touched on the theological question of a divine presence in a defined spatial locus over against the scriptural idea of "Jerusalem on high" (Galatians 4: 26) and "worshiping God as spirit, spiritually" (John 4: 24).[22]

In general, fruitful tensions were preserved between the spiritual and spatial frameworks of understanding God's presence. It was quite apparent that pilgrimage, either to Jerusalem or to local shrines, did not only quite quickly become a religious practice with some valid theological grounds in the first centuries of Christianity,

---

[20] Cf. 1 Peter 1:1; 2:11 and Hebrews 11:13 and St. Augustine's *De Civitate Dei*.

[21] Bitton-Ashkelony, *Encountering the Sacred* (Berkeley, 2005), p. 4; Craig Bartholomew and Fred Hughes (eds), *Explorations in a Christian Theology of Pilgrimage* (Aldershot, 2004); John Inge, *A Christian Theology of Place* (Aldershot, 2003).

[22] Andrew T. Lincoln, "Pilgrimage and the New Testament," and Steve Motyer, "Paul and Pilgrimage," in Bartholomew and Hughes, *Explorations*, pp. 29–49, 50–69.

but it also became highly popular. In this regard, it is crucial to note the role of the complex and particular developments of the respective Christian communities at this time.[23] Also significant here was the fact that this debate had a lot to do with the specificities of the formation of these Christians' religious identity.[24] For this formation of identity was not only based on the data of the New Testament, but also took into account the evolving self-understanding of the Christian community itself as it progressed further in history. By the fourth century, for example, this self-understanding had incorporated the image of Jerusalem as their holy city.[25] Thus, by this time the question was no longer primarily about the sanctity or sacredness of a place *per se*, but rather about the historical significance of this particular place for the community of faith. In this framework, the significance of place is deeply communal and relational. There was an intimate nexus between place, community, and faith. The flowering of the cults around the shrines of the martyrs in early Christian communities should also be understood in this larger framework.[26] By extension and through the eyes of faith, Christian pilgrims also came to see the role of living saints as a crucial part of this dynamic of God's presence in the development of the community of faith.[27] Theologically speaking, the concrete history of the community itself is a locus of the work of the Spirit of God. Thus, the commemorative shrines built on these sites reveal the community's desire to connect with its sacred past. They are memory of God's work for the community. This is precisely the kind of approach that many Christian theologians and authors advocate today.[28] Another important aspect in the historical development of Christian pilgrimage is its personal and spiritual character. In response to the excessive emphasis on the externals of the pilgrimage practice in medieval Christianity—rightly pointed out by Protestant reformers—the personal and spiritual character of pilgrimage came to be emphasized.[29]

This general development of Christian pilgrimage with its major elements has spread widely, and it continues to exist in many parts of the world today.

---

[23] This bigger picture (that includes some element of power struggle and tensions) is necessary to understand, for example, the complex views of Gregory of Nyssa (d. ca. 395) on pilgrimage. For while rejecting the values of pilgrimage to Jerusalem (probably due to his experience with the local church there during his visit), Gregory was an avid proponent of local cult of martyrs in his own diocese of Cappadocia. Bitton-Ashkelony, *Encountering the Sacred*, p. 48ff.

[24] Bitton-Ashkelony, *Encountering the Sacred*, p. 5.

[25] Peter Walker, "Pilgrimage in the Early Church," in Bartholomew and Hughes, *Explorations*, p. 79.

[26] Cf. Peter Brown, *The Cult of Saints* (Chicago, 1981).

[27] Georgia Frank, *Memory of the Eyes* (Berkeley, 2000).

[28] Cf. Philip Sheldrake, *Spaces for the Sacred* (London, 2001); Inge, *A Christian Theology of Place*; also David Brown, *God and Enchantment of Place* (Oxford, 2006).

[29] Cf. Vatican II document on the nature of the Church, *Lumen Gentium* # 50, 67 and *passim*.

Pilgrimage tradition and saint veneration become a crucial part in the formation of Christian identity *vis-à-vis* diverse (local) realities that Christian communities came into contact with in Latin America, South Asia, and so forth.[30]

This book takes seriously the twofold aspect of pilgrimage—as an earthly journey that involves an interior journey—since this is actually what makes pilgrimage so rich as an integral religious practice. Echoing the Protestant concern, it will be shown the deeply personal and spiritual (self-purifying) character of these Javanese pilgrimages. In this regard, it has to be stated that overt polemics on pilgrimage among Christians in Java or Indonesia today is almost non-existent. On the contrary, some Indonesian Protestants become active participants in this tradition.[31]

In the larger Islamic context, any discussion on pilgrimages to shrines and tombs (Ar. *ziyāra*), as distinguished from the canonical pilgrimage to Mecca (the *hajj*), cannot avoid the more heated debate, both past and present, on the propriety of this piety. In this respect, it has become customary among modern scholars to illustrate this debate by examining the critical views of Ibn Taimiyya (d. 1328), a Hanbali jurist of Damascus, on certain aspects of the *ziyāra* tradition or saint veneration in Islam. However, some qualifications need to be made here. First, Ibn Taimiyya's views on the theme represented the minority during his time. Secondly, he did not attack the *ziyāra* tradition wholesale either. He supported what he called the "licit *ziyāra*" (Ar. *al-ziyāra al-shar'iyya*). In this framework, he considered licit the practices of greeting the dead, of making supplications to God on behalf of the dead—but only in the context of a visit that is not specifically meant for offering these supplications for the dead—as well as of making oneself more aware of death or the transitory nature of life. He even permitted visits to the cemeteries of non-Muslims, as far as the Muslim pilgrims did not pray for them.[32] In this regard, it might also be noted that Ibn Taimiyya himself was a member of the Qādirīya Ṣūfī order.[33]

Insofar as his attack on certain aspects of the *ziyāra* tradition is concerned, Ibn Taimiyya's main argument is that many features of his contemporary *ziyāra* tradition were dangerous "innovations." And they were practices not specifically sanctioned by the Qur'ān, the *sunna* and the practice of the *salaf* (the first three

---

[30] In the Latin American context, the case of Our Lady of Guadalupe is very interesting, especially with regard to the question of encounters of Christianity with native identity. On this, see Virgilio Elizondo, *Guadalupe* (Maryknoll, 1997). On the question of encounters of Christian saint veneration with Hinduism and Indian local realities, see Corrine Dempsey, *Kerala Christian Sainthood* (Oxford, 2001); also Margaret Meibohm, *Cultural Complexity in South India* (Ph.D. Dissertation, University of Pennsylvania, 2004).

[31] Beyond Java, the overwhelming presence of Protestant pilgrims in the Marian shrine of Annai Velankani in Medan, North Sumatra, is rather striking.

[32] Christopher Taylor, *In the Vicinity of the Righteous* (Leiden, 1999), p. 188.

[33] George Makdisi, "Ibn Taimīya: A Ṣūfī of the Qādiriya Order," *American Journal of Arabic Studies*, 1 (1973): pp. 118–29.

generations of Islam), and they smacked of polytheism (Ar. *shirk*), and thus go against the principle of the oneness of God (Ar. *tawḥīd*). What made this worse for Ibn Taimiyya was that these practices supposedly bore the influence of other religious groups he detested, such as the Shi'ite Muslims and the Christians.[34]

His basic doctrinal objection was on the propriety of intentionally going to offer prayers or supplications (Ar. *du ʿā'*) in specific places, such as tombs, that are not sanctioned by the earlier tradition, believing that God will be inclined more to these prayers. In this regard, it has to be noted, Ibn Taimiyya recognized that certain *ḥadīth*s hold that certain places are more sacred than others—such as Masjid al-ḥaram in Mecca, Masjid al-Nabawi in Medina, Masjid al-Aqṣā in Jerusalem, the Ka'ba, and other sites in the Hajj pilgrimage—and that certain times are more propitious than others for prayers, such as the entire second half of each night.[35] Again, he did not object *in toto* to the idea of *ziyāra* as visiting a sacred place. His concern in this regard revolved around the suspicion that this desire for traveling to a specific place to offer prayers of supplications smacked of *shirk*. For him, it was a desire for an intermediary between God and the humans.

Over the centuries, many prominent Muslim scholars have of course responded to Ibn Taimiyya. As Christopher Taylor has noted, Taqī al-Dīn al-Subkī (d. 1355), a chief jurist of Damascus, offered perhaps the most detailed and comprehensive responses. In his refutations, al-Subkī identified three "judicial errors" of Ibn Taimiyya. First, Ibn Taimiyya incorrectly interpreted the *ḥadīth*—that says "Do not undertake travel except to three mosques"—to mean banning *ziyāra* altogether, whereas this *ḥadīth* meant that Muslims should not embark on travel to any mosques in order to venerate them, other than the three specifically mentioned. Thus, this *ḥadīth* did not prohibit *ziyāra* to tombs of saints and families out of respect, devotion, and the desire to pray for them. Ibn Taimiyya's second judicial error was nullifying the whole tradition of *ziyāra* based on a few limited examples of excess or improper elements of this otherwise praiseworthy tradition. From al-Subkī's perspective, Ibn Taimiyya's third judicial error was his notion that the *ziyāra* was a form of forbidden innovation, a view that was not supported by the views of any religious scholars or examples from the Prophetic period.[36] In other words, rejecting Ibn Taimiyya's objections, al-Subkī considered *ziyāra* as a lawful and praiseworthy religious practice of *qurbā*—a good deed or pious work that brings to a closer communion with God.[37] Within the category of lawful *ziyāra*, al-Subkī made a strong case for the propriety of doing *ziyāra* for the purpose of being blessed by simply being in the proximity of the righteous dead.[38]

---

[34] Muhammad Umar Memon, *Ibn Taimiya's Struggle Against Popular Religion* (The Hague, 1973), p. 5.
[35] Taylor, *In the Vicinity of the Righteous*, p. 174.
[36] Ibid., pp. 201–8.
[37] Ibid., p. 201.
[38] Ibid., p. 205.

This debate also clarifies some fine points about pilgrimage that are quite important for the subject of this book. For example, Ibn Qayyim al-Jawziyya (1292–1328), himself a staunch critic of certain aspects of the *ziyāra* tradition, reiterated the valid reasons for *ziyāra* according to the *sunna*—i.e., to remember the hereafter, to perform a good deed for the person buried in the grave, and to perform a good deed for the pilgrim himself—and he emphasized that with regard to the remembrance of the dead, connection and communion with the dead would be severed without regular visits, and that the dead would enjoy the visits because they have been separated from family and friends.[39] So, for Ibn Qayyim, one of the underlying spirits of the *ziyāra* was to preserve the existing bonds of friendship and communion, a highly important part of the piety of many Javanese Muslim pilgrims that this book discusses. Along the same line, Ibn ʿUthmān (d. 1218) stressed the necessity of having inner sincerity or pure intentions on the part of the pilgrims, a condition that pilgrims today also strive to achieve, as this book will show.[40]

In this respect, it has to be stated that the debate on *ziyāra* has become so technical and intricate. Since I do not have the space to go deeper into this debate here, it suffices to state that generally speaking Muslim scholars, jurists, mystics, and rulers down to our time have found legal and other grounds within the Islamic tradition itself to defend the validity of the practice.[41] So, in response to this debate and in light of the approach of this book, two observations are in order. First, one needs to approach the *ziyāra* tradition as a complex and integral practice with many layers of meanings and significance. This is the approach I take in this book, which integrates the pilgrims' deep spiritual experience of loving devotion and blessings, both personal and communal, and discusses the creative socio-religious negotiation connected with these practices. To a large degree, the *ziyāra* tradition has become an important aspect of the religious and spiritual formation of many Muslims, including those in Java today. In light of the depth, richness, and complexity of the practice, Ibn Taimiyya's obsession with just one particular doctrinal aspect of the practice—i.e., the legitimacy of intentionally embarking on a journey to offer prayers in a specific place not sanctioned in the Qurʾān and *sunna*—seems to be extremely narrow, and it overshadows or simply ignores other salient aspects of this rich tradition, as al-Subkī rightly pointed out. It is in the

---

[39] Ibid., p. 189.

[40] Ibid., p. 71. Due to the relative purity of the heart during pilgrimage, Ibn ʿUthmān justifies the need for prayers during pilgrimage.

[41] In many pilgrimage guides in the medieval period, for example, Muslim scholars offered a more balanced view of the activities involved in the *ziyāra* as an integral religious practice. These guides also contained particular reasons for certain practices in pilgrimage, such as the need to pray for the dead, a practice that has precedence in the *sunna* of the Prophet. In some cases, these authors were critical of certain questionable practices such as wailing in the cemetery, while allowing for weeping. They argued that the latter had a basis in the *sunna* as well. See Taylor, *In the Vicinity of the Righteous*, p. 70ff.

wider context of this complexity and organic evolution of the practice that one should place the rather dubious aspects of it.[42]

Secondly, one also needs to be attentive to the larger question of the historical development of Islam, including its ongoing and complex interactions with diverse realities such as other cultures and religious traditions in very different local contexts. As some scholars have noted, there are some grounds to believe that interactions with the earlier Eastern Christian tradition of pilgrimage was part of the early development of the practice in Islam.[43] On this point, Muhammad Memon writes of the limitation of Ibn Taimiyya's vision:

> His failure lay in denying any validity to the historical evolution of Islam which had, away from its rigid orthodoxy, taken place in a series of brisk interactions with the traditions and faiths of diverse peoples, and in trying to comprehend the unconscious depths, the irrational side of human mind, through a medium of perception fit essentially for rational thought.[44]

Memon's point on the historical evolution of Islam is especially crucial. In the framework of Islamic theological hermeneutic, the new and local aspects of this *ziyāra* tradition might be understood as "praiseworthy innovation" (Ar. *bid'a al-ḥasana*), which can be explained in terms of the larger and deeper inspirations and aims of the wider tradition of Islam. As al-Suyūti (d. 1505) argued, Muslim festivals were indeed innovation, but a praiseworthy one (Ar. *bid'a al-ḥasana*).[45] As will be shown in many places in this book, Muslim communities in Java have also been attempting to frame the discussion on the various aspects of *ziyāra* tradition, especially those that seem to be coming from outside of the historically preceding Islamic tradition—i.e. local Javanese religio-cultural traditions—within a larger framework of Islam as a comprehensive and inclusive religious tradition with its dynamism toward becoming a blessing for the whole universe (Ar. *raḥmatan lil-'ālamin*). Within the theological framework of the traditionalist Nahdlatul Ulama (the NU) in Java, Achmad Shiddiq (d. 1991), one of its founding fathers, offered a useful hermeneutic based on the principles of tolerance (Ar. *tasāmuḥ*) and moderation (Ar. *tawassuṭ*) that include both the notions of equity or harmony (Ar. *i'tidāl*) and balance (Ar. *tawāzun*). From Shiddiq's perspective, these principles ultimately form a vision of Islam that embraces all manners of good

---

[42] Ibid., p. 79.
[43] Irfan Shahid, "Arab Christian Pilgrimages in the Proto-Byzantine Period (V–VII Centuries)," in David Frankfurter (ed.), *Pilgrimage and Holy Space in Late Antique Egypt* (Leiden, 1998), pp. 373–92; Taylor, *In the Vicinity of the Righteous*, p. 4; von Grunebaum, *Muhammadan Festivals* (London, 1976), pp. 73, 76–81.
[44] Memon, *Ibn Taimiya's Struggle*, p. 6.
[45] von Grunebaum, *Muhammadan Festivals*, p. 76.

things that are found outside of the commonly understood boundaries of Islam, such as the richness of local cultures.[46]

In the context of Java, it also has to be noted that the *ziyāra* tradition until recently has been one of the most important markers of oppositional identity between the traditional and modernist Muslims. In contemporary Java, however, the situation has been changed rather considerably, although not completely. Opposition to the tradition of *ziyāra* from the modernist Muslims can still be found today, although much less polemical in tone. It seems that the most ferocious criticisms come from the much smaller Wahhabi-oriented circles.[47] On the other hand, some traditionalist Muslim scholars and leaders have recently written books and booklets to explain, without adopting polemical frameworks, the nature and legitimacy of the *ziyāra* tradition and its local features.[48]

As far as the pilgrims themselves are concerned, the picture is quite interesting. Of course, the staunch Wahhabi-oriented Muslims take no active part in this tradition. It might be surprising that there are many local Muslim pilgrims today who claim to have stronger religio-cultural identification with the modernist Muhammadiyah than with the traditionalist NU. This phenomenon is reflected as well in the recent discourse within the Muhammadiyah's leadership toward more nuanced and realistic views on the dynamics between Islam and local culture.[49] During fieldwork, I encountered many pilgrims who dismissed this kind of question—"Do you identify yourself with the NU or the Muhammadiyah?"—as largely unimportant. In this regard, it seems that the *ziyāra* tradition has become a deeply personal practice that is shared by many Muslims from diverse affiliations and backgrounds. Even some pilgrims who are deeply into the tradition of *ziyāra* would not necessarily feel the need to identify themselves as belonging to the traditionalist NU.

I have argued that the *ziyāra* tradition has to be treated as a complex, integral, and evolving tradition within Islam. In connection to this, one pivotal aspect of this tradition is the notion of sainthood (Ar. *walāya*). Sainthood is one of the most important theological frameworks of *ziyāra* that requires us to be attentive to its Qurʾānic foundation, as well as to the richness and complexity of its development as a doctrine and practice. For example, the notion of sainthood will help us understand al-Subkī's point about the legality of doing *ziyāra* for the purpose of

---

[46] See Martin van Bruinessen, "Traditions for the Future: The Reconstruction of Traditionalist Discourse within NU," in Greg Barton and Greg Fealy (eds), *Nahdlatul Ulama, Traditional Islam and Modernity in Indonesia* (Clayton, 1996), pp. 163–89.

[47] Cf. the various works of Hartono Ahmad Jaiz, a polemical author who is affiliated with the Salafi-oriented Dewan Dakwah Islamiyah Indonesia (DDII), such as *Tarekat, Tasawuf, Tahlilan Mawlidan* (Solo, 2006); *Mendudukkan Tasawuf* (Jakarta, 1999).

[48] Cf. Madchan Anies, *Tahlil dan Kenduri* (Yogyakarta, 2009); Munawir Abdul Fattah, *Tradisi Orang-Orang NU* (Yogyakarta, 2006).

[49] Abdul Munir Mulkhan, *Islam Murni dalam Masyarakat Petani* (Yogyakarta, 2000); M. Thoyibi et al., *Sinergi Agama dan Budaya Lokal* (Surakarta, 2003).

being blessed by being in the proximity of the saints without being engaged in polytheism or *shirk*.

Although the doctrinal aspect of sainthood might be important to answer Ibn Taimiyya's concerns, it is crucial to take into account the fact that in the larger framework of pilgrimage as an ongoing religious practice, the pilgrims' relationships with God and with the saints (Ar. *awliyā'*) often become inseparable: loving God and His Prophet means fostering a loving devotion and respect for His Friends as well. This feature is ultimately related to the Islamic spiritual cosmology in which the messengers, prophets and *walī*s participate in God's universal protectorship and authority, that is, God as the Protector of all, *al-Walī*. In this Muslim understanding of sainthood, this participatory nature of the saints' authority, which is popularly understood particularly in terms of their power to perform miraculous deeds (Ar. *karāmāt*) or to become intercessors, is the result of their proximity and friendship with God. In fact, proximity, friendship, and authority are at the heart of the Muslim understanding of sainthood. The two fundamental aspects of Islamic sainthood, namely proximity (friendship) and authority, are derived from the verbal root W-L-Y (*waliya*) in Arabic.[50] Thus, a Muslim *walī* is someone who is first of all especially proximate to God, and only then is he given a certain kind of authority from God, the Protector of all.[51] In terms of authority, there is also the sense here that a *walī* is somebody whose affair is taken care of by God.[52]

The paradigmatic role of Muslim saints has also been further justified and explained in terms of the *ḥadīth* literature that further specifies the qualities of God's *awliyā'*. One particular *ḥadīth qudsī* (divine saying) understands the basic qualities of the *awliyā'* in terms of poverty (freedom from earthly possessions), pleasure in prayer, intimate yet "secret" devotion and service to God, and so forth. This particular *ḥadīth* seems to emphasize both the inner qualities as well as the concealment of the true *awliyā'*.[53] The famous "*ḥadīth* of envy" (Ar. *ḥadīth al-ghibtah*) identifies the *awliyā'* of God as God's servants who are neither prophets nor martyrs, but who are envied by the prophets and martyrs for their special position and intimate nearness to God.[54] According to this *ḥadīth*, these saints will be blessed with the thrones of light and their faces will be of light when they see God face to face. This *ḥadīth* seems to be extraordinary in its description of the

[50] Michel Chodkiewicz, *The Seal of the Saints* (Cambridge, 1993), p. 22.

[51] The term "*walī*" is also one of God's names, thus being a *walī* is one aspect of God's being (Qur'ān 2:257, 4:45, 7:196, 42:9, 28, 45:19). See Toshihiko Izutsu, *Sufism and Taoism* (Berkeley, 1983), p. 263.

[52] Chodkiewicz, *The Seal of the Saints*, p. 24.

[53] This *ḥadīth* is included, with minor variations, in the canonical collections of al-Tirmidhī, Ibn Majā, and Ibn Ḥanbal; quoted in James W. Morris, "Situating Islamic 'Mysticism': Between Written Traditions and Popular Spirituality," in R. Herrera (ed.), *Mystics of the Book* (New York, 1993), p. 293.

[54] Chodkiewicz, *The Seal of the Saints*, p. 25.

graces that would be bestowed on the highest saints: they will participate more fully in the *walāya* of God by partaking more intimately in God's glory as light.

All these features of Islamic sainthood have given rise to the highly complex and multifaceted personal, socio-communal and cosmic roles of Muslim saints or *walī*s. Muslim saints have an initiatic or guiding function as well as cosmic role, while they also may become founders and pious ancestors of local communities. Again, the theological ground for all these roles is their special participation in God's own *walāya*. Thus, the saints are not acting on their own.

Recent Studies of Pilgrimage and the Approach of this Book

Due to its universality across religious traditions and cultures, as well as its contemporary rise in popularity, pilgrimage has been taken up as a subject of study in various academic disciplines, such as history, anthropology, sociology, cultural studies, religious studies, as well as theology. On the side of Christian and Islamic traditions, pilgrimage studies tend to be focused on certain regions or historical periods.[55] In this respect, some fine studies have dealt with the question of religious identity and touched on the inclusive nature of shared shrines or on the interaction between pilgrims of different faith traditions.[56] Of course studies of this kind should serve as a reminder that the case of south central Java is not totally unique in terms of the beneficial encounters between Muslims, Christians, and other peoples of different faith traditions in the framework of pilgrimage practice. This book is a modest endeavor to the challenge of doing a full-fledged and focused comparative study of different pilgrimage practices that have been existing in the proximity of each other over a long historical continuum.

---

[55] On the Islamic side, see for example, Taylor, *In the Vicinity of the Righteous*; Josef W. Meri, *The Cult of Saints among Muslims and Jews in Medieval Syria* (Oxford, 2002); Vincent J. Cornell, *Realm of the Saint* (Austin, 1998). Henri Chambert-Loir and Claude Guillot's work, *Le culte des saints dans le monde musulman* (Paris, 1995) is the only work that covers all the principal regions of the Islamic world. On the Christian side, there is no single work with such a global coverage. What we have is regional or historical in nature, such as various works by Diana Webb: *Pilgrims and Pilgrimage in the Medieval West* (London, 1999); *Medieval European Pilgrimage, C. 700–1500* (Oxford, 2000).

[56] Cf. Alexandra Cuffel, "From Practice to Polemic: shared saints and festivals as 'women's religion' in the medieval Mediterranean," *The Bulletin of the School of Oriental and African Studies*, 68 (2005): pp. 401–19; Dionigi Albera, "Pelerinages mixtes et sanctuaries 'ambigus' en Méditerranée," in Sylvia Chiffoleau and Anna Madoeuf (eds), *Les pèlerinages au Maghreb et au Moyen-Orient: espaces publics, espaces du public* (Damas: Institut français du Proche-Orient, 2005), 347–78; H.T. Norris, *Popular Sufism in Eastern Europe* (New York, 2006); Issachar Ben Ami, *Saint Veneration among the Jews in Morocco* (Detroit, 1998).

While following the methodological assumptions of the new comparative theology proposed by Francis Clooney, James Fredericks, and others—such as the importance of doing comparison on a focused, limited aspect of two religious traditions with a view to acquiring theological insights for the enrichment of the comparativist's understanding of his or her home tradition—this book is rather different in terms of its material, since it focuses on a religious practice rather than a religious text.[57] Furthermore, this practice is located in a very particular socio-religious context in which certain dynamics of comparative engagement among religious communities have already happened. Here the concerns that I attempt to address quite obviously fall under the new directions that Clooney observes in younger comparativists: "doctrinal theology remains important, but lived religion and cultural exchange is more central to their work than to mine."[58]

To a certain degree, this book is also an attempt to join the contemporary discourse on the question of identity formation that is becoming more of a problem in the global world of today. One of the reasons why this comparative study takes the case of Java is that the Indonesian society at large has been struggling precisely to understand the relationship between forging a robust identity and taking into account the presence of the other.[59] In this regard, this book offers a theologico-phenomenological analysis of pilgrimage as a privileged—in the sense of rich, authentic, integral, and long lasting—milieu of religio-cultural identity formation. In south central Java, the creativity, authenticity and sustainability of the hybrid religio-cultural identities forged in the pilgrimage practices become especially significant today given the context of "struggle for the soul of Islam" in this area between centuries-old Javano-Islamic tradition and a smaller recent strand of militantly exclusivist Wahhabism.[60]

Organization of the Book

This book is divided into three parts. The first two parts deal with the distinctive pilgrimage practices among Javanese Muslims (Part I) and Javanese Catholics (Part II) in south central Java. These two parts set forth the necessary data and contexts for the comparative theological analysis in Part III.

---

[57] Clooney's major works are textual comparisons, thus privileging the act of comparative reading. Clooney states that this is his preferred method, while also acknowledging that other avenues (based on practice, symbols, images, etc.) are valid as well. See his *Comparative Theology* (Chichester, 2010), p. 58; also James Fredericks, *Buddhists and Christians* (Maryknoll, 2004), pp. ix–xiii, 112–15.

[58] Clooney, *Comparative Theology*, p. 52.

[59] Cf. John Sidel, *Riots Pogroms Jihad* (Ithaca, 2006); Chris Wilson, *Ethno-religious violence in Indonesia* (New York, 2008).

[60] Woodward, "Resisting Wahhabi Colonialism in Yogyakarta," pp. 1–8.

The basic structure of Parts I and II revolves around how the overarching idea of communion with God and His company of saints in pilgrimage, which includes the central identity questions of self and other, is manifested in three major realms: namely, (1) the history of each shrine and its saint; (2) the spatial, ritual, artistic, and architectural features of the shrines; and (3) the experience of the pilgrims and their local communities.

Within Part I, Chapter 1 addresses the understanding and practice of sacred history among Javanese Muslims, focusing on the notion of history as communion and continuity with the past that includes paradigmatic figures and saints. This is the notion of history as a sacred past to be kept alive in the present. This sacred history is not a fixed narrative and legacy of the past, since what is more important is the communal task of continual remaking of connection with it, which includes the presence of the other (the pre-Islamic legacy). It is chiefly through the act of making pilgrimages to the shrines of the paradigmatic figures of the past that Javanese Muslims in south central Java act out this notion of history as memory. In this dynamic, the figures of local saints represent living memories of the embodiments of the Javano-Islamic identity formation. Based on this notion of sacred history, this chapter also explores the historical particularities of the three Muslim shrines and their saints.

As Chapter 2 will show, this general pattern of hybrid identity formation is manifested in many tangible fashions in the ways the shrines and the local Javano-Muslim communities deal with the traces of the earlier other in rituals, arts, and architectures. Again this hybridity is considered to be one of the most enduring and distinctive legacies of the local Javanese Muslim saints such as Sunan Kalijaga, Sunan Pandanarang, and others, whose role as "religio-cultural brokers" ensured the Islamic authenticity of this complex synthesis. This chapter will examine some of the particularities and creative dimensions of this religio-cultural synthesis.

Chapter 3 deals with the experiential world of the Javanese Muslim pilgrims, that is, the many ways in which pilgrims enter into an experience of intimate communion with and devotion to God and His Friends, thus obtaining diverse forms of blessing, while also forming a deeper contact with their own selves as well as other pilgrims from different backgrounds. Special attention will be given to the distinctive intersections between Javanese culture and the wider Islamic tradition, as manifested in the various ways in which pilgrims actually experience different aspects of the pilgrimage.

Part II shares the basic structure of Part I. Chapter 4 discusses the historical formation of a Javano-Catholic hybrid identity by exploring the ways in which the Javanese Catholic pilgrims and their community have understood history as a foundational and sacred past, a past that still has an overwhelming authority over the present and invites deeper reconnection and re-interpretation. Paradigmatic in this past are the founders and founding events of the community, represented and commemorated in the three Catholic shrines and the pilgrimage traditions to them.

As occurs in the Javano-Islamic context, pilgrimage practice among Javanese Catholics has also served as a milieu where their hybrid identity is negotiated in all its complexities and ambiguities by engaging different forms of otherness, especially the Hindu past and the largely Muslim present. So, Chapter 5 will discuss the principal ways in which this complex hermeneutics of identity is operative in the spatial, architectural, and ritual dimensions of the shrines under study.

Following this line of thought, Chapter 6 is an endeavor to delve deeper into the dynamics of pilgrimage practice in the three Catholic shrines under study, as experienced by pilgrims themselves in the context of their shared Javanese religious and cultural sensibilities. This chapter seeks to show how the whole idea of hybrid identity formation and the overarching desire for communion is concretely experienced and negotiated by pilgrims and their communities. Thus it also shows why and how pilgrimage culture, with all its complexities and richness, continues to be a spiritually and religiously rewarding practice, and how it continues to have a religio-cultural significance as a supportive milieu for forging a deeper, inclusive, and lasting identity.

In Part III (Chapter 7), I delve into an explicitly comparative analysis of the data presented in Parts I and II, employing the method of the new comparative theology. The main objective of this chapter is to identify what I consider the most significant similarities and a few observable differences found in the two pilgrimage traditions. These key similarities include: (1) the role of saints and paradigmatic figures as ancestors; (2) the nature of pilgrimage as moment for spiritual renewal; and (3) the deeply sacramental worldview that lies at the heart of these pilgrimage traditions. These insights suggest a major theological argument of this book on the widening dynamic of communion with God that is at stake in the two pilgrimage traditions, a dynamic that in many different ways has been strengthened by and expressed through Javanese culture, a common religio-cultural bond between the two. This comparison is already "theological" precisely because it shows how the underlying sacramental dynamic of fostering an ever deeper and wider communion with God—itself a reality with serious theological import—is deeply shared by Islamic and Catholic pilgrimage traditions as they are practiced in south central Java.

PART I
Javano-Muslim Case

Chapter 1
Formation of Javano-Islamic Identity: Saints, Shrines, and Sacred History

> Remember well, all who are created,
> do not seek permanence in this world,
> as if you were in your dwelling place.
> *Carita Iskandar* (1729)[1]

As the nineteenth-century Javanese text, *Serat Centhini*, narrates, Raden Jayengresmi was a devout and young Muslim prince from the Giri Kingdom, near the present day city of Surabaya.[2] He was the son of the monarch Sunan Giri Parapen.[3] In the wake of the attack of his father's palace by the kingdom of Mataram (1636), Raden Jayengresmi decided to embark on a long period of pilgrimage and wandering throughout Java, while trying to come to terms with his own self after the crisis. During the pilgrimage, this prince dutifully practiced Muslim piety such as reciting the Qurʾān by heart and doing the canonical prayers (Ar. *ṣalāt*) and other supererogatory prayers such as the remembrance of God (Ar. *dhikr*), meditation (Ar. *murāqaba*), intimate conversations with God (Ar. *munājāt*), and the supererogatory night prayers (Ar. *tahajjud*). And he never failed to offer heartfelt personal prayers (Ar. *duʿāʾ*) for his parents and siblings. His visit to the Grand Mosque of Java (the Demak Mosque) was so memorable. Inside this mosque, he was carried over by a profound sense of peace and devotion,

---

[1] Canto XI. *Carita Iskandar* (1729) is a Javanese rendition of the tale of Iskandar dhuʾl-Qarnain (Alexander the Great) and was composed partly as a commemoration of the pilgrimage of Sultan Agung to the shrine of Tembayat in 1633. See Ricklefs, *The Seen and Unseen Worlds in Java* (St Leonards and Honolulu, 1998), pp. 39–53.

[2] The provenance of the *Serat Centhini* goes back to the nineteenth-century Surakarta court. However, the story itself narrated events that occurred in the seventeenth century (1636), namely, the sack of the Giri kingdom in East Java by the Mataram army from south central Java. See Marcel Bonneff, "Centhini, servante du javanisme," *Archipel*, 56 (1998): pp. 483–511. My account of Jayengresmi's journey is based on the condensed translation of the *Centhini* text by Soewito Santoso, *The Centhini Story* (Singapore, 2006).

[3] Jayengresmi's father, Sunan Giri Prapen, should not be confused with his grandfather, the monarch-saint, Sunan Giri I, who was also a prominent saint in the legendary Nine-Saints tradition in Java. Cf. de Graaf and Pigeaud, *De Eerste Moslimse Vorstendommen op Java* (Leiden, 1974), chapter 11.

and saw a miraculous sign from God.[4] Among the Islamic sites that he visited were the tombs of Java's prominent Muslim saints. Very interestingly, however, this pious Muslim prince also visited the ruins of the Hindu Majapahit kingdom and other Hindu kingdoms. At one point he even spent a night in the compound of the Panataran Hindu temple.[5] As a Javanese, he felt profoundly connected to these kingdoms. During this visit he was so taken by a sense of the loss of the grandeur of Java's past while trying to deal with his own uncertain future.[6] However, very often he found profound peace while staying at Hindu hermitages: "the serenity of the place seemed to penetrate into his heart, calming his emotions and driving away all weariness and worry."[7] This prince also tried to pay pious visit to the graves of his distant Javanese ancestors.[8] In this regard, the *Serat Centhini* always envisions this prince's long pilgrimage journey also in terms of forging connection with his ancestors not only by visiting their graves but also by getting in touch with their religio-cultural legacy that had made up the identity of Java.

More than anything else, the particularities of Jayengresmi's pilgrimage reflected the worldview of the Javanese Muslim community in south central Java that was involved in the creation of the work in the nineteenth century. For the figure of Jayengresmi was not a historical figure, but rather a religio-cultural model of a Javano-Muslim identity. His style of pilgrimage—marked by a heartfelt sense of communion with the past events and figures of Java, understood in the most inclusive fashion—was primarily imagined as the kind of pilgrimage that was particularly fitting to a Javanese Muslim sensibility. In the context of the *Serat Centhini*, the inclusivity of this pilgrimage was intimately connected to what the idea of "Java" consisted of and what it meant to be a Javanese Muslim. For the *Serat Centhini*, this religio-cultural hybrid identity was understood in relation to a set of concrete realities: a particular geography with all its natural wonders, a deeply plural society with distinctive religio-cultural customs and lore, a civilization that was extremely proud of its glorious past, and so forth. Hence, pilgrimage was imagined as a way of fostering a deeper connection with this spatial and religio-cultural reality of "Java."

To a large degree, as Part I of this book will show, many crucial dimensions of Prince Jayengresmi's wandering pilgrimage still ring true for many Javanese Muslim pilgrims in south central Java today, particularly the role of pilgrimage as a process of finding one's true self in relation to the wider religio-cultural identity

---

[4] *The Centhini Story*, p. 53.

[5] This Hindu temple is the place where Brawijaya V (d. 1478), the last king of the Hindu Majapahit kingdom, used to pray before converting to Islam. The *Centhini* text describes the atmosphere of the temple as very mystical and sublime. *The Centhini Story*, p. 40.

[6] Ibid., p. 41.

[7] Ibid., p. 55. During his stay at the hermitage, Raden Jayengresmi also learned spiritual wisdom and other forms of knowledge from the Hindu hermits.

[8] Ibid., p. 48.

formation, the practice of pilgrimage as a memory of history and devotion to saint-founders and revered ancestors, as well as the practice of pilgrimage as an intense ascetic or purifying moment.

Focusing on the three Islamic shrines in south central Java as well as taking insights from some others in the area (Map 3), this particular chapter seeks to flesh out the dynamics of multilayered communion in pilgrimage by analyzing the particular understanding of history as a collective memory of, connection with, and participation in the reality of saints and their shrines, marked by its emphasis on the inclusive yet selective continuity between the Muslim tradition and Hindu-Javanese religio-cultural framework.

Since in the Introduction I have presented the identities of the three shrines under study and they will be dealt in detail later in this chapter, it will suffice here to just reiterate the most pertinent information with regard to the shrines' status and geographical location. The first site is the shrine of Tembayat in Klaten regency, midway between Yogyakarta and Surakarta. A major pilgrimage destination with half a million pilgrims per year from all over Java and beyond, the shrine of Tembayat houses the tomb of Sunan Pandanarang. This site has become part of the typical itinerary of the popular *Wali Songo* pilgrimage tradition that draws a large number of pilgrims from outside of Java as well as Malaysia and Singapore. Intimately connected to Sunan Kalijaga, the beacon of Javano-Islamic identity, and to the court of Mataram, this shrine and its pilgrimage tradition are marked by a prominent presence of local Javanese culture (Figure 1.1).

The second site is the shrine of Gunungpring in the vicinity of Muntilan, some twenty-five kilometers to the north of Yogyakarta and a few kilometers away from the Borobudur temple (Map 3). This shrine also shares a geographical proximity to two major Catholic shrines in the area, namely, the Mausoleum of Muntilan and the Marian shrine of Sendangsono. Attracting up to 250,000 pilgrims per annum, this shrine houses the tomb of Raden Santri—considered an ancestor of the Sultanate of Yogyakarta—as well as the graves of Muslim saints from the more recent times. The combination of visits to the Tembayat and Gunungpring shrines is rather common, especially among pilgrims who come in big groups (Figure 1.2).

The third site is the tomb of Mawlana Maghribi, an Arab saint and early missionary who also came to be considered as an ancestor to the royal dynasty of Yogyakarta (Figure 1.3). An old and rather important pilgrimage site in the mythically charged area of Parangtritis on the south coast of Yogyakarta, it draws a continuous stream of pilgrims—perhaps well over 10,000 per year—from all over Java, some of whom stay for a longer period of time as itinerant ascetic pilgrims.[9]

In this chapter I will begin the discourse with history, that is, how the underlying principle of communion is played out in the particularities of understanding and practice of sacred history in south central Java, especially in relation to the

---

[9] The Catholic Sacred Heart shrine at Ganjuran is located a few miles away from Parangtritis (Map 3). As will be shown later, this location is meaningful for the identity and mission of this Catholic shrine in the context of Javanese society and culture.

Figure 1.1   Pilgrims at the grave of Sunan Pandanarang, Tembayat, 2009

tradition of pilgrimage. More specifically, I will explore the notion of history as a constant remaking of communion and continuity with the sacred past, through paradigmatic figures (founders and saints) of the local community, potent sites, and sacred writings. Since this sacred past is also rife with the presence of the Hindu-Javanese other, this kind of history is thus practiced in south central Java as a reaffirmation of a complex Javano-Islamic identity.

Sacred History as Communion and Continuity

Located in the region of south central Java (Map 3), all of the three Islamic shrines under study are intimately connected with the very notion of Javanese history and religio-cultural identity. This is so because this area is historically very crucial in the construction of Javanese identity in engagement with both the Hindu-Buddhist heritage and Islamic element. It covers the region of the former Javano-Islamic kingdom of Mataram (founded in the second half of the sixteenth century) currently represented by the major royal houses of Yogyakarta and Surakarta. As will be made clear later in this book, all these three shrines are intimately connected

Figure 1.2　　Pilgrims reading the Qurʾān at Gunungpring shrine, Muntilan, 2009

Figure 1.3　　Mawlana Maghribi Shrine, Parangtritis, Yogyakarta, 2009

in various ways to the two royal houses of Yogyakarta and Surakarta as the contemporary successors of Mataram. Especially during, and under the influence of, the colonial era, these two courts have come to be identified as the pivots of "Javaneseness" and its most refined religio-cultural achievement (Jv. *adiluhung*). This designation of Yogyakarta and Surakarta as the center of Javanese culture was historically conditioned by colonial discourse on what constituted "Javanese culture," a discourse that involved an othering of Islam.[10]

For Javanese pilgrims, this particular spatial and historical location and a web of connections that comes with it are considered highly crucial for the religio-cultural identity and role of these shrines. In what follows, I will delineate some major elements that contribute to the identity formation of these shrines in terms of their connectedness to the whole history of the realm or the community of south central Javanese people. I will begin with the notion of history in Javanese thinking in general before moving more specifically to how this notion affects the identity and role of the shrines for the self-understanding of the pilgrims themselves.

Among Javanese pilgrims, history is generally understood more as a collective memory that defines their identity, rather than factual and objective events of the distant past. The past is always conceived in terms of sacred events and paradigmatic figures. And history is practiced as a longing for connection and communion with the sacred past that continues to have profound implications for the present as well as the future direction of the community. So there is an obvious search for some sort of contemporaneity of this past with the present, where the vividness of these events can once more be relished. In this framework, the acts of writing and reading history constitute a sacred activity capable of eliciting supernatural blessing, precisely because history connects the readers and writers with the power of the Invisible.[11] By extension, pilgrimage to potent historical sites is an act of making connection to a sacred history through its traces. The connection between pilgrimage and history in Javanese worldview is also illustrated by the fact that both share the same semantic field when pilgrimage is called "*sujarah*," while history is called "*sejarah*." Both words are derived from the same Arabic root of *shajara* that means "to happen" or "to break out," thus, signifying history as events. The derived noun of this verbal root is *shajara*, which means "tree," thus signifying genealogical connections.[12]

---

[10] See Pemberton, *On the Subject of "Java,"* and Nancy Florida, *"*Reading the Unread in Traditional Javanese Literature," *Indonesia*, 44 (1987): pp. 1–15; also her *Javanese Literature*, vol. 1, p. 11ff. The Javanese pilgrims themselves consider "Javaneseness" to be more pronounced, though not necessarily in its most refined manifestations, in the shrines of south central Java, compared to those of other parts of Java. My interviews with pilgrims from East Java as well as my observation with the religious etiquette of visitation (Ar. *adab al-ziyāra*) in East Javanese shrines confirm this impression.

[11] Cf. Ricklefs, *The Seen and Unseen*; and Nancy Florida, *Writing the Past, Inscribing the Future* (Durham, 1995).

[12] Hans Wehr, *Arabic-English Dictionary* (fourth edition; 1994), p. 532.

In this framework of understanding and practice, the past is sacred because it is the moment of foundation, the beginning of the community, corresponding to what Mircea Eliade calls "the Great Time" (L. *in illo tempore*).[13] Again, what is represented by the idea of history is not a factual account of the past, but rather the sacred moment of founding itself as well and the memory of the founders or ancestors.[14] In this respect, connection to the past becomes more crucial to the self-understanding of the community; for it is the moment of founding and the role of founders that laid out the foundation of the identity of the community. This is why the Javanese call their historical accounts "*babad*," a Javanese word that originally means clearing the forest for new settlement, the beginning of a community. Thus, writing history as *babad* is an attempt to foster a connection with that founding moment and the paradigmatic founders of the community. So, in the Javanese culture where communication and communion with the dead and ancestors is essential for the identity and continuation of the community, history is practiced as memorialization, both at personal and communal levels.[15]

That is why historical knowledge alone is never of prime significance in Java. What is more important is the deeper connection and participation.[16] The *Babad*s, the written accounts of Javanese sacred history, as well as other writings, are called *pusaka pinustaka*, namely, a sacred heirloom in the form of a book. For they have "power" due to their connection to sacred moments and figures of the community, and thus invite deeper connection than just reading.[17] In addition

---

[13] Cf. Mircea Eliade, *The Myth of the Eternal Return: Cosmos and History* (first edition 1949; Princeton, 2005).

[14] Hence the crucial role assigned to "genealogies" in the *Babad* literature, that is, a Javanese traditional historical writings in poetic song. The inclusivity of this Javanese genealogy is obvious in the hybrid list of Javanese ancestors in *Babad Tanah Jawi*, as a result of the incorporation of Islamic sacred history (the Prophet Adam etc.) into the existing Hindu-Javanese one. Thus Adam is viewed as the ancestor of *Sangyang Tunggal*, a Javanese deity. See E. Wieringa, "An Old Text Brought to Life Again: A Reconsideration of the 'Final Version' of the *Babad Tanah Jawi*," *BKI*, 155 (1999): p. 250; R. Kevin Jaques, "Sajarah Leluhur: Hindu Cosmology and the Construction of Javanese Muslim Genealogical Authority," *Journal of Islamic Studies*, 17:2 (2006): pp. 129–57.

[15] Cf. Henri Chambert-Loir and Anthony Reid (eds), *The Potent Dead* (Honolulu, 2002).

[16] Florida, "Reading the Unread," p. 4.

[17] "*Pusaka pinustaka*" is also the appellation given by the author(s) of *Babad Tanah Jawi* to the work. In Javanese parlance, an heirloom is also called "*wasiyat*" (Ar. *waṣīya*, bequest), thus stressing its relationship with the dead ancestors (Wieringa, "An Old Text," p. 249). Other historical, religious and mystical manuscripts from Javanese courts are also considered sacred and potent such as *Surya Raja*, *Carita Iskandar*, *Carita Yusuf* (The Story of Joseph) and *Kitab Usulbiyah* (a Javanese rendition of the Arabic Tale of the Prophets, *Qiṣaṣ al-anbiyā'*). In some critical moments of the realm, some of these texts were reproduced to restore order of the realm. See Ricklefs, *The Seen and Unseen*, pp. 28–105; *Mystic Synthesis*, p. 179.

to the nature of the content, the creative process of writing sacred history also involves a certain degree of "sainthood" in the sense of supernatural inspiration and discipline, giving rise to the notion of Javanese poets as saints with prophetic pen.[18] So, it is natural that the tombs of the most accomplished court literary figures (Jv. *pujangga*) quickly become sites for mass pilgrimage.

Thus the *Babad*s keep alive the memory of a community, not primarily by being read widely but by being "participated in" through rituals, pilgrimage, festivals, and so forth. It is in this framework of history as memory of and communion with the sacred past that I discuss the "historicity" of the shrines under study.

Sainthood, Kingship, and the Formation of Javano-Islamic Identity

Javanese historical identity in its south central Javanese conception revolves around two earlier poles. The first locus is Majapahit (1294–1478), the greatest and last Hindu-Javanese kingdom in East Java, whose religio-cultural achievement came to be imagined as the most refined representation of the Javanese classical civilization. This modern recasting of Majapahit also formed the backbone of the politics of culture in the context of the construction of a pan-Indonesian national identity of the New Order Indonesia under President Suharto (1966–98). In this cultural imagination of national identity, Majapahit signifies a founding moment of national unity long before the colonial era.[19] The second locus of identity in south central Java is the kingdom of Mataram, a polity considered the true Javano-Islamic successor to Majapahit, the one that truly succeeds in reconciling the Islamic and Javanese elements into a "mystic synthesis" of Islam in Java. After the split of Mataram in 1755, the royal houses of Yogyakarta and Surakarta are the major representatives of this religio-cultural legacy of Mataram. Here, in talking about "mystic synthesis," I follow the coinage of the term by Merle Ricklefs, a foremost historian of Java. This term obviously avoids the pejoratively inadequate term "syncretism." As Ricklefs points out, this synthesis is anchored in the acceptance of Islam as primary identity in a way that also incorporates older Javanese spiritual forces. Of course, some tension and ambiguity are inherent in such a complex and ongoing synthesis. In general, the mystical Islam at the Javanese courts has accommodated and domesticated much of Java's pre-Islamic high culture. In this framework, the classical texts of Java such as *Dewa Ruci*, *Arjunawiwaha*, *Ramayana*, and others are considered deeply Islamic, while the tutelary goddess of the Southern Sea is often depicted as behaving in the framework of Islam, such as ordering the Javanese to recite the Qur'ān and to pray to God in the battle against the Western infidels.[20]

Furthermore, in the framework of Javanese discourse of history in general as well as in the context of the Islamic shrines under consideration here, the complex historical dynamic of relationship between these two pillars or poles is

---

[18] Florida, *"Reading the Unread,"* p. 5.
[19] Cf. Michael Wood, *Official History in Modern Indonesia* (Leiden, 2005).
[20] Cf. *Serat Surya Raja*; Ricklefs, *Mystic Synthesis*, p. 162; *Seen and Unseen*, p. 220.

represented by two major figures: (1) King Brawijaya V, the last monarch of the Hindu Majapahit; and (2) Sunan Kalijaga, without doubt the most revered and influential Muslim saint (Jv. *wali*, Ar. *walī*) in south central Java and the spiritual protector of Mataram's early founders.

What these political entities and paradigmatic figures represent is actually a complex and long negotiation of what came to be a widespread cultural synthesis between Javaneseness and Islam, or the formation of the hybrid Javano-Islamic identity. In this regard, the figures of Brawijaya V and Sunan Kalijaga symbolically ensure the continuity and authenticity of Javano-Islamic identity, as opposed to any fissure or disruptive break between the old and the new. While Mataram rightfully claims to be able to trace its genealogical lineage to the Hindu Majapahit, its Islamic identity is secured by the crucial role of Sunan Kalijaga as its spiritual protector.[21] This is so because King Brawijaya could not be imagined as having a direct involvement in the founding of Mataram *qua* Javano-Islamic polity. The Muslim identity of this last Hindu-Javanese monarch is a matter of contention in Javanese discourse, since the nature of his conversion to Islam was not without ambiguities, as I will discuss later. Thus, while Brawijaya V was a remarkable figure in this chain of continuity of sacred power in Javanese successions of royal dynasties,[22] Kalijaga is the personification of this dynamics of continuity due to his identity as a truly Javanese figure belonging to the circle of Majapahit court and a prominent Muslim saint at the same time. This twofold identity surely explains why his ubiquity and role in Javanese sacred history is perhaps without parallel. The text *Babad Tanah Jawi* records Kalijaga's legendary role, while his memory is preserved in the Javanese sacred geography through countless sacred places (Jv. *petilasan*) associated with him throughout Java, Bali, and Lombok.

Sunan Kalijaga: Interplay of Javanese and Islamic Themes

Given the importance of his role, one must examine more closely the identity formation of Kalijaga as a Javanese Muslim saint *par excellence*, especially the nature of his sainthood as the Javanese tradition conceives of it, including the

---

[21] Here, the role of Kalijaga as the spiritual protector of Mataram should also be placed within the larger Islamic conception of sainthood (Ar. *walāya/wilāya*), namely, the notions of proximity (friendship) and authority (protectorship; guardianship). In this understanding, Muslim saints can become protectors to kings and their kingdoms as in the case of Kalijaga and Mataram. The spiritual authority of the saint that comes from his closeness to God is needed for the kings to turn their kingdom into a truly a blessed realm. Cf. Chodkiewicz, *Seal of the Saints*; also Gerald T. Elmore, *Islamic Sainthood in the Fullness of Time* (Leiden, 1999).

[22] This is in relation to the notion that royal court and its king are the center of power in the Javanese cosmology. The king is often described as the embodiment of the ideal of Javano-Islamic mystical anthropology. See Ricklefs, *Mystic Synthesis*, pp. 47–8; Milner, "Islam and the Muslim State," in M. Hooker (ed.), *Islam in South-East Asia* (Leiden, 1983), pp. 23–49.

interplay between the Islamic and Hindu-Javanese elements in it. I argue that the interplay of these two dimensions is very helpful in understanding the nature of his role in the larger formation of Javano-Islamic identity in south central Java where the tradition of Javano-Muslim pilgrimage flourishes and in which Kalijaga is still often evoked as a paradigmatic model (Figure 1.4).

Born into a prominent Javanese family that was connected to the court of Majapahit, Kalijaga's Islamic genealogical credential came from the fact that his uncle was Raden Rahmat, a prominent early Muslim saint who married Kalijaga's aunt.[23] Kalijaga may have learned Islam at home, but his transformation to a Muslim *walī* was probably the most spectacular and legendary in Java. Under the tutelage of Sunan Bonang, another prominent member of the legendary Nine Saints of Java, he underwent a dramatic spiritual awakening, coming to be in touch with the Real. Not only did he abandon his former roles as a privileged member of an aristocratic family and then as a Robin Hood-like wayside robber, but he embarked on the cultivation of his new self by going through an extreme ascetic practice of long meditation on the bank of a river. In some versions, his meditation is believed to have taken some years, so much so that by the time his teacher returned to him, vegetation had grown around his body. The film *Sunan Kalijaga* (1984) seems to emphasize the dramatic conflicts of this future saint with his wealthy family as well as his Buddha-like journey to enlightenment and compassion for the poor. In comparing Kalijaga to his Moroccan counterpart, Clifford Geertz argues that Kalijaga had become a Muslim "through an inner change of heart brought on by the same sort of yoga-like psychic discipline that was the core religious act of the Indic tradition from which he came; his redemption, if that is what it should be called, was a self-produced inner state, a willed mood."[24]

As Geertz notes, the affinity between this mode of conversion and its yogic counterpart is rather obvious. But, in my view, Kalijaga's ascetic practices could also be thoroughly understood within traditional Sufi contexts of conversion.[25] In this regard, what is more important is that this type of Sufi conversion presents Kalijaga as a truly Javanese *walī*, a religious virtuoso whose ascetic purification of self (Jv. *laku*) led him to the deepest core of the mystical knowledge of Islam (Ar. *ma'rifa*).

---

[23] According to the text *Babad Dipanagara*, Rahmat's aunt, in turn, was one of the wives of Brawijaya V, making him the nephew of this last monarch of Majapahit. This genealogy also connects Kalijaga to many other members of the *Wali Songo* ("Nine Saints"), such as Sunan Bonang, Sunan Kudus, Sunan Drajat, and Sunan Giri. See James J. Fox, "Ziarah Visits to the Tombs of the *Wali*, Founders of Islam on Java," in Ricklefs (ed.), *Islam in the Indonesian Social Context* (Victoria, 1991), p. 32.

[24] Geertz, *Islam Observed* (Chicago, 1968), p. 27. In this work Geertz seems to assume that Kalijaga did not know Islam at all before his conversion.

[25] Kalijaga's sudden transformation was reminiscent of that of Fudayl ibn 'Iyād. See John Renard, *Friends of God* (Berkeley, 2008), p. 48.

Figure 1.4 Popular depiction of Kalijaga (in the center with Javanese head dress) and other *wali*s of Java on a rug sold at shrines

The nature of Kalijaga's mystical initiation into the spiritual world of Islam is considered pivotal to the specificity of his sainthood and future role in Islamic Java. Under the name of "Sèh Malaya," Kalijaga was said to have been further initiated to Islam by none other than al-Khaḍir—thus putting him in the special company of the disciples of al-Khaḍir, most notably Moses, Ibn al-ʿArabī, ʿAbd al-Qādir al-Jīlānī, and others.[26] There is no shrine associated with al-Khaḍir in Muslim Java, but his role as the teacher *par excellence* of the highest level of Islamic mystical knowledge is secured in various Javanese texts.[27] In Javanese folklore Kalijaga's image as the only *walī* who is closely associated with al-Khaḍir helps secure the truly Islamic nature of his initiation to the spiritual world of Islam, as well as his elevated status among other *awliyā*ʿ in Java.

[26] Originally, the name Sèh Malaya is probably assigned to Kalijaga in the Chinese version of his story. See Hasanu Simon, *Misteri Syekh Siti Jenar* (Yogyakarta, 2008), p. 283.

[27] In Java, al-Khaḍir is always considered a prophet due to his prominent status with regard to esoteric knowledge and revelation. His stories are found in many Javanese texts such as, *Serat Asmarasupi*, *Serat Suluk Musawaratan*, *Suluk Seh Malaya*, and so forth. See Nancy Florida, *Javanese Literature*, vol. 2 (Ithaca, 2000), pp. 201, 205, and 235; Pigeaud, *Literature of Java*, vol. 2 (The Hague, 1968), pp. 445–6; Siti Chamamah Soeratno, "Tokoh Khidlir dan Tradisinya pada Masyarakat Jawa: Tinjauan atas Dampak Penyebaran Islam di Jawa" (Yogyakarta, 1995).

However, it is also crucial to see that even in this framework of Kalijaga's discipleship under al-Khaḍir, a Javanese motif of putting him in the familiar world of Javano-Indic mystical story of Déwaruci is also at play.[28] The story of Déwaruci (or Bhimasuci) is an account of the mystical journey of the Mahabharata hero, Bhima, toward enlightenment. And, more importantly, it forms the backbone of the standard Javanese framework of the mystical union of God and the self. In the story, Bhima's quest for enlightenment is spoken of symbolically as his quest for the water of life (Jv. *tirta perwitasari*) that took him to the heights of the mountains and the depths of the seas before finding out that he had to find it in the core of his very being. Here, it is also insightful to note that an important part of the extra Qur'ānic legends of al-Khaḍir is his search for the water of life.[29] Describing the final phase of Bhima's quest for enlightenment in the Javanese mystical text *Suluk Déwaruci*,[30] Florida writes:

> The hero of the *Suluk*, the Pandhawa Prince Bhima, braves and survives a series of horrible dangers finally to achieve union with God. That union is attained through knowledge gained by means of self-transcendence in the form of the hero's divine fusion with a tiny miniature of himself. Representing the hero's own 'inner self', the miniature's name is Déwaruci. Although the hero at first would prefer to remain suspended at the eternal moment of union, he learns that he must return to the phenomenal world in order to fulfill his duties as a warrior. … The return, then, is to a point from which the hero has yet to depart—and to nowhere. A changed man, he remains 'himself'; his 'return' is to a changed world—and to one he never left.[31]

In the book of *Cabolèk* (eighteenth century), a treatise on Javano-Islamic mysticism and spiritual anthropology that emphasized ascetic practices as conditions for true knowledge of the self and God, this story of Bhima is also foundational. Although the Bhimasuci story originates from the pre-Islamic era, this book of *Cabolèk* argues that the spirit of this pre-Islamic story is thoroughly compatible with the spiritual tradition of Islam, provided one has the skillful interpreters.[32] In this work, echoing the famous *ḥadīth*, ascetic purification is spoken of as "Die before you die!" (Jv. *mati sajroning urip*, or *ngaurip iya urip ing sajroning pejah*). This "death" (of the physical body) is understood as a condition for the spiritual body

---

[28] Leiden Mss (LOr.7510); see Soeratno, "The Figure of al-Khaḍir," p. 14.

[29] Cf. John Renard's entry on al-Khaḍir in J.D. McAullife (ed.), *The Encyclopedia of the Qur'an*, vol. 3 (Leiden, 2003), p. 83.

[30] *Suluk Déwaruci* was composed in the late eighteenth century by the Javanese poet of the Surakarta court, Yasadipura I (1729–1803). See Florida, *Writing the Past*, pp. 257–8.

[31] Florida, *Writing the Past*, p. 261.

[32] See Ricklefs, *Mystic Synthesis*, pp. 116–17; also Soebardi, *The Book of Cabolèk* (The Hague, 1975), pp. viii and 28.

to achieve union with God.³³ It is also highly interesting that Bhima enters into the womb of Déwaruci in order to know himself. For, the Javanese concept of womb is intentionally used to echo its Arabic counterpart, *raḥīm*. Thus, this process is akin to entering into the essence of God as *al-Raḥmān al-Raḥīm*, participating more fully in God's undifferentiated mercy and grace. As a result, Bhima is able to overcome his narrow self-centeredness. The book of *Cabolèk* describes this transformation thus:

> Werkudara's [Bhima's] heart was no longer troubled, now he knew himself. By the power of Déwaruci's words, he could fly without wings, and was able to traverse the entire great universe, he had mastered his body. It is fitting, in the language of poetry, to compare him to a flower, which has been long a bud and now opens and spreads its fragrance, its beauty and perfume ever increasing … the entire world rejoiced.³⁴

In Kalijaga's case, it is the interplay between this earlier Javanese mode of enlightenment and the Islamic one that shapes his identity. For the Javanese tradition also casts Kalijaga (Sèh Malaya) as the new Bhima and al-Khaḍir as the real Déwaruci. One text describes how, during their meeting in Mecca, al-Khaḍir took the form of a child into whom Kalijaga entered to gain a mystical knowledge of the Reality.³⁵ This re-casting of Déwaruci into Kalijaga is eventually made very explicit in another important Javanese text, *Suluk Sèh Malaya* (late nineteenth century), a translation of Déwaruci's Javano-Indic religious and psychological terms into the standard Arabic terminology of Islamic mysticism.³⁶ As I will show later, this traditional archetypal idea of the mystical journey to the self is also quite foundational for my discourse on pilgrimage in Java as the milieu for re-construction of the self or the formation of identity.

It is rather obvious that Kalijaga's mystical relationship with al-Khaḍir and Déwaruci turns him into a remarkable and unique figure in the spiritual world of Java: he became the archetype of Javano-Islamic *wali*. In south central Java, his mythical stature is heightened further by his intimate relationship with the Mataram kingdom and its religio-cultural legacy. As I have argued earlier, it was Kalijaga who provided the link that would make Mataram a truly Islamic polity, a legitimate successor to the Hindu Majapahit. As James Fox has shown, the *Babad Tanah Jawi*—a religio-historical account of the founding of Mataram—narrates

---

³³ *Sèrat Cabolèk*, Canto VIII (51): 38; Soebardi, *The Book of Cabolèk*, p. 126.

³⁴ *Sèrat Cabolèk*, Canto VIII (53): 40; Soebardi, *The Book of Cabolèk*, p. 126.

³⁵ Leiden Mss (LOr 7510); Soeratno, "The Figure of al-Khaḍir," p. 14. See also Anthony H. Johns, "From Buddhism to Islam: An Interpretation of the Javanese Literature of the Transition," *Comparative Studies in Society and History*, 9 (1966): pp. 48–50; Zainul Milal Bizawie, "The Thoughts and Religious Understanding of Shaikh Ahmad al-Mutamakkin: The Struggle of Javanese Islam 1645–1740," *Studia Islamika*, 9 (2002): p. 52.

³⁶ Florida, *Writing the Past*, p. 261; also her *Javanese Literature*, vol. 2, p. 235.

that Sunan Kalijaga was the spiritual teacher of all the founding fathers of Mataram and that he always intervened at critical moments in the history of Mataram since its beginning.[37] These founding fathers include Ki Gede Pemanahan and his son, Panembahan Senapati (r. 1582–1601), and Sultan Agung (r. 1624–45). Right after Panembahan Senapati's encounter with the goddess of the Southern Sea, Kalijaga met with him and warned him not to be overly confident in his supernatural power but rather to be obedient to the will of God. Then he bestowed a prayer mat and the mantle of the Prophet Muḥammad to Senapati. According to legend, Kalijaga himself received this gift during a prayer session with other *wali*s in the Demak Mosque. This gift was considered to be the proof of divine favor on Mataram as an Islamic polity.[38]

Furthermore, according to the legendary history, when the *wali*s in Java gathered in Demak right after the fall of Majapahit to erect the Demak Mosque, Kalijaga was deeply immersed in his ascetic and spiritual practice (Jv. *tirakat*) in Pamantingan, in the Parangtritis area on the south coast (Map 3) before joining the other *wali*s to miraculously contribute one of the main pillars for the grand mosque.[39] The *Babad Tanah Jawi* seems to assume that by this act, Kalijaga had successfully linked the future Islamic kingdom of Mataram in south central Java with the most important Grand Mosque of Java on the north coast. Later on both the Grand Mosque of Demak and the tomb of Kalijaga in the nearby area of Kadilangu are considered to be the main sacred heirlooms of Java that can never be taken away. Famous is the saying of Pakubuwana I (r. 1704–19), the king of Mataram, that even if all the heirlooms (Jv. *pusaka*) of the land of Java are taken away, it will not matter in so far as there are still the graveyard of Kalijaga in Kadilangu and the Demak Mosque.[40] The Demak Mosque is considered a *pusaka*, a concentration of Islamic sacred power in Java, due to the process of its building, involving all the *wali*s and other paradigmatic Muslim figures in Java.[41]

---

[37] Laurie Sears, *Shadows of Empire* (Durham, 1996), p. 54; Geertz, *Islam Observed*, p. 26; Florida, *Writing the Past*, p. 329.

[38] See James Fox, "Sunan Kalijaga and the Rise of Mataram: A Reading of the *Babad Tanah Jawi* as a Genealogical Narrative," in Peter G. Riddell and Tony Street (eds), *Islam: Essays on Scripture, Thought and Society* (Leiden, 1997), pp. 212–14; also H.J. de Graaf, *De regeering van Panembahan Sénapati Ingalaga* ('s Gravenhage, 1954), pp. 76–7; Ricklefs, *The Seen and Unseen*, p. 11.

[39] J. Ras, "The genesis of the *Babad Tanah Jawi*: Origin and function of the Javanese court chronicle," *BKI*, 143 (1987): p. 350; Fox, "Sunan Kalijaga and the Rise of Mataram," p. 202.

[40] Ricklefs, *Mystic Synthesis*, p. 81.

[41] See *Babad Jaka Tingkir* (Florida, *Writing the Past*, pp. 155–63) for a list of all the saints involved in the building. This *babad* also contains the most detailed hierarchy of saints in Islamic Java.

Sunan Kalijaga as the Embodiment of Javano-Islamic Identity

To a large degree, the image of Kalijaga is the personification of the Javano-Islamic identity (the mystic synthesis) that the court of Mataram traditionally endeavors to embody. This mystic synthesis is anchored in the creative—if still ambiguous—interplay between a strong Islamic identity, based on the fulfillment of the five pillars of Islam, and a wide acceptance of an array of local spiritual forces and indigenous culture. Along the same line, Woodward has emphasized the role of a wide-ranging Sufistic interpretive framework for holding together the creative and ambiguous tensions in this synthetic view of Islamization in Java.[42] An important embodiment of this mystic synthesis can be witnessed in the figure of Prince Dipanagara (1785–1855), a Javanese prince of the Mataram court, especially his mystical practices as a wandering pilgrim. On Dipanagara, Ricklefs wrote: "Here was a devout Muslim mystic who travelled the countryside in search of new learning and mystical experiences ... Those visions also brought him into contact both with the spirit of Sunan Kalijaga, and with Ratu Kidul [the Goddess of the South Sea]."[43]

Again, this synthesis is also popularly remembered as the unique religio-cultural legacy of Sunan Kalijaga. In this regard, there is a very unique tradition that narrates a foundational feat of Kalijaga that has helped make him the emblematic personification of Javano-Islamic identity. This legend concerns the achievement of Kalijaga in making a case for the rightful position of Islamic Java *vis-à-vis* the center of universal Islam represented by Mecca. As the nineteenth-century Javanese epic history, *Babad Jaka Tingkir*, narrates, at the point when the council of Muslim saints in Java was dealing with a potentially devastating fiasco in the process of realigning the recalcitrant Mosque of Demak toward Mecca, Kalijaga emerged as an imposing figure with immense powers of reconciliation. It was due to Kalijaga's spiritual power that the Grand Mosque would finally be brought into alignment with the Kaʿba in Mecca (Ar. *qibla*), the material-spiritual center of universal Islam.[44]

This incident is highly revealing about the nature and process of negotiation of Javano-Islamic identity *vis-à-vis* universal Islam, as well as the unique role of Kalijaga in it. On this point, Nancy Florida muses:

> The resistance of this Mosque that embodied the society of new Javanese Moslems who constructed it signifies that the society's work both to define its *Islām* and to establish itself, from its position on the margins of the Islamic world, as a center of authority. The *wali*, who ground that structure of nascent authority, debate among themselves the *kéblat* [*qibla*] thus to negotiate a

---

[42] Woodward, *Islam in Java*, p. 6 and *passim*.
[43] Ricklefs, *Polarizing*, p. 8.
[44] In the *Babad Jaka Tingkir* (XIII. 23), Kalijaga is called the "Substitute Axial Saint" (Ar. *qutub al-abdal*), the sixth rank of the nine saints in Java. See Florida, *Writing the Past*, p. 333.

valid understanding of the Prophet's message that would properly inform the submission, the *Islām*, of those whom they are converting.[45]

It is crucial to point out further that the question of relationship between local Islam (represented by the Grand Mosque as the most sacred heirloom of Islamic Java) and the universal Islam (represented by Mecca) is settled by "the miraculous manipulation of Sunan Kalijaga, a manipulation of both the Meccan Kaʿba and the Demak Mosque."[46] For Kalijaga is said to have grasped the Kaʿba by his right hand, while his left hand took hold of the uppermost peak of the Demak Mosque. Pulling both of them, Kalijaga unified the Kaʿba's roof and the peak of the mosque into one perfect structure or substance.[47]

This legendary feat of Kalijaga in this religio-cultural negotiation and localization of universal Islam in Java—thus, overcoming the binary opposition between center and periphery—is followed by a set of other significant gestures of appropriation of Javanese culture.[48] Known as a Muslim saint who appreciated the Hindu-Javanese shadow theatre (Jv. *wayang*), Kalijaga's mystical interpretation of this religious art is insightful. Quoting a Javanese text, *Babad Cirebon*, the Dutch Javanologist Rinkes summarizes Kalijaga's interpretation thus:

> The *wayang* is indeed a reflected image of the One, so to speak: the image of the Law. The *wayang* [puppet] represents all humanity; the *dalang* [puppeteer] corresponds to Allah, Creator of the universe ... Thus, also the Creatures can only act by the will of the Lord, the Highest, He who manipulates the world.[49]

Furthermore, among the other major saints of Java, Kalijaga is the only one who is always depicted as donning a Javanese traditional outfit (instead of an Arab one) as an expression of his identity (Figure 1.4). The religio-cultural significance of this symbolism becomes rather clear in light of, for example, the criticism by a contemporary reformist writer who muses that although this way of dressing is fine within Islam, it becomes a problem when motivated by an anti-Arab motivation and Javanese culture's superiority.[50]

---

[45] Ibid., p. 334.

[46] Ibid.

[47] *Babad Jaka Tingkir*, XV: 33–4; Florida, *Writing the Past*, p. 167.

[48] On Kalijaga's appreciation of Javanese cultural elements, such as traditional music (Jv. *gamelan*), shadow theatre and so forth, see Kees van Dijk, "Dakwah and indigenous culture: the dissemination of Islam," *BKI*, 154 (1998): pp. 221–2.

[49] Rinkes, *The Nine Saints of Java* (Kuala Lumpur, 1996), p. 130.

[50] See Hasanu Simon, *Misteri Syekh Siti Jenar*, p. 332. Early in the history of Islamization in Java, the issue of clothing was indeed a sensitive one. A text from this era argued: "it is unbelief to dress like an infidel and to speak highly of these clothes"; see G.W.J. Drewes (ed. and trans.), *An Early Javanese Code of Muslim Ethics* (The Hague, 1978), p. 37.

As mentioned earlier, this model of Kalijagan inculturation of Islam in Javanese culture becomes the hallmark of Javano-Islamic practice upheld by the Javanese royal houses in south central Java.[51] In this respect, *Kitab Usulbiyah*, a Javanese reworking of the *Qiṣaṣ al-anbiyā'* (Tales of the Prophets) written at the court of Surakarta offers an interesting iconic image of the Prophet Muḥammad wearing a crown in Hindu-Buddhist style reminiscent of the Majapahit crown: it has the figures of mythical eagles (Jv. *garudha*) facing forward and backward, with teeth of precious rubies, gems for eyes and tongues of water jewels.[52]

King Brawijaya V and the Idea of Hindu and Islamic Continuity

In the previous section, my analysis was focused on the establishment of Kalijaga's image as the originator and embodiment of Javano-Islamic identity, especially in south central Java. This Javano-Islamic identity is, in turn, also anchored in the notion of spiritual and cultural continuity. As the Hindu-Javanese kingdom of Majapahit was subsequently constructed and imagined as the epitome of Javanese culture, it was crucial that Mataram—and the whole idea of Javanese identity that this court was supposed to carry forward—be related intimately to Majapahit. In this regard, somebody other than Kalijaga is needed. For, while Kalijaga is the Muslim Javanese saint *par excellence*, his genealogical location—by virtue of not being a king himself, or genealogically linked to a king—could not put him in the unquestionable line of royal continuity and supernatural power between Majapahit and Mataram.

In the Javanese tradition, this principle of continuity is secured through the figure of Brawijaya V, since he was undoubtedly the progenitor of subsequent Javanese monarchs. I will show later in this chapter that all the Islamic shrines under consideration, as well as many others in south central Java, are connected to Brawijaya V in genealogical terms, a principle that ensures the continuity of supernatural blessings and power through his genealogy and descendants.[53]

However, the relationship between Brawijaya V and later Javano-Islamic identity goes beyond mere genealogy. For, in the Javanese cultural memory, he is also imagined and thus remembered as an accomplished saint whose personal and saintly achievement becomes much more significant precisely because it explains the nature of the highly critical moment of the transition from the Hindu-Javanese period to the new Javano-Islamic one. What is considered particularly important in this memory is not his accomplishment as a Javanese monarch, but rather the nature of the end of his life. A Javanese epic of history and prophecy, the *Babad Jaka Tingkir* mentioned a few times earlier, describes the last moment of Brawijaya's life in the old Indic framework of *moksa* thus: "Vanished from

---

[51] Cf. Pakubuwana XII, *Karaton Surakarta*; Woodward, *Islam in Java*; Hamengku Buwono X, *Kraton Jogja*.

[52] Ricklefs, *Mystic Synthesis*, pp. 46–7; *Seen and Unseen World*, p. 75.

[53] Fox, "Ziarah Visits to the Tombs of the *Wali*," p. 30.

the mortal realm, surging up in lightning body, he rose to the realm of Release (*moksa*), not by way of death; true return consummate, to the realm divinely pure; in absolute perfection, His Majesty Brawijaya perfectly realized *Jatimurti*, knowing the Whence and Whither."[54]

Depicted this way, Brawijaya thus attained the highest stage of a mystical journey of realization of Reality (Ar. *taḥqīq al-ḥaqq*), somewhat parallel to Kalijaga's mystical experience under al-Khaḍir or Dewaruci mentioned earlier. For he realized in his very being the theomorphic nature of humanity, a realization that led him to the final return to the Truly Real. It is crucial to note that the text *Babad Jaka Tingkir* uses the Javanese terms *jatimurti* and *sangkan paran*. *Jatimurti* is derived from two Sanskrit words—*jati*, denoting truth, reality, original state of being, and birth; and *murti*, meaning body, incarnation, and form—while *sangkan paran* is a compound Javanese word, denoting both original source (*sangkan*) and final destination (*paran*). The doctrine of *sangkan paran* forms the pivot of Javanese mysticism and spiritual anthropology since it describes the most fundamental dynamics of the human journey, originating from God and returning back to Him.[55]

However, it is crucial to note that this journey is also intimately connected with the self as well as the role of *rasa*, a very crucial concept in Javanese culture. *Rasa* is originally a Sanskrit word denoting taste, essence, delight and so forth. In Javanese spirituality and theological anthropology, *rasa* points to the deepest intuition and inner sensing. Thus it is at once an epistemological and spiritual category. In the words of Paul Stange, "*rasa* is at once the substance, vibration, or quality of what is apprehended and the tool or organ which apprehends it."[56] This term also acquires much deeper spiritual and mystical meaning in the Javanese

---

[54] *Babad Jaka Tingkir* I.13; Florida, *Writing the Past*, p. 357. In *Babad Jaka Tingkir* XIII. 7 the (Muslim) author of the work tries to account for Brawijaya's religious adherence thus: "His Majesty Brawijaya, though but a heathen *Buda* still was brilliant bright, aware of the Whence and Whither." Although not stated in this work explicitly, this framework of celestial ascension is not foreign to Islam either. In fact, this *moksa* puts Brawijaya in the framework of the ascension to heaven experienced by Enoch (Idrīs) and Elijah (Ilyās), or even Jesus.

[55] The idea of *sangkan paran* is also closely related to the framework of "origin" and "return" (Ar. *al-mabda' wa al-ma'ad*) in the wider Islamic tradition, which points to the fundamental ontological structure and dynamics of human being (spiritual psychology) and the whole reality (cosmology and eschatology). This idea is central in the work of Muslim thinkers such as Mullā Ṣadrā, Najm al-Dīn al-Rāzī, Afḍal al-Dīn Kāshānī, and others. In Java, the creative encounters between Javanese spiritual anthropology and Islam can be found in the Javano-Islamic mystical literature (Jv. *suluk*) and the spiritual doctrines of the *kebatinan* movements (indigenous Javanese mystical brotherhoods). See P.J. Zoetmulder, *Pantheism and Monism in Javanese Suluk Literature* (Leiden, 1995); also Franz Magnis-Suseno, "Javanese *Sangkan-Paran* Philosophy," in his *Pijar-Pijar Filsafat* (Yogyakarta, 2005), pp. 40–57.

[56] Paul Stange, "The Logic of Rasa in Java," *Indonesia*, 38 (1984): p. 119.

culture because it also came to be associated with another Sanskrit term, *rahasya* (secret, mystery). Due to this association, the term *rasa* is then used to refer to the deepest spiritual experience or knowledge that could not be explained by words. This element of spiritual depth gets further intensified when the Javanese use the term *rasa* to translate the Arabic and Islamic concept of *sirr* which, among others, refers to the most subtle and most hidden recess in the human heart in which God is believed to reside, the spot where God and the soul are intimately in contact. In light of this framework of *sirr*, then, *rasa* is the deepest realm in the human constitution where the knowledge and realization of the Whence and Whither (Jv. *sangkan paran*) are sustained. Again, for the Javanese, the journey of the Whence and Whither means going deeper into the self as well, as the stories of Sèh Malaya (Sunan Kalijaga) and Dewaruci describe. It is interesting to see that the book *Usulbiyah* calls the Prophet Muḥammad God's *rasa* (Jv. *rasaningsun*). Echoing the possible meanings associated with the combination of the Sanskrit terms *rasa* and *rahasya* as well as the Arabic term *sirr*, Ricklefs translates this expression as "[God's] secret essence."[57] In this framework, it becomes clearer that the term *rasa* is employed to talk about the familiar Sufi concept of *al-nūr al-Muḥammadī* (the Muḥammadan light) as well as the possibility and mode of union between God and the human person.

In other words, the last episode of Brawijaya's life is depicted both in terms of Javano-Islamic mystical anthropology of *sangkan paran* as well as in the Hindu understanding of *moksa*. It has to be recalled that the *moksa*s of last Hindu-Buddhist kings of Java have been used by certain Javanese texts as a way to assert the unbroken continuity between the dying dynasties and the upcoming ones. This is so because in this framework of *moksa* these kings did not die in the violent battle against the Muslim forces, but rather they disappeared and attained a spiritual height. Thus the idea of *moksa* evades the problem of radical and violent change, something that is culturally troubling for Javanese.[58]

This principle of continuity, however, takes on another different form in Javanese account of Brawijaya, namely, through certain kind of conversion, understood not as a radical break with the past, but rather as a deeper reconciliation and continuity. The accounts of Brawijaya V's conversion to Islam are known in Java, and, very interestingly and probably quite intentionally, are put next to the narratives of his *moksa*. As Rinkes has pointed out, the Javanese seem to see this conversion as continuity on account that "there is little difference between Hinduism in Java and the forms by which Islam found its acceptance, apart from

---

[57] Ricklefs, *The Seen and Unseen*, p. 65.

[58] Soemarsaid Moertono, *State and Statecraft in Old Java* (Ithaca, 1968), p. 55. This strategy of preserving continuity did not necessarily assume conversion. *Serat Cabolang*, for example, narrates that Brawijaya's wife did convert to Islam, while Brawijaya remained true to his ancestral faith. See Drewes, "The Struggle between Javanism and Islam as Illustrated by the *Serat Dermagandul*," *BKI*, 122 (1966): pp. 311–16.

terminology."⁵⁹ In this framework, Brawijaya could have been a Muslim but still had an experience of *moksa*. Again, what is at stake in the various accounts of the last days of Brawijaya V is the idea of continuity with all its possible tensions and ambiguities.⁶⁰

In the context of my argument in this book, the role of the idea of continuity is crucial, precisely since it explains the inclusivity and openness that are still very operative in the whole tradition of Muslim pilgrimage in Java. For instance, it explains how Javanese Muslim pilgrims come to see the role and complex, not to say hybrid, identity of the saints being venerated and the religio-cultural identities of their shrines. Due to this principle of religio-cultural continuity, the Hindu-Buddhist heritage is not considered the totally superseded other, but rather an other that remains a significant aspect of the self. To a certain degree, this pattern foreshadows the dynamics of mutual openness in which Muslim-Catholic encounters occur in south central Javanese society today, as I will show later.

The Three Muslim Shrines and Their Saints

Sunan Pandanarang and the Shrine of Tembayat

This principle of spiritual and religio-cultural continuity between the old Javano Hindu-Buddhist heritage and the new Islamic tradition is also pivotal in the story of Sunan Pandanarang, the saint buried in the shrine of Tembayat. The Javanese account of his legendary ascent to sainthood involves the two personages of continuity mentioned previously, namely the Muslim saint Sunan Kalijaga and the last Hindu Javanese king Brawijaya V.

By all accounts, it can be established that Sunan Pandanarang was the disciple of Kalijaga. Totally immersed in his worldly pursuit as the governor of Semarang, an important port city on the northern coast of central Java, Pandanarang was made to realize the nature of reality (Jv. *sunyata jati murti*) by Kalijaga's display of lofty spiritual feats and utter detachment from wealth and mundane power. However, the *Serat Babad Tembayat*, a Javanese text about this saint, also links him to the Hindu Majapahit royal lineage through its last king, Brawijaya V.⁶¹ In this genealogical account, Pandanarang is believed to be actually none other than Brawijaya V himself or at least his descendant. And it was Kalijaga who brought him to Islam and initiated him, in a way that displays a deeply Javanese spiritual framework, in

---

⁵⁹ Rinkes, *Nine Saints of Java*, p. 72.

⁶⁰ This tension and ambiguity came to the surface in the debate on Javanese identity *vis-à-vis* Islam in the nineteenth century. Here, the exact nature of King Brawijaya's conversion was debated in two controversial works, *Serat Dharmagandul* and *Suluk Gatholoco*. Drewes, "The Struggle," p. 321; Rinkes, *The Nine Saints of Java*, p. 72.

⁶¹ Jamhari, "In the Center of Meaning: Ziarah Tradition in Java," *Studia Islamika*, 7 (2000): p. 65.

the process of becoming the last *wali* (Jv. *wali panutup*) of the venerable council of the Nine Saints (*Wali Songo*) of Java. In this regard, it is very important to notice that *Babad Jaka Tingkir*, a nineteenth-century Javanese text that did not seem to assume the identity of Brawijaya V and Pandanarang, nevertheless keeps a parallelism between the two in terms of the nature of their spiritual transformation on the road to sainthood. As in the case of Brawijaya's *moksa*, this text also insists that it is the knowledge of *jatimurti*, the core of Javanese mysticism and spiritual anthropology, which Kalijaga imparts to his protégé.[62]

Thus one witnesses here once again the Javanese pattern of preserving the continuity of the old religious framework in the identity formation of a new Muslim saint. The same desire to form an inclusive Javanese-Muslim identity is further illustrated in the formative event of Pandanarang's journey to sainthood. As the *Serat Babad Tembayat* narrates, Pandanarang built his first mosque on the top of Mount Jabalkat in order that his call to prayer as well as the light of his mosque could be heard and seen throughout Java. Annoyed by the display of this junior *wali*'s haughtiness, the senior *wali*s reprimanded Pandanarang. And it was Kalijaga who once again made him learn how to understand his identity as a true Muslim *wali* in the Javanese milieu. By telling him to move his mosque to a lower ground and lower the volume of his call to prayer, Kalijaga taught Pandanarang the virtue of humility, not primarily as a personal achievement but rather as a proper expression of Muslim identity.

This lesson of humility is made even more fitting in the context of the *Babad Jaka Tingkir*'s rather unique account of Pandanarang's conversion story. Different from the major versions of his conversion story, this *Babad* presents him as a prince-regent of Semarang who felt sidelined in the new religio-political hierarchy of power in Java introduced by the Islamic *wali*s after the demise of the Hindu Majapahit and the birth of the Islamic polity of Demak. Finding himself without a high position of authority in this new hierarchy, he refused to acknowledge the legitimacy of this new structure altogether. It was, again, Kalijaga who overcame the crisis. Fulfilling Pandanarang's desire for authority, Kalijaga taught him the esoteric teaching of the *wali*-ship and thus moved him up the ladder of the new spiritual hierarchy.[63] On this crucial point of Pandanarang's humility, Jamhari argues:

> *Serat Tembayat* interprets the warning as a means of alerting Sunan Tembayat to the fact that, as a new religion, Islam should not flaunt itself. In other words, *Serat Tembayat* construes the building of the mosque on top of the hill as an

---

[62] *Babad Jaka Tingkir* XVI.12; Florida, *Writing the Past*, p. 357.

[63] Florida, *Writing the Past*, p. 339. In this sense, the *Babad Jaka Tingkir* is unique among other major *babad*s that never mentioned Sunan Bayat's motive for prestige and power in his road to *wali*-hood. However, this story might further explain the reputation of the shrine of Tembayat as a place associated with the *baraka* of prestige and power, including worldly achievements.

arrogant act. As a new religion, Islam should not be expressed in an arrogant way. In other words, the narrative of the moving of the mosque can be interpreted as a kind of cultural alert for the fast-growing Muslim community in the southern area of Central Java.[64]

Thus the nascent Muslim community was being asked to master the art of knowing the dynamic of visibility and invisibility, not only in terms of their relationship with the divine manifestations, but also in terms of forging and expressing their identity and location in the fabric of Javanese society. Pandanarang himself was no stranger to this pedagogy. For he owed his spiritual transformation to the effectiveness of this pedagogy at the hands of Kalijaga, his spiritual master. In the earliest phase of Pandanarang's journey of conversion, the maverick Kalijaga made use of a didactic game of simulacra (Jv. *semu*) and truth (Jv. *sejati*) to lure the future saint to the spiritual path, by skillfully presenting himself as a destitute uninvited guest to Pandanarang's lavish banquet, then minutes later appearing as a rich man dressing in the most elegant robes; or, according to different version, as a poor hay trader whose utter indifference to wealth finally brought Pandanarang to a spiritual discovery of the truly Real (Ar. *al-Ḥaqq*).[65] For Pandanarang, this pedagogy taught him that discerning his master's true identity amounts to discerning the constancy of divine presence in the complex dynamics of visibility and invisibility. Pandanarang apparently took this lesson to heart since he himself made use of it later as a Muslim saint. In this regard, legendary is his victory over a Hindu ascetic in the contest of spiritual power through a game of hide-and-seek. By emphasizing Pandanarang's special power to get to know what is invisible as well as to become invisible himself, the Javanese lore of his sainthood prizes the saint's special powers of true perception of reality.[66]

Pandanarang's relationship with Kalijaga and Brawijaya definitely puts him and his shrine at Tembayat on the spiritual map of Java. However, the shrine's prominence in south central Javanese history is due largely to its connection with the court of Mataram. Among its list of royal pilgrims, the shrine has no less a figure than Sultan Agung (r. 1624–45), the most pious and accomplished monarch of the Mataram dynasty, who visited the shrine following the appearance of the saint in his dream.[67] The timing of this royal pilgrimage in 1633 could not have been more significant. For it occurred during the most fragile moment of Sultan Agung's otherwise glorious reign. After having to swallow a bitter failure in his attempts to subdue the Dutch in Batavia in 1628 and 1629, only with great effort did Sultan Agung finally manage to crush the rebellion of some Muslim leaders

---

[64] Jamhari, "In the Center of Meaning," p. 65.
[65] Rinkes, *The Nine Saints of Java*, pp. 73–4.
[66] Ibid., pp. 78–9.
[67] Ricklefs, *A History of Modern Indonesia since c. 1200* (Stanford, 2008), p. 43; Pemberton, *On the Subject of "Java,"* p. 280.

around Tembayat. So, Sultan Agung's pilgrimage might have been motivated by a sense of acute crisis and a pursuit of supernatural help from the saint.[68]

Regardless of Sultan Agung's exact motive, the effect of this visit is significant in terms of the formation of Javano-Islamic identity. For it was right after this visit that Sultan Agung incorporated the Islamic Hegira calendar to the existing Hindu Caka calendar, giving birth to a hybrid Javano-Islamic calendar.[69] The fact that Sultan Agung opted not for a replacement but rather an inclusion is telling about the larger spirit of inclusivity and continuity in the Javano-Islamic identity that the court of Mataram endeavored to embody. In this respect, the Hindu-Javanese style of the ceremonial gate in the shrine that Sultan Agung erected as a memory of his visit could well serve as a symbolic and tangible testament to Javano-Islamic identity at the shrine of Tembayat.

Mawlana Maghribi: An Arab Saint and the Javano-Islamic Tradition

So far, I have touched on the historical significance of the Tembayat shrine, where one also finds the centrality of Kalijaga and Brawijaya in the framework of continuity between Hindu-Javanese Majapahit and Javano-Islamic Mataram. The two other Muslim shrines under study here, the shrines of Gunungpring and Mawlana Maghribi, did not really have the same "historical" stature compared to the shrine of Tembayat. However, both are also symbolically related either to Kalijaga or Brawijaya, or both.

In terms of genealogy, Mawlana Maghribi belongs to an important line of the Arab family from whom nearly all early Muslim saints in Java descended. According to the genealogy posted in the shrine, he was the grandchild of Sèh Jumadil Kubra.[70] As van Bruinessen has pointed out, Jumadil Kubra is the ancestor of many members of the Nine Saints of Java.[71] In general, however, the

---

[68] Fox, "Ziarah Visits to the Tombs of the *Wali*," p. 29.

[69] In addition, around the time of his pilgrimage to Tembayat, two explicitly Islamic works were composed at the court of Mataram, namely *Carita Sultan Iskandar* (the tale of Alexander the Great) and *Carita Yusuf* (the story of Joseph). These writings are considered spiritually potent and were reproduced and redacted in the court of Surakarta in 1729, as the centennial year of Sultan Agung's pilgrimage to Tembayat approached. Yet another writing, *Suluk Garwa Kencana*, is associated with Sultan Agung's pilgrimage to Tembayat. This text is believed to contain the spiritual lessons that the saint of Tembayat confided to Sultan Agung. See Ricklefs, *Mystic Synthesis*, pp. 43 and 186.

[70] According to the text *Babad Dipanagara* (nineteenth century), Mawlana Maghribi was the father of two important saints, Sunan Ampel and Sunan Giri (Fox, "*Ziarah* Visits to the Tombs of the *Wali*," p. 32), and in *Serat Sèh Dul Kadir* (nineteenth century), Mawlana Maghribi is related to ʿAbd al-Qādir al-Jīlānī, the famous saint from Baghdad, who is also very popular among Javanese pilgrims. See Florida, *Javanese Literature*, vol. 1, p. 299.

[71] van Bruinessen, "Najmuddin al-Kubra, Jumadil Kubra and Jamaluddin al-Akbar," p. 320; also de Graaf and Pigeaud, *De Eerste Moslimse Vorstendommen op Java*, chapter 1 (note #2).

exact genealogical relationship between Jumadil Kubra and early Muslim saints in Java—such as Mawlana Maghribi, Ibrahim Asmaraqandi, Mawlana Ishaq, and Sunan Giri—is never made very clear in Javanese historiography. There are too many inconsistent stories.

According to Pigeaud, Jumadil Kubra (or Jumadil Akbar) stayed in China and converted a Chinese emperor before coming to Java. In this respect, it is more important to understand the significance of this figure in the Javanese historical imagination. Van Bruinessen writes, "The range of the legends and the extent of the geographical dispersion suggest that the archetype of Jumadil Kubra must have enjoyed great prestige in early Indonesian Islam."[72] Many pilgrimage sites in Java are associated with Jumadil Kubra, such as the one in Turgo hill, on the slope of Mount Merapi, to the north of Yogyakarta, where he is believed to have been the spiritual adviser of Sultan Agung (r. 1613–46), certainly not in a historical sense but rather in a mystical framework. In this genealogy, although Maghribi was younger than Jumadil Kubra, he still belonged to the earliest era of Muslim presence in Java. Attesting to this would be the fact that his name appeared in the oldest surviving texts from that era such as the Ferrara Manuscript.[73] And, despite the confusions and inconsistencies in the Javanese accounts of the genealogy of Mawlana Maghribi, it is generally accepted that he was none other than Mawlana Malik Ibrahim, the most senior member of the Nine Saints. Tradition has it that he hailed from Central Asia, but might have come to Java in the last decades of the fourteenth century via Gujarat (India) and Champa (Vietnam). He apparently had a cordial relationship with the Hindu court of Majapahit due to his peaceful manner in his missionary work. As the inscription on his tombstone in Gresik, East Java, attests, he died in 1419.

In the context of the supernatural worldview of south central Java, shared by typical pilgrims to Maghribi's shrine, emphasis is generally placed on Maghribi's genealogical connection to Kalijaga and Brawijaya V (and Mataram) as well as the geo-spiritual location of his shrine. Maghribi was married to Kalijaga's sister (Roro Rosowulan),[74] and one of his grandchildren (Dewi Nawangsih) became the wife of Prince Bondan Kejawan, the son of Brawijaya V, from whose line the Mataram dynasty descended. In the Parangtritis area (see Map 3), the connection between the Brawijaya clan and Mawlana Maghribi is further established through

---

[72] Martin van Bruinessen, "Najmuddin al-Kubra, Jumadil Kubra and Jamaluddin al-Akbar," p. 324.

[73] Mawlana Maghribi is mentioned by name in this manuscript as one of the seven saints that were present during the so-called "synod of the *walis*" in which a verdict on Sèh Lemah Abang, an allegedly heterodox saint, was passed. See Drewes, *An Early Javanese Code of Muslim Ethics*, pp. 9 and 13.

[74] This tradition is based on the *Babad Tanah Jawi*; see Soewito Santoso, *Babad Tanah Jawi* (Surakarta, 1979), pp. 80ff; also Klaus Fuhrmann, *Formen der javanischen Pilgerschaft zu Heiligenschreinen* (Ph.D. Dissertation, Albert-Ludwigs-Universität, Freiburg im Breisgau, 2000), p. 269.

local legends, according to which two of Brawijaya's children became the students of Maghribi, following the defeat and eventual conversion to Islam of their former Hindu teacher at the hands of this Muslim saint. The alleged tombs of these two revered students of Maghribi—known as Sèh Bela-Belu and Sèh Gagang Dami Aking—still stand today in the same area and are popular among Javanese pilgrims. In short, this complex genealogical line makes Mawlana Maghribi a unique Arab ancestor (Jv. *pundhen*) of the Yogyakarta sultanate that descended from the Mataram dynasty. For this reason, his shrine in Parangtritis is also under the jurisdiction of this royal house.[75]

As mentioned, the location of Maghribi's shrine on the southern coast of Parangtritis (Map 3) is also very crucial. This shrine shares physical proximity with three mythical places in this area that are associated with the founding of the Mataram dynasty. The first is the venue where Panembahan Senapati (r. 1588–1601), the legendary founder of Mataram, sealed a political and romantic pact with the goddess of the Southern Sea; the second is the site where Panembahan Senapati received the divine omen (Jv. *wahyu*) of his future kingship from the invisible world at Lipura;[76] and the third is the tomb of Sultan Agung in Imogiri (Map 3). Furthermore, in light of Mawlana Maghribi's genealogical connection with Jumadil Kubra, his shrine at the southern coast would be spiritually connected to Jumadil Kubra's shrine on the slope of Mount Merapi in the north. In the context of Mataram's traditional sacred cosmology, this genealogical relation also means connecting two important supernatural-geographical poles of the realm, namely the Indian Ocean (Southern Sea) and Mount Merapi in the north, thus forming south central Java as a unified spiritual cosmos (*mandala*).[77] All these factors seem to explain the curious fact that although this saint was of Arab descent, Javanese culture and history provide the main framework of the pilgrimage tradition to this shrine.

Raden Santri and Other Javanese Muslim Saints at Gunungpring

This linkage to Brawijaya and Mataram is also crucial for the identity of Pangeran Singasari (Raden Santri), the most senior saint of the Gunungpring

---

[75] Carey, *The Power of Prophecy*, pp. 141 and 781.

[76] For the significance of Lipura and the southern coast for Javanese identity, see H.J. de Graaf, *Awal Kebangkitan Mataram* (Jakarta, 1985), p. 74ff; Ricklefs, "Dipanagara's Early Inspirational Experience," *BKI*, 130 (1974): pp. 227–58. The Catholic Sacred Heart shrine under study is precisely located in Lipura (Map 3). Since Panembahan Senapati's role in the history of Java is seen also as a fighter for a Javano-Islamic identity, this spatial and spiritual proximity has been interpreted as a call for the Sacred Heart shrine to be a place where this kind of inclusive identity is fostered.

[77] This *mandala* has four guardians—the Queen of the Southern Sea (Jv. *Ratu Kidul*), Sunan Merapi (the spirit king in mount Merapi in the north), Sunan Lawu (the spirit of Brawijaya) in the east, and Semar (an indigenous Javanese divine figure). See Woodward, *Islam in Java*, p. 199.

shrine. According to the official genealogy of the saint, Pangeran Singasari also descended from Raden Bondan Kejawan, the son of Brawijaya V, and more specifically he was the brother of Panembahan Senapati. Thus, through the line of Raden Bondan Kejawan, Raden Santri is also connected, albeit very indirectly, to Mawlana Maghribi and Sunan Kalijaga.[78] According to the standard version of his hagiography, after some years of helping out his brother in subduing some outlying Javanese principalities, Raden Santri devoted his life as a Muslim ascetic and teacher, and finally settled in the Gunungpring area. At Gunungpring, this royal connection is made more formal by the establishment of the Raden Santri Foundation (Jv. Yayasan KR Santri Puroloyo Gunungpring) that operates under the auspice of the royal house of Yogyakarta. As Stuart Robson remarks, there are some rather peculiar legends around this saint, the chief among which is that there will always be a "holy madman" (Ar. *majdhūb*) among his descendants.[79] In the 1960s, it was Gus Jogo (*Mbah* Jogoreso, also buried in Gunungpring) who was believed to be the mad saint. Together with *Mbah* Dalhar (d. 1959) from the nearby Darussalam Islamic boarding school (Jv. *pesantren*),[80] they were two famous contemporary saints who attracted large numbers of students from all over Java, including the next generation of *wali* such as Gus Miek (Kyai Haji Hamim Djazuli, a maverick and controversial saint with a large following across Java who died in 1993; more on this figure below) and Kyai Chudlori (d. 1977), the founder of the famous Tegalrejo Islamic school (Jv. *pesantren*) in Magelang regency, Central Java.[81] During his lifetime, *Mbah* Dalhar had been rather widely known as a *wali*, an expert in the science of Reality (Ar. *ḥaqīqa*), a disciple of al-Khaḍir, and a teacher (Ar. *murshid*) in the Shādhiliyya Sufi order. He left behind a work

---

[78] See "Silsilah Kyai Raden Santri (Eyang Pangeran Singasari) Puroloyo Gunungpring Muntilan" (published by the Association of the Yogyakarta Court's Attendants). This genealogy is consistent with the *Babad Tanah Jawi*, which lists Raden Santri as the third son of Kyai Ageng Pemanahan. However, according to other texts, he was the brother of Sultan Agung. See Stuart Robson, "Kjahi Raden Santri," *BKI*, 121 (1965): 259–64.

[79] Robson, "Kjahi Raden Santri," p. 260. In Sufism, the *majdhūb*—literally, those who are completely drawn to God—refers to a particular kind of saints who exhibit shocking behavior under ecstatic mystical influence. Due to this behavior, they sometimes would be regarded as mentally deranged. See Annemarie Schimmel, *Mystical Dimensions of Islam* (Chapel Hill, 1975), pp. 19 and 105.

[80] Forming one of the central pillars of traditional Islam in Java, the *pesantren*s are Islamic religious schools that also become, in most cases, centers of mystical learning and practice, associated with local and international orders (Ar. *ṭarīqa*). Many contemporary saints in Islamic Java come from these networks of families who own the *pesantren*s. In many cases, the *pesantren* compound in which the tombs of these saintly *kyai*s become new pilgrimage centers.

[81] For a biography of Gus Miek, see Muhamad Nurul Ibad, *Perjalanan dan Ajaran Gus Miek* (Yogyakarta, 2007). For a brief sketch of Kyai Chudlori's life and work, see Bambang Pranowo, "Islam Faktual: Antara Tradisi dan Relasi Kuasa" (Adicita Karya Nusa, without year), pp. 53–74; see also his *Memahami Islam Jawa* (Ciputat, 2009).

in Arabic called *Tanwīr al-maʿānī* on the life and virtues (Ar. *manāqib*) of Abū al-Ḥasan al-Shādhilī (d. 1258), the Egyptian founder of the Shādhiliyya Sufi order. Adding to his charisma among the Javanese people in the area, *Mbah* Dalhar was also a distant descendant of a Mataram king, Amangkurat III (d. 1734).[82] His grave at Gunungpring has become a focal point of pilgrimage among those who are more attracted to him due to their connection to him via their teachers in the networks of *pesantren*s, rather than to Raden Santri. The former students and followers of Gus Miek, for example, become familiar with pilgrimage to *Mbah* Dalhar's tomb because their teacher taught them to do so.

At this point, it is crucial to see the confluence between the court culture and the *pesantren* culture in the pilgrimage tradition in south central Java. As I have shown, the figure of Raden Santri largely represents the court culture while the figures of Gus Jogoreso, *Mbah* Dalhar, and Gus Miek represent the *pesantren* culture. For the most part, the two go hand in hand, making the tradition of pilgrimage more rich, intense, and widespread. Due to this confluence, the hybridity of the practice becomes noticeable. The *pesantren* culture, due to its strong master-student relationship, also connects a particular saint and his shrine to a chain of other saints and their tombs. For example, because of the role of Gus Miek, the tomb of Gunungpring is related to the cemetery of Tambak (Makam Tambak) in Kediri regency, East Java, where his tomb is located, together with the tombs of other Javanese *wali*s. The networks of pilgrims to this cemetery grow significantly due to the popularity of the special gathering of Qurʾānic recitation (Jv. *Sema'an al-Quran*) and prayers of remembrance (*Dzikrul Ghofilin*) initiated in the 1970s by Gus Miek. This cemetery is in fact the place where the gathering took place.[83]

Concluding Remarks

This chapter deals with the crucial question of sacred history in the context of pilgrimage tradition among Javanese Muslims in south central Java. In this regard, I have attempted to show that in this context, a particular understanding of history is at work, namely history as a memory of sacred past and collective task. History is not a fixed narrative and legacy of the past that a generation would readily receive, but rather the communal task of continual remaking of connection and continuity with the complex past where the other (the pre-Islamic legacy) is not only present, but constitutively so. Concretely, it is through the act of making pilgrimages to the shrines of the paradigmatic figures of the past that Javanese Muslims act out this notion of history as memory. In this dynamic the figures

---

[82] For a brief biography of Mbah Dalhar, see Muhammad Wafa al-Hasani, "Waliyullah Mbah Kyai Dalhar Watucongol", http://al-kahfi.net/tarikh-wa-tsaqafah/waliyullah-mbah-kyai-dalhar-watucongol/ (accessed September 2009).

[83] Muhamad Nurul Ibad, *Perjalanan dan Ajaran Gus Miek*, pp. 113–54, and *passim*.

of the saints then represent living memories of the embodiments of this creative process of Javano-Islamic identity formation.

Foundational in this identity formation was the role of Sunan Kalijaga. So singular was his role that the hybrid Javano-Islamic identity in south central Java continues to be identified largely with this particular saint. In general, due to this role, saints like Sunan Kalijaga and Sunan Pandanarang continue to have a religio-cultural authority for the community in the present. On the basis of the prominence of this kind of religio-cultural patterns, I argue that the Javano-Muslim pilgrimage tradition in south central Java is, by and large, governed by the principle of communion and continuity with the sacred past. In this overarching framework of communion, the newer saints and their religio-cultural legacies are creatively placed and interpreted.

Chapter 2
Muslim Self and Hindu-Javanese Other: Spatial, Architectural, and Ritual Symbolisms

> Gone, vanished without a trace, are the works of the (worldly) realm!
> Javanese Chronogram[1]

In the earliest history of Islamization in Java, it was the legacy of the Hindu-Javanese polity of Majapahit that for the most part became the "other," a foil against which Islam set itself. Thus the transition from the fall of Majapahit (1478) to the first Islamic sultanate of Demak is curiously marked by the above mentioned chronogram: "Gone, vanished without a trace are the works of the (worldly) realm" (Jv. *sirna ilang pakartining bumi*). However, if one takes this chronogram to refer specifically to the vanishing of the Hindu-Javanese kingdom of Majapahit, a question arises: is there really no trace left behind by this once mighty kingdom? The previous chapter has made clear that the principles of continuity, connection and communion with the sacred past that includes the pre-Islamic legacy have become the principal ways in which the so-called Javano-Islamic identity is founded and negotiated. In the kind of model pilgrimage that the *Serat Centhini* advocates, one sees how Jayengresmi, a Muslim prince-cum wandering pilgrim, in his longing for the sacred past, visited the ruins of Hindu-Javanese sites, as well as learned some wisdom lessons from the living Hindu teachers in their hermitages. The *Serat Centhini* seems to argue that there were legitimate reasons why this pious Muslim prince lamented the loss of the grandeur of this sacred past and why he was still able to imbibe in its power in the present.

This chapter takes the discussion of the formation of Javano-Islamic identity further by examining the spatial, artistic, and architectural symbolisms, as well as the ritual activities, of the shrines under study. In this framework, these symbolisms and rituals are understood as tangible and material expressions of a Javano-Islamic collective self that is marked by an appropriation of Hindu-Javanese tradition of the past that in turn, can be taken as a larger and enduring symbolic hospitality to the other. In various ways, this chapter carries further the argument that pilgrimage

---

[1] This chronogram is found in many Javanese texts, for example in the *Babad Jaka Tingkir* (canto I.19). Here I use Nancy Florida's translation in her *Writing the Past* (p. 94) with a slight alteration, as I translate the Javanese word "bumi" as realm, rather than earth.

in south central Java has always been imbued with the desire to commune with, and to make present, the authoritative and sacred past that includes the founding events and figures such as the saints and kings. Maintaining a connection with this sacred past that includes forms of otherness definitely makes this religio-cultural identity formation richer and complex at the same time. That is why it raises the issue of continuous discernment on the part of the pilgrims and their communities with regard to finding creative ways of interpreting anew the extremely rich yet complex (not to say, ambiguous) aspects of this identity formation in the artistic, architectural, and ritual realms.

Spatial, Artistic, and Architectural Traces of the Other

As examined in Chapter 1, it is in the framework of negotiating a complex Javano-Islamic identity that the practice of pilgrimage in south central Java in the present finds its framework of meaning. In this framework, traces of the past are not only carefully kept alive, chiefly through pilgrimage tradition to these sites, when they are available, but they are also sought after, or "invented," when they are not readily available.

In this regard, the Javanese penchant for finding "traces" of the sacred past as well as forms of otherness contained in it, is illustrated well in the role of the "*petilasan*" (derived from Jv. *tilas*, trace). These are particular places normally associated with the particular deed of important historical or mythical figures in certain location, perhaps corresponding to the more general notion of *maqām*, understood as a place where paradigmatic figures have stayed or passed, in the Islamic tradition. The shrine of Mawlana Maghribi (Map 3) is a good example of a *petilasan* that has become a major pilgrimage site. However, for the most part, *petilasan*s in Java are very simple, seemingly having nothing much to offer to sight-hungry pilgrims, even evoking more absence than presence.[2] As Chambert-Loir shows, in some cases these *petilasan* "may materialise a sacred place; in others it may be the means to revere a sacred mythical figure."[3] By visiting these mostly unassuming places, Javanese pilgrims (not only Muslims) seek to commune with a sense of sacred and potent presence, however dim it would appear to be. The Javanese have a special term to designate this particular kind of pilgrimage as a reenactment of history. It is called *napak tilas* (Jv. literally means "walking in the footsteps" of paradigmatic figures). In this regard, the parallelism between this Javanese practice and Michel de Certeau's understanding of historiography as "a treatment for absence" is striking. For *napak tilas* is nothing other than walking

---

[2] For example, the *petilasan* of Sunan Kalijaga in Cawas, Klaten (not far from the shrine of Tembayat) consists of just a stone with some holes. It is believed to be the place where this saint stopped to do the prayer.

[3] Chambert-Loir, "Saints and Ancestors: The Cult of Muslim Saints in Java," in Chambert-Loir and Reids (eds), *The Potent Dead*, p. 136.

along, in the sense of re-tracing, the footprints of the vanquished.[4] In the context of Muslim Java, the vanquished includes the other, such as the historical and mythical figures of the Hindu-Javanese past as well as this Hindu-Javanese past as a whole.

Among the three shrines under discussion, it is in the shrine of Tembayat that the traces of the Hindu-Javanese "other" are the most conspicuous.[5] Historically speaking, this character stems from the fact that most of its architectural remains date back to the early Mataram period (seventeenth century) when the so-called "mystic synthesis" between Islam and aspects of Hindu-Javanese tradition, i.e. cultural synthesis between Islam and Javaneseness that is grounded in a mystical worldview shared by Sufism and Javanese culture, was flourishing under Sultan Agung (r. 1613–46) who himself made a historic pilgrimage to the shrine in 1633 and became its royal patron.[6] And in this mausoleum, as in the royal mausoleums in Imogiri and Kotagedhe (Map 3), the most conspicuous traces of the other are the Hindu-styled gateways with all the delicate ornaments.[7]

The shrine also incorporates more aniconic images that can be striking. For example, in front of the inner pavilion (Jv. *bangsal lebet*), just below the mausoleum of the saint, there stands a short obelisk with a familiar ornament of Kala's head on the bottom. Then, on the bottom of the door of the hall, on both sides, one finds two images of a turtle head, one with mouth open and the other with mouth closed. In the same area, stands also the legendary water barrel (Jv. *genthong sinaga*) for ritual purification that has a shape of a dragon's head as the channel for the flowing water in the base. Then, just before entering the chamber where the graves of the saint and his family members are located, one finds the Gate of the Dragon (Jv. *regol sinaga*). This gate is not in the Javano-Hindu Majapahit style—a fact that might suggest its more recent origin—and it is partitioned into three smaller gates. On the very top of these smaller gates, one finds three sets of interesting ornaments. The right and left gates have the ornaments of two wild beasts guarding a Hindu temple (Jv. *candi*), while the one at the center has the

---

[4] Illustrating his understanding of historiography as "a treatment for absence," de Certeau argues: "Like Robinson Crusoe on the shore of his island, before 'the vestige of a naked foot imprinted upon the sand', the historian travels along the borders of his present; he visits those beaches where the other appears only as a *trace* of what has *passed*." De Certeau, *L'Absent de l'histoire*, pp. 8–9; quoted in Jeremy Ahearne, *Michel de Certeau* (Stanford, 1995), p. 10.

[5] When speaking about the religio-cultural legacy of Hindu-Buddhism in Java as "the other," I do not imply a total otherness precisely because the principle of continuity is at work, meaning that this other has become an inherent part of the self. Even in the framework of the Javano-Islamic "mystic synthesis," there is a persisting sense of alterity, ambiguity and tension, on account of the lack of "total" identity between Hindu-Javaneseness and Islam.

[6] Ricklefs, *Mystic Synthesis*, p. 39.

[7] These Hindu-Javanese style gateways (Jv. *gapura*) are designed and placed to mark a spatial movement from outer to inner part of the shrine. And if these gates are put in the context of the mystical ascent to Jabal al-Qāf, one sees how an interesting Hindu-Muslim architectural metaphor is displayed at this shrine.

image of two dragons becoming one, forming a shape of a royal crown filled with lotus flowers, flanked by two buddha-like figures in deep meditation.[8]

The architectural features of the gates in non-Majapahit style that hold these images do give the impression of more recent origins. In general, the artistic and architectural features of this shrine exhibit a remarkable influence of the royal courts of Yogyakarta and Surakarta. Strikingly similar hybrid artistic patterns are found the Yogyakarta palace.[9] Interestingly, in the Yogyakarta palace, these hybrid artistic patterns are also placed in the most Islamic part of it, that is, the Grand Mosque (Jv. *Masjid Agung*). For instance, on the pillars of this mosque, one finds decorative designs ("Putri Mirong") that incorporate various central symbolisms of the Hindu and Buddhist traditions, such as the lotus flower and the stupa-like golden leaf. Quite intentionally, these non-Islamic symbolisms are taken as a sign of acknowledgment on the part of the court of all goodness in Hinduism and Buddhism.[10] In this hybrid decorative design, the Islamic framework is expressed in the inscription of the words "Allāh" and "Muḥammad," as well as the Arabic letters "Alif Lām Mīm Rā"—the mysterious letters that are found in the beginnings of some chapters of the Qurʾān. These central Islamic symbolisms are also taken as a reminder for the sultan that his power is limited and God is truly the Lord of the world.[11]

In light of this connection, one might assume that the same interpretive framework has been at work in the incorporation of the Hindu-Javanese symbolisms in the Tembayat shrine as well. One example of possible interpretation of this hybrid art at the Tembayat shrine—particularly the symbolism of the mountain, Jabalkat—will be offered later. At this point, some general observation about the patterns of hybrid Javano-Islamic arts in Java would be helpful to situate the case of Tembayat and to show that this shrine is not an isolated case, both in terms of its historical location and its hybrid artistic pattern.

Generally speaking, Islamic architecture in Java from the earliest period (fifteenth century) is marked by the concerns to find its distinctive identity. In this

---

[8] Still, in yet different parts of the compound, one finds the traces of pre-Islamic artistic patterns such as head of a buffalo and head of an ogre (Jv. *raseksa*). One of the white gates (called *Bale Kencur*) features the ornamental images of two dragons (Jv. *naga*) and two eagles (Jv. *garudha*) on the top of the *naga*s. Images of two dragons are also found on the top of the main white gate after the pavilion (Jv. *bangsal*) for ritual meal and communal prayers.

[9] The ornamental motifs of two dragons, in the same shape as the ones in the Tembayat shrine, are also found in various places in the Yogyakarta palace compound, for instance in the Magangan Gate (Jv. *regol magangan*). It is also used in the chronogram signifying the year of the erection of the palace, which in Javanese reads: "*Dwi naga rasa tunggal*" (two dragons united in profound sensation), referring to the year of 2861 Caka (1760). See Hamengku Buwono X, *Kraton Jogja*, pp. 57 and 154.

[10] Sultan Hamengku Buwono X, *Kraton Jogja*, p. 62.

[11] Ibid.

framework, there was obviously a desire to minimize the aniconic motifs. However, it is very interesting to see that within this general pattern, cases of exceptional presence of the Hindu-Javanese artistic motifs in the forms of human and animal images could still be seen. This hybrid art is found in many important mosques and court edifices throughout Java. Even the Demak Grand Mosque (fifteenth century), the oldest and most sacred mosque in Java, exhibits this hybridity. It has a unique main door called *lawang bledhek* (the door of thunders), featuring images of dragons; while its prayer niche (Ar. *miḥrāb*) features a chronogram cast in the image of a turtle, one of the sacred animals in Hindu Java.[12] Along the same line, the mosque of Kajen, in north central Java, has a Javanese style pulpit (Ar. *minbar*) that features woodcarvings in Javanese traditional cloth patterns (Jv. *batik*) and a depiction of two birds holding the ends of a crescent moon. According to popular belief, the provenance of this *minbar* goes back to Kyai Ahmad Mutamakin, a rather famous and controversial seventeenth-century saint whose tomb is located nearby.[13] Images of dragons and ogres are also found in the main door of the tomb of a saint-monarch, Sunan Prapen (d. 1527) in the town of Gresik, East Java.

In East Java, remarkable traces of early Javano-Islamic hybrid art are also found. In this respect, the case of the Sendang Dhuwur Mosque is rather interesting, both in terms of its artistic and architectural particularities as well as its connection with Sunan Kalijaga, the legendary founder of the hybrid Javano-Islamic identity (Chapter 1). Located in the Lamongan regency in East Java, this mosque, being one of the oldest Islamic edifices in Java, exhibits this early Javano-Islamic hybrid architecture and ornaments in remarkable ways. Built on a former Hindu site, the mosque of Sendang Dhuwur contains a highly decorated wooden pulpit that is composed of diverse motifs such as mythical crocodile (*makara*), the Majapahit-style sunburst (*surya*), as well as the lotus and *kala* motifs.[14] As is common in the Hindu edifices in Java, the *makara* monsters guard the staircase leading to the gateway of the mosque. The monumental gate of this mosque features two gigantic wings and a truncated pyramid, i.e., a mountain with curving peaks in whose midst is placed a bird-like figure with outstretched wings. The bas-relief has images of peacocks and lions. The familiar Islamic element of this mosque is observable in the crescent moon shape carved on a tombstone.[15]

---

[12] Sugeng Haryadi, *Sejarah Berdirinya Masjid Agung Demak dan Grebeg Besar* (Jakarta, 2003), pp. 34, 58, and 67; also Zakaria Ali, *Islamic Art in Southeast Asia 830 A.D –1570 A.D.* (Kuala Lumpur, 1994), pp. 279–93.

[13] Ricklefs, *The Seen and Unseen*, p. 132.

[14] In Hindu Javanese temples, the *kala* ornament is the mask of a demon, that is, Batara Kala, originally the god of time in Hinduism. Placed above doorways or niches, it usually goes together with the *makara* ornament, i.e., the depiction of the mythical crocodile with an elephant's trunk. See Ann R. Kinney et al., *Worshiping Siva and Buddha* (Honolulu, 2003), pp. 288–9.

[15] John Miksic, "The Art of Cirebon and the Image of the Ascetic in Early Javanese Islam," p. 136; Zakaria Ali, *Islamic Art in Southeast Asia*, pp. 320–21.

As mentioned earlier, the role of Sunan Kalijaga in the founding of this ancient hybrid mosque (and grave) of Sendang Dhuwur is worth noting. As local legend has it, the saint of Sendang Dhuwur (d. ca. 1585) was trying to purchase the original mosque from its proprietor, Queen Kalinyamat of Jepara. She refused at first and then only let it go due to the power of Sunan Kalijaga who intervened, helping the saint of Sendang Dhuwur relocate the mosque from its original location to the top of the hill at Dhuwur. As it stands now, this mosque is attached to the grave of this saint. Again, this rather typical story reveals the religio-cultural memory of Kalijaga as the originator of hybrid Javano-Islamic identity, including its artistic and architectural manifestations.[16]

In this continuum of hybrid art and architecture that is marked by combinations of Hindu, Buddhist, Chinese, and Islamic motifs, one sees the crucial role of the royal houses of Surakarta and Yogyakarta as the heirs of the Mataram dynasty that continue this pattern beyond the earliest phase in the late fifteenth or early sixteenth century. As examined in Chapter 1, the Javano-Islamic identity has been the religio-cultural hallmark of the Mataram dynasty since its foundation, and the role of Sunan Kalijaga in this regard is always regarded to be so foundational and paradigmatic. It is in the framework of this wider tradition of Javano-Islamic art, as well as the particular role of the courts of Yogyakarta and Surakarta, that the artistic and architectural specificities of the shrine of Tembayat should be understood.

In my view, what one sees here, both in the Tembayat shrine and the Yogyakarta and Surakarta palace, is the expansion of the religio-cultural dynamic of inclusivity and connection with the past. While the whole interpretive framework at Tembayat is largely Islamic—which makes sense given the identity of the saint being venerated here—there is an intentional effort to maintain connection with the Hindu-Javanese past. In this regard, the name of the mountain, Jabalkat, is insightful since it puts the whole shrine into an explicitly Islamic sacred geography. This name is clearly a Javanese corruption of the Arabic *Jabal al-Qāf*, which according to the Muslim tradition is the mother of all mountains, encircling most of the inhabited world.[17] Placed in this cosmic framework, the shrine of

---

[16] At times, this identity is contrasted to the notion of "pure" Islam, and in this regard, the superiority of Kalijaga over other more "pure" saints of Arab origins in Java is also seen as a proof of the superiority of the hybrid Javano-Islam. See John Miksic, "The Art of Cirebon and the Image of the Ascetic in Early Javanese Islam," p. 138; also Zakaria Ali, *Islamic Art in Southeast Asia*, p. 325.

[17] Ibn Faḍl Allāh al-'Umari (d. 1349) describes this mountain thus: "All mountains are branches of the range which encircles most of the inhabited world. It is called Jabal al-Qāf, and is the mother of mountains, for they all stem from it. It is in some places continuous, in others interrupted. Like a circle it has, to be precise, no recognizable beginning, since the ends of a circularity of the Jabal al-Qāf is not that of a sphere, yet it is a bounding circularity, or almost so." See N. Levtzion and J.F.P. Hopkins (eds), *Corpus of Early Arabic Sources for West African History* (Princeton, 2000), p. 254.

Tembayat becomes a kind of liminal space. This designation of Jabalkat is made more meaningful in the context of pilgrimage understood as an ascent to God and the true self, a journey that involves an intense process of ascetic purification, as many Javanese pilgrims would like to understand it. As has been mentioned in the previous chapter, ascetic purification is so central in the ascetic understanding of pilgrimage as *tirakat* and *laku* among Javanese Muslims in south central Java.

In this regard, the journey of the saint of Tembayat (Sunan Pandanarang) is exemplary. As discussed in Chapter 1, Sunan Pandanarang's ascent to sainthood under the tutelage of Sunan Kalijaga began with an arduous journey from the city of Semarang to Tembayat. In popular hagiography of this saint, this journey has always been understood as a journey of intense purification of the soul from its lower self (Ar. *nafs*), something that is necessary to pursue true friendship with and proximity to God (Ar. *walāya*). Only after he was able to purify himself, Sunan Pandanarang was allowed to reside in the peak of the Jabalkat hill. So, his residing in the hill is a symbolic sign of his status as a *walī*, an intimate friend of God.

This understanding of spiritual journey as an ascent to God is of course very familiar in the wider mystical tradition of Islam. In Farīd al-Dīn ʿAṭṭār's *Manṭiq al-ṭayr* (*Conference of the Birds*), this ascent is described so dramatically in terms of the journey of the thirty birds (representing different psycho-spiritual types of human being) to the Sīmurgh, the king of the birds, a symbolic representation of God, who resides in Jabal al-Qāf. In ʿAṭṭār's mystical framework, this arduous and purifying journey to the Sīmurgh or God occurs as a journey of discovery of the true self in its relation to God and other selves.[18] On this central relationship between the self and God in ʿAṭṭār, James Morris argues:

> The central—indeed the unique—subject of the poem is the intimate relation of God and the human soul, a relation that he describes most often in terms of the mystery or secret of divine Love. ... For the love that concerns him throughout this work is not simply a particular human emotion, or even the deeper goal of man's striving, but rather the ultimate Ground of all existence: the birds'/soul's pilgrimage itself turns out to be the unending self-discovery of that creative Love.[19]

In this framework, then, the human persons, both individually and together (the thirty birds of ʿAṭṭār), become a privileged site where manifestation and traces of God can be encountered.[20] In this respect, the mystery of the human person

---

[18] James Morris, *The Reflective Heart* (Louisville, 2005), p. 16; also his, "Reading ʿAṭṭār's 'Conference of the Birds'" in Wm. Theodore de Bary and Irene Bloom (eds), *Approaches to the Asian Classics* (New York, 1990), pp. 77–85.

[19] Morris, "Reading ʿAṭṭār's 'Conference of the Birds,'" pp. 78–9.

[20] Thus, on a deeper level, the whole symbolism of Jabal al-Qāf then still shares the basic Hindu-Javanese understanding of Mount Meru as macrocosm and its counterpart,

becomes like Jabal al-Qāf, that is, the very context of the ascending journey to God. As mentioned previously, this theological anthropology is the backbone of traditional Javanese mysticism. In this framework, such a spiritual and mystical interpretation of pilgrimage as ascending the Jabal al-Qāf seems to be natural.

What is unique about Tembayat in this respect is that the meaning of this Islamic symbolism of Jabal al-Qāf becomes more complex due to its spirit of including the other, namely the various Hindu-Javanese symbolisms, including the symbolism of Mount Meru in the form of the Hindu temple with its various gates. Perceptive pilgrims who ascend the hill of Tembayat as the symbolic Jabal al-Qāf have to take into account the symbolism of Mount Meru in the Gate of the Dragons (Jv. *regol sinaga*), just before they enter into the inner chamber that houses the grave of the saint. This symbolism could be a strong reminder that there is some possibly deeper affinity between Meru, the Hindu mountain, and Jabal al-Qāf, the Muslim mountain. In particular, the need for asceticism and the purification of soul in the ascent to the spiritual realm of God and His saints that these two symbolisms represent seems to stand out as a possible meeting point. It is worth noting that in the familiar Hindu-Javanese depiction, this sacred mountain is guarded by wild beasts or ogres at the lowest gate.

In the Javanese culture in general, under the influence of Indian cosmology, the symbolism of the Meru is very significant, both as the macrocosmic mountain and microcosmic map of spiritual ascent. The Meru symbolism is replicated in the Hindu and Buddhist temples throughout Java, as well as in the various architectural and ritual elements of the royal court culture. In this regard, the Borobudur temple is iconic because this Buddhist temple is structurally built in the template of Mount Meru (both in its overall structure and its thousands of stupas), and it also features, in the stories of the bas-reliefs as well as in the dynamic of movement from one layer to the next, the archetypal story of the spiritual ascent and enlightenment of the Buddha, a spiritual journey marked by intense purification.[21] Beyond the realm of these temples, the Meru symbolism finds its way into the Javanese culture in the central image of the *gunungan*, which literally means "the image of a mountain" in Javanese, found most significantly in the traditional shadow puppet theatre (Jv. *wayang*).[22] In the framework of its meaning as a cosmic mountain, the *gunungan* also symbolizes the mystical ascent of the human person to God. This is so because on the summit of this cosmic mountain stands the Tree of Life. However, in order to reach this peak, one has to overcome the wild beasts and ogres that guard the mountain. In this framework,

---

namely, the human person as micro-cosm. Cf. I.W. Mabbett, "The Symbolism of Mount Meru," *History of Religions*, 23 (1983): pp. 64–83.

[21] Cf. Julie Gifford, *Buddhist Practice and Visual Culture* (New York, 2011); Jacques Dumarcay, *Borobudur* (Oxford, 1992).

[22] Cf. Sumastuti Sumukti, *Gunungan: The Javanese Cosmic Mountain* (unpublished Ph.D. Dissertation, University of Hawaii, 1997). On the symbolism of the Tree of Life in Islam, see Schimmel, *Deciphering the Signs of God* (Albany, 1994), p. 17.

anyone who aspires to embark on a mystical ascent should take an arduous journey analogous to climbing up the mountain, reaching its peak which symbolizes the nirvanic experience of liberation, thus achieving the true destiny of his existence (corresponding to the Javanese *sangkan paran* mystical doctrine mentioned in the previous chapter).

Thus, in the framework of one's spiritual journey or pilgrimage to God and the true self, the symbolism of wild beast might be easily taken as a reminder for the pilgrims for the need to overcome the temptations of the egotistical self (Ar. *nafs*).[23] To return to ʿAṭṭār's mystical framework, the pilgrims are the "birds" who have to fight these wild beasts inside themselves in order to be able to embark on the journey toward the Sīmurgh. Armed by this victory over their own *nafs*, pilgrims would be ready to reach the liminal sphere of the true Jabal al-Qāf.

At this point, it has to be stated that this pattern of symbolic relationship between Islamic artistic tradition and other artistic traditions on the idea of purification is by no means peculiar to Java. Particularly insightful for the symbolisms of dragons found in the shrine of Tembayat as well as other shrines or mosques in Java are the various meanings of the dragon image in Islamic art. As Abbas Daneshvari has noted, the image of the dragon is a recurring and popular image in the arts, architecture, and literature of Islam.[24] To a certain degree, this image of the dragon and its various meanings are taken from non-Islamic cultures. In the framework of Islamic spirituality, however, the dragon had become the symbol of greed, attachment, and love for the worldly life; it was also used to describe the destructive aspect of human desire.[25]

Particularly pertinent to the image of the dragon at the Tembayat shrine—that is, the image of a royal crown guarded by two dragons—is the widespread depiction of the dragon as guardian of treasures and royal power. This belief might stem from the popular notion that dragons coil upon treasures, due to their greed and attachment to them. Thus, in this framework, to get access to these treasures, one needs to slay the dragons, an idea found in Muslim poets and mystics such as Nāṣir Khusraw, Farīd al-Dīn ʿAṭṭār, and ʿAbd al-Raḥmān Jāmī.[26] In the context of Islamic spirituality, then, it is the process of "slaying" these dragons that becomes much more important. The spiritual journey of purification, the pilgrimage of each human being, is nothing other than a transformation of this desire, the distorted human *nafs* represented by such "wild dragons." It is through this process that

---

[23] At Tembayat, through the symbolism of a crown guarded by two dragons and flanked by two meditating Buddhas at the center of the Gate of the Dragon, the end of the journey of true pilgrimage is imagined in terms of "power," a very crucial category of the manifestation of sainthood in Java.

[24] Abbas Daneshvari, "The Iconography of the Dragon in the Cult of the Saints of Islam," in Grace Martin Smith and Carl W. Ernst (eds), *Manifestations of Sainthood in Islam* (Istanbul, 1993), pp. 16–25.

[25] Daneshvari, "The Iconography," pp. 18–19.

[26] Ibid., pp. 19–20.

the spiritually enlightened persons like the saints become the true guardians of spiritual treasures. This idea is by no means alien to the wider Islamic tradition where the dragons are also believed to guard the spiritual treasures.[27] This feature might also be related to the popular pre-Islamic belief that the dragons were responsible for the eclipse of the "sun." However, it should also be pointed out that the employment of the "sun" as a symbol for God is known in the Islamic tradition as well.[28]

In light of this, one can understand the reasons why the image of the dragon is quite popular in shrines and tombs of Muslim saints.[29] For the saints as God's friends (Ar. *awliyā'*) and spiritual company can be seen as the real "dragons" who gather around the divine treasure. Like the dragons, they are powerful. But their power and authority are derived from their very participation in and proximity to God. This is the foundation of their power to perform miraculous feats (Ar. *karāmāt*). In this respect, the shrines of the saints also participate in this Divine treasure, turning into a milieu in which the blessings of God could be attained. Thus one can make sense of the aforementioned insight about the Tembayat shrine as a kind of liminal space in the sacred mountain (*Jabal al-Qāf*) where pilgrims find their true selves in God. The shrine only becomes liminal on account of the presence of Divine treasure there, a treasure that the saint(s) participate in and something that the pilgrims could obtain only through purifying their *nafs* along the ascent.[30]

At this point, it has to be stated that the interpretation of the possible symbolic meanings of the artistic decorations at the Tembayat shrine offered here is just one example of how the spatial and architectural pattern of including the other could mean for the pilgrims to this shrine. The presence of the other could simply complicate things, but it could also enrich the whole experience of pilgrimage, provided one has the right spiritual disposition. It is also crucial to recall here the nature of Islamic art as deeply contemplative and transforming, as James Morris argues: "What is essential in these arts is always what goes on inside each viewer or auditor, the mysterious inner shift in awareness from the sensible material, temporal forms in 'this world' (*al-dunya*) to their transcendent Source and Reality among the archetypal divine Names."[31]

---

[27] In the *Tales of the Prophets* (Ar. *qiṣaṣ al-anbiyā'*), for example, it is said that the Divine Throne is surrounded by mighty serpents. See Annemarie Schimmel, *Deciphering the Signs of God*, p. 25.

[28] Ibid., p. 14.

[29] As Daneshvari points out, there are many stories about the close friendship between Muslim saints and dragons. See his, "The Iconography," p. 23.

[30] In certain patterns of Safavid rugs, the idea of the purification of the soul is also described by using animal images for the snares of worldly temptations. See Schuyler V.R. Cammann, "Religious Symbolism in Persian Art," *History of Religions*, 15 (1976): p. 198.

[31] James Morris, "Remembrance and Repetition: Spiritual Foundations of Islamic Art," *Sufi* (Autumn 2000): p. 18.

In this framework, the inclusion of the other in the Islamic arts as found in the shrine of Tembayat could be particularly significant. First, for the contemplative pilgrims, this inclusion of the other could mean that the religious other is included in their very ascent to God, whatever this might mean. Secondly, this contemplation should also help the pilgrims purify their hearts *vis-à-vis* the Hindu-Javanese artistic symbolisms, that is, finding their deeper meanings, rather than seeing them merely as an extraneous or "un-Islamic" representations of things. As has been shown previously, many of these Hindu-Javanese symbolisms themselves point to the need of this purification of the hearts. This point is particularly relevant given the fact that as I will discuss in Chapter 3, purification is such a central aspect in the experience of Javanese Muslim pilgrims who practice pilgrimage as an intense period of spiritual cultivation (Jv. *tirakat*) accompanied by purifying practices of prayers, meditation, and asceticisms (Jv. *laku*).

Although, for the most part, typical Javanese pilgrims would not articulate their experience of this complex religious world in any systematic fashion, its effect in terms of the formation of a distinctive Javano-Islamic identity is quite real. For one thing, this inclusion of the other can be taken as a creative realization of the prophetic admonition of Kalijaga when he told the future saint of Tembayat to remove his mosque from the top of the hill to the lower ground. Now, it becomes entirely proper, even desirable, for the body of the saint to repose on the very top of the hill, precisely because the whole shrine has served as a sign of inclusivity, rather than haughtiness.

Due to the limitation of space in this book, I could not do justice to the complex topic of the development of Islamic arts *vis-à-vis* other religio-cultural traditions, such as Byzantine and Buddhist traditions.[32] However, what is crucial here is to never lose sight of the role of local society in the creation of this Islamic art and architecture. For as Grabar has argued, "monumental architecture has a close relationship to the society which surrounds it, sponsors it and uses it."[33] In this respect, what I have shown so far is the role of the Javanese culture and society in the creation of hybrid art that has both Islamic and Hindu-Javanese elements.

My basic argument here is that behind the creation and maintenance of such a hybrid art lies the local Javanese Muslim society's rather distinctive understanding of Islamic identity. Now a question might arise as to the role of such a hybrid art precisely with regard to formation and expression of Islamic identity. Due to its hybridity, can this art still be considered a true representation of Islam? On this question, Titus Burckhardt's categorical argument is worth noting:

> If one were to reply to the question "what is Islam?" by simply pointing to one of the masterpieces of Islamic art such as, for example, the Mosque of Cordova,

---

[32] Oleg Grabar, *Early Islamic Art, 650–1100*, vol. 1 (Aldershot, 2005), pp. 3–41; Géza Fehérvári, "Islamic Incense-burners and the Influence of Buddhist Art," in O'Kane, *The Iconography of Islamic Art*, pp. 127–41.

[33] Oleg Grabar, *Islamic Art and Beyond*, vol. 3 (Aldershot, 2006), p. 248.

or that of Ibn Tulun in Cairo, or one of the *madrasah*s in Samarqand or even the Taj Mahal, that reply, summary as it is, would be nonetheless valid, for the art of Islam expresses what its name indicates, and *it does so without ambiguity*.[34] (emphasis added)

In light of Burckhardt's statement, the shrines and tombs of Muslim saints in south central Java, or in the whole Java for that matter, have never been called "the masterpieces of Islamic art." For the most part, they are architecturally unassuming and modest. But, to return to Grabar's point on the relationship between Islamic architecture and its society, one can say that these shrines of the saints, in terms of their artistic and architectural forms as well as historical significance, are intimately related to the process of identity formation or self-understanding of the Javano-Islamic society that built them.

And, as has been discussed in the previous chapter, since the society itself is not free from creative tensions and ambiguities *vis-à-vis* the pre-Islamic traditions, then its architecture could not afford except to be so. While it is often harder to understand the deeper—as opposed to the practical or technical—reasoning behind some examples of hybrid art in other parts of the Islamic world during the more distant historical periods,[35] the case of south central Java is rather different largely because we have some knowledge about its underlying logic, that is the principle of continuity and communion with the complex heritage of the past, a principle that is kept alive in the court culture and pilgrimage tradition. Contrary to Burckhardt's notion of the non-ambiguous character of the masterpieces of Islamic art, the application of the principle of continuity in Java is not without ambiguities.

This ambiguity allows for some room for continuous discernment and negotiation on the part of the Javanese Muslim community, a complex process that also involves the active participation of the pilgrims, as I will discuss in the next chapter. In light of this, one can say that the hybrid architecture and art of these Islamic shrines not only answers the question of "what is Islam?" but also does it in a very concrete yet open fashion in the particular context of south central Java, precisely due to its complex ambiguity, understood positively as a result of a religio-cultural negotiation of identity that in south central Java has been associated with the paradigmatic roles of Sunan Kalijaga and other *wali*s and perpetuated by the Javano-Islamic courts of Yogyakarta and Surakarta. Precisely in this sense, this hybrid art expresses the universal spirit of Islam as an inclusive spiritual as well as a complex and enduring cultural force, a true blessing for the whole cosmos (Ar. *raḥmatan lil-'ālamin*).

---

[34] Burckhardt, *Art of Islam: Language and Meaning*, Commemorative edn (Bloomington, 2009), p. xv.

[35] Géza Fehérvári, "Islamic Incense-burners and the Influence of Buddhist Art," in O'Kane, *The Iconography of Islamic Art*, p. 138.

The Self and Other in Javano-Islamic Rituals and Festivals

As noted previously, the Muslim pilgrimage tradition in south central Java has been known for its bolder and richly elaborate Javanese character, compared to its counterparts in East and West Java. This characteristic is displayed mainly in the local pilgrimage rituals. In this section, I will illustrate how the complex dynamic of inclusive identity, involving Javanese and Islamic elements, occurs in the rituals and festivals of the shrines under study, by focusing on: (a) the ritual etiquette of making pilgrimage; (b) the role of the ritual communal meal (Jv. *slametan*) as the meeting point between veneration of saints and memory of ancestors; and (c) the influence of the distinctive Javanese court culture of imperial festivals (Jv. *garebeg*) and its concomitant veneration of sacred heirlooms (Jv. *pusaka*) in the major festivals of shrines.

Javano-Islamic Etiquette of Pilgrimage and Shrine Festivals

At the shrines of Tembayat and Mawlana Maghribi, a great number of Javanese pilgrims would continually follow a largely Javanese ritual etiquette of tomb visitation combined with the more standardized Islamic ritual etiquette (Ar. *adab al-ziyāra*). Typically, after climbing the hundreds of steps to the top of the Jabalkat hill where the grave of Sunan Tembayat is located, pilgrims take off their shoes to enter the compound; then they do the ablution in the area next to the old Javanese style mosque. Many would change their clothes, and some would go to the old mosque to do the prayer (Ar. *ṣalāt*). All pilgrims would then proceed to the registration desk where the custodian of the outer area (Jv. *juru kunci jaba*) records their data, typically their name, address, intention of the visit, and the amount of donation. This custodian would not typically don the traditional Javanese outfit. As I will show below, it is the inner area custodians (Jv. *juru kunci jero*) who have to put on the traditional Javanese clothing. Apparently, this distinction has much to do with the ritual function and perception of sacredness. For the rites that the inner area custodians perform occur in the area closer to the sacred tomb of the saint, and thus requires more respectful etiquette that is outwardly expressed in the various element of the rituals including a variety of Javanese cultural elements (more on this below). It is very interesting that this respect for God and His saint is symbolically represented, among others, by the donning of Javanese traditional clothing. After recording their visits, pilgrims have the choice either to use the service of the inner area custodian of the shrine, or to proceed to the mausoleum of the saint through various gates on their own. Many ordinary Javanese pilgrims to this shrine would opt for the former. The incorporation of local Javanese culture into this ritual etiquette is rather striking. It makes use of the Javanese language and other culturally symbolic gestures and items such as the *sembah* position,[36] incense and certain kinds of flowers that are considered ritually fitting in Javanese culture (Jv. *kembang telon*). Donning a Javanese traditional outfit and sitting cross-legged in a Javanese style, the inner area custodian helps the pilgrims with their visitation (the *jawab* ritual). After asking the pilgrim's intention of making the *ziarah*, the custodian would lead the recitation of petition prayers in a hybrid mix of the highest register of Javanese—the only appropriate linguistic tool for addressing God and the saint in Javanese—and broken Arabic.[37] The pilgrims would then go to the inner chamber of the mausoleum, passing through the last gate, the Gate of the Dragons (Jv. *regol sinaga*) and the very small door. Once inside, sitting in the Javanese meditation position (Jv. *sila*) and facing the dark wooden chamber that houses the sarcophagus of the saint, they would offer personal prayers (Jv. *donga*, Ar. *du'ā*).

Just outside the door of the dark chamber, another custodian will be available to help the pilgrims with their visit. He would typically lead the ritual prayer together with the pilgrim(s) who ask for his service. Generally, this ritual consists of greetings to the saint, request for God's forgiveness for the saint, expression of the pilgrim's intentions, and gratitude to the saint. Then the pilgrims finally get inside the dark chamber through a very narrow and low door, so that they have to literally bow down to reach the graves of the saint and his two wives. Many would rub the tomb three times with their hands, then wipe their faces three times as a gesture of securing the *baraka* of God and the saint.[38] Most pilgrims would then put the flowers on the graves of the saint and his two wives while murmuring some prayers. Pilgrims would normally set aside some flowers to be placed on the other graves of the saint's family members in the outer part of the chamber. Believing that the flowers now contain the *baraka* of the saint, pilgrims take some flower petals from the gravestones and bring them home as a memorial and portable blessing.[39] Many pilgrims would spend a considerable time on private prayers in silence before they leave to ensure the personal character of the visit.

---

[36] In religious or ritual context, *sembah* is a ritual hand-gesture of respect, devotion and adoration made by holding the hands before the face, palms together, thumbs touching the nose, and bowing the head slightly. Some Javanese Muslim pilgrims would do the *sembah* when approaching the gravestone of the saint. Rather surprisingly, it is the Catholics who make use of this gesture more abundantly during mass and other devotional prayers including pilgrimage. Its origin is most probably pre-Islamic because of its similarity with the Hindu hand-position during the *puja* worship.

[37] Jamhari, "The Meaning Interpreted: The Concept of *Barakah* in *Ziarah*," *Studia Islamika*, 8 (2001): p. 92.

[38] Ibid., p. 77.

[39] The centrality of flowers in the pilgrimage culture at Tembayat has a lot to do with Javanese understanding of pilgrimage as *nyekar* (from the word *sekar*, meaning "flowers"), that is, visitation to the tombs of ancestors that includes putting the flowers on the graves. For these pilgrims, the saint of Tembayat has become a revered ancestor of the community. See Jamhari, "In the Center of Meaning," pp. 70–78.

Although the hybrid *ziyāra* rituals are so prevalent at the Tembayat shrine, there is no fixed ritual for all pilgrims in this shrine.[40] In fact, one finds other types of pilgrims who do not follow the hybrid Javano-Islamic ritual etiquette, and instead would stick to the more standardized Islamic ritual etiquette of tomb visitation (Ar. *adab al-ziyāra*), that is, with minimal influence from local culture. When they come in groups, the leader would lead the standard prayers for shrine visitation (mostly in Arabic) that are used widely in other shrines throughout Java. The basic structures of this *adab* could be found in the popular pilgrimage guidebooks. In terms of the prayers, it typically consists of: the *tahlīl* prayer (the recitation of the formula "no god but God") and other short prayer formulas like the *tasbīḥ* (prayer for the glory of God), *istighfār* (request for God's forgiveness); the recitation of Qurʾānic chapters, typically the 36th chapter, the *Sūra Yā Sīn*, or the 112th chapter, the *Sūra al-Ikhlāṣ*, or at least the Throne Verse (Ar. *āyāt al-kursī*) from the second chapter of the Qurʾān; the *ṣalāḥ* (prayer for blessings on the Prophet Muḥammad); the *tawassul* prayer (the intercessory invocations of prophets, saints and other righteous persons).[41] These kinds of pilgrims would also perform other additional prayers together inside the inner chamber of the mausoleum. In some cases, this prayer session can be reasonably long. Some of them would also start the visit by praying the *ṣalāt* in the old mosque in the shrine. Within the plurality of rituals at the shrine, the case of Chinese pilgrims is very interesting. Since Sunan Pandanarang was a former prince-regent of Semarang, many Chinese merchants from this city would pay a visit to him in Tembayat for homage and blessings. They consider him as their ancestor whose intercession is particularly potent due to his former position. Of course, the great majority of them are not Muslims, so they would follow their own way of doing the rituals, mostly in the form of a Buddhist or Confucian ritual that is common among the Chinese in Java.

In the context of my argument in this book, it is important to see that this standardized Islamic ritual etiquette of tomb visitation is in fact a combination of prayers of supplications and intercessions (Ar. *tawassul*) to God and His spiritual company, particularly the prophets and saints, and prayers for the dead. In this framework, the invocations of the prophets and saints are always done in the framework of praise and prayers to God. The underlying logic at work is that of a prayerful remembrance of the prophets and saints in the form of offering prayers and blessings to them. In this respect, visitation to the dead is conceived as no different from visiting living persons. The pilgrims greet the dead, both the pious and the ordinary, in direct speech because the dead are present or aware of their visits. It is for the same reason that pilgrims have to bring a gift (of prayers) as a sign of love, respect, and connection.

Only within this framework of prayerful remembrance of God and His spiritual company could one understand the intercessory part of the prayer. Sometimes in

---

[40] This is what Jamhari calls "a polyphony" of rituals. See his "The Meaning Interpreted," p. 91.

[41] See Labib M.Z., *Tuntunan Ziarah Walisongo* (Surabaya, 2000).

very general terms, pilgrims ask the intercessions of the Prophet(s) and saints before God. In this connection, the dynamic of inclusivity of the list of the holy and paradigmatic figures being invoked in the prayer is worth noting. It starts with the Prophet Muḥammad and his family; it then proceeds to other prophets, angels, saints and martyrs, and all the righteous (Ar. *ṣaliḥūn*), before mentioning particular saints, typically ʿAbd al-Qādir al-Jīlānī and the local saint whose tomb is being visited. The list then continues with all the inhabitants of the graves (Ar. *ahl al-qubr*), both the *muslimūn* (literally those who submit to God) and the *muʾminūn* (those who have faith), before it concludes with the immediate ancestors, teachers, and parents of the pilgrims. The universal tone of this concept is made clear in the prayer. For it specifies further that these figures are both men and women, from East and West, those in the sea and on the land.[42] Very interestingly, a specific mention is made about all those persons who have been instrumental in the lives of the pilgrims. Again, the inclusive scope of this list is striking, while the sense of lively and overwhelming communion with all these figures is so remarkable.[43]

In the next section I will deal with the question of how these two features are at work in the Javanese ritual-communal meal (Jv. *slametan*). However, before delving into this very important ritual-communal meal and its intimate relationship with saint veneration and loving remembrance of ancestors, I will briefly discuss another crucial aspect in these dynamics of blessings and intercession (Ar. *tawassul*) in pilgrimage tradition, namely, the regular celebration of the saint by the pilgrims and their communities.

In Tembayat, the blessing of the saint is believed to be abundantly available for all and takes on a very communal character on the eve of Friday *Legi* in the hybrid Javano-Islamic calendar (once every 35 days). During this night, local devotees as well as pilgrims from near and far form a single community in celebration of the saint. In general, the atmosphere of this night is ludic, festive, and serene. A large crowd of locals and pilgrims would gather in the plaza, the outermost part of the whole shrine compound at the foot of the hill, where they can enjoy all sorts of entertainment and converse with one another. Then, as the night goes deeper, the crowd would do the ascent (Jv. *munggah*) to the peak of Jabalkat to the grave of the saint, trekking through hundreds of steps.

Souvenirs shops and food stalls are still to be found on both sides of these steps, but upon reaching the inner compound of the grave, marked by the area of ablution, the worldly festive character at the foot of the hill changes into a

---

[42] Labib M.Z., *Tuntunan Ziarah Wali Songo*, p. 57. The concept of *īmān* (and its derivation, *muʾmin*) is central to the Qurʾān, and it does not primarily refer to "belief" but rather faith, inner peace and absolute assurance, total trust, granted by God. Thus it is foundational and existential disposition of human being *vis-à-vis* God. Cf. Farid Esack, *Qurʾan, Liberation and Pluralism* (Oxford, 1997), pp. 117–26; also Toshihiko Izutsu, *The Concept of Belief in Islamic Theology* (Tokyo, 1965).

[43] On the *tawassul* prayers used in West Java, see Julian Millie, *Splashed by the Saints* (Leiden, 2009), pp. 101–7.

communal celebration of spiritual devotion to the saint on the top of the hill. The cacophonies of loud music and chatters are replaced by unison of communal ritual chants and divine invocations (Ar. *dhikr*) in a mix of Javanese and Arabic in the Surakarta melody in the big prayer hall, led by a group of custodians donning green Javanese traditional outfits. While this *dhikr* is underway, throngs of pilgrims continue to flow in. Some pilgrims would stop by to participate in this rather long session of prayer, then proceed to the inner chamber of the mausoleum, to do their own group *dhikr* or other forms of prayers in front of the grave of the saint.

During this celebration, most pilgrims would come with their families, including children. In rural Java, at few other occasions would they bring children out this late. While most of them would leave the shrine an hour or two after midnight, believing that the *baraka* of the saint would descend to them during this particular time period, a large number of pilgrims even spend the whole night in the shrine doing vigil (Jv. *tirakat*).[44] During this night, the boundaries between the tomb as the place for the dead and the community of the living seem to disappear, as the tomb-shrine becomes a lighted city where the dead are brought back to life in the memory and devotion of the living.

Thanksgiving to God, the Saints and Ancestors (the Slametan *Ritual)*

As has been mentioned earlier, the ritual activities in the Islamic shrines in south central Java have another crucial and distinctive feature. It is the *slametan*, that is, a communal and ritual meal. In accordance with the wider Javanese ritual etiquette of holding this *slametan* as a thanksgiving meal to God, the prophets, saints and ancestors, some pilgrims at Tembayat whose prayers have been granted would also return to the shrine, bringing traditional food for this ritual-communal meal.[45] The custodian on duty will also officiate at this hybrid ritual meal. Pilgrims interpret this ritual meal not only as a sign of gratitude to the saint, but also a sharing of the blessing of the saint to the others.[46] In this way the communal character of this meal is completed. A rather grand *slametan* ceremony, where more pilgrims and local devotees bring food offerings and abundant flowers, is held regularly in late

---

[44] The same ritual was also held regularly on Friday eve at the court of Mangkunegaran in Surakarta in the eighteenth century. This ritual was followed by a regular *slametan* after the Friday prayer at the court's main mosque. This shows a close relationship between the Javano-Islamic culture of the court and that of the shrines. See Ann Kumar, *Java and Modern Europe: Ambiguous Encounters* (Richmond, 1997), pp. 57–60.

[45] At Tembayat, some pilgrims would hold a *slametan* at the beginning of the *ziarah*, as a means of declaring their intention and readiness to receive the *baraka* of the saint. See Jamhari, "The Meaning Interpreted," p. 109.

[46] In this respect, *slametan* food is often referred to as a "gift of the heart" stemming from a deep desire to help one's fellow humans. Woodward, "The 'Slametan': Textual Knowledge and Ritual Performance in Central Javanese Islam," *History of Religions*, 28 (1988): p. 64.

afternoons of the Friday *Legi*, to begin the communal celebration at the shrine that I discussed in the previous section.

Before proceeding further, it should be noted that there is an ongoing debate among scholars with regard to the nature of this ritual-communal meal of *slametan*. Mark Woodward argues for the truly Islamic character of this ritual meal, i.e., that it could be explained fully within the larger Islamic framework (the textual and mystical tradition), while Andrew Beatty emphasizes its multivocal character.[47] In my view, this debate further reinforces the centrality of the *slametan* in the Javano-Islamic complex identity, so much so that when a shrine holds the *slametan* regularly, one can be sure that this shrine and its pilgrims understand themselves as *Javanese*-Muslims, as opposed to just "Muslims." Although this practice is also known in other parts of the Muslim world, it has become one of the most important features of Javanese ritual and communal life. Traditionalist Muslims in Java consider this ritual-communal meal as a crucial part of their identity and thus from time to time have to defend this practice against the assaults from the modernist Muslims. The same can be said of Catholic shrines in Java where a regular *slametan* is also held (more on this in Chapter 5).

Against the background of this debate and in light of the subject matter of this book, it is crucial to see the particular role of the *slametan* as a particular expression of religio-cultural habit of devotion among pilgrims. For the nature of *slametan* is a thanksgiving meal where the community comes together in the presence of God and His spiritual company or court: prophets, saints, as well as all members of the invisible world, including the ancestors. It is one of the most central ways in which the Javanese express their relatedness with God and His saints as a community through the categories of "*slamet*" (derived from the Arabic *salāma*, the Javanese holistic notion of well-being) and "*berkah*" (Ar. *baraka*, blessing, blessedness).

In this respect, one should not fail to notice the centrality and ubiquity of the *slametan* in Javanese religious tradition, beyond the particular context of pilgrimage, but still in an organic relationship to the larger veneration of saints and loving devotion to (and remembrance of) ancestors. Traditional Javanese of all faiths hold the *slametan* in the face of every important life event such as rites of passage, communal festivities and so forth, in order to secure the blessing of God and His spiritual company of saints and their ancestors, precisely because these figures are an integral part of their community, on whose blessings the wellbeing of the community depends. Crucial in this ritual meal is the invocation of the saints and spirits to whom the ritual food is symbolically offered, before being shared to the participants. Interestingly, at least in the original and complete form, the saints and spirits have to be invited by name to the ritual. In this connection, it is crucial to note as well that the *slametan* is practiced in different ways among contemporary

---

[47] See Woodward, "The *Slametan*," pp. 54–89; Beatty, "Adam and Eve and Vishnu: Syncretism in the Javanese *Slametan*," *The Journal of the Royal Anthropological Institute*, 2 (1996): pp. 271–88.

Javanese. However, the original and complete form of it has the feature of calling the prophets, saints, Javanese kings, spirits of the ancestors, local guardian spirits, and so forth by names to ensure the personal character of the invitation.[48] In this regard, the *santri* Muslims—namely those who are not so much influenced by the Javanese culture—generally invite more Arabic saints, while the more Javanese-influenced Muslims would also invoke the spirits of Hindu-Javanese kings, many of whom are said to have been converted to Islam after death.

It should be noted that this feature of invocation of saints and spirits is strikingly similar to the pilgrimage ritual etiquette (Ar. *adab al-ziyāra*) discussed earlier, especially the direct and personal greetings of pilgrims to the prophet(s), saints and all the "people of the graves" (Ar. *ahl al-qubr*). The invocation of these figures is a pivotal part of the prayer of supplications in the Islamic pilgrimage etiquette.[49] So, in this regard, one sees a deeper organic connection between pilgrimage tradition and ritual-communal meal. Both are marked by the spirit of communing with God and His spiritual company of prophets, saints, and ancestors of the community. More specifically, this communion is done through prayerful remembrance of these figures in the presence of God. During the occasion, the community gathers to offer prayers or praises to these figures, and to receive blessings in return.

In south central Java, the intimate relationship between veneration of saints, remembrance of ancestors, and the *slametan* finds its most communal and ritual expression in the celebration of *ruwahan* (or *sadranan*) that occurs on the twenty-seventh of the Islamic month of Shaʿbān, immediately preceding the fasting month of Ramadan.[50] This annual ritual for the dead has two major elements, namely, visiting the grave of the ancestors and the holding of the *slametan* in the cemeteries or mosques nearby. At Tembayat, this *ruwahan* ritual is central and quite elaborate because it coincides with the anniversary of the death of Sunan Pandanarang.[51] It normally begins with the cleansing of the graves by the community, and culminating in the offering of the food to the saint (and the

---

[48] Woodward, "The *Slametan*," p. 76.

[49] For a roughly similar pilgrimage etiquette in the medieval Syria and Egypt, see Meri, *The Cult of Saints*, pp. 145ff; Taylor, *In the Vicinity of the Righteous*, p. 70ff.

[50] The Javanese word *ruwahan* is derived from the Arabic word for soul or spirit (sg. *rūḥ*, pl. *arwāḥ*). The spirit of this celebration is strikingly similar to All Souls Day in Christianity. In the larger context of Muslim piety, the month of Shaʿbān (called "Ruwah" in Java) is considered a special month for self-purification and tomb visitation. In Java, this month is traditionally connected to the communal ritual of village cleansing (Jv. *bersih desa*). By visiting and cleansing the graves of the ancestors and saints, Javanese Muslims seek the special blessings that they need to undergo a process of self-purification in the month of Ramadan.

[51] The tradition of holding a *slametan* on the occasion of the anniversary (Jv. *haul*) of the death of the saints is popular in Java. Cf. Ann Kumar, *The Diary of a Javanese Muslim* (Canberra, 1985), p. 154.

subsequent distribution of the food to all present) and the ritual of changing the cloth of his grave, accompanied by various performances of Javanese traditional music and dances. This is the biggest annual celebration in the shrine when the whole community of local Muslims and other pilgrims express their common devotion and relatedness to the shrine and its saint, in a way that puts this saint in the company of their dead ancestors.[52]

In this regard, then, the holding of the *slametan* at the shrine could be understood perfectly within the larger Javanese tradition of saint veneration and remembrance of ancestors. Shrines and sacred tombs are places where the *slametan* acquires more specific meanings due to its location in the devotion and connectedness of the pilgrims and their communities to a particular saint. However, it is also through this ritual that the particularity of this devotion is put in a larger framework of saint veneration and loving remembrance of ancestors. This is so partly due to the inclusive nature of sainthood (in the sense of protectorship) and the list of the saint-protectors invoked in the *slametan* ritual. The Javanese proclivity to expand the list of saints and ancestors invoked in the *slametan* could be explained in several ways. Obviously, it is an attempt to embrace the universal and cosmic power represented by paradigmatic figures and saints from different religions, whether historical or legendary. Thus it is not surprising that the most comprehensive list would start with Adam, the prototype of the human person but also the first prophet in the Islamic tradition, then go down to different prophets, the Prophet Muḥammad and his early companions, the Islamic saints and monarchs in Java and also some figures from the Javanese-Hindu tradition, such as Vishnu and others.[53]

Saints and Communal Identity: The Haul *Festivals*

The inclusive and communal nature of the *slametan* is displayed in its most splendid grandeur during the imperial festivals of *garebeg*, held three times a year on the occasions of the three major Islamic feasts (*'Īdu al-Fiṭr*, *'Īdu al-'Aḍḥā*, and *Mawlid al-Nabī*) by both the royal houses of Surakarta and Yogyakarta. Here, the spirit of the *slametan* becomes the pivot of the festivals of the realm since the peak of this festival is the offering of the gigantic food-mountains (Jv. *gunungan*) as a symbol of thanksgiving to God for the wellbeing of the realm and the distribution

---

[52] Every year during the *ruwahan* or *sadranan*, the royal house of Yogyakarta would send some financial support and ritual items to the shrine of Mawlana Maghribi because the saint is considered the revered ancestor (Jv. *pundhen*) of this court.

[53] Ann Kumar, *Java and Modern Europe*, p. 60. It seems that the model for inclusivity of this pantheon of saints and prophets is to be found in the court tradition of identifying two sides in their ancestral genealogy. The right side (Jv. *panengen*) of this genealogy includes the prophets and saints descended from Adam via Islamic figures, while the left side (Jv. *pangiwa*) is the line of descent from Adam through Hindu-Javanese gods, including Javanese kings. See Ricklefs, *Mystic Synthesis*, p. 171.

of these food-offerings to the people as a symbol of the generosity of the king to his people. Employing a vast array of Javanese symbolisms, these festivals also feature another ritual element of sainthood, understood specifically in terms of sacred power that becomes a rather distinctive hallmark of the anniversary festival of the saints (the *haul* festival) in Java, namely, the cleansing of the sacred heirloom (Jv. *jamas pusaka*) and the subsequent heirloom procession (Jv. *kirab pusaka*).[54]

Modeled on the court rituals and festivals, the *haul* festivals of saints in various shrines in south central Java have two major elements, i.e., Islamic and Javanese. In both Tembayat and Gunungpring shrines, the *haul* celebration includes recitation of the Qur'ān, the reading of the al-Barzanjī text[55] and a short biography of the saint; communal *dhikr*; traditional Islamic musical performance (Jv. *terbangan*); circumcision of boys and so forth. It also includes Javanese cultural performances, such as the *wayang* shadow theater, traditional dances, ritual procession using abundant Javanese cultural symbolisms, from clothing to gestures, and so forth. At the Gunungpring shrine, this celebration occurs on the same day of the Islamic New Year, a very important day in the Javano-Islamic calendar. On the eve of this day, the royal houses of Surakarta and Yogyakarta would send offerings to a number of sacred places, including the mausoleums and shrines of saints connected to the royal court such as the shrines of Gunungpring and Mawlana Maghribi.

Another distinctive aspect of the *haul* celebration in Java has to do with the ritual of changing the cloth that covers the sarcophagus of the saint and the rite of heirloom cleansing. Obviously, there is a rather close relationship between these rituals and the Javanese royal ritual of heirloom cleansing that occurs typically during the Islamic New Year.[56] Furthermore, extension of Muslim veneration of saints to objects that were connected to the saints or prophets is not unheard of in many other parts of the Muslim world.[57] In the context of Java, this interconnection among categories of sainthood, certain weapons as the most potent heirlooms,

---

[54] Hamengku Buwono X, *Kraton Jogja*, pp. 114–25.

[55] Composed by the Shāfi'ī *muftī* of Medina, Ja'far ibn Ḥasan ibn 'Abd al-Karīm al-Barzanjī (d. 1764), the al-Barzanjī's text is one of the most beloved traditional panegyrics to the Prophet Muḥammad. In many parts of the Muslim world, this text is recited during the celebration of the Prophet's birthday (Ar. *mawlid*). By participating in this celebration, many Muslims believe they obtain the blessings and intercession of the Prophet. In this respect, the spirit of the *mawlid* celebration is in line with the framework of the *tawassul* prayer discussed earlier.

[56] In some major shrines, this ritual is called "*buka luwur*." At the tomb of Sunan Kudus, this also occurs on the first of Muharram. The connection to the Javanese ritual of heirloom cleansing (Jv. *jamas pusaka*) is very obvious at this shrine. In fact, the *haul* celebration begins with the cleansing of a Javanese dagger believed to be the possession of the saint during his lifetime. The ritual of heirloom cleansing is also held in other major shrines in Java. See Inajati A. Romli, *Jejak Para Wali dan Ziarah Spiritual* (Jakarta, 2006), *passim*.

[57] This practice should also be understood in relation to the veneration of the Prophet Muḥammad's "relics" such as his hair, beard, mantle, sandal, footprint, and so forth. See Annemarie Schimmel, *And Muhammad Is His Messenger* (Chapel Hill, 1985), pp. 39–45;

and the court culture might stem from both the fact that some of the major local saints were also kings or heads of independent communities or polities, and the widespread belief that kings are considered "saints" due to the supernatural power they obtain *qua* kings.

In many shrines that hold the heirloom cleansing ceremony, another feature of court culture is also adopted, namely the grand public procession of the heirlooms (Jv. *kirab pusaka*). During this moment, the sacred objects that generally are kept out of public sight become visible. Thus, the *kirab pusaka* is a ritual moment where a normally hidden aspect of sainthood is unveiled. For most Javanese today, the ritually traveling "relics" serve more as a memory of the founding of the realm and the community, although the aspect of sainthood in the form of relics has not completely disappeared either. It is the aspect of paying homage to the ancestors and preserving the tradition in memory of them that come to be emphasized in the contemporary practice of this ritual. The *kirab pusaka* of Ki Ageng Pandanarang, the saint of Tembayat, in the regency of Semarang is also presented as an expression of communal identity by returning to the founder and founding moment of the community (Jv. *asal-usul*). Prior to the ritual, the regent, considered to be a successor to the saint, would perform a *ziarah* to the tomb at Tembayat. The cleansing of six heirlooms lasted for 15 days. After being cleansed, they are then presented to the current regent, before being taken for procession that culminates in the main plaza (Jv. *alun-alun*). The tone of the whole ritual is Javanese—obviously patterned on the grand royal procession of the Javanese courts—except for the Arab-style clothing of some of the heirloom bearers.[58] In general, this annual ritual has much to do with fostering a local identity around the figure of the saint as the founder.

In this regard, the wider context of Islamic tradition could help us understand the dynamics of this symbolism (dagger and the procession) better, especially in terms of its function as a memory of the founding of the community. The veneration of relics in the form of a sacred sword is rather well known in the Islamic tradition, for example in the discovery by ʿAbd al-Muṭṭalib of swords and armor in the treasure of the Kaʿba, as well as the sword of Muḥammad and ʿAlī. In general, a sword is used in many cultures as a symbol of royal and religious authority. However, as Wheeler has argued, the discovery of a sword at the Kaʿba is taken as a symbol of the dawn of the Islamic civilization.[59] The public display and procession of the relics of the Prophet Muḥammad's hair is also a known part of the *mawlid* celebration in some places.[60]

---

also Ignaz Goldziher, "The Veneration of Saints in Islam," *Muslim Studies*, 2 (1971): pp. 255–341.

[58] *Suara Merdeka Daily*, December 20, 2003.

[59] See Brannon Wheeler, *Mecca and Eden: Ritual, Relics, and Territory in Islam* (Chicago, 2006), p. 43.

[60] Wheeler, *Mecca and Eden*, p. 75.

In relation to our discourse on identity and alterity, festivals have a unique role to play due to their inclusive aspect as well as their significance as celebrations of the founding moment of the entire community. Clearly, the hybridity of the festivals is consistent with the complex identity of the community, precisely because the "festival is a special context for the construction of ethnicity and socio-religious behavior and experience."[61] The Javanese pattern of "including" is clearly at display during these most splendid festivals. Modeled on the court *garebeg*, the various festivals at Muslim shrines in south central Java become rather unique moments where the foundational interconnection between ethnic and religious identities is re-enacted. The centrality of the *slametan* in such festivals also reinforces a sense of inclusivity precisely because the blessings that it brings are deeply universal in their scope.

Muslim Saints as Religious Guarantors and Cultural Brokers

In the previous section I have discussed that the inclusivity and hybridity of the shrine rituals in south central Java are a remarkable participatory element in constituting and affirming Javano-Islamic identity. The first part of this chapter has also shown how Kalijaga and other *wali*s are seen to be the propagator of this Islamic inclusivity in the adoption of local Javanese cultures, arts and festivals. The continuation of the *garebeg* festivals is also attributed to their support and initiative. Indeed, this is probably the most public aspect of the Javano-Islamic identity.

The power of this particular framework of identity seems to lie in its ability to create room for diverse understandings and practices. Thus pilgrims who feel more as a Muslim than a Javanese would still be able to be fully present at the shrines, largely due to the fact that the interpretation of the symbols of these rituals is not monolithic; and thus concrete participation always allows for many different interpretation and meanings.[62] In this regard, Javano-Muslim shrines in south central Java continue to be sites where different ways of engagement with regard to the notion of sainthood, rituals, histories, and other features are not only allowed but also welcome and celebrated. It is even possible to see these sites as the embodiment of the deep, complex, and at times ambiguous intersections of religion and culture. By ambiguity, I refer to the fact that some of the features of this framework can be taken in different directions. Arguably, this ambiguity also

---

[61] David D. Harnish, *Bridges to the Ancestors* (Honolulu, 2006), p. 3.

[62] In this respect, my fieldwork confirms Beatty's observation (in his "Adam and Eve and Vishnu") on the plurality of interpretive frameworks on Javanese rituals, for example, about the role of the Goddess of the Southern Sea. The Javanese pilgrims in Parangtritis who did not personally subscribe to the belief in the existence of this goddess could still understand the religio-cultural spirit of Javanese courts' practice of making annual offering to this figure of tutelary spirit. They could also understand the local belief in the sacredness of the place.

accounts for its ability to unify, or simply to change itself overtime in response to different needs. As a religio-cultural practice of memory, these shrines present the past not for the sake of the past but rather in response to the need of the present day Javanese society that continues to be pluralistic albeit in different and shifting senses. So these shrines have served as in-between spaces or interstices, in the sense that they authentically belong to both the local world of the Javanese as well as the wider tradition of Islam.

This way, the Javanese case makes it harder to talk about the clear-cut boundaries between self and other, between Islam and Javaneseness (or *vice versa*). From a sociological or anthropological point of view, the *walis* are considered as religio-cultural "brokers" who smooth out the complex intersecting of boundaries.[63] While, on the more theological side, these saints are guarantors of the authenticity of the Muslim character of the intersections.

Concluding Remarks

I have attempted to show in this chapter the rich and complex picture of Javano-Islamic pilgrimage tradition in south central Java in terms of arts, architecture and ritual. Particular emphasis has been given to the significance of these features of the pilgrimage tradition in the process of the religio-cultural identity formation of the Javano-Muslim communities. In this framework, the principle of continuity and communion with the other, done always in extremely complex ways, is also at work in the material and ritual culture of the shrines and the pilgrimage tradition among Javanese Muslims in south central Java. To a large degree, this principle is considered to be one of the most distinctive legacies of the local saints like Kalijaga, Pandanarang and others. The result is the formation of a hybrid Javano-Islamic identity marked by an overwhelming respect for the richness of the Javanese local culture and the desire to appropriate the goodness of this culture into the practice of Islam. In south central Java, this religio-cultural process has been supported and smoothed out by the Javano-Islamic courts of Yogyakarta and Surakarta, as well as by the traditionalist Muslim organization (the Nahdlatul Ulama).

This religio-cultural synthesis is unique in terms of its concrete contents and particularities. It is about the particular encounters between Islam and the Javanese culture, itself a synthesis of different religio-cultural traditions such as native spirituality, Hinduism, Buddhism, and so forth. This framework explains the presence of some distinctive ritual, artistic, and architectural features native to Java. For instance, I have discussed the distinctive role of the *slametan* as a ritual invocation and memory of the local ancestors, together with the prophets and saints. The ubiquitous presence of this ritual meal in the pilgrimage tradition

---

[63] The notion of the role of traditional Muslim leaders (Jv. *kyai*) in Java as cultural brokers was coined by Clifford Geertz: "The Javanese Kijaji: The Changing Role of a Cultural Broker," *Comparative Studies in Society and History*, 2 (1960): pp. 228–49.

in south central Java gives this tradition of saint veneration a more distinctive quality as a memory of ancestors as well. For although the basic form of this ritual meal is known in other parts of the Islamic world, this memory of local saintly and paradigmatic ancestors—as well as the distinctively hybrid lists of prophets and saints being invoked in the ritual—makes the Javanese case rather unique. In the same vein, I have also shown how the veneration of relics of the saints and ancestors takes a distinctively local form in south central Java due to the influence of the Javano-Islamic royal courts of Yogyakarta and Surakarta.

However, as far as the general pattern of appropriation is concerned, the case of south central Java is not completely *sui generis* because it could be understood within the more widespread patterns of encounters between Islam and other religio-cultural traditions in other parts of the world and across historical periods. As far as the specificities of the case of Java are concerned, they can still be understood within the larger Islamic interpretive framework, such as the Islamic mystical tradition, more particularly its various symbolic devices such as mystical mountain, spiritual ascent, animal symbolisms and so forth. As always, a certain degree of ambiguity is embedded in this kind of creative religio-cultural synthesis. In this respect, Javano-Islamic pilgrimage culture in south central Java continues to take as a paradigm the kind of synthesis that the earlier *walis* as the "religio-cultural brokers" have achieved. For many Javanese Muslims, it is the role of these *walis* that ensures the Islamic authenticity of the synthesis. However, this does not mean that the understanding and interpretation of this synthesis have been finalized. This religio-cultural interpretive framework should be considered a living legacy of these saints and founders, and within this framework, ambiguities are embraced as both sign of complexities but also openness toward further and diverse interpretive engagements in response to the dynamics of contemporary society.

Chapter 3
The Richness of Pilgrimage Experience: Devotion, Memory, and Blessings

> Whenever he sets off from home to wander in lonely places,
> [He] imbibes the old lessons, seeking ecstasy with clear intention,
> With great disciplines, reining in the passion, both day and night,
> Molding works pleasant to the heart of his fellow human beings.[1]

Employing thoroughly Javanese idioms, the text quoted above is meant to describe a personal habit of spiritual journeying (Jv. *ziarah*, *tirakat*) of a rather famous Javano-Muslim figure, Kyai Chudlori (1912–77), the founder of the influential Islamic education center (Jv. *pesantren*) at Tegalrejo in Magelang regency, central Java. During his life Kyai Chudlori played a paradigmatic role in attempting to strike a religio-cultural synthesis of Islam and Javanese culture in his *pesantren* as well as the wider local society. Due to his pioneering work, his school has been known for its excellence as a traditional Islamic boarding school that combines comprehensive Islamic learning with deep appropriation of Javanese culture. In a rather iconic way, Kyai Chudlori placed a shadow puppet image of Bhima, the most admired hero of the Mahabharata epic whose mystical experience is central to Javanese mysticism, on the wall of his room.[2]

However, the quotation is also striking in a different sense. For in attempting to describe the dynamics of extended pilgrimage (Jv. *ziarah*, Ar. *ziyāra*) as a process of spiritual journey, it starts with the experience of strangeness (being a wanderer) and of loneliness but ends with a sense of being in communion and friendship with fellow human beings. This dynamic is remarkably similar to the experience of al-Harawī (d. 1215) that I mentioned in the Introduction. It is insightful that the identity of Kyai Chudlori is presented in the text quoted above in terms of his practice of spiritual and ascetic journeying, using the all too traditional Javanese idioms. This way, it has already pointed to one of the most crucial questions of this

---

[1] M. Bambang Pranowo, "Traditional Islam in Contemporary Rural Java: The Case of Tegal Rejo Pesantren," in Ricklefs (ed.), *Islam in the Indonesian Social Context*, p. 39; also his *Memahami Islam Jawa*, p. 157. I altered Pranowo's translation slightly.

[2] So, by choosing the image of Bhima, Kyai Chudlori was revealing the nature of his project of creating Javano-Islamic identity that was also based on his own extended spiritual journey. On the role of this *kyai* and the Tegalrejo *pesantren* in the synthesis of Islam and Javanese culture, see Bambang Pranowo, *Memahami Islam Jawa*, pp. 159–235.

chapter, namely, the richness of pilgrimage experience. For within the framework of Javanese culture, the text identifies fundamental elements of pilgrimage experience, namely, solitude and loneliness, spiritual lessons, devotion, purity of intention, disciplines of purification and asceticism, and so forth. Furthermore, in relation to the identity of Kyai Chudlori, the text also indicates further how the tradition of Muslim *ziyāra* or spiritual journeying as it is practiced in Java could become a milieu for forging such a complex identity that embraces dimensions of "otherness," more specifically some allegedly "non-Islamic" categories, such as the various aspects of the Javanese culture.

As has been mentioned, this chapter deals with the experiential world of the pilgrims, that is, the many ways in which pilgrims get into an experience of intimate communion with and devotion to God and His Friends (Ar. *awliyā'*), thus obtaining diverse forms of blessing, while also getting into a deeper contact with their own selves as well as other pilgrims. Special attention will be given to the distinctive interplays between Javanese spiritual and cultural heritage and the wider Islamic tradition in the various ways in which pilgrims actually do different aspects of the pilgrimage practice, especially how they interpret the various aspects of God's blessings, the role of the saints and so forth.

At this point it has to be noted as well that the general argument of this chapter has to be placed within the larger and deeper framework of communion that has become the underlying principle at work in the pilgrimage tradition among Javanese Muslims in south central Java. As shown in the previous chapters, it is the underlying principle of communion, understood broadly, that makes pilgrimage tradition able to forge such a hybrid and inclusive Javano-Islamic identity. In the dynamics of pilgrimage in south central Java, this complex and rather elusive notion of identity is shaped and acted out within this framework of attaining deeper and more integral communion and connectedness with God and His company of saints in the context of a complex tapestry of devotion to and spiritual intimacy with God, oneself, and other pilgrims. Furthermore, pilgrimage also involves a significant level of participation in the personal and communal memory of saint-founders, founding moments, holy places, and sacred landscape. As I have attempted to show, the practice of pilgrimage as memory involves a certain degree of engagement and hospitality to the presence and traces of the other, such as the other religious traditions or local cultures.

In light of this larger framework, this chapter continues the discussion by focusing on the pilgrims themselves, the most important agents of this tradition, especially in terms of the richness of their experience. Recent statistical data at the Gunungpring shrine, for example, shows a rising pattern in the number of pilgrims during the peak months of pilgrimage to this shrine.[3] In light of the role of these

---

[3] The following is the statistics on the number of pilgrims to this shrine, posted on the wall of the shrine itself, during the peak months of the pilgrimage season (not the whole year). In the year of 2000, the shrine was visited by 31,000 pilgrims; in 2001, 35,000; in 2002, 35,000; in 2003, 34,000; and in 2004, 38,000. So, there is an increasing trend

pilgrims, my principal questions can be formulated as follows: how pilgrimage has become what it is in Java; more specifically, why pilgrimage continues to be a personally, culturally, and religiously meaningful practice for these Muslims; and how it serves as a means for the identity formation of these individuals and communities. Naturally, such a treatment of the experience of the pilgrims involves a good amount of complexity, in the sense of richness and plurality of the experience. However, it is still possible to look for a certain degree of shared experience, illustrated by personal accounts of some pilgrims that I interviewed during fieldwork.

Employing two rather broad categories that in their interconnections to each other hopefully represent the salient elements of the pilgrimage experience, I attempt to put some structures to the vast and complex experiential world of the pilgrims. The first category has something to do with the complex motivation of the pilgrims, captured by the notions of devotion, needs, and blessings. And the second comprises the various spiritual lessons and personal growth, in tandem with the rather intense practice of asceticism and purification. Roughly, these two categories correspond to the two general types of pilgrim: (1) pilgrims of devotion, and (2) ascetic and soul-searching pilgrims. I will deal more with sub-classifications of these types later. However, it has to be noted that this classification is based on the more dominant feature of each category; thus they are not mutually exclusive. In fact, the ascetic and soul-searching pilgrims also foster deep devotion, while the pilgrims of devotion embrace ascetic purification as an important part of the pilgrimage as well.

It should be recalled as well that other type might exist, such as tourist-pilgrims. However, I have found that the number of such casual pilgrims is quite limited in the three shrines under discussion in this book, since these shrines are not the most popular tourist destinations, although to a certain extent, these shrines are obviously part of tourism industry as indicated by the fact that most group-pilgrims combine these shrines with other more touristy places nearby as destinations.[4] Furthermore, some people who would be present during festivals might qualify as local tourist-pilgrims, but they are more aptly considered as members of the local

---

in the number of pilgrims. During the busiest months, this shrine would have more than a thousand visitors per day. Given the stature of the shrine of Tembayat, the number of pilgrims would be more numerous there. This figure could be easily doubled in the most popular shrines in Java, such as the shrine of Sunan Ampel in Surabaya and the shrine of Sunan Gunungjati in Cirebon.

[4] This feature is related to the status of Yogyakarta as a unique destination for cultural tourism in Indonesia. As noted in the Introduction, the New Order government of Indonesia (1967–98) promoted Yogyakarta as a unique place for the so-called "Pancasila" tourism. *Pancasila* is the Indonesian national principle, representing, among other things, the idea of unity in diversity. In this framework, Yogyakarta was imagined as a kind of national symbol of an ideal harmonious existence amidst diversity and plurality that should be the hallmark of the whole Indonesian society. So, many pilgrims to Yogyakarta combine religious pilgrimage with cultural tourism.

community. In this regard, it is crucial to note that not only does the relationship between visitors and the saints vary greatly—making it hard to set rigid boundaries between the devout pilgrims and more superficial tourists—but it also develops over time. Many seasoned pilgrims ascribe their penchant for pilgrimage to an initially very casual visit to certain shrine.

Motivation: Devotion, Needs, and Blessings

In my view, it is highly appropriate to begin the discussion on the experiential world of the pilgrims with the category of devotion, understood here as deeply personal connectedness with God and the paradigmatic figures of the community. This is so because devotion is key to understanding the many significant behaviors of pilgrims, both outward and inward, inside and outside the shrine. For, without taking devotion seriously, one could barely understand the dynamics of pilgrimage itself, namely, the initial intention and the whole process, its aftermath as well as the next round of pilgrimage.[5] It is devotion that brings the saints and their shrines to the hearts of the pilgrims and to places beyond the shrines. It explains the motivation of so many pilgrims that would come to shrines on a regular basis, simply because this practice has become the habit of their hearts, so to speak. It, for instance, explains the motivation of a group of illiterate elderly Javanese Muslim pilgrims who chose to spend the government's aid on making *ziarah*, rather than on buying new uniforms for their association.[6] It also helps us understand the motivation of a group of pilgrims who felt the need to stop by the shrine of Gunungpring as they happened to attend a wedding celebration in the area.[7] This personal and communal sense of devotion and connectedness to saints, the habit of the heart, could be puzzling to some people.

In this regard, the story about the former president of Indonesia, Mr. Abdurrahman Wahid (1940–2009), is rather interesting. Mr. Wahid—who was also a highly respected Muslim scholar and former leader of the Nahdlatul Ulama,

---

[5] In a rather direct relation to the sensitive nature of pilgrimage, some Muslim pilgrims come to base their habit on a strong personal religious conviction and belief (part of devotion), at times coupled with theological arguments drawn from within the tradition. For example, Ms. Wiwik, an owner of a small business, argued that although she is a member of the modernist Muhammadiyah—in fact, she hails from Kotagedhe in Yogyakarta, the very place where the modernist Muhammadiyah movement was founded in 1912—she keeps doing some Javanese religio-cultural practices because of her personal conviction and experience. Interview, Mawlana Maghribi shrine, June 5, 2009.

[6] This particular group came from Tegalrejo, Magelang. They decided to visit the shrines of Tembayat, Mlangi (the tomb of Kyai Nur Iman in the outskirt of Yogyakarta), and Gunungpring. Interview, Gunungpring, May 30, 2009.

[7] This group was from Salatiga, located around 20 miles from the shrine. Interview, May 27, 2009.

the biggest Muslim organization in the country—was reported to have abruptly left his presidential palace just few hours before an important cabinet meeting was supposed to start, simply because he felt compelled to pay a visit to the tomb of a deceased leader of his Nahdlatul Ulama. Throughout his life, Mr. Wahid had been known as a progressive traditionalist Muslim leader and non-sectarian thinker with a deep personal piety and devotion of visiting the tombs of some prominent leaders of his organization as well as other saints and paradigmatic figures.[8] In this particular instance, Mr. Wahid felt he had to visit the tomb because his close confidante had reportedly told him that the deceased spiritual leader was unhappy that Mr. Wahid had not visited his grave for a while. In response, his staff had to mobilize three presidential helicopters to rush him to the tomb where he prayed earnestly. Moments later he emerged with new confidence and resolve, and then he announced the dismissals of his cabinet ministers immediately thereafter.[9] Again, to those unfamiliar with the rather intense and distinctive piety and devotion of many traditional Muslims like Mr. Wahid, this event will indeed look bizarre, superstitious, and suspect, especially its connection with politics. However, considered by many as a living *wali* himself, Mr. Wahid had no need to explain this to the public.[10]

Although the case of Mr. Wahid was definitely more complicated and controversial than the first two examples of ordinary pilgrims mentioned earlier, there was a common feature that they shared. Together with many other Javanese Muslim pilgrims, all of them would understand their *ziarah* basically in terms of devotion understood as personal connectedness to God and His spiritual company, the saints and paradigmatic figures of the community.

In this respect, more particularly, many Javanese Muslim pilgrims would describe the particular nature of pilgrimage in the framework of Javanese cultural practices of *sowan* and *nyekar*. The Javanese word *sowan* denotes a dutiful visit of a subject to his master; it is an acknowledgment of dependence and duty, and it will result in the harmonious relationship between the pilgrims as subjects and the saints as masters and protectors. Here, the idea of Islamic "sainthood" (Ar. *walāya*) as protectorship seems to be particularly relevant. Due to their proximity to and friendship with God, Muslims *wali*s participate in the authority (Ar. *wilāya*) of God as the supreme Protector (Ar. *al-walī*). In south central Java, this notion of

---

[8] For example, while serving as the president of Indonesia (1999–2001), Mr. Wahid visited the Tembayat shrine as well as the royal cemetery of the Mataram kings in Imogiri (see Map 3), drawing some severe criticisms from his political opponents. See *The Republika Daily*, April 22, 2000.

[9] Chambert-Loir and Reid, *The Potent Dead*, p. xv.

[10] Since his demise in 2009, Mr. Wahid's tomb in East Java has become a major pilgrimage site. At some point, it was drawing two thousand pilgrims per day according to some reports (*The Jakarta Post*, December 22, 2010). There has been some suggestion for calling Mr. Wahid the tenth *wali*, thus putting him in the famed tradition of Javanese Nine Saints (Jv. *Wali Songo*). *The Jakarta Post*, December 19, 2010.

sainthood and its corresponding idea of *ziyāra* as *sowan* echo the religio-cultural tradition of the royal courts, especially the belief that kings are saints endowed with special supernatural powers.[11]

When this notion of *ziyāra* is combined with the word *nyekar*—literally means placing flowers on the graves of deceased ancestors and family members as a sign of loving remembrance—one sees how this dutiful visit occurs in the framework of more intimate, familial, intergenerational, and communal framework of relationships. While the notion of *sowan* denotes dutiful reverence (Jv. *urmat*), *nyekar* is an outward display of devotedness (Jv. *bekti*) as a result of personal connection.[12] Connected to my previous discussion on the Javanese etiquette of *ziyāra*, this attitude would be offered also to parents, living and deceased, to whom Javanese would have heartfelt personal relationship. When the term *nyekar* is used as a designation for visiting the tomb of the saint, it points to pilgrimage as a natural extension of loving remembrance of ancestors.

It is in this complex framework of relationship that most Javanese pilgrims would understand their more mundane intentions. For many pilgrims, their relationships with God and the saints develop around the dynamics of devotion and supplications. In this respect, the basic issue is not so much about the granting of their specific prayers, but rather about the dynamics and effects of such a communication, basically an unveiling of self, in the continuum of one's relationship and devotedness to God and His saints. This is the larger context of spiritual growth that particular pilgrimage finds itself. In general this dynamic is true for all kinds of pilgrims. In Java, quite a few ordinary pilgrims would be drawn, initially at least, to particular shrines due to their legendary power of fulfilling mundane requests. However, once a relationship of devotion is established, fulfillment gradually ceases to be the sole aim of the pilgrimage. This is so precisely either because other features of true devotion come to the surface, or because the pilgrims would understand the true meanings of the supplications and their fulfillments on a different level, perhaps in a more existential and integral framework of their complex lives, as I will illustrate later.

This process often includes a deeper realization of the necessary growth of the pilgrims' own understanding of life. In this framework, even in the case when mundane supplications seem to have been deferred, pilgrims continue to show devotion by going to the shrines over and over again as part of the larger process of understanding the complexities of their lives in relation with God and His saints. In this dynamic, pilgrimage is personally revelatory insofar as it serves as the milieu through which the hitherto hidden aspects of the pilgrims' lives are unveiled by the grace of God.

---

[11] Woodward, *Islam in Java*, pp. 163–77.

[12] In relation to my previous discussion on the Javanese etiquette of *ziyāra*, this attitude would be offered also to parents, living and deceased, to whom people have personal relationship, but not to government officials, for example. Cf. Jamhari, "In the Center of Meaning," pp. 70–78.

Let me illustrate this crucial point by the story of a middle-aged woman pilgrim that I encountered at the shrine of Gunungpring. This woman has been coming to this shrine since she was a small girl. She has continued to come here, more in earnest when her daughter was having a mental breakdown recently. Obviously the fact that her daughter's recovery is nowhere in sight did not prevent her from coming to the shrine. On the day when I met her, she paid a visit to the saint because her daughter would soon be transferred, probably permanently, to a mental hospital. When I asked her about the fact that her request has not been granted by the saint, she bluntly said that she has been asking God for some explanation. She has lost everything in the pursuit of her daughter's recovery, even the money she originally saved for the *ḥajj* pilgrimage to Mecca. Furthermore, her daughter's son, who was also her only grandchild, had to die on her lap due to the maltreatment and neglect from his own mother. On top of this, she has suffered considerably from social stigma. Her neighbors accused her of neglecting her daughter and her grandchild. However, despite her protest to God, she said she could not help coming to this shrine because she has put her daughter in the protection of the saint. She has been committed with the saint and the saint has been part of the life of her daughter who herself was also a devotee of the saint before the breakdown. She confided to me, while sobbing, that the situation has been so hard now, but she was resolute in keeping her faith in God and His blessing through Raden Santri, one of the Javanese Muslim saints buried here and her beloved saint. She believed that if her daughter would eventually be healed, it would be at the hands of Raden Santri, due to his superior sanctity over other saints.

In other words, in the very dynamics of her habit of making pilgrimage over the years, this woman has learned to understand better the various aspects of having faith in God and the virtues of fidelity to and trust in the saint. The intergenerational aspect of this devotion to God and the saints is also apparent in her practice. She also learned how to place her personal needs in the larger framework of devotion.

All these stories of pilgrims, within their limitations, show that devotion is very personal and highly complex. It also necessarily develops over time in the context of the personal growth of the pilgrims themselves. In many ways, a particular visit or pilgrimage is connected to the previous and future visits, as well as the larger development of the pilgrims' understanding of their lives in connection with God and the saints. In most cases, this devotion is not about a relationship of equal friendship. It is a loving devotion of course. However, most Javanese Muslim pilgrims continue to display a sense of being dependent on the saints in their journey of drawing near to their protectorship. In my view, it is in the framework of the real yet complex dynamics of proximity, friendship, and protectorship— covered by the Islamic term for sainthood, *walāya*—that one should understand, as the pilgrims themselves do, the "transactional" character of pilgrimage.[13]

---

[13] Interview, April 20, 2009. In this sense, contemporary Muslim pilgrims are not unlike their Christian counterparts in Roman late antiquity, as Peter Brown has argued in his work *The Cult of the Saints*.

In this connection, some Javanese pilgrims that I encountered at the shrine of Mawlana Maghribi explained the naturalness of the logic of proximity to God and the saints (Ar. *qurbā*) and intercession (Ar. *tawassul*) by using a metaphor of approaching the village leader (Jv. *lurah*) through his right-hand man (Jv. *carik*). In a society where human relation and connection forms a crucial part of its fabric, this metaphor shows how a largely religious practice like saint veneration reflects social expectations and structures.

Especially among Javanese pilgrims who get used with the practice of shamanism or magic, the temptation to turn this friendship with the Muslim saints to a *do-ut-des* transaction seems to be more real at times.[14] However, on the whole, this transactional model is largely inadequate in helping us understand the complexity, deep significance, and overall structure of the pilgrimage experience in these Muslim shrines under study. As the above-mentioned examples have indicated, the element of "otherness" is quite inherent in this relationship. Even the most ordinary pilgrims know all too well that God is the one in charge, and they simply do not know the scope of the mystery and vastness of His will. The saints themselves do not have power to grant their prayers apart from God's, hence the idea of participation of the saints in God's power.[15] The awareness of pilgrims in Java in this regard is surprising; even the most simple ones seem to be quite informed about this orthodox framework of understanding the relationship between God and the saints. During the fieldwork I was continually surprised at the naturalness of pilgrims' explanation that they are, strictly speaking, seeking God's favor through the mediation (Ar. *tawassul*) of the saints. In this regard, the dispute and controversies about the propriety of *ziyāra* that has marked much of the interaction between the traditionalist and reformist Muslims in Java in the past probably has a good effect on pilgrims now.

In general, pilgrims are aware that contrary to magic, even the most meticulous executions of ritual precepts would not guarantee that supplications are granted the way the pilgrims would expect initially. Learning from their own experience, they realize that mere ritual orchestration is simply not the best way to deal with this complex relationship. Naturally, it is a sincere friendship (Ar. *walāya*), expressed in the devotion of the pilgrims to God and His saints, that pilgrims feel to be the most appropriate response to this dynamic of relationship. Thus, in the bigger picture, it is the sincerity of this relationship that becomes the pivot.

---

[14] This practice becomes much more prevalent in the Javanist shrines that have a very slight or no connection with Islam, such as the tomb of Panembahan Jaka Bodo in Bantul (Yogyakarta), the shrine of Gunung Kawi in East Java, and the tomb of Pangeran Samudra in Kemukus, Sragen, Central Java. On the shrines at Kemukus and Gunung Kawi, see Fuhrmann's *Formen der javanischen Pilgerschaft zu Heiligenschreinen*, pp. 193–265, 317–68; on Gunung Kawi, see also Huub de Jonge, "Heiligen, middelen en doel: ontwikkeling en betekenis van twe islamitische bedevaartsoorten op Java," in Willy Jansen and H de Jonge (eds), *Islamische Pelgrimstochten* (Muiderberg, 1991), pp. 89–95.

[15] See Introduction.

In the experience of the pilgrims, the antidote to pure transaction is the cultivation of pure intention. As expressed in the etiquette of the Muslim *ziyāra*, right intention (Ar. *niyāt*) is an essential part of this friendship and devotion. Interestingly, the purification of intention can happen in the repetition of pilgrimage to the same shrine, since unanswered prayers or supplications might be signals of flawed intentions. It is also in this framework that a transformation of the motivation of the pilgrims could occur. Many pilgrims expressed how they came to know their true need only as a result of their long struggle to purify their hearts and intentions, a process of spiritual transformation or growth that can be triggered by a series of outward rejection of their requests by God and the saints.

Moreover, there is another aspect in the dynamic of supplication that is crucial for my discussion here, namely supplication as an expression (unveiling) of self in the context of intimate conversation. As I have illustrated in the case of the Tembayat shrine, some pilgrims would do this unveiling of self through specific rituals: the ritual where the pilgrims formulate their personal intention to God and the saint through the custodian, as well as personal prayers (Ar. *du'ā'*). However, certain type of pilgrims (see the next section) would continue this unveiling of self through intimate prayerful conversations (Ar. *munājāt*) at the shrine. For many pilgrims, it is this unveiling of self that helps render the visits more personal, putting them in a lasting and deeper relationship with God, the saint and his shrine. It is also the place where the path of spiritual renewal often begins.

In the experience of so many pilgrims in Islamic Java, this unveiling of self can at times occur in a deeply interpersonal atmosphere. Indeed, shrines could turn into an intimate space where pilgrims converse not only with God and the saints but also with one another. It is rather surprising that during pilgrimage, "strangers" could confide, albeit gradually, some aspects of their most personal lives to one another. The dynamic of this rather intimate conversation seems to revolve around mutuality and trust. Typically, however, it starts with mundane conversations and then it takes only a person to open up to turn them into interpersonal communication and connection. For other pilgrims, this unveiling of self signals a humble plea for help, to which they would respond not by giving direct advice, but rather by narrating their own life stories as an expression of connection and solidarity. There is also a rather profound awareness that they need one another, precisely at the time when they feel so helpless and overwhelmed by all sorts of life problems. A middle-aged woman pilgrim at the Mawlana Maghribi shrine explains the spirit behind this, thus: "Being a pilgrim is to share with other pilgrim, because we all have problems and sharing them could ease us out!"[16] This interpersonal unveiling of self results in a sense of mutual solidarity among pilgrims. In the presence of the friends of God (Ar. *awliyā'*), strangers become friends quite literally. This friendship might or might not continue beyond the shrine, but what is more lasting is the experience of friendship itself. At this moment of friendship, communion with God and His saints means communion with one another.

---

[16] Interview, June 5, 2009.

For many pilgrims, this experience of encounter and friendship with other pilgrims is one of the many forms of divine blessings (Ar. *baraka*). In Java and elsewhere, the category of *baraka* is quite central to the motivation and experience of the pilgrims. The Javanese term *ngalap berkah*—more or less equivalent to the Islamic notion of *tabarruk*—expresses a popular understanding of the pursuit of the divine blessing which is universally available and could be obtained in many possible ways, not only through pilgrimage as such, but also participation in public rituals and festivals at shrines, courts, mosques, and so forth. In the framework of the pilgrimage tradition to the tombs of the Nine Saints (the *Wali Songo*), the theme of *ngalap berkah* is constant in the fliers or small posters for group pilgrimage since it is the most popular spiritual framework for mass pilgrimage. These fliers are glued to the walls of major shrines throughout Java, a practice that resembles the old tradition of writing one's name on each site visited as act of remembrance. This theme would appear in different wording such as *lampah mubarokah* (blessed journeying), *expedisi ngalap berkah* (the expedition in the pursuit of Divine blessing), and so forth. One curious example is the flier from an Islamic high school in East Java.[17] Framed in an Islamic theme of "*Ngalap Pangestu Dateng Para Wali*" (seeking the blessings of the saints), it features a curious depiction of a man praying under a big tree, on a mountain at night, a typical Javanese description of the natural setting of ascetic practice (Jv. *tirakatan*).

In the eyes of many, one of these possibilities of being blessed is related, mostly in ways that are beyond words, to some materiality, for example in the forms of the ritual food being distributed at the festivals, or the flower petals from the grave of the saints mentioned above. Of course they know that these petals are not "sources" of *baraka per se* and did not contain the whole *baraka* and its efficacious power, but they are somehow related to the world of divine *baraka*. For many pilgrims, these petals become a tangible memory of pilgrimage blessings. When they give these petals to family and friends, the web of persons affected by the blessings of pilgrimage widens out.

In this connection, highly popular among Javanese pilgrims is the notion of *kesawaban*. This notion expresses the belief that Divine blessings could be obtained through various degrees of connectedness to the saints and shrines as channel of those blessings, for example, through physical proximity, personal dedication and service, genealogical connection, and so forth.[18] This word might have been originally derived from the Arabic *ṣāba*, that means "to be right, to obtain or to bestow," but also "to wound, to injure," and so forth. This is why the Javanese also understand "*sawab*" as ambiguous. For it could bring about either true blessedness or misfortunes.[19] In order to obtain this *baraka* as a positive force,

---

[17] This was the Islamic school, Madrasah Aliyah al-Manar, Nganjuk, East Java.

[18] Jamhari, "The Meaning Interpreted," p. 96.

[19] The negative aspect of this is expressed in the word *musibah* (misfortunes, disasters), derived from the same Arabic root. In the same semantic field, the word *uṣība* means to be stricken, attacked, and afflicted. Wehr, *Arabic-English Dictionary*, p. 617.

one has to possess the right intention and proper inner disposition. One should not abuse this *baraka*, once obtained. Thus, it is simultaneously a gift and a demand.

This ambiguous semantic field is insightful because it shows the double-edge sword of the saint's spiritual power. As Jamhari shows, *baraka* is a multivalent term and many pilgrims at the shrine of Tembayat differentiate between "true blessing" as such (Jv. *berkah*) and "boon" or worldly gain (Jv. *perolehan*).[20] Pilgrims believe that while both are bestowed by God to them, the two differ in their effect. For the *berkah* effects a true spiritual peacefulness (Jv. *slamet* or *tentrem*) whose effect goes beyond the boundaries of one's life on earth (Jv. *donya*; Ar. *dunyā*), while *perolehan* is worldly and ambiguous in terms of its effect on the integral welfare of the person. Some pilgrims would speak of the former in terms of a general education and purification of their hearts or souls. Their principle is simple: the more one spends time in sacred places and performs spiritual exercises, the more one's heart would be purified.[21] This is the notion of *baraka* that I discussed previously, namely the sense of peacefulness of the heart at the shrine (Jv. *tentrem*), as the result of being in touch with the Divine.

With regard to the relationship between true spiritual blessings (Jv. *berkah*) and worldly boon (Jv. *perolehan*), pilgrims believe that this spiritual blessing would not only naturally bring about worldly boon but also helps them manage it better. Mr. Parjono, a food-peddler at the shrine of Tembayat remarks that when his heart is purified, this would be reflected in his outward behavior that customers find attractive or pleasant. Furthermore, once his heart is purified and filled with thankfulness to God, he would then have the right inner disposition to make use of this boon more wisely.[22] In this respect, pilgrims seem to be aware that specific requests for worldly gain would be inadequate and even dangerous without the grace of the more fundamental state of blessedness. This is why a purely transactional model fails to describe the dynamics of *baraka* in the experience of the pilgrims.

I will examine in the next section how this transactional model fails to explain the complex and rich experiential world of ascetic pilgrims whose fulfillment of the goal of their *ziyāra* is intimately intertwined with the whole range of educational dimension of the visit itself. Before delving into this particular kind of pilgrimage where the experience of blessedness is highly internalized and intensified, it should be noted that in the worldview of the pilgrims, *baraka* has probably become the most inclusive category. Flowing from God's boundless mercy, in the Islamic sense of *raḥma*, it is cosmic in its scope, transcending the

---

[20] Jamhari, "The Meaning Interpreted," p. 87.

[21] It is in this framework of the more fundamental divine *baraka* that some pilgrims would visit the shrines of the other. Here, "sacredness" of the shrine that ultimately is derived from the Divine is measured by its effect in the kind of inner transformation that the pilgrims experience. Most of these pilgrims would rarely engage in the rituals of the religious others, but they feel they partake in the sanctity of the Divine in these traditions by being there. This pattern is more generally true to these border-crossing pilgrims.

[22] Interview, Tembayat shrine, June 25, 2009.

formal or outward borders of religious traditions. In Java and elsewhere, this explains the practice of shared shrines among various religious traditions. In this context, the Javanese ritual meal of *slametan* seems to provide a model of shared blessing. The universality of Divine blessing is also the reason why the custodians at Tembayat shrine insist on the inclusive character of the shrine, saying: "This is a *Pancasila* shrine!"[23] In other words, the saint is for everybody, regardless of formal religious affiliations. At Tembayat, this inclusivity explains the presence of Chinese pilgrims who would perform their own rituals at this shrine.

Having said this, it has to be stated that even the most ordinary pilgrims experience the highly personal nature of *baraka* since its effectiveness and impact also depend on the persons in their relationship with God and His spiritual company of saints. It is this context of personal relationship and connectedness that I call devotion. Understood this way, devotion is a personal milieu for this *baraka* to work in a complex and dynamic web of correlation with personal needs, inner disposition and intentions, and so forth.[24] Furthermore, devotion also explains, at the deeper and more personal level, the reason why pilgrims come to express their "selves" in the Javano-Islamic rituals: because these rituals belong to who they are, that is, their identity. It helps us understand why they did not really become easily distracted by outward forms of otherness or alterity, precisely because what matters most is what they feel in their hearts with regard to their enduring relationship with God and His saints.

Pilgrimage, Asceticism, and Spiritual Moments

In the previous two chapters, I have pointed out that Javanese Muslims put an emphasis on the ascetic and purifying element of pilgrimage. This is the Javanese understanding of pilgrimage as *laku* or *tirakat*, a serious and focused period of spiritual cultivation aided by intensive spiritual and ascetic practices (Jv. *tapa*). It is a moment of intensive solitary withdrawal from the humdrum of the world. Normally taken as a preparation of important undertaking, the *tirakat* is also aimed at purging the self (Ar. *nafs*) of distorted egotistical interests, thus putting oneself in a proper disposition to discern the right ways to proceed in view of the true goals of the undertaking. Traditionally crucial in this process of *tirakat* is its particular setting, typically sacred sites associated with prominent ancestors and

---

[23] As noted previously, *Pancasila* is the Indonesian state ideology that, among others, guarantees the freedom of worship among the adherents of major world religions, based on the common principle of faith in the One God. Together with the state motto of "Unity in Diversity" (S. *Bhinneka Tunggal Ika*), *Pancasila* has become the basis for religio-cultural pluralism and harmony in the Indonesian society.

[24] In light of this notion of devotion, I find insightful Christopher Taylor's more comprehensive designation of *ziyāra* as a mode or style of pious expression, rather than a specific action. See his *In the Vicinity of the Righteous*, p. 62.

saints. This is so because the *tirakat* is traditionally connected to the larger idea of communing with the ancestors and spiritual guardians of Java, a communion that can impart diverse forms of spiritual blessings and power.[25] In this respect, the Javanese use the word *laku* to talk about this extended period of self-purification. For in the Javanese sensibility, *laku* is a framework of movement, an active process of self-transformation toward a goal in which self-denial and asceticism forms an inherent part.

The *tirakat* or *laku* is deeply embedded in the Javanese culture, practiced by paradigmatic figures in the past such as kings, paradigmatic ancestors and saints, to gain spiritual or supernatural power that often translated to political power as well. In general, the traditional Javanese believe that true spiritual power only comes through self-restraint in all things, not only food, drink, or sleep, but also various forms of improper self-interest (Jv. *pamrih*). Thus, in this respect, the practice of *tirakat* (or *tapa-brata*) is essential for the spiritual formation of all. In the book *Serat Sasana Sunu* (nineteenth century) as in other Javanese works, for example, this period of purifying ascetic practice (Jv. *tapa*) is frequently glossed as "death in life" (Jv. *mati ing sajroning ngurip*), echoing the famous ḥadīth: "Die before you die." On the centrality of purifying asceticism, the *Serat Sasana Sunu* argues categorically:

> He who has great abilities, he who has supernatural power, and he who becomes a *priyayi* (nobleman), all have their roots in *tapa* (asceticism). Every great matter has its origin in *tapa*, which is followed by happiness. Even if one is very able, and even if one becomes a *priyayi*; if this does not originate in *tapa* it is riches from the devil.[26]

This text argues that this ascetic practice is a crucial part of the formation of Javanese leaders. They are advised not to concern themselves with worldly things. Instead they should live as if they were dead. I have shown in Chapter 1 how this understanding of spiritual purification was at work in a paradigmatic fashion in the spiritual formation of Sunan Kalijaga as well as Sunan Pandanarang.

It is important to note that even in the context of popular group pilgrimage to the tombs of the major Muslim saints in Java, this purifying and ascetic aspect is maintained to a certain degree. Pilgrims would travel by bus, covering a dozen of sites within the span of four days. Under this condition, pilgrims sleep either on the bus or very briefly in various places in the shrines they visit. Food is mediocre, to say the least. However, this arrangement is intentional. On this point, a pilgrim reasons: "All these hardships should be considered normal; after all, this is a *ziarah*, so we have to do a lot of *tirakat* practices."[27]

---

[25] Cf. Carey, *The Power of Prophecy*, p. 131.
[26] See Kumar, *Java and Modern Europe*, p. 404.
[27] As told by a pilgrim in his blogspot, "Ziarah Wali Songo 2008": www.edipsw.com/opini/ziarah-wali-songo-2008/ (accessed July 2010).

For some pilgrims, the ascetic aspect of the pilgrimage might be understood more as a necessary means for a specific goal, such as to obtain a special divine favor or supernatural power. However, there is another longstanding group of Javanese-Muslim pilgrims who cultivate this type of ascetic pilgrimage as a long period of spiritual education. Indeed, shrines in Java continue to be a privileged space where a deep and sustained spiritual experience and formation can naturally and spontaneously happen more frequently. I have previously mentioned the distinction between pilgrims of devotion and soul-searching/ascetic pilgrims. It is the latter who consciously cultivate this practice of pilgrimage as an extended period of soul-searching and spiritual education, practicing rather intense asceticism and spiritual exercises. Their numbers might be smaller compared to the more numerous pilgrims of devotion. But it is obvious that these pilgrims and their mode of doing pilgrimage form a very significant part of the pilgrimage tradition in Java. Furthermore, based on the difference in the mode and duration of their pilgrimage, one can differentiate between "soul-searching pilgrims" and "ascetic-wandering pilgrims." The former are pilgrims who spend a longer period of time (days or weeks) at a certain shrine for an intensified period of spiritual practice. They tend to have more specific goals, typically in response to a particular personal situation, and do not normally move from one shrine to the next in a long journey away from home. The ascetic-wandering pilgrims, on the other hand, would travel a great distance over a much longer period of time (months or years), staying in various shrines and doing a series of ascetic and spiritual practices along the way, as part of a more comprehensive spiritual pursuit.

Furthermore, among these two categories of pilgrims, one also finds two different styles of religio-cultural orientation along the continuum of the Javano-Islamic mystical synthesis, namely the *santri*-type who follows more normative Islam and the Javanist type who combines normative Islamic practices with Javanese traditions (or *vice versa*). In what follows I will provide a brief survey of the world of their experiences. Since in many ways they overlap in terms of spiritual practices and experience, I will emphasize the heightened sense of spiritual experience in both, but will also pay attention to the significant differences.

Soul-Searching Pilgrims

For soul-searching pilgrims, the shrine is primarily a space of solitude and intimacy with God (and His saints) and the self. Ms. Yuni, a young woman entrepreneur from Jakarta who spends much time periodically at the shrine of Mawlana Maghribi, remarks that there is no gap between her words and her heart while she is at the shrine. It is at the shrine that she can be really alone with God for an extended period of time.[28] This explains why some pilgrims of this type do not like crowded shrines or crowded visiting times at certain pilgrimage sites. This

---

[28] When I interviewed her on June 20, 2009, Yuni had spent ten days at the shrine. Her habit of making ascetic pilgrimage was propelled by her conversion from being a drug

sentiment confirms the experience of a pilgrim to Tembayat who said that it is at the shrine that he can maximize his concentration, in order to see and get in touch with his life's problems more clearly.[29]

Most pilgrims would associate this pacifying and enlightening effect of the shrine to the natural location and environment of the shrine, as well as its sacredness. Some women pilgrims at the shrine of Mawlana Maghribi, for example, argued that this shrine gives them so much peace because it is far from the all-too-familiar domestic world where they at times would feel so choked with problems and struggles.[30] It is this distance from the humdrum daily life that helps them to get focused on their encounter with God and the saints. Especially for urban pilgrims, the natural beauty and freshness of these sites also contribute to the aura of the shrines as a different place. In this regard, the atmosphere of solitude and loneliness also helps pilgrims considerably. Mr. Pinasti, a wandering pilgrim from East Java, expresses his profound experience of finding God and his own self thus: "People say that although I try to search for God everywhere, I fail; yet, they didn't know that during the hardest times of being ill, helpless, rejected, and outcast, I experience being alone with God: just God and myself."[31]

The shrine is indeed a different place.[32] This aspect of distance and difference, interestingly enough, is combined with the experience of closeness and proximity to, and intimacy with, God, the saint, and self.[33] Earlier I have illustrated this kind of dynamic in al-Harawī and Kyai Chudlori. Thus actual distance facilitates inner

---

addict to a spiritually attuned person under the guidance of a Muslim master in Jakarta. Every time she visits the shrine here, she would spend at least a week.

[29] Jamhari, "The Meaning Interpreted," p. 114.

[30] Interview with Ms. Wiwik, Mawlana Maghribi shrine, July 5, 2009. Another pilgrim at Gunungpring, a construction worker, said that pilgrimage refreshes him so much, taking him out of his daily toil at the construction sites (Interview, Gunungpring shrine, May 10, 2009). Another group of construction workers I encountered in the Mausoleum of Kotagedhe remarked that they need this peaceful space due to the hardship of their daily work as well as the crowdedness of their homes in the inner city of Yogyakarta. Interview, May 14, 2009.

[31] See the article "Ziarah: Sepotong Surga Para Musafir," *Kompas Daily* (Yogyakarta edition), May 5, 2009. The motivation to seek solitude leads some pilgrim-seekers to avoid popular shrines or to avoid the crowds during the peak of visiting times. Mr. Agus, a Muslim pilgrim from Surabaya said that he would even go to certain Hindu or Buddhist temples in the Dieng plateau in central Java solely in pursuit of this solitude. Interview, July 2, 2009.

[32] I use this term in reference to Jill Dubisch's work, *In a Different Place: Pilgrimage, Gender and Politics of a Greek Island Shrine* (Princeton, 1995). This notion of shrine as a different place is closely related to the understanding of pilgrimage as a therapy of place, an important approach to pilgrimage in anthropology.

[33] Many ordinary pilgrims, including those who come in groups, would also have this special moment of spiritual proximity. In the shrines of Tembayat and Gunungpring, I observed how many groups of pilgrims have a quite long meditative moment (silence) after the group prayers.

proximity. There is also the pursuit of an intensified sense of divine presence. These pilgrims speak about the fact that they become much more receptive to divine presence in the shrines, although they keep praying at home as well.

Among these pilgrims, this spiritual experience of closeness and divine presence is normally obtained through a rather structured order of daily activities. At the shrines of Gunungpring and Mawlana Maghribi there are always pilgrims who follow a retreat-like pattern: their days revolve around major spiritual exercises, such as the canonical prayers (Ar. *ṣalāt*), personal meditation and reflection (Ar. *tafakkur*), intimate and personal conversation with God (Ar. *munājāt*), fasting, manual work (such as cleaning the shrine compound), conversation with other pilgrims and the custodians, and so forth. Again, this pattern sets the extended pilgrimage apart from daily life. A woman pilgrim remarked that while staying at the shrine, she would be able spend two hours from one to three in the morning in prayers, doing the devotional night prayers of soul-purification (Ar. *tahajjud*), thousands of prayers of God-remembrance (Ar. *dhikr*), and some specific Qur'ānic recitations or prayer formulae (Ar. *wirid*).[34]

Among these soul-searching Muslim pilgrims, the Javanist type would sometimes do the ascetic practice of total (24-hour) fasting (Jv. *pasa ngebleng*) as well as burning incense during meditation. With regard to these local practices, the more conservative *santri*-type pilgrims would normally stay away from these, but neither do they strongly condemn them. As Javanese, they certainly understand the underlying religio-cultural assumptions behind these practices. Ms. Yuni, a pilgrim mentioned before, said that she, as a Javanese, could not run her life without doing *laku* (asceticism) such as periodical fasting and meditation. But her *santri*-type of religiosity leads her to do them in the spirit of Islamic laws. So, she would not do the Javanese total fasting. But she tolerates this practice by other pilgrims. On the use of incense by Javanist pilgrims, she argued that it can be justified in the Islamic framework because God, the Prophet, as well as all the inhabitants of the invisible world, love fragrance. In general, this kind of tolerance seems to be one of the hallmarks of Islamic pilgrimage tradition in south central Java.[35]

Ascetic-Wandering Pilgrims

As I have mentioned, a second category of pilgrims who cultivate this spiritual experience is the ascetic-itinerant pilgrims (Jv. *musafir*; Ar. *musāfir*).[36] Before

---

[34] Interview, Mawlana Maghribi shrine, June 5, 2009.

[35] This might explain why in south central Java, there is no shrine that prohibits incense burning, in comparison with the shrines of Ampel and Bonang in East Java. Cf. de Jonge, "Heiligen, middelen en doel," pp. 83–9.

[36] In Arabic, the word *musāfir* means traveler, visiting stranger, or guest. In light of the purifying function of this kind of pilgrimage, it is also insightful to note that this word is derived from the verbal root S-F-R whose semantic field also covers the meaning of "remove the veil or disclose" (see Wehr, *Arabic-English Dictionary*, p. 481).

discussing the experiential world of these pilgrims, it is important to note that this idea of "itinerant or wandering pilgrimage" is one of the major themes in Javanese classical literature, especially the mystical literature (Jv. *suluk*). Here, the idea of wandering pilgrimage is employed largely as a framework for spiritual and mystical quest for God and the true self.[37] The practice of wandering pilgrimage was also very popular in the *pesantren* culture in the nineteenth century; and, to a certain degree, this phenomenon continues until the present, as I will illustrate later.[38] In the nineteenth century, this type of religious travel existed alongside the wider pattern of travel as a means to get the more intimate knowledge of the so-called "Java", that is, Javanese identity and reality during the high colonial times.[39]

In light of this historical background, it might not be all that surprising that in contemporary Muslim Java, we still find the presence of itinerant pilgrims in many pilgrimage sites. Staying true to the spirit of asceticism, they would walk on foot from shrine to shrine all over Java, and sometimes in the neighboring islands of Madura, Bali, and Lombok to the east, as well.[40] Most of them are solitary pilgrims, although they may experience a kind of temporary *communitas* while residing in those sites. Defining themselves sometimes as *gembel* (Jv., meaning "filthy and destitute people"), they would at times depend on the generosity of the people for sustenance, but usually try to exchange manual work for food along their long journeys from home.[41] However, it is not rare that some have to eat from the garbage bin. The hardships of the journey are intentionally embraced as

---

[37] Just to mention two examples of the *suluk* literature from the court of Surakarta: *Suluk Makmunuradi Salikin* about the spiritual adventures of the wandering Arab prince Makmunuradi Salikin and his two servants; *Suluk Jati Sampurna* about the adventures of the Javanese princes Sèh Mudha Jatisampurna and Ki Jatisurti. On the mysticism of the *suluk* literature, see Zoetmulder, *Pantheism and Monism in Javanese Suluk Literature*.

[38] An interesting example of this *santri*-type itinerant pilgrim in the nineteenth-century Java is Mas Rahmat, a Javanese Muslim who traveled throughout Java and Madura, visiting sacred places and Islamic centers for religious learning, and serving as a spiritual advisor to the Madurese courts. See Kumar, *The Diary of a Javanese Muslim*.

[39] An interesting example here is Raden Purwa Lelana, a Javanese Muslim traveler of aristocratic birth and high administrative rank. In Javanese, his name means "the first traveler." His account is ethnographically detailed, reflecting the changing times that Java had undergone under the colonial rule. There are a number of historical accounts of such travels in nineteenth-century Java. This was also the tradition that the *Serat Centhini* was part of. See Bonneff, *Pérégrinations javanaises* (Paris, 1986).

[40] The recent creation of the tradition of making *ziyāra* to a series of shrines in Bali (the shrines of the Seven Saints, *Wali Pitu*) and Lombok (the shrines of the Three Saints, *Wali Telu*) has given further impetus to both group-pilgrimage and ascetic pilgrimage to the shrines outside of Java. See my article, "Perjumpaan Yang Tak Biasa: Tradisi Wali Pitu di Pulau Dewata," *Basis*, 11–12 (2012): pp. 32–8.

[41] This phenomenon of becoming a destitute pilgrim in contemporary Java could be understood within the wider phenomenon of *faqīr* or *derwīsh* in the larger Muslim tradition. The conversion narrative of Sunan Tembayat (Chapter 1) also follows this pattern.

moments for spiritual growth, especially in acquiring and practicing the virtues of total trust in God (Ar. *tawakkul*), perseverance, patience (Ar. *ṣabr*), and so forth. For female itinerant pilgrims, this journeying can be a lot tougher. That is why they are believed to be more firmly trained in the virtues of *tawakkul* than their male counterparts. On this ground, male *musafir*s tend to respect the women pilgrims more, believing that their mystical stations (Ar. *maqām*) are higher.

Here are two examples representing two different orientations in the continuum of Javano-Islamic mystical synthesis. The first is a stricter Muslim *santri*, the other a more "Javanist" Muslim pilgrim. Mr. Hussein Astawati has been an itinerant pilgrim for practically twenty years, with only a brief interval when he got married. When I saw him in the shrine of Sunan Geseng in June 2009, he had been staying there for over a month.[42] With a sense of pride, Mr. Hussein told the story of his association with Gus Miek, a maverick and idiosyncratic saint of recent memory (Chapter 1). He often wandered all over Java with Gus Miek, and his most memorable ascetic practice with him was going for 17 days without food (just drinking to work the fasting hours in the line of the Islamic law) while meditating at the shrine of Jumadil Kubra in Turgo hill in Kaliurang, on the slope of Mount Merapi, north of Yogyakarta (see Map 3). Then, one day, a woman with a delicious marinated whole chicken appeared because she had been ordered by the Almighty to do so for Gus Miek.[43]

When I asked him about his motivation for doing this extended wandering pilgrimage, his answer was brief, yet profound: there is something amiss about his life when he did not do pilgrimage. Being a son of a Muslim religious master (Jv. *kyai*), he became deeply immersed in the tradition of *ziyāra* through his family. His love for pilgrimage has led him to faraway shrines in Sumatra, something very rarely done by pilgrims from Java. He even went as far as Medina and Yemen where he visited the tomb of Prophet Hud and that of the Prophet Muḥammad. In this respect, like many other *musafir*s, Mr. Hussein did not have a very particular "worldly" request to bring to the saints or prophets. The intercessory prayer ritual (Ar. *tawassul*) that he does every night, the remembering and invocations of a long list of saints whose tombs he has visited, has become a pious habit of his heart, a habit of communion, rather than petition. He considers these saints as moral and spiritual models to follow.[44]

In general, he likes pilgrimage because he learns so many things in life through long travels, including his ugly confrontations with reformist Muslims who, he

---

[42] Sunan Geseng was one of the most famous disciples of Sunan Kalijaga in south central Java. His shrines can be found in many places in this area, such as Piyungan (Yogyakarta), Purworejo, and Grabag, Magelang. Cf. Rinkes, *Nine Saints of Java*, pp. 49–68.

[43] This marinated whole chicken (Jv. *ingkung*) is considered a delicacy in Java, and it is an obligatory component in the food offering during the communal meal of *slametan*.

[44] In some cases, this motivation leads this type of pilgrim not to visit shrines of saints whose historical identities are not known, because it would be difficult to follow in their footsteps. Interview with Mr. Subaki, Gunungpring, May 10, 2009.

said, have taken over some pilgrimage sites in Java. However, this confrontation has confirmed his long practice of following the prescriptions of the Islamic law while doing pilgrimage in order to strike a balance. He always tries to be attentive to his own personal style in doing pilgrimage and to the specific reasons and prescribed behavior for *ziyāra* that the Islamic tradition delineates, namely, to remember death, to pray for the dead, and to emulate the examples of these saints. When I was staying with him in the shrine of Sunan Geseng in Magelang, it became obvious that Mr. Hussein has become a sort of spiritual master for other itinerant pilgrims. Around him gathered some of the younger Javanese *musafir*s whose knowledge of the Muslim tradition barely goes beyond the basics.[45] Every night Mr. Hussein would lead the prolonged communal prayer (Ar. *mujāhada*) at the shrine.[46] In my view, he represents a wandering pilgrim whose adherence to the Muslim principle of *tawḥīd* and the *sharī'a* goes hand in hand with his deep attunement to the Invisible World in the context of pilgrimage to shrines that feature a more conspicuous Javanese character, such as the Mataram royal mausoleums in Kotagedhe and Imogiri (see Map 3).

As indicated previously, shrines in Java are also natural homes to yet another different kind of *musafir*, the Muslim-Javanist type. Mr. Kasiyo is a simple Javanese villager from the vicinity of Yogyakarta who likes to spend his days in shrines and holy tombs, including the shrines of Mawlana Maghribi and Sèh Bèla-Bèlu, in the Parangtritis area (see Map 3).[47] Representing a rather different Muslim personage from that of Mr. Hussein, Mr. Kasiyo never studied Islam formally, and he did not even finish elementary school. Framing his natural penchant for pilgrimage in Javanese terms, he anchors its dynamics (in terms of motivation, process, and goal) to the world of "inner sensing and intuitive/spiritual knowledge" (Jv. *rasa*). Every time he was moved by the subtle stirrings and spiritual desire in his heart, he would embark on an extended pilgrimage, sometimes completely on foot. He got the first taste of the art of doing pilgrimage when as a young boy he went with his grandmother on her ascetic pilgrimage journey (Jv. *tirakat*) around Yogyakarta area, passing through some uninhabited forests. Lacking a proper education in Islamic learning, Mr. Kasiyo is in fact content with uttering some basic prayers in Arabic, and would mostly express himself in Javanese while doing the pilgrimage.

---

[45] The motive for learning has actually become a major reason for these simple itinerant pilgrims to stay longer in the shrines where they could learn first-hand knowledge from different "masters" for free and without having to enter a formal school. This is so partly because the sons of prominent *kyais* in Java would be spending their formative times in shrines as itinerant pilgrims themselves and serve as informal teachers to other pilgrims.

[46] Among many pilgrims of this type, the *mujāhada* prayer is central. Mas Rahmat, a Javanese itinerant pilgrim who presented himself as a *walī* to the readers of his pilgrimage diary, believed that his sainthood (*walāya*, understood as proximity to God and the power that comes with it) was achieved through his perfection in the *mujāhada*. See Kumar, *The Diary of a Javanese Muslim*, p. 89.

[47] See my article "Ziarah Kasiyo Sarkub," *Basis*, 56 (2007): pp. 14–19.

However, he never entertains any doubt with regard to his Islamic identity. Speaking as an adept in the knowledge of Javanese mysticism, he understands the ultimate goal of pilgrimage in terms of seeking *Kyai Slamet* ("integral wellbeing") and *Nyai Tentrem* ("true peace"), two concepts that express the existential homeostasis and the sense of profound personal and cosmic harmony that Javanese mysticism always strive to achieve.[48]

As I have argued, these two individuals exemplify two kinds of itinerant pilgrims, as well as the possible forms of intersections between the two. The first category, the *santri* type, consist of the students and former students (Jv. *santri*) of Java's network of Islamic religious boarding schools (Jv. *pesantren*), as well as other persons who are connected in one way or another to this network and come to adopt its style of Islamic observance. They embark on the long journey of pilgrimage in the quest for growth in spirituality and knowledge (Ar. *'ilm*) in the footsteps of their former teachers. Many of these religious schools actually urge some of their students to lead a life of being itinerant pilgrims during a specific period of time each year. In some cases, this practice of ascetic pilgrimage occurs in the larger context of seeking Islamic knowledge from the right masters, something that requires these students to move frequently from one religious school to the next.[49] Thus many of these students continue this practice of wandering pilgrimage long after their formal graduation.

The second type is what I have called Javanist-Muslim wandering pilgrims.[50] Exploring their particular identity as *Javanese* Muslims, they cultivate some Javanese religio-cultural practices alongside the standard Islamic ones. Of course, the degree of their regularity in practicing the normative Islamic *sharī'a* such as the canonical prayers (Ar. *ṣalāt*) and Ramadan fasting varies greatly from person to person. They are naturally more inclined toward the mystical side of Islam. Most of them are not associated formally with the Javanist mystical brotherhoods

---

[48] *Kyai* and *Nyai* are titles of high respect for male and female respectively. Normally designated for persons of high religious and social status, these terms would also be used for things believed to possess supernatural power, such as sacred heirlooms. Thus, by designating wellbeing as *Kyai Slamet* and true peace as *Nyai Tentrem*, Mr. Kasiyo holds them as personified sacred pillars of true human existence as the Javanese would understand it.

[49] This practice is deeply rooted in the Javanese tradition of *satriya lelana* and *santri lelana* (wandering prince or religious student), exemplified by the famous Muslim rebel prince, Dipanegara (1785–1855).

[50] Here I follow Woodward (*Islam in Java*, p. 2ff), instead of Geertz (*The Religion of Java*). For it is clear that this type of pilgrim does not neatly belong to Geertz's typologies of *santri* (orthodox Muslims), *priyayi* (the nobility influenced largely by Hindu-Javanese traditions), or *abangan* (village animists). While highly influenced by Javanese tradition, they do not come from noble families and are far from being animists or "heterodox" Muslims. They clearly identify themselves as *Javanese* Muslims, emphasizing the Javanese way of being Muslims, more in the style of what Ricklefs calls "mystical synthesis of Islam and Javanese tradition" (see his *Mystic Synthesis*).

(Jv. *kebatinan*) although they might share some of their basic tenets of Javanese spiritual teachings. Among the three shrines under study, the tomb of Mawlana Maghribi is without doubt the most commonly frequented by this type of wandering pilgrims who would visit other Javanese sacred shrines nearby as well (see Map 3).[51]

Different as they are in terms of their religio-cultural orientations and sensibilities, these two types of wandering pilgrims would often meet with each other. The *santri*-type would also visit some sacred places that are more Javanese than Islamic, for example the many *petilasan*s (Ar. *maqām*) of legendary Hindu-Javanese figures. Simple Javanist pilgrims with just basic knowledge of Islam would also learn a lot from their more textually learned (Jv. *santri*) friends in some shrines. This rather informal and spontaneous encounters of either master-disciple relationship or *santri*-Javanist exchange of views occur very frequently in shrines in Java. In general, these groups tend to have an inclusive view of sacredness with regard to shrines of the other. At least some of them would pay short visits to the shrines of other religious traditions, such as Javanese indigenous shrines, Hindu-Buddhist temples, Catholic Marian shrines, Chinese temples, and so forth.[52] These visits would generally be short and might stem partly from mere curiosity, due to their hunger for looking for and being in the sacred precincts, but they can also lead to a deeper relationship. These wandering pilgrims often discover hitherto unrecognized sacred sites and then initiate a novel tradition of pilgrimage to these sites.

In this respect, it is remarkable to see how these wandering pilgrims come to recognize the sacredness of hitherto unknown sites. In the case of the *santri*-type pilgrims, it is still true that despite their typically deeper knowledge of Javano-Islamic history, they do not base their recognition on history understood as an objective account of past events. Rather, as I argued in Chapter 1 on the Javanese notion of history, they rely on the experience of being connected to spiritual presence, something that they feel in the deeper recess of their heart (Jv. *rasa*).

---

[51] The Parangtritis area is known as one of the most potent areas in the entire Mataram region. Many of these Javanist Muslim wandering pilgrims would also visit other Javano-Islamic shrines here, such as Parangkusumo, Guwa Langse, and so forth. Prince Dipanagara also visited these sites in his spiritual wandering in preparation for leading the Java war (1825–30). Dipanagara was a pious Muslim aristocrat with a strong connection with the *pesantren* world, yet he visited these sites that were associated mainly with indigenous Javanese spirit-figures. See Ricklefs, *Mystic Synthesis*, p. 209; Carey, *The Power of Prophecy*, p. 140.

[52] In this regard, some itinerant pilgrims come to develop an adaptable and personal way of praying, depending on the nature of the shrine they visit. Mr. Agus, a pilgrim from Surabaya, said that when he visits an indigenous Javanese shrine, he adjusts his way of prayer by using Javanese rather than Arabic and so forth. When he goes to the shrines of Islamic *wali*s, he would use Islamic manners of prayers. Interview, Pengging Shrine, July 2, 2009.

This is why their favorite sites might be not those favored by the general public or those sites whose historical background and Islamic identity are unambiguously established.[53] They also tend to understand the charismatic grace (Ar. *karāma*) of the saints not in terms of their outward "miracles," but rather the virtuous qualities of their personalities, especially their love (Ar. *maḥabba*) and proximity (Ar. *walāya*) to God.

In the context of pilgrims of both types, the depth of this spiritual experience is also normally connected with a special cultivation of sensitivity toward dreams, inner visions and signs (Jv. *wisik*), different stirrings of the heart, and so forth.[54] As Jamhari noted, many pilgrims at the Tembayat shrine consider these forms of inner communication with the invisible world very crucial in their pilgrimage and the achievement of the true *baraka*. Pilgrims talk about this type of experience and sometimes consult the custodian or one another to arrive at the proper meanings. One pilgrim at the Tembayat shrine, for instance, narrated his experience with dream and its interpretation thus:

> I came to this shrine because I was urged by a pious man in my dream. I could not recognize the person clearly. The man told me that this shrine is the right place to search for an amulet. After performing *ziarah* to the Sunan [saint], I slept in the corner of the main building of Sunan Tembayat's tomb. A person with a nice smile and wearing white clothes approached me. He did not say anything to me, but he gave me a hoe. I did not understand the meaning of this symbol. Therefore, I asked the custodian (Jv. *juru kunci*).[55]

Then, through the help of the custodian who firmly believed that the saint advises visitors to his tomb through dreams, this pilgrim came to understand that the saint was very happy with him and urged him to work harder in life, achieving his purpose through the hoe, rather than the amulet. Thus, for this pilgrim, the true *baraka* of God and the saint ultimately comes from this kind of spiritual assurance and support from the saint, and should be achieved in the larger framework of his life.

Mr. Hussein, whom I mentioned previously, also had a memorable experience with dreams during pilgrimage. He claimed to have met with a famous Javanese saint, Sunan Drajad, during a visit to his tomb in Lamongan, East Java. Later on

---

[53] Another example that I encountered is Zuhdi, a young *santri*-type wandering pilgrim from Magelang, who loves to visit the tomb of Kyai Nur Iman in Mlangi, Yogyakarta, and other less well-known sites in Pati and Juwana (north central Java). Interview, May 26, 2009.

[54] Ms. Wiwik, a woman pilgrim who was on the brink of financial bankruptcy, argued that focused meditation could serve as the best condition for right interpretation of dreams because it cultivates a particular sensitivity to inner movements of the soul, including dreams. She believed that God and the saint give signs through these dreams. Interview, Mawlana Maghribi shrine, June 5, 2009.

[55] See Jamhari, "The Meaning Interpreted," p. 93.

he would attribute his personal liking of *ziyāra* to this initial encounter with the saint. With regard to the interpretation of dreams, he explained that the full range of meanings of these "signs," might not always be self-evident when they first occur, so that they need to be interpreted in the larger continuum of one's life, namely before, during and after the outward act of pilgrimage.[56] Many pilgrims would confirm Mr. Hussein's point. The fuller meanings of God's blessings communicated through dreams have to be discerned in the context of one's own life. In this sense, *baraka* is always a mystery that can be unraveled only through more serious spiritual discernment.

At this point, it is also crucial to note that due to their intense cultivation of spiritual life, it is only natural that these true ascetic pilgrims become in some sense "spiritual masters", sought after by ordinary pilgrims for advice, spiritual and otherwise. Popular shrines in Java are places where such communication between ordinary pilgrims and spiritual "masters" continue to occur. And this role of informal spiritual master or counselor applies to both the *santri*-type and the Javanist one, as the experiences of Mr. Hussein and Mr. Kasiyo exemplify. In contemporary Java, this role is both real and rife with problems, as some itinerant pilgrims themselves realize.[57]

One defining feature of the *santri*-type soul-searching pilgrims as well as the itinerant ones is their mastery of and devotion to the Qur'ān. In the proper ritual etiquette of *ziyāra* in general, the recitation of Qur'ānic verses is considered the most meaningful spiritual gift to the dead.[58] However, for many of these pilgrims, Qur'ānic recitation has become the main pillar of their spiritual sojourn at the shrine. They develop some deep spiritual communion with God and the saints through the Qur'ān. Considering Qur'ānic recitation as a valuable and effective offering to the deceased saints and former teachers, they also believe such sacred recitation can bring blessings to themselves. At the shrine of Gunungpring, a large number of *santri* pilgrims spend their whole time of visitation reciting the Qur'ān

---

[56] Mr. Agus, an itinerant pilgrim mentioned previously, said that he often got lost in interpreting this kind of communication with the invisible world. At times, only a cultivation of *rasa* and the perseverance to always look for diverse signs in life could help him figure out the true meanings of that spiritual communication. Interview, July 2, 2009.

[57] For the most part, these problems are associated with the gullibility of some simple pilgrims, but also with the tendency of some fake "spiritual masters" to exploit these credulous people. Due to their religio-cultural status as sacred precincts where supernatural energies are concentrated, shrines and holy tombs possess a natural appeal for both true pilgrims and more superficial visitors who search for shamanic assistance or magical feats from all sorts of masters of the supernatural world.

[58] Many Javanese Muslims commemorate the anniversary of the death of relatives through offering prayers and Qur'ānic verses printed on small booklets. Interestingly, this recitation is done not only in the grave of these relatives but also at the tombs of the saints. This is why one finds these booklets in almost all Muslim shrines in Java. These booklets would also be useful for other pilgrims who had no relation with the dead being commemorated. Thus, the prayers for the dead can potentially expand.

at the tomb of *Mbah* Dalhar, with whom they are related in one way or another through the chain of teacher-disciple (Ar. *silsila, isnād*). They often undergo the ascetic practice of vigil, staying up the whole night (Ar. *ṣahr al-layal*), following the personal example of *Mbah* Dalhar.[59] Many of the *santri*s also have the pious habit of completing the recitation of the whole Qur'ān (Ar. *khatamāt al-Qur'ān*) at the saint's grave.

Concluding Remarks

By way of conclusion, three points need to be noted. First, among Javanese Muslim pilgrims in south central Java pilgrimage is a rich and complex mode of religiosity and piety that is both personal and communal, religious and cultural. It is motivated by spiritual devotion and love, but it also includes a very real search for blessings and blessedness that in turn involves a rather profound process of self-transformation and understanding. Pilgrimage is a space where a sheer human desire for all too mundane fulfillment is often transformed into a much more exciting lifelong journey of self-discovery and spiritual growth. To a large extent, the dynamics of pilgrimage are governed by the Islamic idea of *walāya*, in the sense of proximity to God and His saints as well as participating in the authority of God and His spiritual company. Javanese Muslim pilgrims treat the saints as having real authority and continuous presence. For the most part, these saints also belong to the category of revered ancestors or founders, spiritual intercessors and protectors, paradigmatic exemplars, and so forth. In practicing asceticism and purification in the understanding of pilgrimage as *laku* and *tirakat*, pilgrims become closer to God and their true selves.

Secondly, I have shown how pilgrims experience and express the Javano-Islamic aspect of pilgrimage. This hybrid aspect is not practiced or experienced all in the same way and to the same degree, given the diverse religio-cultural orientations of the pilgrims and the corresponding plurality of modes of doing the pilgrimage. Rather, what one sees in these diverse types of pilgrims is the remarkable richness of pilgrimage experience itself. Pilgrimage tradition appeals to a wide variety of people for many different reasons. Crucial in these diverse experiences are the ways in which many facets of Javanese culture get appropriated both naturally and intentionally, such as the cultivation of *rasa* and the search for true peace and wellbeing (Jv. *tentrem* and *slamet*).

---

[59] *Mbah* Dalhar is known as an accomplished ascetic. While in the Hejaz, he underwent a retreat for three months. His penchant for silent *dhikr* would sometimes keep him in that state of intense God-remembrance for three days and nights without interruption. His descendants and students remember him as a saint who performed ascetic and spiritual practices (Ar. *riyāḍa*) for their wellbeing. See Muhammad Wafa al-Hasani, "Waliyullah Mbah Kyai Dalhar Watucongol", http://al-kahfi.net/tarikh-wa-tsaqafah/waliyullah-mbah-kyai-dalhar-watucongol/ (accessed September 2009).

Thirdly, in many ways, my discussion on the practice of pilgrimage has shown the various manifestations in which the idea of communion—in the forms of inclusivity, continuity, adaptation, connection with the past, spiritual communion with God, the self, and other pilgrims—is at work as a principle in the face of complex relationships involved in the pilgrimage experience. Due to all of this, the whole pilgrimage tradition has become a milieu in which a complex Javano-Islamic identity is forged, not superficially and instantly, but rather through a long personal and communal engagement in the multifaceted elements of this very old tradition.

PART II
Javano-Catholic Case

Chapter 4
Identity as Memory: Sacred Space and the Formation of Javano-Catholic Identity

> This grotto is not only a source for the great joy of Catholics, but also a very beautiful and suitable advertisement for those who are not Catholic yet; for the Virgin would be the missionary there.
>
> J.B. Prennthaler, S.J. (1928)[1]

This chapter explores the relationship between the history of the three Catholic shrines under study and the identity formation of the local Javanese Catholic community. From the outset, it has to be noted that the Javanese Catholic community in south central Java came into being through a very complex and rather dramatic process of formation in which they engage different challenges. The setting of this formation was also very crucial, namely, the first three or four decades of the twentieth-century Java. During this time Dutch colonialism was on the way out, but in the eyes of the Javanese, Christianity was from the very start associated with the menacing power of colonialism and the West. Consequently, the greatest challenge faced by the nascent Javanese Catholic community had to do with this double alterity: being a Christian meant following a foreign religion brought to Java by a menacing colonial power with its anti-Islamic agenda.[2]

A Brief History of Javano-Catholic Community

In its initial phase (1920s–30s), this challenge was faced with a sense of determination, even confrontation, as indicated in the *Swara-Tama*, the mouthpiece of the first generation of Javanese Catholic intellectuals and leaders,

---

[1] Letter of Father Prennthaler, March 24, 1928 in *Brieven van Pater J.B. Prennthaler aan Pater Directeur van de St. Claverbond* 1922–1937 (hence *Brieven*), p. 65.

[2] Cf. Steenbrink, *Catholics in Indonesia*, vol. 2, p. 406. As illustration of the foreignness of Christianity, the new Catholic converts in the town of Ambarawa were accused of having abandoned the faith of the Javanese, arguing vehemently that the Europeans were meant to be Christians, while Divine Providence had decreed that Javanese followed the Prophet Muḥammad. See J.A.C. Schots, S.J, "Eerstelingen te Ambarawa!" *St. Claverbond* (1923): p. 292; Jos Gitsels, S.J., "'N Eeenzaam Afsterven," *St. Claverbond* (1923): pp. 271–4.

during this period.[3] Always accused of being sympathetic to the Dutch, the *Swara-Tama* continued to be critical and combative in its debate with other native media.[4] This might indeed be shocking, especially when one sees it from today's vantage point. But the historical context was very conducive for this kind of confrontational style of identity formation. For this was the age in motion in the Netherlands East Indies, a tumultuous period in which the identity formations of various ethnic or religious groups (the Javanese, Chinese, Arabs, the Muslims, and so forth) were first negotiated in the context of their own group as well as over against each other.[5]

One of the most defining challenges faced by the first Javanese Catholic community was the tension between cultural hybridity and religious purity. They were aware of the necessity of cultural hybridity: they wanted to stay Javanese and yet to be open to Western cultures as well.[6] However, in the realm of religion, they initially seemed to say that this was not negotiable, and wanted to live out the "purity of the Catholic religion." But then the community adopted some creative strategies of making sense of their Javaneseness and Catholicity. In the words of Soegijapranata, the most articulate among the first group of Javanese Catholic intellectuals, the principle of this hybrid vision is formulated succinctly as follows: "We become Javanese Catholics, not Catholic Javanese" (Jv. *Djawi Kathoelik sanes Katholiek Djawi*).[7] Thus, there is also a sense of inevitable hybridity here that they negotiated from both sides, Catholicism and Javanese culture. They opted for the priority of Catholic element as the main framework in this hybrid identity. In the process, the first generation of Javanese Catholic intellectuals were proud of the nimbleness, versatility, and inclusivity of their "catholic" tradition ("catholicity") in appropriating the Javanese culture and people. They believed

---

[3] The *Swara-Tama* (Jv., Good News; henceforth *ST*) was a Javanese publication that was in circulation from the 1920s to the 1940s. Started by the students of the Catholic mission school in Muntilan (Xavier College), the editorial board moved to Yogyakarta later and connected for a while with the Jesuit house of formation there. In this book, I call the Javanese Catholic writers who contributed to these publications "the first Javanese Catholic intellectuals"; not only did they voice the nascent Javanese Catholic community's concerns and aspirations and engage the general public, they also went on to become leaders of this community both on the ecclesial and political realms, like Soegijapranata (the first native and Javanese bishop) and I.J. Kasimo (founder of the Catholic Party).

[4] Cf. *ST*, March 1921.

[5] Cf. Takashi Shiraishi, *An Age in Motion* (Ithaca, 1990).

[6] Cf. *ST*, March 1921.

[7] Soegijapranata argued that this kind of identity was the vision of van Lith for his Javanese students. The principle was to build a thoroughly Catholic Javanese, that is, a solid Catholic identity that preserves the good of the Javaneseness or ennobles it. See his "Pastoor van Lith als onze opvoeder," *Berichten uit Java* (1952): p. 101; also his article "Missi kalijan Kaboedajan: Agami Katholiek saged mengkoe sadajaning kaboedajan," *ST*, June 26 and July 4, 1940.

that Catholicism was able to enhance what is good in Javanese culture.[8] However, this determination was coupled by a general sentiment to be authentically Javanese as opposed to becoming Western or Dutch—sometimes not primarily because Dutchness or Western culture was seen as something undesirable, but because they had to prevent the suspicion about the hidden agenda of the Catholic mission *vis-à-vis* local culture and identity. The following warning reflects this concern: "Don't become a fake Dutch (Jv. *Walandi tetiron*), lest people say: 'The [Catholic] mission destroys culture'" (D. *De Zending bederft de cultuur*).[9]

In making a case for the necessity and authenticity of this identity, a Javanese Catholic intellectual put forth his argument thus:

> I have argued over and over again that if we want to become truly Catholic in the deepest sense, to the marrow, it is not sufficient for us to perfect our religious knowledge. We must baptize our morality and culture. This means, we transform our Javanese culture and morality into Javano-Catholic morality and culture. This is so on account of the fact that Javano-Catholic morality and culture are not the same as that of the Dutch, British, Chinese, Japanese and so forth.[10]

In looking for the ways of negotiating this hybrid identity that was eventually governed by the principle of communion and continuity, this community actually took Father Franciscus van Lith (1863–1926), their beloved founder, as the paradigm, especially his masterful combination of modern (Western) education and genuine care for the indigenous people and their culture. It was this paradigm and principle that enabled the first Javanese Catholics to unabashedly embrace foreign elements—that is, the Dutch Church and the positive values of the Western culture brought by the Dutch—as well as to back the nationalist aspiration and to remain true to their Javanese cultural identity. Since some other aspects of the figure of van Lith will be discussed later in this chapter as well as Chapters 5 and 6, in the following I will offer a brief sketch of his life in the memory of the local Javanese Catholic community.[11]

---

[8] *ST*, September 15, 1921.

[9] *ST*, February 19, 1926.

[10] *ST*, June 26, 1940. This discourse was extended to the next edition (*ST*, July 3, 1940) which forcefully argued that European missionaries did not have the business of making other nations and peoples European or European Catholic, but rather, making them distinctively Catholic in terms of their own cultures.

[11] For historical and biographical accounts of van Lith, see Hasto Rosariyanto, *Father Franciscus van Lith, S.J.: Turning Point of the Catholic Church's Approach in the Pluralistic Indonesian Society* (Doctoral Dissertation, Gregorian University, Rome, 1997); Gerry van Klinken, "Power, symbol and the Catholic mission in Java: The Biography of Frans van Lith, S.J." *Documentieblad voor de Geschiedenis van de Nederlandse Zending en Overzeese Kerken*, 1 (1997): 43–59.

By his former students, van Lith was fondly remembered as an accomplished priest and teacher as well as their most beloved spiritual father. This was largely due to his self-sacrificing love for the Javanese. Always portrayed as a man of total detachment from worldly and self-pursuits, van Lith is also remembered as a white Catholic missionary whose life was devoted fully to accomplishing a lofty mission (Jv. *pakaryan luhur*), not only for the Javanese Catholics but also for the whole Indies.[12] His former students who lived closely with him for some years in the mission school at Muntilan were moved by the quality of his personality: socially likable, simple, humble, and entirely dedicated to the cause.[13]

Indeed, van Lith's long sojourn in central Java—from 1896 to 1926 with just few years of absence—was marked by a personal and professional immersion into the Javanese world. He was an active member of the *Java Instituut* where he shared common concerns for reviving the Javanese culture of the classical age, understood as relatively devoid of Islam, with some prominent members of Javanese elite and Dutch Orientalists.[14] He also contributed a few articles to the scholarly discourse on the Hindu-Buddhist element of the Javanese culture.[15] Van Lith's membership in the *Java Instituut* and his scholarly contribution might be arguably seen as an evidence of his Orientalist tendency, something that was not without its ambiguous ramifications on the question of Islam.

---

[12] Despite his apparent preferential love for the Javanese, van Lith's concerns went beyond the confines of Java. His friendship with Haji Agus Salim, a prominent Muslim figure of the Sarekat Islam, was due to their common concerns for the welfare of Indonesians in general. Sukarno, a prominent nationalist activist who would eventually become the first Indonesian president, quoted van Lith's political views in his defense speech during his 1929 trial and considered van Lith as a true saint due to his preferential love for cause of the natives. See van Klinken, "Power," pp. 55–6.

[13] *ST*, August 24, 1934.

[14] The *Java Instituut* was established in 1919 following The Congress for Javanese Cultural Development in Surakarta in 1918, for the revival of Javanese classical (Hindu-Buddhist) culture (cf. Ricklefs, *Mystic Synthesis*, p. 242; also Laurie Sears, *Shadows of Empire*, p. 145–6). In this context, van Lith came to foster deeper friendship with Suwardi Suryaningrat, Suryopranoto, and Prince Sasraningrat, all proponents of Javanese culture from the Pakualaman royal house (the minor court) of Yogyakarta. This Institute also listed some prominent Dutch orientalists of the day among its members, such as Bosch and Schrieke. See Gerry van Klinken, "The Power," p. 50.

[15] Two articles of van Lith on old-Javanese (Hindu-Buddhist) themes are: "Raden Larang en Raden Sumana," *Tijdschrift voor 'Indische taal-, land- en volkenkunde*, 66 (1926): pp. 435–46; "Het gebed van Ardjoena tot Ciwa," *Studiën*, 56/101 (1924): pp. 362–75. He also wrote an article on Javanese grammars: "De Javaansche grammatica op Javaanschen grondslag," in *Handelingen van het Eerste Congres voor de Taal-, Land- en Volkenkunde van Java, Solo, 25 en 26, 1919* (Weltevreden, 1921), pp. 273–85. For van Lith's role in the subsequent congresses of this institute, see also *Verslagen der Javaansche Cultuurcongressen 1918–1921* (Weltevreden, ca. 1922), p. 318.

Learning from van Lith, the Javano-Catholic intellectuals and their community understood the complex principle of communion as a guide for their identity formation, in the cultural, political, and religious realms, giving rise to forms of hybridity. However, ambiguities and tensions do exist in this historical process. In the rest of this chapter I will explore the ways in which these tensions, ambiguities, and limits of the Javano-Catholic identity formation have been dealt with and made fruitful by the community itself, especially in the history of the building of the three shrines under study, that is, the Sendangsono Marian grotto (1929), the Sacred Heart Shrine at Ganjuran (1930), and the Mausoleum in Muntilan.

In this regard, the statement of Father Prennthaler (1885–1946), a prominent Jesuit missionary in the post-van Lith era and the founder of the Marian grotto of Sendangsono, quoted above is highly instructive. For he understood the significance of the grotto precisely in terms of the symbolic and material dimension of the Catholic identity formation of the community, especially *vis-à-vis* the religious other. For him, the grotto was not only a source of joy for the community but also a beautiful and suitable advertisement for non-Catholics in the surrounding area due to the role of the Virgin as the missionary. However, it is clear that this conception is not without its ambiguities and tensions. For it raises different questions: what does it mean for the Virgin to be the missionary among the non-Catholic Javanese? How would she exactly accomplish her role as the missionary? Does it mean that Mary would draw these people into the Church through baptism, or also through some other ways that simply are beyond our immediate understanding? When non-Catholic pilgrims are drawn to the grotto and come to revere Mary in their own way without formal conversion to Catholicism, does it mean that Mary's role as the missionary fails? Or, does this show a different aspect of Mary's role as the Mother of all nations (Luke 1:48)?[16] And, what are the roles of the Catholics themselves in this dynamic?

Obviously, this set of questions can only be answered by exploring the ways in which the Javano-Catholic community itself has been grappling with them since its foundation. In this regard, once again, the three shrines can be taken as crucial historical and material expressions of the tensions and ambiguities embedded in the identity making of this community. I will illustrate further the major ways in which this communion and connection to the sacred past represented by the three shrines works in terms of the whole community's self-understanding in the present. This hermeneutical process of returning to the founding sources (*resourcement*) is a crucial part of the negotiation of communal identity that makes possible the communion with the religious other. I will identify how this process of reinterpretation provides some directions to the potentialities, tensions, and ambiguities inherent in the story of the shrines.

---

[16] Cf. Alexandra Cuffel, "'Henceforward all generations will call me blessed': Medieval Christian Tales of Non-Christian Marian Veneration," *Mediterranean Studies*, 12 (2003): pp. 37–60.

Figure 4.1   Pilgrims at the Sendangsono Marian Shrine, 2009

Before moving to the first section, some basic information about the three shrines under study is in order. The first shrine is the aforementioned Marian grotto of Sendangsono (Figure 4.1), the so-called "Lourdes of Java."

Modeled after the famous Marian shrine in France, this is the most important as well as the oldest Marian shrine in Java. Most importantly, its consecration in 1929 memorializes the birth and foundation of the indigenous Javano-Catholic community. For, it was on this very site that in 1904 a large group of Javanese (171 persons) received their baptisms into the faith through Fr. Franciscus van Lith (1863–1926), the founder of the Java mission. This shrine is located in the hamlet of Sendangsono that is part of the larger area called Kalibawang, on the hills of Menoreh, some twenty miles to the northwest of Yogyakarta and around seven miles away from the Borobudur temple (Map 3). The shrine draws a stream of pilgrims every day but the months of May and October, the Marian months, are the busiest period.

The second pilgrimage site is the Sacred Heart Shrine of Ganjuran (Figure 4.2), located some twenty miles to the southwest of the royal city of Yogyakarta, a few miles away from the Parangtritis coast in the south that is also the home to various Javanist and Muslim sacred sites (see Map 3).

Built by the Schmutzer family, a prominent Dutch family whose role as laity in the Jesuit mission in Java was surpassed by none, the shrine is also considered to be the sister shrine of the Sendangsono grotto. It was consecrated in 1930, a year after the Sendangsono grotto. During the consecration, the island of Java as a symbol for the whole of Indonesia was placed under the protection of the

Identity as Memory 111

Figure 4.2   The Sacred Heart Shrine at Ganjuran with the Sacred Heart Statue in the Inner Sanctum, 2009

Sacred Heart.[17] The foundational spirit of this shrine is that the growing Javano-Catholic community in Java whose foundation is commemorated in Sendangsono is called now to become a blessing to all people and the whole nation. This shrine was from the very beginning known to be a model for Catholic inculturation into Javanese culture since it makes abundant use of Hindu-Buddhist symbolisms and architectures. After a period of neglect and decline, the shrine experienced a spectacular revival since the late 1990s and it now draws a larger number of pilgrims than the other two. An important part of this revival is the growing presence of non-Catholic pilgrims, mostly Javanese Muslims.

The third site is the Mausoleum of Muntilan (Figure 4.3). This mausoleum is located in the small town of Muntilan, which is the original site of the Catholic mission center of the van Lith era. So, the place holds a very special significance in the identity formation of the Javano-Catholic community. Sharing a geographical proximity to the Borobudur temple, this small shrine is the mausoleum of some of the most prominent figures in the history of the Catholic Church in Java, including

---

[17]   Karel Steenbrink, *Catholics in Indonesia*, vol. 1, p. 396.

Figure 4.3   Pilgrims at the grave of Father Sanjaya in the Mausoleum of Muntilan, 2009

Fr. van Lith and that of Fr. Sanjaya, the first "martyr" of the young Catholic community.[18] It also shares a geographical proximity with the Gunungpring shrine, an important Muslim pilgrimage site discussed in Part I. Traditionally, pilgrims would visit this mausoleum in tandem with the Sendangsono grotto.

At the Origin of the Community: The Lourdes of Java

Memory of and Communion with the Founding Moment and Founders

The year of 2004 was declared a "Year of Gratitude for the Gift of Faith" by the Archdiocese of Semarang, under whose ecclesiastical jurisdiction the Marian grotto of Sendangsono falls. This "gift of faith" refers to nothing other than the foundational event that occurred a hundred years before at the site of what is now the Sendangsono grotto, namely, the aforementioned baptisms of the first largest

---

[18]   The site is also popularly known as the grave of Father Sanjaya (I. *Makam Rama Sanjaya*) due to the fame that this slain priest holds among Catholics in the area. Although the grave of Father Sanjaya typically becomes the focus of the pilgrimage, more and more pilgrims would also pay special visits to the grave of Father van Lith as well as other graves of prominent Church personnel there.

group of Javanese by Father van Lith in 1904.[19] Historically speaking, this baptism was not really the first among the Javanese, but it was considered to be singularly foundational because it saved the Java mission from utter failure during its most crucial juncture and thus marked the real beginning of the Javanese Catholic community in south central Java.

In words that have also become legendary in the history of the community, Father van Lith described the providential event thus:

> The visit of the people from Kalibawang was for me an unexpected and inexplicable event. I have visited lots of places, treading miles of missionary path, but to no avail. But look, in a region with which I have never had anything to do, there arose suddenly a desire for our religion. This was a sign of providence that the Java mission would continue to exist. In and of itself, the conversion of this relatively small group was of little meaning for the enormous mission work among millions of the inhabitants of Java. But it was very important, because now I can continue my already matured plans for the schools in Muntilan.[20]

Here, one sees how van Lith connects the Sendangsono event with the other foundational moment in the history of Javano-Catholic community in south central Java, namely, the establishment of the mission school, the Xavier College, at Muntilan. As mentioned before, the alumni of this school would become the first intellectuals of the Javano-Catholic community and play a crucial role in its subsequent involvement in the larger Javanese and Indonesian society. In the mind of van Lith, the event of Sendangsono was intimately and architectonically related to Muntilan.

Historically, the Sendangsono baptism was a miracle needed to confirm the validity of the particular missionary method of Father van Lith. What the 2004 centenary celebration primarily shows is the continued significance of this foundational event in the present identity of the local Catholic community. As this community understands it, the event has provided a solid theological foundation for its *raison d'être*. For the miracle of baptism was taken as a clear sign of divine confirmation and protection of the community's existence and future. Its "spectacular" growth is a living testament to this foundational assurance.[21] In a proper theological framework, the event marked the moment of the descent of the gift of "faith," the most defining aspect of the identity of the community.

---

[19] Mgr. Ignatius Suharyo, "In Gratitude for the Gift of Faith" (I. "*Syukur atas Karunia Iman*"), a pastoral letter on the occasion of the centenary of the Sendangsono baptism (2004), in Wismapranata Pr et al., *Kenangan atas 100 Tahun Sendangsono* (Yogyakarta, 2004), pp. 8–10.

[20] See the Jesuit newsletter, *Berichten uit Java* (1956): p. 100.

[21] The term "spectacular" is used here in reference to Karel Steenbrink's evaluation on the growth of the indigenous Catholic community in Indonesia, not only Java, from 1903 to 1942. See his *Catholics in Indonesia*, vol. 1, p. xii.

Thus it is no wonder that in the centenary celebration of the Sendangsono baptism, Father van Lith was remembered as the main channel through which the gift of faith had been passed down to the subsequent generations. As I will show later, there are two other paradigmatic figures, or founders of lesser degree, of both the Javanese Catholic community and the Sendangsono grotto. The first is a Javanese man named Barnabas Sarikrama (1874–1940). He was the first catechist in the area, the right hand man of Father van Lith in the formation of the newly baptized Catholics in Kalibawang. The second is the aforementioned Father Johannes Prennthaler (1885–1946), an Austrian born Jesuit missionary who worked in the area for over 15 years, under whose initiative and leadership the grotto came into being.

Within only a few years after its foundation in 1929, this shrine quickly became the major pilgrimage site among Catholics in Java, both European and Javanese. During its earliest phase (ca. 1930s) pilgrimage to this site was known also for its asceticism, due to the arduous journey, which pilgrims had to undertake, mostly on foot, through the rough terrain of the Menoreh hills that could be really nightmarish during the rainy season.[22] Furthermore, the shrine has also become a popular site for communal and ecclesial events at the level of the local diocese.[23] During these events, an important message was normally being retold, that is: "Don't come to Sendangsono to ask for miracle, but rather focus your attention on your relationship with Mary!" More generally, the deeper and wider spiritual nature of the grotto is emphasized over against the popular proclivity to turn it into a place of magic.

The grotto has undeniably become a privileged milieu vested with a vast range of symbolisms and deeper meanings. This is why the centenary celebration of the foundational baptism was centered on the shrine. The spirit of the whole celebration was intimately connected with the shrine, such as emphasizing the symbolic messages of holy water of the grotto, of pilgrimage to the site, the role of Mary as an exemplar of Christian life, as well as the role of the shrine and its pilgrimage tradition in light of contemporary concerns for the preservation of local culture, environment, and interfaith dialogue.[24] Thus, pilgrimage to Sendangsono is clearly understood as an act of communing with the sacred past, the founding moment of the whole community, not for the sake of communal nostalgia, but rather for a better understanding of its identity in the contemporary society. This way pilgrimage is practiced as the moment of the community's returning to its spiritual source (*resourcement*).

Before tackling the question of the other that is intimately implicated in this foundational story of the Sendangsono grotto, I will first delve more into the communal memory of the two other founders of the community and the grotto,

---

[22] Cf. *ST*, January 16 and 26, May 1, 1935.

[23] Cf. *ST*, May 29, 1935. During the celebration of the Marian Year of 1954 an average of a thousand pilgrims visited this grotto in May. See "Maria Koningin der Volkeren," *Berichten uit Java* (1954): pp. 97–9.

[24] See Wismapranata et al., *Kenangan*, p. 19.

namely the Jesuit Father Prennthaler and Barnabas Sarikrama. For the ways in which these two personages are imagined today are revelatory of the ongoing process of the identity formation of this community. As happens among Javanese Muslims (Chapter 1), Javanese Catholics also understand shrines as being imbued with sacred history and as a living legacy of past authoritative events and paradigmatic founder-figures. In this framework, pilgrimage acquires the meanings of memory and communion, including communion with these founders with the purpose of, among others, re-interpreting or broadening their legacy in light of contemporary questions with regard to the relationship of the community with the religious other.

The Javano-Catholic community portrays Barnabas Sarikrama (1874–1940) as a pilgrim in the most fundamental sense of the word, that is, a person seeking to commune with God. He is seen as an important founder of the community because his relentless search for the Truth that originated from the depth of the spiritual world of the Javanese finally led him to the bosom of the Church. Thus his pilgrimage is a proto-type of the community's own journey. In this master narrative, Sarikrama was described as a dedicated and accomplished layman whose life-changing transformation to a pilgrim-apostle was sparked off by the miraculous cure of his feet at the hands of Brother Kersten, a Jesuit nurse-missionary at the mission center of Muntilan.[25] Upon the cure, he used his feet to walk the rough road of mission in the Sendangsono area. He brought the first large group of Javanese to the Church in 1904 (the aforementioned baptism) and since then continued his crucial role in the formation of this newly born congregation.

Perhaps more importantly, Sarikrama is also portrayed as a bridge between the Javanist religion and Catholicism. For it was his pilgrimage and meditation in the Javanist shrine of Den Baguse Samijo near the Borobudur temple, as part of his search for healing that eventually led him to the mission center of Muntilan.[26] Reaching Muntilan as a disabled man, hardly capable of walking, he came out as a sound and healthy man, both physically and spiritually. So Sarikrama was both a pilgrim *par excellence* and a bridge or road that connects the two spiritual worlds at the founding moment of the community. Here one sees the framework of continuation and fulfillment between the two traditions. For Sarikrama took up the spiritual tradition of the Javanese (Jv. *ngelmu urip*) seriously as the necessary soil for the inculturation of the Catholic faith.[27]

---

[25] Tartono, *Barnabas Sarikrama* (Muntilan, 2005), pp. xii–xv.

[26] Den Baguse Samijo is an ancestor-spirit (Jv. *pundhen*) who is believed to have had his abode in the Sendangsono spring before the arrival of Mary. To emphasize the depth of Sarikrama's location in the Javanese spiritual world, it is mentioned that his father (Kyai Mertaleksana) was an accomplished Javanist master (Jv. *guru*) and his grave continues to be a minor pilgrimage site for the locals until today. See Tartono, *Barnabas Sarikrama*, pp. 6–7.

[27] This aspect of harmonization between the two traditions is emphasized in the historiography of the shrine. See Sindhunata, *Mengasih Maria: 100 Tahun Sendangsono* (Yogyakarta, 2004), p. 40.

As previously mentioned, the second founder of the grotto and its community is Fr. Johannes Prennthaler (1885–1946), arguably the most outstanding Jesuit missionary in the area in the post van Lith era. Born to a simple family of farmers in Tirol, Austria, he entered the Jesuit Order of the French Province in 1904 and was initially destined to work as a missionary among Muslims in Syria or the Near East. He knew Arabic and worked in Beirut for three years (1914–18), but could no longer stay in the Middle East in the wake of World War I. His love affair with the Java mission then began with an article on this mission that he read in Vienna. Captivated by the story of this mission, he asked the Jesuit general superior for transfer to the Dutch Province. Arriving in Java in 1920, he eventually worked for many years in the parish of Bara, near Sendangsono, while also teaching Arabic to young Jesuit seminarians in Yogyakarta. However, Prennthaler did not seem to show a keen interest in things Islamic during his sojourn in Java, despite his mastery of Arabic language and three years of experience in the Middle East.[28]

Together with Barnabas Sarikrama, Father Prennthaler was not only instrumental in building the Sendangsono shrine in 1929, but he put a very personal stamp on it. He unabashedly pleaded with his Dutch benefactors to give funds and sundry items needed in his missionary work. His concerns over his destitute flock struck by the economic hardship of the great depression in 1930s would include: securing their crops, staple food, water supply and medicines, helping out with their debt, fighting against the liberal colonial regulation on opium use, and overseeing their spiritual wellbeing. Unlike van Lith, he was certainly no deep thinker or progressive missionary-theologian, but his work was so remarkable due to his total immersion in the reality of his people.[29]

Father Prennthaler has been remembered fondly by the local Javanese Catholic community as their saintly founder. The memory of his persona was made very clear in 2002 as the parish he founded celebrated their seventy-fifth anniversary.[30] The community remembered him as a hardworking missionary, a man of prayer, totally dedicated to the divine cause, and completely abandoning his own worldly interest for the sake of the welfare of his flock. One of his former aides wrote: "Father Prennthaler was like a saint; he was no longer concerned with [his own] worldly needs."[31] His poverty and frugality is as legendary as that of van Lith.[32] Highly insightful among his portrayals is his image as a pilgrim, a traveling missionary who would cover a distance of almost a thousand miles annually.[33] His

---

[28] Robert Hardawiryana, S.J., *Romo J.B. Prennthaler, S.J.* (Yogyakarta, 2002), p. 49ff.

[29] Hardawiryana, *Romo Prennthaler*, p. 110.

[30] See the foreword of the committee of the anniversary celebration in Hardawiryana, *Romo Prennthaler*, p. 4.

[31] This same person also narrates a story of miracle that Father Prennthaler performed during one of his missionary travels. See Sindhunata, *Mengasih Maria*, p. 60.

[32] Hardawiryana, *Romo Prennthaler*, pp. 110–11.

[33] Letter of Prennthaler, January 24, 1928; *Brieven*, p. 55; also F. Knooren, S.J., "Bijzonderheden over den Dood van Pater Prennthaler S.J. – RIP," *St. Claverbond* (1946): p. 93.

collapses from fatigue that led to his eventual demise in 1946 reinforced his image as a thoroughly ascetic missionary, always on the move despite the setbacks and hardships that at times became unbearable.[34]

The lasting power of his memory among his people is made manifest in the fact that his tomb in the cemetery of the parish in Bara, two miles to the east of the Sendangsono grotto, has become a rather popular site of local pilgrimage in recent years. The 2007 novena in his name at his tomb was clearly an attempt by the community to not only remember him as the founder but also to commune with him as an intercessor. He himself promised to pray for his little flock after his death, as well as assured them of the continued help of Our Lady of Lourdes in Sendangsono.[35] There has been some effort to widen the scope of Prennthaler's memory as to include all the peoples of the area, due to his concerns for the integral wellbeing of the people during his tenure as pastor.[36]

Encounter with the Other: From Mimetic Rivalry to Communion

In the previous section, I discussed how the major dynamics of the memory of founders and founding moment, as well as their memorialization at the sacred site of Sendangsono, have been governed by the widening principle of communion and continuity. Thus the identity of the community is largely formed in the framework of fostering diverse forms of communion and interconnection, including with the Dutch benefactors. However, inherent in this story is also the question of otherness that manifests itself in different forms, but mainly through the categories of "other religion," particularly the Javanist religion and Islam.

In the story of Sendangsono, this complex question of alterity has two major dimensions. The first dimension lies in the fact that the Marian grotto replaces a Javanist shrine. As noted earlier, the statue of Our Lady of Lourdes at Sendangsono was intentionally placed at the site of the baptism of the Javanese in 1904. However, this site used to be the abode of two ancestor-guardian spirits, Den Baguse Samijo and his mother, Dewi Lantamsari, and was still visited by local population, both "pagan" and Muslim. In the distant past it had been used by Buddhist monks as a resting place on their way to and from the Borobudur temple.[37] For this reason,

---

[34] The *Swara-Tama* (November 9, 1934) reported that Prennthaler had to take some rest in the Netherlands after his hardworking years in Java since 1920. In his letters he was quite frank about the hardships of being a missionary in this area: physical fatigue from the travels, psychological depression and distress from the financial difficulties as well as the competition with the Muhammadiyah etc. See his letters of February 15, March 27, and June 12, 1929; *Brieven*, pp. 112–15, 117–20, and 131–5.

[35] See Prennthaler, "Het Testament van Pater Prennthaler," *St. Claverbond* (1946): p. 203.

[36] During his tenure, Prennthaler paid great attention to the socio-economic development of his flock, such as fighting against the take over of the land by industrialists. His letter of June 26, 1930; *Brieven*, p. 211.

[37] Letter of Prennthaler, March 24, 1928; *Brieven*, p. 65.

the building of the grotto, together with the baptism, was also meant as a story of triumph of Christianity over "paganism" or the religious other. In this regard, Fr. van Lith is reported to have said: "Because the spring is considered sacred by the locals and the Buddhist monks, let me baptize it also [together with the people]."[38] After the Sendangsono grotto was built, this Christian triumph took a deeply Catholic form as it was Mary who occupied the central symbolic role. On this point, Fr. Prennthaler wrote categorically: "By virtue of being located at this site [of paganism], the grotto of Lourdes, with the statue of Our Lady of the Immaculate Conception, should always remind us that Mary is the woman who crushed the head of the snake, that Mary has driven out these pagan evil ancestor-guardian spirits (Jv. *pepundhen*)."[39]

Due to the significance of this location as the abode of the ancestor-guardian spirits, namely the founders of the local pagan community, the replacement of them through the building of the grotto also signals a different foundation of a new community. Again, this aspect of difference and newness is explained in the history of Sendangsono mostly through baptism and the installment of Mary. However, it is crucial not to overlook the subtle way of explaining the transition between these two religio-cultural frameworks in the foundational story of the grotto. For the two ancestral spirits were believed to have moved out before the arrival of Mary. And later, when Dewi Lantamsari, the mother, wanted to return to her former abode and found out that Mary was more potent, she voluntarily relinquished the site forever.[40]

An interesting point here is also the subtle suggestion that it might have been the pagan ancestral spirit of Den Baguse Samijo who led the Javanist Sarikrama to his eventual baptism. In his quest for healing, as mentioned before, Sarikrama was meditating at the site of Den Baguse Samijo near Borobudur temple area, and it was during this meditation that he received a supernatural omen to go to the direction of the Catholic mission.[41] Thus there is some pattern in which the transition from Javanism to Catholicism is conceived in a peaceful manner, rather than in a violently triumphant way.[42] Furthermore, Sarikrama would also appropriate important facets of the Javanese spiritual tradition in his work among the Javanese.[43]

---

[38] G. Vriens, *Seratus Tahun Misi* (Yogyakarta, 1959), p. 77.

[39] Letter of Prennthaler, May 23, 1929; *Brieven*, p. 130.

[40] Sindhunata, *Mengasih Maria*, pp. 16–17.

[41] Tartono, *Barnabas Sarikrama*, p. 19; also Wismapranata et al., *Kenangan*, p. 25.

[42] At Sendangsono, although Mary was presented as a slayer of the snake's head, she was never imagined, at least explicitly, as Slayer of Muslims and heathens, in contrast to, for example, the metamorphosis of St. James into *Santiago Matamoros* (St. James, Slayer of the Muslims) in the Iberian Catholicism. See, Jerrylynn D. Dodds et al., *The Arts of Intimacy* (New Haven, 2008), pp. 100–101.

[43] Tartono, *Barnabas Sarikrama*, pp. 27 and 30.

The prevalence of the principle of continuity, rather than conflict, might also help explain the relative absence of demonization of the (Muslim) other in Sendangsono, compared to other contexts such as medieval Egypt or present day Sri Lanka.[44] In the history of the encounter between Christianity and Islam in Java, the demonization of the other has very rarely been conceived in terms of the fight between God and the demons belonging to the false religion. Even if there are some Muslims who regard Christians as "infidels," these Christians are not imagined in terms of demons. And *vice versa*. Although he called the cult of ancestral spirit among the Javanese "paganism," Fr. Prennthaler never considered the Muslims as inspired by demons.

The second dimension of the way in which the religious other was reckoned with in the Catholic self at the foundation of this grotto stems from its "missionary" nature as its founder conceived of it. The grotto was expected to serve as a beacon of self-identity, endowed not only with a dominant agenda of marking the existence of a self against the backdrop of the other, but also of turning and converting this other to the self. In the vision of Fr. Prennthaler, the Sendangsono grotto was not only conceived as a sign of a great joy and gratitude of the Javanese Catholics, but more importantly, as a proper advertisement (D. *passende reklame*) for the non-Catholic population, as the quote at the beginning of this chapter makes it clear. He declared with conviction: "Our Lady would be the missionary among these people."[45] In the mind of Prennthaler, the missionary, this was of course meant in the plain sense that Mary would not only subdue the local ancestral spirits but also convert the local Muslim and Javanist population. His hope was that this grotto, the "Lourdes van Java," would eventually become a major pilgrimage site, the first in the land of the "heathens" (D. *heidenen*).[46]

This was how Fr. Prennthaler conceived this shrine as a sign of the existence of a Catholic self over against the other. During his lifetime, the grotto did indeed attract a constant flow of non-Catholic Javanese pilgrims, including some local high-ranking government officials.[47] The popularity of the grotto among the Muslim population was strongly indicated by the fact that at some point a local government official felt the need to tell his subjects that a visit by non-Christians to the grotto would only result in disaster and curse. Apparently there had been some Muslims who would send out their representatives to do the visit to the grotto. Fr. Prennthaler did not in fact believe in the sincerity of these non-Catholic pilgrims. He was also worried that the Javanese Catholics would also treat the grotto as some kind of pagan shrine where a magic power would erupt. His local

---

[44] Frankfurter, *Pilgrimage and Holy Space in Late Antique Egypt*, p. 38; Stirrat, "Demonic Possession in Roman Catholic Sri Lanka," *Journal of Anthropological Research*, 33 (1977): p. 137.

[45] Letter of Father Prennthaler, March 24, 1928; *Brieven*, p. 65.

[46] Ibid.

[47] Cf. Letter of Fr Prennthaler, October 16, 1930; *Brieven*, p. 231.

cathecists assured him that there was no ground for this fear, arguing that the Javanese Catholics had pure faith in Mary.[48]

As mentioned, competition with the Muhammadiyah had become a special source of anxiety for Fr. Prennthaler.[49] Almost daily he felt he had to race against them, observing that they intentionally prevented the spread of the mission. They built up schools in places where the mission also planned to work.[50] In this regard, his meticulous and rigorous Catholic formation program for his Javanese community, centered around the grotto and Mary—the regular communal pilgrimage under his leadership, the festivals and processions, the three-time-a-day *angelus* prayers and so forth—could not be separated also from his concern to lay a solid Catholic foundation of the local church, a community that had to be strongly visible in its Catholic identity, in light of the "aggressive" presence of the other, in particular the Muhammadiyah.[51]

Before moving on to the second shrine under study, it is crucial to note that while much of Sendangsono's sacred symbolisms was originally conceived in a rather narrow and exclusive framework for the identity formation of the Catholic community, the development of the shrine, as it stands now, is geared toward offering hospitality to the other. In fact, the commemorative publication of its 2004 centenary celebration is filled with the stories of Muslim pilgrims to the shrine.[52] This book ends with an interesting article on Mary that emphasizes her universal motherhood by Fr. Bernhard Kieser, a senior Jesuit theologian of the Sanata Dharma University in Yogyakarta and a regular pilgrim to the Sendangsono grotto himself. Fr. Kieser speaks of Mary as the mother of all, weaving a Mariology that is ecumenically sensitive as well as taking into account the role of Mary in the Islamic tradition. Taking a major insight from the Qur'ān (21:91), he underlines the role of Mary and Jesus as sign of God's power, a powerful sign that gives rise to true faith.[53]

While formal conversion through baptism was a crucial part of the foundational story and master narrative of the shrine at the beginning, the contemporary local Catholic community put this concern in terms of the spread of the Kingdom of God. Mgr. Ignatius Suharyo, the then Archbishop of Semarang, remarked during the centenary celebration of the foundational baptism at the Sendangsono grotto:

---

[48] See his letter of October 16, 1930; *Brieven*, p. 231.

[49] See his letters of September 9, 1927; May 13, 1928, June 1928, January 13 and 19, 1929, February 15, 1929, October 10 and 28, 1930; August 24 and September 8, 1936; also his letter, "Open Brief van Pater J. Prennthaler, S.J.," *St. Claverbond* (1935): p. 171.

[50] See the letter of Father Prennthaler, October 28, 1930; *Brieven*, pp. 233–4.

[51] It was rather common among the Dutch missionaries at the time to view the Muhammadiyah as being strictly Muslim and thus fiercely anti-Catholic. Cf. F. Dirks, S.J., "'N Christen onder Mohammedanen," p. 62.

[52] See Sindhunata, *Mengasih Maria, passim*.

[53] Bernhard Kieser, S.J., "Maria, Siapa Punya? Orang Kristiani dan Orang Muslim Menghormati Maria," in Sindhunata, *Mengasih Maria*, pp. 189–204.

"The perspective of the Church's mission now is the Kingdom of God, not primarily baptism, although it is always good if God leads people to the Church through baptism."[54]

The Sacred Heart Shrine at Ganjuran: A Community Being Sent

It has become clear that the initial phase of the history of the Javanese Catholic community in south central Java was marked by tensions as it wobbled between security and insecurity, deep faith and self-doubt, as well as communion and exclusion. In what follows I will illustrate how the community came to terms with these tensions in a rather different spirit in the context of the Sacred Heart shrine in Ganjuran, where the identity of the community was negotiated within the larger and more integral context of a Catholic existence anchored in structural charity and inculturation. As also happened at the Sendangsono grotto, the current communal discernment of the community has significantly broadened the underlying principle of communion.

Both in terms of history and its role in the identity formation of the Javano-Catholic community, the Sacred Heart Shrine at Ganjuran—located some twenty miles to the southwest of Yogyakarta, a few miles away from the southern coast where some Javanese and Muslim sacred sites are found (see Map 3)—is intimately connected to the Sendangsono grotto. Consecrated on February 11, 1930, the feast day of Our Lady of Lourdes, the shrine was also expected to be like Lourdes: that is, to be blessed with miracles.[55] The shrine was an important pilgrimage site since its foundation, although it experienced a period of decline before becoming very popular from the late 1990s until the present.[56] Conceived and built chiefly by the Schmutzer family in their estate, the shrine acquired an ecclesial significance since it was conceived as a monument or memorialization of the "apostolic" moment of the identity formation of the community: that is, when the whole community was being sent out on a mission to the larger society, after being founded, so to speak, at Sendangsono. At the dedication ceremony of the shrine, the whole realm of Java and the Dutch East Indies was also consecrated to the protection of the Sacred Heart of Jesus. Therefore, the concerns went beyond the narrow confines of the Javano-Catholic community in Java or the Catholic Church in the Indies, but rather to the whole "nation" (I. *Nusantara*).

Given this foundational spirit, the shrine was meant to be a sign of the maturity of the Javanese Catholic community, its coming of age, marked by the greater sense of responsibility for the much wider society. This foundational spirit is of course subject to the same complex process of communal discernment that

---

[54] See his interview in the video program by S.A.V. Puskat, *Sendangsono* (Yogyakarta, 2004).
[55] *ST*, February 14, 1930.
[56] Cf. *ST*, June 19, 1935; November 16, 1934.

includes theological hermeneutic of self and otherness. However, from the outset one can say that the spirit of communion with the other—however it was meant originally—had been at the heart of this shrine since its foundation under the framework of channeling the Divine blessings, the merciful embrace of the Sacred Heart of Jesus, to the larger Javanese or Indonesian society.[57] The direction of this communal hermeneutic has been from the very start governed by the spirit of including the other, while immersing oneself more deeply into this reality of the other. More concretely, this foundational spirit has been translated into a structured program of charity and education for all, as well as inculturation of Catholic faith in the local Javanese culture, as I will show below.

In what follows, my historical analysis of these dynamics at the Ganjuran shrine will be focused on three elements. Preceded by a brief account of the historical context of identity formation of the Javano-Catholic community in the 1920s and 1930s, I will examine the community's discourse against the other, namely, the argument that presented the Ganjuran shrine as a living proof of the Catholic appreciation of the Javanese culture, arguably one of the most crucial beneficial manifestations of the Catholic mission in colonial Java. Then, I will discuss the role of the founders of the shrine, the Schmutzer family, in the formation of the identity of the community in the socio-political realm, as well as in the field of inculturation of the Catholic faith in Javanese culture.

The immediate context of the birth of the Ganjuran shrine is the first two or three tumultuous decades of the early decades of the twentieth century. As I have noted briefly at the beginning of this chapter, during this time period the Javanese society and the whole Indies were experiencing deep fissures, not only in terms of differing religions but also conflicting political and economic ideologies. Particularly crucial for my discussion here is the ideological enmity between the socialist/communist groups and their enemies (Islamic, Christian, and nationalist groups) that came to be much more pronounced in the 1920s.

It was in this context of sectarian political struggle that the Ganjuran sugar factory, owned by a religiously pious and socially progressive Dutch Catholic family (the Schmutzers), was presented as an example of the goodness of Catholicism by the Javano-Catholic intellectuals and community which was under serious attack due to its connection with the local Dutch industrialists. In the socio-economic realm, the Javanese Catholic community was often accused of being the lapdog of Dutch capitalists.[58] Thus, against the backdrop of rampant capitalist exploitation of the Javanese populace by the sugar factories in Java in the late nineteenth century and early decades of the twentieth century, and the specter

---

[57] In its current formulation, this spirit is expressed thus: "Becoming a Blessing for All Creatures, Everyone and Everything" (I. *Menjadi Berkat Bagi Siapa dan Apa Saja*; or *Menjadi Berkat untuk Segala Mahkluk*). See the official brochure of the shrine, *Gereja Hati Kudus Tuhan Yesus Ganjuran: Rahmat Yang Menjadi Berkat* (henceforth *Rahmat Yang Menjadi Berkat*; Yogyakarta 2004), p. 5.

[58] Cf. *ST*, October 15 and November 30, 1921.

of influential socialist and communist ideas, the first Javano-Catholic intellectuals proudly presented Ganjuran as a good exemplar of a factory that highly benefited the Javanese population, namely, bringing in a good irrigation system, sparing special funds for charity and education, and actively responding to social concerns of the surrounding society.[59] The practice of "solidarity"—as opposed to gross capitalism, socialism or communism—was taken up by the Catholic *Swara-Tama* as a distinctive marker of the Catholic socio-economic enterprise, its socio-political identity.[60]

In the story of the Ganjuran shrine, this practice of solidarity was rooted in the personal as well as professional lives of the Schmutzer family, a prominent Dutch Catholic family whose contribution to the Javanese (Indonesians) was expressed in the realms of politics (public service), economy (sugar factory), as well as religion and charity (parish church, hospitals, orphanage, and schools). I will delve a bit into the Schmutzer family because of their role as founders, not only of the shrine but also of the wider Javano-Catholic community, as well as their paradigmatic status as the most accomplished lay apostles in the history of the Catholic community in Java in colonial times. Surely their image as religiously pious and socially progressive founders continues to play a paradigmatic role in the ways in which the shrine understands itself and functions today, as I will illustrate later.[61]

In the realm of socio-political thought, the Schmutzer family was influential in shaping the identity and outlook of the Javano-Catholic community in this period. The two Schmutzer boys, Josef and Julius, were born in Java and only went to the Netherlands to pursue their university studies at the prestigious Polytechnic School in Delft. After graduation, the older Josef went on to Paris to pursue another course of studies in mineralogy at the École Nationale Supérieure des Mines de Paris, and then returned back to Delft for his doctorate. He then stayed at that school as a lecturer, before returning to the Indies with his younger brother, Julius. In the Indies, Josef was a member of the *Volksraad* (People's Advisory Council). The *Volksraad* was the first institution set up with an eye toward self-governance in the Indies. Opened in 1918, it was the first significant initiative of the Dutch progressive politicians (the Ethici) to enhance the conditions of the colony.

---

[59] *ST*, September 1920; Steenbrink, *Catholics in Indonesia*, vol. 1, p. 486.

[60] In the context of the Jesuit mission in colonial Java, plantation enterprise (D. *onderneming*) often functioned as a place of making fruitful contact with the Javanese natives, and a privileged avenue in which the laity and the missionaries were working hand in hand, united among others by the same concern against the spread of communism. See Kimmenade-Beekmans, *De Missie van de Jezuiten op Midden-Java tijdens het Interbellum*, p. 83.

[61] See the brochure, *Rahmat Yang Menjadi Berkat*, p. 13ff. This official publication of the shrine regards the Schmutzer family's socio-religious concerns, namely, their response to the call of Pope Leo XIII's social encyclical *Rerum Novarum*, as the embodiment of the Sacred Heart spirituality.

However, among Indonesian radical activists, the *Volksraad* was considered a largely symbolic institution.

Josef was a prominent Catholic layman not only in the Indies where he was a leader in the Dutch Catholic Party in the Indies (D. *Indische Katholieke Partij*), but also in the Netherlands, where he was involved with the Catholic Party and held a brief ministerial post during World War II. He returned to Utrecht from the Indies in 1930 to become a professor in mineralogy before assuming a ministerial post. An accomplished scholar and public servant, Josef was also interested in various aspects of Catholic theology, mission, arts, and so forth.[62] His younger brother, Julius Schmutzer (1884–1954), was the one who practically ran the sugar plantation in Ganjuran while also being very involved in various ways with the Jesuit mission in south central Java, especially in the realm of social and charity works.[63]

In particular, Josef Schmutzer is remembered for his visionary views on the question of colonialism and the rights of the natives. Drawing insights from Thomas Aquinas, he defended the natural inclination and rights of the peoples to organize themselves in the pursuit of common good. He saw the common identity of the people as something more primordial and important—based on the natural love for and attachment to homeland—than government and state. Thus, he argued, duties to the homeland should take precedence over duties to the (colonial) government and state. Government was only a means for the common good and it should be changed in accordance with the choice of the peoples, even by force, if necessary. On the contrary, when a colonial government fulfilled its duties toward the native peoples, it could be justified, but only until the peoples themselves became ready to have their own government (D. *zelfbestuur*).[64] Already in the late 1920s, Josef Schmutzer expressed his belief that the necessary maturity had been reached for the Indonesian people to decide on their own needs through the exercise of modern self-governance.[65] This was also the vision that the first Javano-Catholic intellectuals came to embrace.

---

[62] His relevant works in this area include: "Leekenarbeid in het Indische Missiegebied," in *Eerste Nederlandsche Missiecongres* (Leiden, 1921); *Un Art Javanais Chrétien*" (1922); "Bezieling en Arbeid," in *Eerste Internationaal Missiecongres in Nederland* (Utrecht, September 25–29, 1922), pp. 193–208; "Javaansche Madonna's" *St. Claverbond* (1935): pp. 214–22; "Het Apostolaat der Kunst," *St. Claverbond* (1935): pp. 53–68; "Irene Peltenburg en de Aangepaast Missiekunst," *St. Claverbond* (1934): pp. 65–8. For a brief sketch of Josef Schmutzer's life and work, see also C. van der Deijl, S.J., "Geloof en Wetenschap," *St. Claverbond* (1930): pp. 150–58.

[63] For a sketch of Julius Schmutzer's life and work, see van Kalken, S.J., "Hunne Werken Immers Volgen Hen," *St. Claverbond* (1930): 142–9.

[64] *ST*, August 2, 9, and 16, 1929. Also Josef Schmutzer, "Het Algemeen Regeeringsbeleid en het Arbeidsvraagstuk in den Volksraad," in *Publikaties der Indische Katholieke Partij* (1929), vol. 1, p. 84; Eduard Schmutzer, *Dutch Colonial Policy and the Search for Identity in Indonesia 1920–1931* (Leiden, 1977), pp. 102–4.

[65] *ST*, August 23, 1929.

In Josef Schmutzer's thoughts, this down-to-earth and nuanced view of colonialism and native nationalism was coupled with an adherence to the Catholic principle of solidarity.[66] The many activities and public service that he performed during his long sojourn in the Indies were nothing other than his attempts to apply this principle in the colonial context of the Dutch East Indies. In the context of Catholic mission in south central Java, this vision of solidarity was made much more concrete and far reaching by his younger brother and his wife, Julius Schmutzer and Caroline van Rijckevorsel. Julius was a pious Catholic industrialist who managed the sugar factory in Ganjuran.[67] Under his direction, the plantation and sugar factory of Ganjuran were guided by an integral practice of Catholicism, marked by concerns for the spiritual and material wellbeing of the whole community, including the Muslim population. It was a place of solidarity where the workers were treated humanely, and where a large part of the profit of the capital was returned to the community in the forms of education, health service, and infrastructure development.[68] Another aspect of this solidarity is the Schmutzers' concerns for the preservation of Javanese culture as well as the inculturation of Catholic faith in Javanese soil (more on this in the next chapter).

In the memory of the local Javano-Catholic community, all of these philanthropic activities have given rise to the image of the Schmutzer family as pious and hardworking Catholic pilgrims from the Netherlands whom God used in His salvific plan for the Javanese people. They felt forever indebted to this family as their founders.[69] The Schmutzer family was a paradigm of what it meant to be a good Dutch Catholic layperson in colonial Java.[70]

In the life and dynamics of the shrine today, this historical aspect in the sense of keeping the memory of the founders alive is quite pronounced. I will discuss in the next chapter how memory of the Schmutzer family features rather prominently in the prayer of the Sacred Heart of Jesus, one of the most distinctive rituals at the shrine. Beyond these rituals, this memory of the founder is largely governed by the master narrative of the Sacred Heart's spirituality, namely, the spirit of sharing the gift of God, of becoming the channel of God's outpouring grace for all, the grace of reconciliation and universal harmony (I. *Menjadi Berkat Untuk Segala Mahkluk*).[71] The spirit of the Sacred Heart is taken as the deepest driving

---

[66] J. Schmutzer, *Solidarisme in Indië* (Leiden, 1922).

[67] Cf. van Kalken, S.J., "Hunne Werken Immers Volgen Hen," pp. 142–9.

[68] In terms of infrastructure and community development, the Schmutzer family built 12 schools in the area, two hospitals, one in the area and another in the city, and a water irrigation system. Due to his service to the community, he obtained a personal appreciation and favor from the Sultan of Yogyakarta.

[69] Cf. *ST*, June 22, 1934.

[70] Cf. *Rahmat Yang Menjadi Berkat*, p. 26. The stature of the Schmutzer family became more paradigmatic as the Pope honored Julius Schmutzer with a title of a knight in the Order of St. Gregory. Cf. *ST*, December 6, 1929.

[71] See *Rahmat Yang Menjadi Berkat*, p. 7.

force of the Schmutzer family.[72] Crucial in this *resourcement* movement is the role of Father Gregorius Utomo, the shrine's current and longtime chaplain, whose quest for the so-called "Ganjuran legacy" has become the backbone of the identity formation and practice of the shrine today.[73]

In recent years, this *resourcement* results in a renewed practice of integral Catholicism around the shrine, in which nothing good for the full flourishing of the human person in the context of its relationship with God, the self (individual and communal), the neighbors (including the religious other), the local culture, and the cosmos, should be excluded. This dynamic can be found more concretely in the realm of the rituals of the Sacred Heart, the hybrid architectures of the shrines, and charity program for the sick and the poor, and so forth.

The Mausoleum of the Martyr and the Founder: The Community Being Tested

In the previous section, I have attempted to flesh out the central notion that history, understood as the founding moment of the shrine and its community, becomes a reality of the present that continues to define the very identity and mission of both. While the Javano-Catholic community at the Ganjuran shrine seems to have no trouble finding the *resourcement* for their understanding of mission in today's world by expanding its foundational vision, the dynamics of the third shrine under study, the Mausoleum of Muntilan, presents rather different dynamics. Although at the end of the process the principle of communion with the other remains normative, the mausoleum represents a phase in the history of the community's identity formation that was marked more by tensions and struggle that involved martyrdoms at the hands of the Muslim other. As mentioned, the mausoleum houses the tomb of the Javanese martyr, Fr. Richardus Sanjaya, who was murdered in the area by an Islamic militia group in 1948, as well as the tombs of other Dutch Jesuit missionaries killed in the same event as well as the incident of 1945 in the aftermath of Indonesia's declaration of independence.

Thus, on one level, the mausoleum of Muntilan represented a quite complicated moment of self-reckoning on the part of the Javano-Catholic community precisely because it had to square its very identity with the acute sense of its own alterity at a critical time when the new, yet fragile, identity of "Indonesia" as a nation state had just come into being. In this way, the Mausoleum of Muntilan represents a delicate question of alterity to the Javano-Catholic community, not the alterity

---

[72] The shrine brochure, *Rahmat Yang Menjadi Berkat*, p. 57.

[73] See *Rahmat Yang Menjadi Berkat*, p. 38ff. Father Gregorius Utomo began his tenure in Ganjuran in 1988 when the shrine had been dormant as a site of pilgrimage for some years. An important part of Father Utomo's *resourcement* of the shrine, in the sense of reconnecting it with its foundational past, is to keep a personal connection with the surviving Schmutzer family.

of another group, but rather its very own. Here the endurance of the framework of communion that had become the backbone of the identity formation of the community was tested. I will later discuss how the community came to terms with this rather troubling event.

However, on another level, the Mausoleum of Muntilan is also endowed with an aura of the great and sacred founding moment of the community. For Muntilan is "the Bethlehem of Java," a site associated with the origin of the Javano-Catholic community. At the mausoleum, this idea of origin is closely related to the idea of development and struggle, due to the variety of the tombs found in this cemetery. For besides the tombs of the martyrs mentioned above and those of Fr. van Lith and Fr. Mertens, the two great founders of the Java mission, it also houses other graves of important figures of the community, both European and Javanese.[74] In this framework, then, the struggle of the community to come to terms with the question of alterity also happens in the context of coming back, both spiritually and hermeneutically, to the founding moment and the founders.

In my view, the community came to be able to cope very fruitfully with the question of alterity in the wake of the troubling event of Fr. Sanjaya's martyrdom— not only in the sense of strengthening their identity, but also of preventing them from withdrawing from the larger framework of communion—precisely because they did not lose sight of the sense of divine assurance of the community's future that had became very clear at Sendangsono (and had been strengthened at Ganjuran), as I have shown in the preceding sections of this chapter.

As mentioned previously, the murders of Father Sanjaya (a Javanese diocesan priest) and Herman Bouwens (a young Jesuit seminarian) in 1948 were a test for the endurance of the complex identity formation of the Javanese Catholic community, particularly the principle of communion with all its elements. The blow to the community was felt so much harder because just three years earlier several Dutch Jesuit priests in the neighboring town of Magelang were also murdered on All Saints Day.[75] During the tumultuous period of the revolutionary wars against the Dutch (1945–49), the question of "foreignness" that stemmed from any kind of association with the colonial power became politically acute, largely due to the refusal of the Dutch to recognize the independent Indonesia (declared in 1945) and to their attempts to retake Indonesia by military force. Still quite fresh in the

---

[74] Among the local Church luminaries buried here are Henricus van Driessche (the pioneering missionary who worked in Yogyakarta, and who opened the mission station of Ganjuran), Piet Zoetmulder (the most accomplished Jesuit Javanologist and Islamologist in Java), Matthias Jonkbloedt and Jan Weitjens (two saintly Jesuit missionaries), and Justinus Cardinal Darmojuwono (the first cardinal of Indonesia) more recently.

[75] In all, there were ten Church persons who were murdered (the majority of whom were Dutch). Only on August 1950, in a solemn ceremony, their bodies were re-buried in the mausoleum in Muntilan, together with Sanjaya and Bouwens. See the article "Martelaren?" in *Missienieuws*, 71 (1963), p. 11; also J. Hadiwikarta Pr (ed.), *Mengenal dan Mengenang Rama R. Sanjaya Pr* (henceforth *Rama Sanjaya*; Jakarta, 1984), p. 23.

memory of the Indonesian people was Japan's anti-Dutch and pro-Islamic campaign during the brief Japanese occupation (1942–45). In this regard, it should be noted the particular challenge of foreignness faced by the Javano-Catholic community in the early 1940s as the Second World War began. The community was attacked because of its intimate connection with the Christian Europe.[76] Then, during the political chaos under the Japanese occupation, the Catholic Church found itself in a difficult situation in the Indies because most of Dutch missionaries were interned due to their Dutchness and their (presumed) connection to the Allies.

Around this time, Mgr. Soegijapranata, the first native bishop, spoke about the imminent dangers that the Catholic Church faced from the whole political chaos, resulting particularly from the tension between the Dutch and the Muslim communities, brought about by the wrong colonial policy toward the Muslims. In a critical tone, he remarked:

> The Catholic community in Indonesia realizes that there have been indeed some danger and threat for the Church, coming especially from the Muslim community. However, precisely in this connection, the international interest on Indonesia could prevent such threat. … We have anxieties that in no small measure come from the Dutch-controlled areas [which are also heavily Muslim] because the Dutch government always wants to find (and control) thoroughly Muslim community. They consider what is now normal in the Republic of Indonesia [i.e. after its independence] as impossible, dangerous or untactical. The Dutch could attempt to make the Muslims favorable to them by promoting all the old conditions that have been introduced, but this attempt is in itself laden with guilt.[77]

Rather clearly, the event of martyrdom in Muntilan shows the fragility of the kind of hybrid identity that the Javano-Catholic community came to adopt during its formative years. As I have mentioned, this principle basically argued that the community wanted to become truly Catholic, but also to stay authentically Javanese. Driven by the spirit of communion, it was also founded on the intimate relationship with the Dutch Church, trying hard under the colonial condition to make a case of differentiation between the generous and well-meaning Dutch Church and the self-preserving Dutch colonial government. What the martyrdom particularly revealed was the fragility of this differentiation, but perhaps also the kind of delicate struggle that the Dutch missionaries themselves had to undergo with regard to their personal political stance.[78] Writing some years after the event, two Javanese priests argued:

---

[76] *ST*, May 22; October 23, 1940.

[77] G. Vriens, S.J., *De Javanen-Missie der Jezuieten in de Republiek* (no place and date), p. 18. This quote was originally part of the interview that Mgr. Soegijapranata gave to a Dutch journalist working for the newspaper, *Gelderlander-pers*, in the 1940s.

[78] See the account of Willy Setiarja, "Kesaksian Kecil untuk 'Calon Orang Besar,'" in Hadiwikarta, *Rama Sanjaya*, p. 54.

The aggression of the Dutch in a bid to reclaim Indonesia provoked a rather intense anti-Dutch sentiment among the Indonesian population. The problem was that they did not differentiate between the Dutch as the colonial power and the Dutch in general: they became anti-Dutch without discrimination, rejecting all things that come to be associated with the Dutch. Therefore, the Catholic mission that was largely staffed by Dutch missionaries was viewed with so much suspicion, although there was really no reason for this because the Church's activity was universal (not bound by nationalities or race).[79]

Under such conditions, the perception of Christianity's foreignness was becoming more intense. Confrontations between Muslim youth from the neighborhood and the seminarians in the mission compound also took a turn for the worse. The mostly verbal confrontations over the use of the football field led to occasional open brawls. The seminarians were naturally accused of taking the side of the Dutch.[80] However, some believed that the seeds of the hatred actually hearkened back to the early days of the mission under van Lith, reflecting the anger and jealousy on the part of the Muslim community over the growth of the mission.[81] In addition, the mission compound had a history of prior incidents of vandalism in 1942.[82]

In the standard historical account of the 1948 event, the murders of Sanjaya and Herman Bouwens were believed to have been perpetrated by the members of an Islamic militia group (I. *Laskar Hizbullah*), most probably with a rather strong element of anti-Dutch as well as anti-Christian sentiment, in the context of the political chaos surrounding the birth of the Indonesian state (1945) and the end of Dutch colonialism. Having refused to recognize the sovereignty of Indonesia, the Dutch returned with fresh military attacks, targeting among others the city of Yogyakarta. The newly born Indonesian government instructed the burning down of all public buildings and big structures, for fear of confiscation by the Dutch troops. In Muntilan, clashes broke out between the seminarians who tried to put out the fire in their building and the Hizbullah militia who attempted to stop them. Previously, this militia group had also asked to use the seminary building. This request was denied, making the tensions worse. Then, one fateful night, a group of these Muslim militiamen asked all the priest-staff at the seminary to attend

---

[79] Kachmadi, O. Carm, and J. Hadiwikarta, Pr, "Menjelang hari-hari terakhir," in Hadiwikarta, *Rama Sanjaya*, p. 25.

[80] Hadiwikarta, *Rama Sanjaya*, pp. 24–5.

[81] Hadiwikarta, *Rama Sanjaya*, p. 21. Related to this question is the tension between the Catholic mission and the anti-mission Regent of Magelang (Mr. Danoesoegonda) in the 1930s. Feeling threatened, the Jesuit Father Spekle complained about the aggressiveness of this regent in building mosques in areas in which the adherence to Islam was so weak. See Steenbrink, *Catholics in Indonesia*, vol. 2, pp. 511–14.

[82] Kachmadi, O. Carm, "Pastor Paroki Muntilan," in Hadiwikarta, *Rama Sanjaya*, pp. 19–21.

a meeting at a local mosque and demanded especially that all the Dutch priests without exception be present at the meeting.

The Dutch missionaries became very suspicious of the meeting, partly because it would be held in a mosque. Father Sanjaya was the only Javanese priest on the seminary staff and had been the liaison between the seminary and the local neighborhood on the dispute over the football field. Thus, it was naturally expected that he would go to the meeting. He did and was accompanied by a Dutch Jesuit scholastic, Herman Bouwens, who himself had a personal history of confrontation with the local Muslim youth. A Javanese Jesuit lay brother, Kismadi, also joined the delegation. The hope was of course that the presence of a local Javanese priest would make a difference in such a precarious situation.[83] As it turned out, they were not escorted to the mosque but rather to an undisclosed site where Sanjaya and Bouwens were violently murdered. The immediate circumstances of the murder were not clear. However, the traces of the horrible violence were unmistakably displayed in the corpses of Sanjaya and Bouwens that were found in shallow graves by none other than Sanjaya's own father the next day. Apparently, they were tortured violently before being shot dead.[84]

As has been mentioned, most sources attributed the cause of the murder to two factors, i.e., the political chaos as well as the longstanding antagonism between the Catholic community and their Muslim counterparts in Muntilan, aggravated by the wider public image of the menacing foreignness of Christianity due to its association with the Dutch as well as its missionary success in Java.[85] Quite naturally, the perception of otherness was mutual. For the Catholic sources of that time normally identified the Muslim militia as extremists and religious fanatics.[86] And the majority of the local clergy thought that the murder was religiously motivated (L. *odium fidei*), while the lay members of the Javano-Catholic community were convinced immediately that they had their first "martyrs" and started to flock to their graves.[87]

In general the tone of the Javanese Catholic reaction to the incident was very careful and subdued, compared to the combative style of the *Swara-Tama* in the 1920s and 1930s. Surprisingly absent was the sense that the community was under serious and systematic attack from the Muslim community. Rather, a basic standpoint of acceptance of the unfortunate incident and forgiveness for the perpetrators was embraced. Attempts were made to grasp the complexity of the situation and what the fateful event meant for the long-term growth of the community. The "martyrdom"

---

[83] See the article "Martelaren?" p. 9.

[84] Hadiwikarta, *Rama Sanjaya*, pp. 27 and 58.

[85] Kardinal J. Darmojuwono, "Proses yang berhenti di tengah jalan," in Hadiwikarta, *Rama Sanjaya*, p. 61.

[86] See *Voorzetting van het "Chronologisch Overzicht" van de werkzaamheid der Jesuieten in de Missio Bataviensis, 9 Juli 1934–12 Maart 1956* (Archive, the Jesuit Provincial Office, Semarang, Indonesia), p. 123; "Martelaran?" p. 9; Hadiwikarta, *Rama Sanjaya*, pp. 34 and 38.

[87] Hadiwikarta, *Rama Sanjaya*, *passim*.

was then understood as part of a period of suffering that the community had been enduring since the Japanese occupation, a cross that it needed for its growth *qua* Christian community. A particularly troubling aspect of this cross was also recognized, namely, the antagonism between the East and the West, the "brown" (D. *bruin*) and the "white" (D. *blank*). They accepted this as a natural consequence of their identity as a Christian community founded by a European mission under colonialism.[88]

Rather than focusing on the murky and politically sensitive circumstances of the murders, the communal memory of the event was quickly turned to the figure of the slain martyrs and the significance of their lives and deaths, especially Father Sanjaya. The hagiographical image of Father Sanjaya (1914–48) was then quickly formed. In the eyes of the community, Father Sanjaya was a priest who obediently offered his life for the Church at a critical juncture on the land of his own birth, the land that had become the site of the birth of the Javano-Catholic community.[89] Thus the seed of martyrdom fell down on the very soil of the foundation of the whole community. On this point, an author wrote:

> We placed our first martyrs of Java on the very location that the first pioneers of the Java mission, Father van Lith and Father Mertens, had chosen to be the soil of God, because it was there that the first seeds of the faith were planted. Here, on the same soil, we now entrusted the seeds of martyrdom. Thus, the abundant harvest came immediately to the soil.[90]

Echoing the Tertullian dictum on martyrdom and the growth of the Church, the Catholic community in south central Java hoped that the seed of Sanjaya's martyrdom at Muntilan would also fecundate the local church. It is interesting here to see how this community interpreted this whole idea of "fecundation." Obviously the hermeneutic principle of communion with the other has been a constant governing principle, even when the community has to come to terms with its most troubling period, that is, the legacy of its martyrs, as I will show below.

In the framework of a close connection between the idea of foundation and fecundation, it is crucial to note that Sanjaya was a native of Muntilan, the son of a first generation Catholic family in the area. His grandfather was described as a strict and pious Muslim who died in Mecca during the *ḥajj*, while his father, like Sanjaya himself, was baptized by Father van Lith and later worked at the mission. Sanjaya's father was described as a simple and ordinary man, yet possessing a deep spiritual life.[91] The young Sanjaya was remembered as a brilliant and industrious student, yet very humble, with a sincere religious sensibility showed by his regular

---

[88] W. Nijs, S.J., "Moentilan," *St. Claverbond* (1946): p. 77.

[89] Cf. Dwidjasoesanta, "Rama Sanjaya, zijn levensschets en roemvol einde: Het martelaarschap van de eerste Javaanse seculiere priester," *Berichten uit Java* (1949): 54–8.

[90] "Martelaren?" p. 12.

[91] Kachmadi, O.Carm., "Muntilan Tempat Bersejarah," in Hadiwikarta, *Rama Sanjaya*, p. 6.

attendance at early morning mass and particularly by his strong devotion to Our Lady. From childhood, he forged a personal habit of making pilgrimage to the Sendangsono grotto during school breaks, walking on foot for nine hours roundtrip undeterred by the worst tropical weather. As a priest, Sanjaya kept his simplicity and gentleness, his mild rigidity and shyness. People remembered him as bookish, negligent about his outward appearance and rather clumsy in practical and social affairs. Many people were struck by the rare combination of virtuous traits in his personality. For Sanjaya was definitely a man of reason and understanding (L. *lucerna lucens*) who also possessed a warm heart (L. *lucerna ardens*). He was also portrayed as a young and virtuous Javanese priest, simple in his lifestyle but very profound in his thinking; outwardly meek yet brave in spirit. In the eyes of the community, he is now "a shining light" (D. *een licht dat brandt*) due to his exemplary life.[92]

Quite clearly, the community was more interested in the role of this martyr for the faithful, rather than pursuing the murderers. Sanjaya's grave in Muntilan quickly became a new central point of communal identity as well as of divine succor and providence. His relics were rather popularly sought after.[93] An author put this sentiment this way: "Our prayers for the martyrs are not 'May they rest in peace!' but rather, 'Remember us in your glory with the Lord!'"[94] Within the span of two decades, the process of possible beatification of Sanjaya was initiated, but then abandoned while the popular cult around him continued to grow.[95] On this abortive attempt of beatification, Cardinal Darmojuwono, the former Archbishop of Semarang, remarked:

> Personally, I prefer that we return to the spirit of the early Church. Let the faithful revere and ask the intercessions from those priests who were slain on December 20, 1948 without necessarily giving them the titles of saint or blessed. They earned the respect from the people who always say the name of "Father Sanjaya" with devotion and awe. So, let us go on a pilgrimage to Father Sanjaya, the holy man of the people! *Vox Populi Vox Dei*: the voice of the faithful is the voice of God.[96]

---

[92] Cf. "Martelaren?" p. 9.

[93] Stories about the power of his relics circulated among Javanese Catholic community. See Hadiwikarta, *Rama Sanjaya*, pp. 45–7.

[94] "Martelaren?" p. 12.

[95] Initiated in 1962, the process of Father Sanjaya's beatification was aborted because of the many difficulties, mainly in terms of providing direct eye witnesses who could testify that the slain priest was murdered because of his Catholic faith and that he was faithful to the Catholic faith until his death. Cf. "Martelaren?" p. 9; also Kardinal J. Darmojuwono, "Proses yang berhenti di tengah jalan," pp. 61–2.

[96] Kardinal J. Darmojuwono, "Proses yang berhenti di tengah jalan," p. 62.

Thus, in the framework of the traditional Christian hermeneutic on martyrdom, Sanjaya's violent death did not represent a loss but rather a new addition to the already quite rich tapestry of the community's founders and paradigmatic figures. To the local community, this addition makes the Catholic notion of *communio sanctorum* (communion of God and the Holy, including the saints) much more real.

In this framework of the *communio sanctorum*, the principle of communion is at work, by which the community tries to keep alive the memory of their paradigmatic figures through pilgrimage to their tombs and other communal means of reappropriating the legacies of these figures. *Communio sanctorum* is a complex and rich framework for fecundating the life of faith of the community by making connections to different yet interrelated sets of sacred realities, among others, the grace of God through these paradigmatic figures and events.[97] It is in this context that the Mausoleum of Muntilan plays a very crucial role for the Javano-Catholic community. As mentioned, it houses many tombs of these paradigmatic figures, especially Father van Lith. Long before the addition of Father Sanjaya, the tomb of Father van Lith had become an important site of pilgrimage. Only three years after van Lith's demise, one of his former students wrote a highly personal account of the intercessory role of this missionary.[98] The process of designing a hybrid Javano-Catholic style gravestone for van Lith also involved the participation of non-Christian and even non-Javanese young people.[99] On the occasion of the centennial celebration of van Lith's birth in 1963, two thousand people gathered around his grave.[100]

In recent years the memorialization of the legacy of the founders in Muntilan took on an ecclesial level with the creation of the Muntilan Museum of Mission (I. *Museum Misi Muntilan*), whose vision is precisely returning to the foundational sources (*resourcement*), mainly in the sense of retrieving the spirit of the founders, communing with them in various possible ways. Highly crucial among the initiatives of the Muntilan Museum of Mission is its attempt to embrace otherness, including the Muslim people and their tradition, for instance by incorporating the Islamic musical performance (J. *terbangan* or *slawatan*).[101] Thus, very interestingly, the tomb of the martyr fecundates the Church not by setting an opposition between this Church and the religious other, but rather by becoming a site of identity formation where otherness is embraced in different ways.

---

[97] Elizabeth A. Johnson, *Friends of God and Prophets* (New York, 2005), especially pp. 94–7.

[98] *ST*, March 29, 1929.

[99] Cf. *ST*, March 12, 1926; also April 16 and March 26, 1926.

[100] Cf. the article, "Pastoor van Lith (1863–1963)," in *Missienieuws*, 71 (1963): pp. 54–8.

[101] This facet of including the Muslim other became apparent in the novena of van Lith held at the mausoleum in 2009 in which the *terbangan* was performed and a special session was devoted to the theme of interfaith dialogue.

Concluding Remarks

As this chapter has shown, the three shrines under study now have become historically significant due to their crucial role in the process of the negotiation of the Javano Catholic community's identity. The Sendangsono grotto represented the beginning stages where the tension between the particularity and universality of "Catholic" identity was taken up for the first time in the form of a material-symbolic monument, a Marian shrine. This shrine was meant both as a sign of the particularity of a Catholic identity as well as a sign of the universal mission of the Church among the people of Java. Naturally, the focus of the community was still largely inward. In this ongoing dynamic, the Sacred Heart shrine at Ganjuran is a manifestation of the community's decision to take up the call toward the universalization of its mission. Framed in the language of Catholic piety and the integral practice of Christian charity as well as the inculturation of Christian faith, the shrine's mission was from the start understood as deeply outward looking, that is, to become a vehicle of God's blessings for all, as the Javanese Catholic community tries to negotiate its proper place and role in the wider Javanese society and beyond. In this dynamic, the Mausoleum of Muntilan that commemorates both the idea of foundation (with the grave of van Lith) and martyrdom (the grave of Father Sanjaya) can be seen as the monument of the struggle of the community to maintain its creative fidelity to the mission.

As this chapter also makes clear, the history of these three shrines is the story of how the Javano-Catholic community has made sense of the tensions and ambiguities that were involved in the foundation of the shrines, as well as the history of the community. In this regard, the community has employed a hermeneutic principle that is based on the spirit of communing with founders, founding moment, and the benefactors. I have attempted to illustrate how the spirit of communion has become widened in today's practice and vision of the shrines and the surrounding community. Otherness is perceived differently now. While Father Prennthaler, the missionary, was taken aback by every move of the Muslim other, the Javano-Catholic community of today looks forward to having the presence and participation of their Muslim neighbors and others, not only in the shrines, but also in the larger dynamics of their community. In this very process, they come to know the fuller scope of the inclusiveness of Divine grace, the grace of the Sacred Heart of Jesus that flows through Mary, the saints, and their own local pious ancestors such as Father van Lith and Father Sanjaya.

Chapter 5
The Trace of the Other in the Javano-Catholic Identity

> In the luminous clarity of Revelation and through prayer and work, the science of the Occident and the art of the Orient merge to form a new culture, rich in living forces, which will assure to the highly gifted Javanese people an honorable place among the peoples in the world.
>
> Josef Schmutzer (1882–1946)[1]

In the 1930s the Dutch missionary journal, *St. Claverbond*, often featured a curious image that depicted differences among Christianity, Islam, Hinduism, and Buddhism in terms of architectural symbolisms. This image had a large Western style church (with the words "*Lumen Gentium*" and a shining cross placed on top of it) flanked by a Javanese style mosque (with the word "Mohammed" written on top) on the left and a Hindu-Buddhist temple (with the word "Boeddha" placed on top) on the right.[2] This image would normally be used as the main illustration and imaginative framework for articles written by Jesuit missionaries about other religions in Java.

Against the background of this evocative image, one could pose the following question: what happens when Catholic edifices, the material-symbolic manifestation of the "*Lumen Gentium*," are built in the style of the Hindu-Buddhist temple or the Islamic mosque, as had occurred in south central Java since the earliest Catholic mission in the area? On a certain level, then, not only does the neat division between the three that seemed to lie at the heart of the *St. Claverbond* symbolism disappear, but also the Church itself as "the light of nations" (L. *lumen gentium*) seems to be paradoxically invisible due to the unfamiliar local appearance that it took. Instead, what appears to be dominant on the visual surface of things is the face and trace of the religious other. In the eyes of the other, though, the Church becomes rather familiar.

Upon deeper examination, as I shall suggest below, a rather complex constellation of diverse intentions and elements was at work in this process of realizing what I call "Javano-Catholic" identity in architectural forms. Genuine respect, humility, and a desire for closeness with the other existed together with a hidden agenda of moderate triumphalism, something that was not unusual in the

---

[1] Josef Schmutzer, *Un Art Javanais Chrétien* (Paris and Louvain, ca. 1929), p. 86.
[2] See *St. Claverbond* (1937): p. 60.

encounters between different ethnic and religious groups in colonial Java at the time. In many ways, this new image surely represents complexities—ambiguities, tensions, and promises—in the relation between the Church's identity and the religious other. For one thing, the trace of the other becomes embedded in the self, whatever this might mean for the community as well as other beholders. Furthermore, the dynamics of this complex relationship might lend themselves to new interpretations and could be taken in different directions by subsequent generations of the respective communities.

As mentioned in the previous chapter, the Javano-Catholic community today understands the sacred history of the shrines mainly in the sense of coming to terms with the foundational events and paradigmatic figures and their message for the whole community as it responds to the present. The shrines and the tradition of pilgrimage to them then become highly communal and ecclesial, since they are understood as the memorialization of these key foundational historical events and figures. The story of the shrines is intertwined with the ongoing struggle of the community. What is born out of this understanding of and involvement with this sacred history is a hermeneutic whose dynamics are intentionally geared toward fuller self-understanding and the widening communion with the neighboring other at the same time. This chapter explores further this hermeneutic of communion that has become the underlying principle of the formation of the Javano-Catholic identity in south central Java, more specifically how it has been operative in the spatial, architectural, and ritual dimensions of the shrines under study.

Meanings of Spatial Location

In Chapter 4, I have indicated that the spatial locations of all the three shrines under study are meaningful and intentionally chosen, serving as important sources for the hermeneutics of identity of the local Javano-Catholic community. The shrines and their locations are intimately connected to the very foundation of the community in the case of the Sendangsono grotto and the Muntilan mausoleum, and to the eventful growth of the community in the context of Javanese culture and society in the case of the Ganjuran shrine. These spatial locations are also made meaningful in the encounter with other, reflecting the idea of Christianity aligning itself with the spirit of the local (Javanese) culture, or the notion of Christianity absorbing and fulfilling the religious other.

Since the case of Sendangsono has been dealt with rather intensively in the previous chapter, I now turn to the spatial dimension of the Sacred Heart temple-shrine of Ganjuran. From the very beginning, it was intentional that the Sacred Heart shrine should be built in Ganjuran (originally called "Gondang-Lipura"), due to its proximity with the Javanese sacred site of Lipura, now located a mile away from the Sacred Heart shrine. Josef Schmutzer, the founder of the shrine, made this point clear on the occasion of the consecration of the shrine, arguing that

Lipura was the origin of the Javano-Islamic Mataram court.[3] Lipura is indeed a foundational place for the formation of Javano-Islamic identity represented by this court. During his early formative years, Panembahan Senapati (ca. seventeenth century), Mataram's founder, underwent a series of ascetic meditations at the site during which he received a supernatural sign of kingship.[4] Many subsequent kings of the Mataram dynasty as well as other prominent figures in south central Java down to the present would also visit this site for ascetic pilgrimage (Jv. *tirakat*).[5] Schmutzer mentioned the fact that the area has other sites connected to foundational figures of the Mataram dynasty, such as Ki Ageng Pemanahan and Sultan Agung, two crucial figures discussed in Chapter 1.[6] It was also believed that the crown jewel of the Javano-Islamic Mataram kingdom was kept in the same area.

Moreover, the site is also endowed with a sense of continuity with the Hindu past. For since the Hindu times, this area has been a special territory, as shown by the presence of the various Hindu temples and so forth. In the present context of the Sacred Heart shrine, the memory of Lipura and its role in the hybrid Javano-Islamic identity formation of Mataram is made alive and more meaningful by the fact that the shrine is meant to carry on the religio-cultural spirit of Mataram, centered around the propagation of the Javanese culture and marked by inclusion of the other.[7]

In the same dynamic of inclusion, the whole compound of the shrine is now called "the *mandala* of the Sacred Heart," understood as a sacred milieu of encounters between God and humans in all its complexities.[8] Of course the origin and meaning of *mandala* in South Asian and East Asian religions is very complex. As Bühnemann argues, *mandala* is an important ancient Hindu practice and is central in the Tantric tradition of Buddhism.[9] Tantrism was an important part of the religious life of the Javanese population under the Hindu and Buddhist dynasties; and it was a significant ritual background for the Hindu-Javanese temple (Jv. *candi*).[10] For my discussion here, this ritual background is crucial because the Sacred Heart shrine in Ganjuran is also called "*candi*" (temple). Quite clearly, the use of the words "*mandala*" and "*candi*" is part of the effort of the shrine's

---

[3] *ST*, February 14, 1930.

[4] de Graff, *Awal Kebangkitan Mataram*, p. 74.

[5] The list of these figures includes Prince Dipanagara; see Carey, *The Power of Prophecy*, p. 127ff; also Ricklefs, "Dipanagara's Early Inspirational Experience," pp. 227–58.

[6] The original site of Mataram's first court was located not far from Ganjuran, in a place called "Kerto."

[7] See interview with Fr. Gregorius Utomo in the documentary on the shrine by Komunitas Tusing Kandha, *Candi Hati Kudus Yesus Ganjuran* (Yogyakarta, 2005).

[8] See *Rahmat Yang Menjadi Berkat*, p. 8.

[9] Gudrun Bühnemann, *Mandalas and Yantras in the Hindu Traditions* (Leiden, 2003), p. 1ff; Martin Brauen, *The Mandala* (Boston, 1998), p. 61ff.

[10] Kinney, *Worshiping Siva and Buddha*, pp. 19–27.

community to preserve relevant features of the Javanese culture. To a large degree, it is an expression of connectedness to the spirit of the place.

In its Tantric framework, *mandala* is a plan of both macrocosm and microcosm and functions to bring the two together. It consists of a spatial or mental map of constellation of divinities in the sacred space, with a governing divinity in the center that should become the identity of the practitioner during the meditation or ritual.[11] Thus it has an integrative power. The *mandala* practice also has a deeply personal element in that the human body (microcosm) can be imagined as a *mandala*, a constellation of diverse elements and realities that need to be integrated.

Furthermore, it is also crucial to note that one of the underlying principles in the practice of *mandala* is the reality of structural correlations and parallels among all things and in particular between the universe, the *mandala*, and the human body.[12] There is rich and integral sense of communion embedded in the conception and practice of *mandala*, that is, communion with the Divine and true self, paradigmatic figures or teachers, fellow human beings, as well as with the entire cosmic reality. The interconnectedness of the ritual, spatial, and meditative elements of the *mandala* practice is also noteworthy.[13] For these features constitute major aspects in the pilgrimage tradition in both Catholic and Muslim contexts in south central Java.

In the next chapter, I will explore the rich and inclusive meaning of the *mandala* symbolism through an analysis of the experience of the pilgrims. This is because at the Ganjuran shrine, the whole gamut of meanings of the *mandala* symbolism only becomes clearly integrated when the spatial and architectural elements are looked at from the existential framework, namely the experience of the pilgrims. For now, my analysis will be focused on the hybrid Javano-Catholic architecture of the Ganjuran shrine, which includes the main temple (Figure 4.2) as well as the various statues housed in the shrine and the adjacent parish church.

Self and Other in Hybrid Architecture and Religious Arts of the Shrines

My argument here is that hybridity in the architecture of the Ganjuran shrine is an expression of the spirit of forming the self that involves the acts of including and embracing the other, i.e., the whole dynamic of communion with self and other. It is also due to its status as the architectural icon of Javano-Catholic identity in south central Java that I focus my analysis in this section on the richness and complexities of the hybrid architecture and religious arts of the Ganjuran shrine. As noted in the previous chapter, inculturation (D. *aanpassing*) of the Catholic faith in Javanese reality is one of the most important legacies of the Schmutzer family, the

---

[11] Kate O'Brien (trans.), *Sutasoma* (Bangkok, 2008), pp. 169–70.

[12] Brauen, *The Mandala*, p. 51.

[13] Brauen, *The Mandala*, *passim*; Bühnemann, *Mandalas and Yantras*, pp. 57–118, 153–78.

founders of the Ganjuran shrine. This shrine was taken up by the first generation of Javanese Catholic intellectuals in the 1930s as a proof of the goodness of the Catholic mission *vis-à-vis* local Javanese culture. Against those who accused the Catholic mission of destroying local culture, these intellectuals proudly embraced the hybrid Javano-Catholic arts and architecture at Ganjuran as an incontestible expression of Catholicism's genuine respect for local culture.[14]

The shrine-temple is now called "*Candi Hati Kudus Tuhan Yesus,*" the Sacred Heart Temple. Architecturally, it was built on the model of the Hindu Panataran temple in East Java.[15] It is for this mimetic reason that the shrine is called *candi*. In ancient Java, a *candi* was typically built as a replica of Mount Meru, the mythic and cosmic mountain; and functioned as a house of worship, an abode of a deity, or a mausoleum of deceased kings who were divinized in the edifice. So it would normally have a statue of a certain god or the monarch in the form of a god. When it served as a mausoleum, it would become a center of ancestor cults because the spirit of the king became the most important representative of all the ancestors. And here the ritual worship of a god would be integrated with ancestor worship.[16] To a certain degree, this dual function is replicated in the Ganjuran temple-shrine. For it houses a statue of the Sacred Heart of Jesus in the form of a Hindu-Javanese king in the inner sanctum. Another replica of the same statue is placed in the foundation of the shrine, a practice that was unknown in the Hindu-Javanese context. Its pinnacle is a cross. Thus it is obviously meant to be the abode of Christ, the Lord and the King. It also becomes a center for the development of a renewed rite of saint veneration in which the memory of ancestors and founders of the community also forms an important part, as I will discuss later in this chapter.

As will become clearer below, the hybrid Javano-Catholic style of this temple and its statuary should be placed in the dynamics of a discerning quest for an identity of the community, a religio-cultural negotiation of self in the face of otherness. On the theological plane, it is part of the communal discernment of the Church on what it means to be a Catholic community in the particularities of Java. In its initial phase, the complicated encounter between the West and the East under the colonial condition was a rather major theme in this whole dynamic. In the previous chapter, I have attempted to show that the basic standpoint of embracing the reality of "Java" continues to be done in several ways in the context of the shrine and its community. On the part of the Javanese-Catholics, the decision to

---

[14] *ST*, May 11, 1934.

[15] The Panataran temple was built circa the fourteenth century by the Hindu Majapahit dynasty. Now located in the regency of Blitar, East Java, it is a Shivaitic temple and used to be quite important in the cultic life of the Majapahit court. See Kinney, *Worshiping Siva and Buddha*, p. 181.

[16] On this, see Natasha Reichle, *Violence and Serenity* (Honolulu, 2007), pp. 112–13; Kinney, *Worshiping Siva and Buddha*, p. 25; W.F. Stutterheim, "The Meaning of the Hindu-Javanese Candi," *Journal of the American Oriental Society*, 51 (1931): pp. 1–15; Nancy Dowling, "The Javanization of Indian Art," *Indonesia*, 54 (1992): pp. 117–38.

take up and develop further the Hindu-Javanese tradition of religious arts and architecture could be considered as an act of coming to self and other at the same time. This is so because for them the Javano-Hindu religious culture is part of who they are in terms of their traditional religio-cultural environment, but not completely either, due to their Catholic identity that has been rather intimately connected with the Western tradition of Catholicism. So even as a cultural artifact (as opposed to a religious one), a Hindu Javanese temple is still endowed with visible traces of otherness for Javanese Catholics qua Catholics. There is a naturally delicate tension between self and other involved in such an identity formation. It is an act of embracing a certain otherness, but this process becomes all the more complicated because this very otherness is rather uneasily related to self.

On the part of the Schmutzers and the Dutch Catholic community, the whole process was no less complicated. There was a sense of embracing otherness and self-emptying in the fact that they refused to just impose the familiar European style of their own, and instead adopted indigenous cultural expressions. This process, however, also involved a subtle and complicated need for self-searching. In the previous chapter I have mentioned the cultural vision of Father van Lith and his fellow Dutch missionaries—that is, the Orientalist vision of the Javanese culture that favored the Hindu-Buddhist legacy to the relative exclusion of Islam. In the Dutch East Indies, this cultural vision served as the framework of the archeological excavations of the Hindu-Buddhist remnants of Java's antiquity.[17] This cultural movement in the colony was in turn part of the larger archeological project since the 1900s in Europe and the Netherlands that could be viewed as an effort to come to better terms with the origin of Europe, a particular search for identity that cannot be separated from the archeological excavations of Greek, Roman, Egyptian, Babylonian, and Mesopotamian sites. In this regard, the connection with the Hindu-Buddhist world came with the discovery of Sanskrit and the ancient Hindu civilization of India as "the primeval source of all these other civilizations."[18] On this point of self-searching, Marieke Bloembergen wrote: "Those engaged in both these types of research were chiefly concerned to discover more about the origins and ancient history of their own civilizations. So essentially they were conducting a form of self-examination."[19]

The significance of this archeological past in this search for civilizational origin and national representation became rather obvious at the World Exhibition in Paris in 1900. Here the Hindu-Javanese antiquity was chosen as the representation, not only of the grandeur of the civilization of the Dutch colony, but of the Netherlands

---

[17] Cf. the articles on archeology in *Djawa* and the papers presented at the first congress of the *Java Instituut* by F. Bosch, Purbacaraka, and Thomas Karsten, in *Handelingen van het Eerste Congres voor de Taal-, Land-, en Volkenkunde van Java (Solo, 25 en 26 December 1919)* (Weltevreden, 1921).

[18] Marieke Bloembergen, *Colonial Spectacles* (Singapore, 2006), pp. 195–6; also Tomoko Masuzawa, *The Invention of World Religions* (Chicago, 2005).

[19] Bloembergen, *Colonial Spectacles*, p. 196.

itself.[20] The Dutch pavilion in Paris in 1900 was centered on Hindu-Javanese antiquity. This was a sign of appreciation and desire of *rapprochement* with this antiquity. There was a nationalistic motif and international competition involved in this, namely, to show the cultural dignity of the Netherlands over against its competitors such as France and Britain. In this framework, the more antique the archeological artifact was, the more valuable it would be. The Dutch took pride in the fact that Candi Sari, the major artifact displayed in the Dutch pavilion, was much older than the pagoda of Phnom-Penh that the French put out in the same exhibit.

In light of this historical data one can say that on the part of the Dutch, what happened in Ganjuran could be related, albeit very subtly, to this whole search for self-understanding. A crucial factor that might have played a rather direct role here is the personal friendship between Josef Schmutzer and Henri Maclaine Pont (1884–1971), an influential Catholic architect who was the pioneer of indigenous architecture in the Indies and was also involved in the archeological excavations of Java's Hindu-Buddhist past. From this vantage point of identity quest, the inculturation at Ganjuran was a decision to recast the image of the self in the unfamiliar form of the other, a form which was then made intimately connected to that self through a process of discernment that was not completely free of ambiguities and tensions.

Maclaine Pont was involved in the discourse on architecture in the Indies, particularly between the school that advocated European architecture in the Indies—arguing that there was no indigenous architectural tradition in the Indies, hence the need and propriety of building "a Tropical Netherlands"—and the school that advocated the hybrid Indies architecture. To a large degree, the Ganjuran shrine belonged to the latter, in which the local Hindu-Javanese tradition was blended with the "European" element, in this case the Catholic framework of representation and meaning.[21] In this regard, Maclaine Pont was the proponent of the latter school, and he fostered a personal friendship with the Schmutzers. Since his student days in the Netherlands, Josef Schmutzer maintained a personal connection with Maclaine Pont. Born in Batavia but trained as an architect at Utrecht in the Netherlands where the Schmutzer boys were educated as well, Maclaine Pont was also involved in the archeological excavations (and reconstruction) of the capital of Hindu-Javanese kingdom of Majapahit in Trowulan, East Java. Eventually baptized a Catholic in the church of the Schmutzer family's estate in Ganjuran in 1931, he played an important role in the designs of some Catholic churches in Java, including the church and Marian shrine of Puhsarang, Kediri, East Java.[22]

---

[20] Ibid., p. 195.

[21] Abidin Kusno, *Behind the Postcolonial* (New York, 2000), p. 29ff.

[22] Steenbrink, *Catholics in Indonesia*, vol. 2, pp. 367–70; also Ben F. van Leerdam, *Architect Henri Maclaine Pont* (Den Haag, 1995), pp. 143–60. Father van Lith also had a personal relationship with another proponent of this architectural school, Thomas Karsten, through the *Java-Instituut* in which both were members.

While Josef Schmutzer's vision of inculturation was motivated more by his Catholic tradition, Maclaine Pont seemed to be more influenced by the ethical movement among the Dutch colonialists in the first decades of the twentieth century. In the realm of culture, this period was a time when "the colonizers reorganized their attitudes by courting what was identified as 'local' cultures and traditions," and a time when "architecture became profoundly political in its role in responding to the demand of the 'new age' and remolding an ideal colonial society based on 'ethical' principles."[23] On the imperative of creating a hybrid architectural tradition, Maclaine Pont argued:

> The invading people ultimately have an eye for the culture of the conquered and may prove to be receptive to it ... Then no clash, no demonstration of supremacy is necessary, and the peoples draw together ... If there is a living architectural tradition, a new mighty architecture can arise, *heterogeneous and not pure* in style.[24] (emphasis added)

Maclaine Pont's insights were perfectly in line with the spirit of deeper and more comprehensive "unification" between the East and the West, between the natives and the colonialists, which was espoused by the Javanese Catholic community. However, this hybrid architecture movement as an appropriation of indigenous culture was of course still within the limits of colonialism. For one can argue that a crude colonial domination in the realm of material culture was here replaced by a kind of colonial ennoblement of the native culture.

As the following section will show, the language of ennoblement was also used by Catholics in the Indies to talk about inculturation of the faith. However, from within the dynamics of Catholic theology of inculturation, the emphasis would normally be placed on the truly "catholic" and incarnational dimension of the faith that allows for more genuine respect for the religio-cultural tradition of the other. Here, ennoblement becomes spiritual revivification. And this process also amounts to the complex dynamics of "Christianization" of indigenous culture and "indigenization" of Catholic faith, with more emphasis on the former (Chapter 4). In what follows I will delve a bit deeper into the logic, theological and otherwise, of this two-dimensional process of Christianization and indigenization by exploring the vision of Josef Schmutzer, the founder of the Ganjuran shrine.

The Religio-Cultural Vision of Josef Schmutzer

In their effort to initiate the indigenous Christian art, Josef Schmutzer and his circle had to define first what constituted a proper "Javanese" culture. Here, the Orientalist vision on Java—centered around the project to retrieve and revive the

---

[23] Kusno, *Behind the Postcolonial*, p. 16.

[24] Quoted in Kusno, *Behind the Postcolonial*, p. 33. See also Helen Jessup, "Dutch Architectural Visions of the Indonesian Tradition," *Muqarnas*, 3 (1985): p. 144.

Hindu-Javanese glory of the past—came to be the dominant framework among the Dutch literati in the Indies, including the missionaries and prominent laymen like the Schmutzers and Maclaine Pont. Due to his travels throughout Java and his friendships with Dutch Orientalists, Josef Schmutzer had a quite deep and wide exposure to the Hindu-Buddhist archeological remnants of Java. His personal admiration and love of this culture was remarkable, lamenting the fact that the Javanese people had forgotten the meanings and significance of their great monuments of the past, due to the coming of Islam.[25] Then aligning his artistic and cultural interest with those of a small number of Javanese princes who became the "promoters of modern Javanese art with classical inspiration," Schmutzer was glad to see that there arose a generation with a nationalist sentiment who appreciated more and more the great works of the past era.

However Schmutzer rightly noticed that the nascent Javanese Catholic community did not seem to be part of this movement at first. For during their initial formative years, their religious artistic taste was largely satisfied with foreign religious arts of low quality.[26] A fascination with the high culture of the Hindu-Buddhist heritage was not really part of the mentality of the first Javanese Catholic community at the very beginning. But then, partly due to the influence of such great figures like van Lith, Schmutzer, and Maclaine Pont, they came to see that heritage as part of their identity. As mentioned, Schmutzer's argument for an indigenous Christian art as well as his experiments in this area were embraced by the Javanese Catholic intelligentsia to boost their argument for cultural hybridity.

But, why did Schmutzer come to choose the Hindu-Javanese tradition as it was found in the Hindu-Buddhist archeological remnants of Java as a vehicle for his project of inculturation of the Christian faith in Javanese soil, rather than other available forms? While the Orientalist framework certainly had its role, the process of discernment was for Schmutzer both natural and selective. It was natural because his extended stay in Central and East Java had exposed him to a vast array of Hindu-Javanese architectures and arts. He was captivated and personally touched by the remarkable and exquisite quality of these arts and by the way in which they helped to convey the presence of the "eternal."[27]

---

[25] Josef Schmutzer, "Christelijk-Javaansche Kunst," in J. Schmutzer and J. Ten Berge, *Europeanisme of Katholicisme?* (ca. 1929), p. 59. This text of Schmutzer on indigenous Christian art appeared the first time in the journal *Gemeenschap*, 7–8 (1927): pp. 230–51. Then, it was published separately as a book, *Europeanisme of Katholicisme?* (Utrecht, no date) together with a long chapter by J.J. ten Berge on indigenous Christian art in other mission territories, entitled "Christelijk-Inheemsche Kunst in de Missie." This book was translated into French as *Europeanisme ou Catholicisme?* (Paris and Louvain, 1929). The French translation of Schmutzer's article is entitled *Un Art Javanais Chrétien*, which I use rather extensively in this chapter.

[26] Schmutzer, *Un Art Javanais Chrétien*, p. 61.

[27] Schmutzer, *Un Art Javanais Chrétien*, p. 69.

For Schmutzer, the process was selective as well because he had tried, in collaboration with a local Javanese catechist, different avenues using other forms of Javanese arts, namely the world of the shadow puppet theater (Jv. *wayang*). For this purpose, the Trinity was rendered in the style of the shadow theater. But Schmutzer did not find this attempt satisfactory because, among others, it aesthetically failed to convey the sacredness of the Divine Mystery, perhaps due to its highly abstract and flat depiction of divine and human figures in this artistic framework.[28]

So, he was looking for an appropriate artistic framework that could serve as a vehicle for Christian inspirations, rather than just an indigenous architectural tradition. Understandably, the Islamic artistic tradition in Java did not naturally lend itself to him as an alternative because of its specificities in expressing the Divine. In this sense, the exclusion of Islamic art did not solely stem from the bias of a colonial discourse on Javanese culture.[29] Schmutzer argued further that, although the Hindu artistic tradition was brought from a foreign land, it has secured an indigenous cultural patrimony for the Javanese. In his view, Islam had to destroy the Hindu-Javanese statues and architectural edifices, but this did not mean destroying all the links that connected the Javanese to their ancestral culture. Thus, from his perspective, there was a good reason to revive the interest of contemporary Javanese people in the artistic dimensions of this heritage.

However, Hindu-Javanese art still retained too much trace of the religious other to be properly used in unchanged form in the Catholic context. To deal with this challenge, Schmutzer employed an interesting principle: "[Once we] take away the elements that were the reminders of the ideas and attributes of paganism, then artistic forms will lend themselves to Christian ideas."[30] Thus, what he considered most useful in the heritage of the Hindu-Javanese arts for his project was their forms that he thought could be severed from their original religious or theological settings. As mentioned earlier, he was genuinely touched by the spiritual atmosphere that these arts exuded, but for some reasons he did not seem to connect this spiritual atmosphere with the particularities of Hinduism or Buddhism *qua* religion. He even used the word "paganism" in this context. Apparently he did not want to explore the possibility of theological similarities as background for formal artistic appropriation.

As I shall demonstrate below, Josef Schmutzer was very meticulous in choosing particular symbolic forms out of this vast world of the Hindu-Javanese arts, looking for the proper ones that could convey the particularities of the Christian message at stake. In reality, what he ignored or removed from earlier Hindu Javanese temples were mostly the stupas of the Buddha, the statues of the Hindu deities, the reliefs containing the stories of the Buddha or Vishnu's avatars, the terrifying faces of the ogres (Jv. *raseksa*), and so forth. In the realm of statuary, he also took away all the

---

[28] Ibid., p. 62ff.
[29] Ibid., p. 70.
[30] Ibid.

forms that appeared to be rather offensive or improper to his European Catholic sensibility, most notably the bare breasts of the goddesses.

In Schmutzer's conception, these purified forms should then be re-vivified by the spirit of Christian truth. He argued:

> But, Christianity, which teaches the people the truth at the same time as its regeneration, necessarily makes new life bloom everywhere where it radiates its light and warmth. So, why could Christianity not accomplish in the East what it has realized in the West? Why could it not, to honor the truth, vivify through its spirit the pagan forms of art that were lost in error and that have been dead for centuries?[31]

Here Schmutzer talked about the appropriation of local culture as a Christian revivification of the forms of the other. The term of rebirth or renaissance is crucial. Although the whole logic could not be completely separated from the colonial mindset, this process was clearly not meant to be a simple borrowing or plundering of the treasure of an actual Hindu community in Java, largely because the Hindu religion *qua* religion was already dead in Java by the time this idea of renaissance was gaining ground among Catholics there.

On the contrary, the notion of revivification was presented as a noble idea of taking the dignity of the local culture to a higher level. It was seen as an act of ennoblement in the spiritual or religious realm. In the next chapter, I will illustrate how the pilgrims would testify to the effect of this revivification, how the presence of God's blessings effectively revivifies the sacredness of the Hindu-Javanese architectural forms and the whole spatial ground. In the preceding chapter, I have shown how the contemporary community of the shrine also attempts to respond to the broadening horizon of the Sacred Heart's undiscriminating blessings by continuing this principle of revivification. On the spiritual and existential levels, this revivification happens in different directions as various kinds of pilgrims come to be in contact with the Spirit of this new life. For the Buddhist, Hindu, and Muslim pilgrims come to the shrine for various reasons and go away with a set of different experiences.

To a certain degree then, Christianity is also being reborn in the same process, revivified in a new soil by new people with different religious sensibilities. Thus, as it turns out, the process of "renaissance" is a two-way street. This particular dynamic is something that Schmutzer might not have thought when he founded the shrine. But on the theological plane, he anticipated this in a way when he emphasized the work of the Holy Spirit, the Uncreated Love and Grace, as the most crucial theological dimension in many of his experiments in Javano-Catholic religious arts.

In this regard, the Javano-Christian artistic panel of the Holy Trinity that Schmutzer designed, with the help of the Sundanese Muslim sculptor Iko, offers

---

[31] Schmutzer, *Un Art Javanais Chrétien*, pp. 61–2.

a crucial pneumatological framework.[32] Emphasizing the priority of Love in the theological understanding of the Trinity, Schmutzer put the figure of the Holy Spirit in the middle, flanked by the Father and the Son. This type of artistic work is insightful in relation to the propriety of the word "vivify," because, as Irenaeus of Lyons argues, it is the Spirit who vivifies the body and gives it its true life beyond the biological. The Spirit is the Giver of life, and her work knows no fixed bounds.[33]

In Schmutzer's conception, this pneumatological framework is also deeply christological. For the role of the Spirit is intimately connected to the wider spirituality of the Sacred Heart. He remarked:

> It is to the Holy Spirit that we are indebted in the event of the Incarnation of the Word; for, although the Spirit does not have a power to send the Son from whom he proceeds, we can say that he is, as the Uncreated Love, the primordial cause of the divine act which gave us a Savior; and thus, he is also the cause of the effects of mercy that followed the divine mission of the Son. ... It is the Holy Spirit who keeps the sacred heart of Jesus overflowing with mercy.[34]

As this passage reveals, the pneumatological aspect of Schmutzer's vision is anchored on the dynamics of Divine Love and Wisdom, because the Spirit is the Love between the Father and the Son. In the context of the contemporary development of the Ganjuran shrine, this intimate relationship between pneumatology and Christology is maintained. For at this shrine, it is the Sacred Heart of Jesus who is perceived to be the vehicle for the outpouring love of God to humanity and the whole cosmos.

Within this theological framework, the experiments in indigenous Christian arts that Josef Schmutzer undertook were not merely an inculturation of Christian arts simply as aesthetic forms, but also an occasion for deeper engagement with the presence of God through the categories of love and mercy. Therefore, the fuller meanings of these hybrid arts and architecture have to be found through deeper and wider engagements as well. That is why Schmutzer emphasized the importance of this art in inducing a meditative and prayerful atmosphere.[35] To a large degree,

---

[32] Schmutzer met with Iko, a talented Muslim sculptor who was familiar with Hindu-Buddhist artistic styles, in 1924. By then Iko's artistic genius had been known among a circle of Dutch art specialists and connoisseurs. It was in Iko's works of indigenous art that Schmutzer found the most promising platform for his project. See his *Un Art Javanais Chrétien*, p. 69.

[33] In this respect, it is telling that the Federation of Asian Bishops' Conferences (FABC) has also developed a pneumatological theology of religions in response to the awareness of the Spirit's overwhelming presence beyond the formal boundaries of the Church in the context of Asia where Christianity constitutes a tiny minority. See my licentiate thesis, *The Spirit at Work: Asian Pneumatology from Below and the Problem of Religious Pluralism* (Cambridge, MA: The Weston Jesuit School of Theology, 2005).

[34] Schmutzer, *Un Art Javanais Chrétien*, pp. 75–6.

[35] Ibid., p. 74.

it is the underlying force of love and mercy that really inculturates the Catholic faith into the local context, rather than just the artistic expressions of it. That is why one should be attentive to the wider and deeper dynamics of pilgrimage to this shrine, especially the experience of pilgrims from various backgrounds. For their experiences could serve as a better indicator that a true inculturation or revivication has taken place, namely, a process in which the Trinitarian reality of grace becomes rooted in the local people, their culture, and their daily lives. As I will discuss in the next chapter, pilgrims of all faith backgrounds at Ganjuran come to be in touch with the reality of the healing power of God's love in different ways. Also crucial in this regard is the role of the shrine as a center of charity works for the larger local community, through which God's grace becomes a reality to many people across religious boundaries. As Schmutzer himself seemed to have anticipated, this widening influence of divine love is the work of the Spirit whose work knows no boundaries.

The Expressions of Hybrid Religious Arts at Ganjuran

As concrete illustrations of Schmutzer's experiments in Christian indigenous arts, I will examine two of the most iconic and theologically insightful examples from his collections, namely the image of the Sacred Heart or Christ the King (Figure 5.1), and the image of Madonna with Child (Figure 5.2).

The design of the Sacred Heart at Ganjuran is definitely a hybrid Javano-Christian work of art. Clothed in a Hindu-Javanese royal robe, Christ is seated on his throne; his left hand holds the robe on the chest, opening it a little bit to show the image of the Sacred Heart, while his right hand points to this image. The luminous image of the Sacred Heart is encircled by a crown of light. In Schmutzer's conception, this luminous crown of love is a symbolism of how a meditation of the love of Christ should be elevated to the contemplation of the Uncreated Love, the Holy Spirit, through which the Father and the Son love each other as well as humanity. Without the image of the Sacred Heart in the breast, this statue might only effuse the aura of a Hindu-Javanese king in all his glory and power. Obviously Schmutzer attempted to present a rather different image of kingship, one that is based solely on love. This design has been sculpted and the statues are now housed in the inner sanctum of the temple-shrine and the parish church (Figure 4.2).

The second sample is the design of Madonna with Child (Figure 5.2). Employing the template of Prajnaparamita (or Laksmi), Mary is represented as a queen, clothed in classical royal robe with a shawl and long corsage, holding the Child on her lap.[36] The robe is made of two layers of cloth in the traditional Javanese *batik*, that is, patterned cloth design. The upper layer is in the pattern

---

[36] The statue of Prajnaparamita (ca. thirteenth century) has been called "arguably Java's greatest single stone sculpture" and has been replicated continuously. In present day Indonesia, this iconic Buddhist sculpture is used to reinforce notions of ancient history and contemporary statehood. See Reischle, *Violence and Serenity*, pp. 69–70.

Figure 5.1   Statue of Christ the King and the Sacred Heart in the Hindu-Javanese Style, Ganjuran

of overlapping circle called *kawung*, on top of the royal pattern of *parang rusak*, signifying that Mary's position is less elevated than that of Christ.[37] But the shawl is ornamented with the royal pattern of *parang rusak* because the Virgin holds the Divine Son in her heart. Furthermore, the Child looks straight ahead with the aura of authority, while the Virgin keeps her eyes semi-closed in a serene and meditative position. The Child has a streamlined halo and sacerdotal sash on his breast. The throne is ornamented with blossoming water lilies, symbols of purity.[38]

---

[37]   The styles of *parang-rusak* and *kawung* are the two most traditional and oldest patterns of Javanese cloth design (Jv. *batik*). The provenance of the *kawung* dates back to the Hindu Majapahit era (1294–1478) when this style was worn by kings. The courts of Yogyakarta and Surakarta reserve the use of the *parang-rusak* pattern only for the highest strata of the royal family. In this context, the *parang-rusak* style is considered more glorious and royal than the *kawung*. Cf. Sylvia Fraser-Lu, *Indonesian Batik* (New York, 1986), pp. 34, 37 and 57; also Pepin van Roojen, *Batik Design* (Boston, 1997), pp. 50 and 59.

[38]   This model has another variation where Mary is depicted as sitting on a throne crafted on the model of the seat of Prajnaparamita that was found in the Singasari temple

Figure 5.2   Statue of Madonna with child in a Hindu-Javanese style, Ganjuran

In this respect, the role of Prajnaparamita as the template for the image is noteworthy. Given its intrinsic quality as a work of art as well as its historical role in the religious history of Java, one can understand why Josef Schmutzer decided to employ this statue as a model for his depiction of Mary. With regard to the motherhood of Prajnaparamita, Mahayana Buddhism does indeed consider her as the "spirit representing matter, from which everything in heaven and earth sprung, the supreme self existent-power of nature, the universal mother, the first cause."[39] In Java, Prajnaparamita is also related to the Hindu goddess Laksmi or Bhagavati, the consort of Vishnu.[40]

---

in East Java (Schmutzer, *Un Art Javanais Chrétien*, pp. 76–7); Cf. Reischle, *Violence and Serenity*, pp. 51–3.

[39]   W.F. Stutterheim, "Note on Saktism in Java," *Acta Orientalia*, 17 (1938): p. 150; Nancy Dowling, "Javanization of Indian Art," p. 20.

[40]   Stutterheim, "Note on Saktism in Java," p. 148; Dowling, "Javanization of Indian Art," p. 19.

On the Catholic side, although Schmutzer did not explicitly mention, this particular depiction of Mary is surely connected to the traditional image of Mary as the Seat of Wisdom or a Virgin of Majesty. In this image, the Virgin and Child are depicted in the same position of enthronement, a representation that has become common since the seventh and eighth centuries in the Christian West. Originally, this image was part of the traditional portrayal of the Adoration of the Magi; it then became a freestanding image, without the presence of the magi. In this regard, comparison with the image of the Virgin in Majesty, designed for the Clermont cathedral in France would be insightful.[41] It is rather clear that this kind of image was the Catholic prototype for the Prajnaparamita Mary of Ganjuran.

For my discussion here, it is crucial to notice that traditionally the magi represented a non-Jewish presence and acknowledgment of the authority of Jesus; thus theirs is the presence of the other. Matthew's Gospel identifies them specifically as being from the East (Matthew 2:1). That is why in the traditional depiction of the scene, their images are cast as the images of the Eastern other, typically as an Arab, Persian, or Indian. In this respect, then, the image of Prajnaparamita Mary at Ganjuran might represent a rather unique dynamic. For now it is the Virgin and Child who have become the other since they have assumed the forms of the other. This way, the difference between the adorers and the adored is less visible, assuming the invisible adorers or "magi" here are the Javanese themselves. So there is no need to describe the adorers as being from the East anymore, because Mary and the Child are now in the East, among these very people. Read against this background, the Javano-Catholic image at Ganjuran becomes an image of Mary and the Child's visit to the other, rather than the other way around. This logic is part of an incarnational dynamic that forms the backbone of Christian theology in general as well as the theology of inculturation that Josef Schmutzer embraced.

So, this image of the Prajnaparamita Mary turns out to be a result of a pilgrimage, a visit to the other that leads to a transformation. On the artistic plane, this transformation is visible when Mary takes the framework of beauty and wisdom of Prajnaparamita. However, this transformation seems to have deeper meaning. For, in the framework of the incarnational dynamic of Catholic theology, the seat of Mary and the Child is represented as a lotus flower. This is significantly different from the traditional Western image where the Child rests on the lap of Mary while his bare feet (signifying Christ's humanity) do not rest on another throne (that is why Mary is called the Seat of Wisdom), and where Mary sits on the Solomonic throne.[42] This unique feature of the Prajnaparamita Mary might signify the spirit of learning from the wisdom of the other.

---

[41] In this portrayal, the Child is also depicted as having the royal authority, with his hand gesture of giving blessings. See Sarah Jane Boss, *Mary* (London and New York, 2003), p. 107ff.

[42] Boss, *Mary*, p. 109.

Although Schmutzer spoke more about the role of Christianity in teaching the nations about the truth when it came to the topic of the theology of mission, this spirit of learning from the richness of the earlier Javanese culture has been very much at work in his works of Javano-Catholic arts. For his appreciation of the Hindu-Javanese arts went much deeper than mere aesthetic amazement. Although he did not take the time to delve into the richness of the Hindu and Buddhist traditions in terms of religious teaching and practice, he was profoundly captivated by the spiritual atmosphere, the sense of being in touch with eternity, that these arts evoked. This spirit becomes more apparent in the development of the shrine.

Here I do not have enough space to do justice to the enormous potential of a comparative theological discourse on Prajnaparamita and Mary.[43] It suffices to say at this point that the image of the Prajnaparamita Mary at Ganjuran seems to invite a deeper meditation on the confluence of Prajnaparamita and Mary. Both are extolled as pure, and serve as a cosmic place of refuge. Both are protecting Mothers in their own rather distinctive ways. Prajnaparamita is the mother of all bodhisattvas due to her role in bringing enlightenment, while Mary is the Mother of God and all His children due to her radical openness and connection to God as well as her loving compassion and motherly care. It is insightful here to see how Prajnaparamita is described in the framework of Buddhist soteriology in the *Astasahasrika Prajnaparamita* text:

> Perfect Wisdom spreads her radiance ... and is worthy of worship. Spotless, the whole world cannot stain her ... . In her we find refuge; her works are most excellent, she brings us safely under the sheltering wings of enlightenment. She brings light to the blind, that all fears and calamities may be dispelled ... and she scatters the gloom and darkness of delusion. She leads those who have gone astray to the right path. She is omniscient; without beginning or end is Perfect Wisdom, who has Emptiness as her characteristic mark; she is the mother of the *bodhisattvas* ... . She cannot be struck down, the protector of the unprotected, ... the Perfect Wisdom of the Buddhas, she turns the Wheel of the Law.[44]

---

[43] Following the lead of Francis Clooney's insightful comparative theological study of the Hindu goddess tradition and the Catholic Marian tradition in his *Divine Mother, Blessed Mother* (Oxford, 2005), a comparative theological treatment of Prajnaparamita and Mary is, I believe, not only possible, but also desirable. It would be interesting to see how Buddhist goddess tradition could enrich our Christian understanding of Mary, just as the Hindu goddess tradition does in Clooney's account. In the context of Indonesia, this kind of comparative project should also take into account the role of Mary in the Muslim tradition. This way, the comparative project will be more complicatedly rich, since it involves more than two traditions.

[44] Wm. Theodore de Barry (ed.), *The Buddhist Tradition* (New York, 1969), p. 103; quoted in Reischle, *Violence and Serenity*, p. 56.

With the presence of the Prajnaparamita figure, detachment and enlightenment as aspects of true wisdom are added to the Marian compassionate protection and involvement in the very messiness of human affairs. These combined attributes are of course appropriate for Mary, who at Ganjuran is venerated together with the Sacred Heart of Jesus. A Buddhist detachment coming from a deep realization of the nature of reality through the mind is matched with a Christian spirit of compassionate involvement with the day-to-day plight of the world in fidelity with the dynamics of the overflowing love and grace from the Sacred Heart of Jesus. As the next chapter will show, enlightenment in the sense of finding the direction of life amidst confusions and the peacefulness that this enlightenment brings, constitute some of the most paradigmatic spiritual experiences of the pilgrims at the Ganjuran shrine.

Recently this spirit of learning from the other at Ganjuran has been displayed by the local community in their decision to build the new parish church in the Javanese style, in place of the old one destroyed during the 2006 massive earthquake. This architectural design allies the community once more with the religio-cultural spirit of the Javano-Muslim sultanate of Yogyakarta since the style of the church resembles its palace (Jv. *kraton*). In fact, in the conception of Father Gregorius Utomo, the style was the manifestation of a religio-cultural mission of retrieving the Javanese culture as a foundation of fostering brotherhood among diverse religious communities in Java. This hybrid architecture is understood as a combination of a Javanese court palace (Jv. *kraton*) and the biblical symbolism of the vineyard. That is why many features of Javanese royal palaces are incorporated.[45] This design might also help resolve certain tensions in the earlier Orientalist-colonial vision of Javanese culture that had affected the earlier self-understanding of the Javano-Catholic community in Java. For due to its terraced roof and open space inside, this church edifice now resembles the traditional mosque designs in Java, most notably the Demak Mosque.

On the Hybridity of Jesuit Mission Art in Java

Earlier in this chapter, I have touched briefly on the question of the Dutch fascination with Hindu-Javanese antiquity in terms of their quest for national identity. As Bloembergen has pointed out, this colonial fascination was rather complex. This complexity was rather well illustrated in the display of the replica of *Candi Sari* (the temple of Sari) at the Exhibition in Paris in 1900.[46] Clearly

---

[45] Here I do not have the space to enumerate all the hybrid symbolisms in the new Ganjuran church. Basically, since the church is conceived both as a vineyard and a Javanese palace, the ornamental motifs on the canopy are floral patterns, featuring the three most ritually important flowers in the Javanese culture (Jv. *kembang telon*) as well as the Christian symbolisms of vines and wheat. The chief artist, a Javanese Catholic, has also worked for the court of Yogyakarta, including the designing of major mosques in Yogyakarta.

[46] *Candi Sari* is a small Buddhist temple (eighth century) located in the northern vicinity of Yogyakarta, near Prambanan. Excavated by the Dutch archeologists toward the

there were some disparate elements involved in this decision. It showed that the Netherlands imagined the Netherlands East Indies, particularly Java, as part of its identity. This decision might have also been motivated by a genuine respect for the high and ancient culture of the colony. As it turned out, this exhibition also drew some criticisms, such as that it was a bastardization of the original, a vulgarization of a solemn sanctuary, a banal, demeaning, and tasteless replica of an exquisite artistic work for mass consumption, something that was out of place with the surroundings at the Trocadéro Square in Paris.[47]

In my view, the same question of bastardization can also be raised about the Catholic mission art in Java, precisely due to the same dynamics involved. Are the Ganjuran shrine and its statuary merely a bastardization of the Hindu Javanese original?[48] Is it a tasteless replica for mass consumption of pilgrims? Here, a crucial category to take into account is the specifically religious nature and context of this hybrid art. For it is this religious dimension that gives a distinctive characteristic and quality to this art. This religious aspect is none other than the Christian revivification of indigenous art that I elaborated previously, in contrast to the fully secularized replica of the Buddhist temple of Sari in the Paris Exhibition. The working principle of Schmutzer was such that the Christian revivification of the Javanese Hindu arts had to be done by allowing the forms and sacred context of the indigenous art to take precedence. That is why he wanted to put the Hindu-Javanese inspired statuary in its spatial framework of a Hindu-styled temple, located in its original location in the land of Java, among the Javanese people, its original proprietors.[49] As the next chapter will illustrate, pilgrims come to the Ganjuran shrine for deeper reasons than just looking at the statuary and temple with aesthetic admiration. For many pilgrims, it is the hybrid architecture of the shrine that helps create a particular ambiance of spiritual serenity and peace. Even in the Catholic context of a Sacred Heart shrine, these traditional local artistic forms retain their power. In the words of Schmutzer, it brings a deeply spiritual

---

end of the nineteenth century, it had never been exposed to the European gaze before. At the Paris Exhibition in 1900, however, the replica of Candi Sari was in fact made of a combination of different features from other Buddhist or Hindu temples found in Java; it also featured glass roofs, a modern addition to the ancient looking replica. Bloembergen, *Colonial Spectacles*, pp. 201–2.

[47] Ibid., p. 210.

[48] Schmutzer tackled up the question of bastardization of Javanese art by taking the example of the depictions of Christian themes by Cajus Rahid, a local artist who also experimented with indigenous Christian arts. In one of his works, Jesus is portrayed as holding a chalice. This painting is totally Western, including the face and the gesture of Jesus, except for the frame that employs a Javanese *batik* style. Thus, the Javanese element was relegated to just a minor decorative motif. Schmutzer argued that nothing like this happened at Ganjuran because of the prominence of the Hindu-Javanese motif over the Western one. *Un Art Javanais Chrétien*, p. 67.

[49] Schmutzer, *Un Art Javanais Chrétien*, p. 79.

atmosphere.[50] Thus in this framework of religious experience, the architecture is not really out of place.[51] On the contrary, it renews the spiritual presence in the place. As mentioned, the Ganjuran shrine-temple is intentionally erected in Ganjuran because of the sacredness of the area, something that the experience of contemporary pilgrims from diverse backgrounds confirms.

As a result of Schmutzer's commitment of giving formal space to the indigenous arts, the Javano-Catholic hybrid arts at Ganjuran subsumed the Western appearance under the indigenous canon. As Gauvin Bailey has shown, this same pattern has happened in different Jesuit mission territories.[52] Thus in general, the initial aesthetic appearance of these Javano-Christian arts in Ganjuran is overwhelmingly Javano-Hindu. Here, Jesus and Mary are still visible of course, but their visibility is shrouded in their invisibility, due to the fact that they have here taken on the unfamiliar appearance of the other. This is part of the dynamics of visibility and invisibility that also happened in the course of the history of the Islamization of south central Java. In Part I of this book I have attempted to show this dynamic in the hagiography of Javano-Muslim saints, which in turn is instructive as to the nature of the process of the Islamization in south central Java, i.e., the gradual formation of a distinctive Javano-Muslim identity.

Self and Other in Local Catholic Rituals and Festivals

While architecturally the Sendangsono shrine does not offer eye-catching traces of the religious other, it boasts a rather unique appropriation of a form of Islamic musical performance called *terbangan* or *slawatan*. In Java, this genre is now considered a distinctively Islamic music. Although its origin was apparently foreign, it was gradually accepted in some central Javanese Muslim courts and larger society around the eighteenth and nineteenth centuries, at times even blended with the Javanese traditional music (Jv. *gamelan*). Historically it may have come to Java in connection with Sufi *dhikr* sessions.[53] The core of the performance consists of the chanting of Arabic praises for the Prophet Muḥammad (Ar. *salawāt*) or of the Muslim credo (Ar. *shahādah*) with the sole accompaniment of tambourines. The Javanese text, *Serat Centhini*, informs us that in certain areas people believed in

---

[50] Ibid., p. 70.

[51] Although not specifically related to Ganjuran shrine, one major criticism of the Catholic hybrid architecture in Java was that it tended to be elitist, impractical, and costly. Thus it was not criticized for being a cheap bastardization of the original. A case in point is the Javanese design of the parish church in Bara, near the Sendangsono grotto in the late 1920s, which was criticized by Fr. Prennthaler. See Letter of Fr. Prennthaler, February 15, 1929; *Brieven*, p. 113.

[52] Bailey, *Art on the Jesuit Missions in Asia and Latin America 1542–1773* (Toronto, 2001), p. 13.

[53] Sumarsam, *Gamelan* (Chicago, 1992), pp. 22–3, 26.

the efficacious and sacred character of the *terbangan* performance. Many Muslim students (Jv. *santri*) would even perform the *terbangan* for their livelihood. The *terbangan* was both a religious activity performed during important occasions such as rites of passage and a great public spectacle in rural Java at the time. Combined with magic show, it could lead the crowds to trance and commotion.[54]

The Javanese Catholic community at Sendangsono appropriates the form of *terbangan* to perform the rhythmic chanting of verses from the Scriptures. Here the practice of this hybrid music—called the *Shalawat Katolik* (The Catholic *Shalawat*)—began quite early in the 1930s. The local Catholics are very proud of this hybrid music, largely because it is very rare that Catholics would adopt this music of the Muslim other. However, there is also a mimetic dynamic going on. For the local Catholics try to maintain this music because they have seen that the Muslims are able to preserve it from generation to generation.[55]

Being a unique feature of the ritual life at the shrine for decades, it also undergoes an interesting development in recent years, as the Catholic group would collaborate with the Muslim one in performing the music. On this point, Ien Courtens writes:

> Bonds between Muslims and Christians are strengthened on these occasions, as Muslims are invited to accompany the Catholic players [of the *slawatan*]. The Muslim community welcomes these invitations, and during the Catholic *slawatan*s Muslim people not only play the instruments but also join in singing the lyrics. The people perceive the lyrics not as stemming from an entirely different religion but as beautiful religious stories. While performing them, they experience the similarities in their faith.[56]

To a large degree this friendly collaboration signals that the Catholic appropriation of the Islamic music is not considered an illicit borrowing of the other. This distinctive hybrid music has also spread to a few other places in recent years including the Mausoleum of Muntilan. In the 2007 novena at the mausoleum, for instance, the Catholic *terbangan* music was performed and it was explicitly meant also as a sign of openness and generosity toward the Muslim other.[57]

---

[54] Santoso, *The Centhini Story*, p. 175.

[55] Sindhunata, *Mengasih Maria*, pp. 73, 75; cf. *ST*, April 24, 1940.

[56] Ien Courtens, "Mary, Mother of All," in Anna-Karina Hermkens et al. (eds), *Moved by Mary* (Aldershot, 2009), pp. 113–14.

[57] One of the novena sessions was specially devoted to the theme of interfaith dialogue with the theme "Following Christ, Respecting the Religious Other" (Jv. *Ndherek Gusti Urmat Agama Liya*). This respect comes from the realization that God in Christ works in the world consisting of different religious communities. Thus it is grounded in a Christian theology of incarnation and the reality of religious pluralism. The presiding priest, the director of the Museum of Mission of Muntilan, based the practice of borrowing from the religious other at the shrine on the long standing Catholic tradition of openness to all goodness from the other.

When placed in its historical continuum, this development is remarkable. As I have argued in the previous chapter, this is of course part of the ever widening communal hermeneutic of openness to the other around the three shrines under study. However, it is particularly striking to see this development at Sendangsono shrine. For during its earliest phase, Catholic rituals at this shrine were performed not just as purely religious ceremonies, but also as a public display of a local Catholic existence, a political statement of identity over against a rival group. Fr. Prennthaler, the founder of the shrine, employed the *angelus* bells that he brought from Europe to counter the mosque drum of the Muslims.[58] Then, in 1930, he wrote of his effort to counter the boisterous, provocative, and triumphant sound of the Javanese traditional music from the Muhammadiyah camp: "Definitely we must display our own music and songs against them and our music got to be so much louder, more provoking, intimidating, and triumphant!"[59]

Thus, in light of this early mimetic rivalry, the gradual Catholic appropriation of the Islamic music and the ensuing recent collaboration with Muslim groups are truly remarkable. In this new framework of amicable mimesis, the hybrid *terbangan* serves as a living memory of the other. In a sense, it still sounds rather "strange" in typical Catholic ears, but it is also becoming more and more familiar. In the Catholic adoption of this music, otherness is recognized, that is, the fact that it is normally associated with Islam; however, a deeper connectedness is also becoming more important, as the reason for the adoption is formulated in terms of sincerity in praising God, rather than mimetic rivalry.[60]

Inculturated Saint Veneration

At the Sacred Heart shrine at Ganjuran, the movement of inclusiveness toward the other becomes very visible in the entire inculturation of Catholic faith into the local culture. For the limited purpose in this chapter, I will focus my analysis on the particular ritual of saint veneration and the annual festival of the Sacred Heart of Jesus at this shrine.

Created in the late 1990s by Father Gregorious Utomo, the aforementioned pastor who revived the shrine, this ritual is called "The Prayer of the National Sodality of the Sacred Heart" (I. *Doa Umat Hati Kudus se-Nusantara*). Motivated by the desire to forge wider and deeper solidarity and communion in and through prayer, the basic idea of this movement is to pray together and for each other at the same time (at seven in the morning). As I will discuss below, the complete form of this prayer includes Marian devotion, veneration of saints, remembrance of founders and ancestors, as well as prayers for integral healing. That is why I call this prayer a ritual of saint veneration.

---

[58] Prennthaler, "Open Brief van Pater J. Prennthaler, S.J.", *St. Claverbond* (1935), p. 171; his letter of September 9, 1927; *Brieven*, p. 33.

[59] Letter of Prennthaler, October 10, 1930; *Brieven*, p. 228.

[60] Sindhunata, *Mengasih Maria*, pp. 71–6.

The simplified form of the prayer that the devotees are expected to say daily in their hectic schedule is very brief, yet loaded with biblical and eucharistic overtone: "The Sacred Heart of Jesus, have mercy on me!" (I. *Hati Kudus Yesus, kasihanilah kami!*). As a kind of *mantra*, this prayer is supposed to become the focal point of the spiritual lives of the members of the Sodality. The complete ritual of this prayer is regularly performed at the shrine on the eve of every first Friday of the month and during the annual festival of the Sacred Heart in June. In both occasions, this special prayer forms an integral part of the Eucharistic celebration and lasts for more than thirty minutes.

What is rather striking about the creation of this Sacred Heart prayer is its foundational spirit: "We ask for God's blessings so that we become a blessing for others in turn."[61] This spirit of receiving and channeling divine blessings is symbolized in the particular position of the hands during the prayer. The devotees would normally sit on the mats, with legs crisscrossed and right palm hand rested on the right knee, facing up, symbolizing the reception of God's blessings, while left palm hand rested on the left knee, facing down, symbolizing communion and solidarity with all humanity and the transfer of divine blessings to all. In the ritual, this last point is understood as a heartfelt communion despite the distance. This hands position is interestingly very similar to the Buddhist ritual hand position (S. *mudra*), particularly the *varada mudra* that signifies the gesture of giving whatever is necessary to bring all beings to enlightenment.[62] In light of the foundational spirit of the Ganjuran shrine as a channel of the mercy of the Sacred Heart for the whole cosmos, this Buddhist connection might signify something deeper.[63]

In its complete form, this ritual starts with the blessing of the shrine's water of life (Jv. *perwitasari*) taken from the ground beneath the temple-shrine. After the blessing of the water, then begins the prayer to the Sacred Heart, followed by veneration of Mary, Joseph, and a long list of saints and guardian angels. Thus this form of prayer session can be seen as a revival of traditional Catholic ritual of saint veneration in the form of invoking the saints' intercessions, while combining it with contemporary concerns for integral well-being and other pressing needs of the community.[64]

---

[61] See the shrine's official brochure, *Rahmat Yang Menjadi Berkat.*

[62] O'Brien, *Sutasoma*, p. 171. This position is also identical to the symbolism of hand positions in the Mevlevi ritual.

[63] This particular *mudra* is intimately connected, in the framework of the cosmic Buddha Ratnasambhava, with the elements of water and earth and with the *skandha* of feelings. See O'Brien, *Sutasoma*, p. 171.

[64] As can be seen in the newly formulated roles of these saints below, the ritual is a renewed form of otherwise traditional Catholic veneration of saints. The list of saints and their roles includes: St. Peregrine, healer of cancer; St. Bernadette of Lourdes and St. Catherine Laboure, for healing in general; St. Benedict, for fighting the evil spirits; St. Scholastica, for good "weather," both in the physical and spiritual sense of the word, freed from natural disasters etc.; St. Jude, for lost cause; St. Anthony, for lost items, but also

An important dimension of this ritual is also remembrance and memory of ancestors, founders, and pioneers of the local community. In this category, the Schmutzer family occupies a central stage, followed by the deceased priests who worked in the parish, as well as some first local Javanese Catholic families. Remembrance and gratitude of the generosity of "the mother Church" in the Netherlands is also a constant feature, mostly in the form of praying for priestly and religious vocations for that church in crisis. There is an obvious desire to pay back what the community has received from this Church in the Netherlands.

Toward the end of the ritual, the devotees are expected to feel the reception of God's blessings through their whole body in some way. A period of silence follows, allowing the participants to symbolically feel the blowing of the wind, a traditional Christian symbolism of the Spirit, as a sign of their personal and cosmic communion with God's presence. The ritual closes with hymns of the Sacred Heart and Mary in Javanese.

After the closing hymns, the Eucharist celebration would resume. What is noteworthy here is that toward the end of the Eucharist, after communion, a procession of the Most Blessed Sacrament is held. It circumambulates the temple-shrine three times as it also happens in Hindu rituals in Java and Bali.[65] This procession is followed by the sprinkling of the blessed water of life over the pilgrims. This moment can be rather chaotic because many pilgrims will rush to the temple, trying to grab the flowers and other items that they believe retain particular blessings of God. However, a serene night vigil around the Blessed Sacrament would then ensue. A great number of pilgrims would stay longer in the shrine's compound after the mass, either for praying the novenas from small booklets or doing other spiritual practices (Jv. *tirakat*). Certain pilgrims would also take the occasion to seek the blessing and advice of the priests who are still around. Pilgrims from far away places would also stay overnight in vigil at the shrine.

Annual Festival of the Sacred Heart

The annual festival of the Sacred Heart is the largest religious feast at the Ganjuran shrine, held on a Sunday in June on the Solemnity of the Sacred Heart. Historically

---

for those who lost their spouses due to infidelity; St. Francis of Assisi, for environment, organic farmers etc; St. Francis Xavier and St. Therese of Lisieux, for the mission, understood as the spread of the Kingdom of God.

[65] All Hindu temples in Java have processional paths (S. *pradakshinapatha*); pilgrims or devotees would do the homage to the god by performing the rite of clockwise circumambulation (S. *pradakshina*) along this processional path before ascending to the central chamber where the image of the god has been placed. See Soekmono, "Notes on the Monuments of Ancient Indonesia," in Jan Fontein et al. (eds), *Ancient Indonesian Art of the Central and Eastern Javanese Periods* (New York, 1971) p. 15. The ritual of (individual) circumambulation is also popular in Muslim shrines in Egypt. Cf. Valerie J. Hoffman, *Sufism, Mystics, and Saints in Modern Egypt*, p. 333.

this festival and procession has long been part of the popular practice of Catholics in Java.[66] In its current form, the annual festival of the Sacred Heart at the Ganjuran shrine is basically a solemn and prolonged mass, attended by some two thousand people, in which the aforementioned prayer session of the Sacred Heart constitutes an important and distinctive part, making the connection between the veneration of the saints and its Christological framework more manifest. In the context of this festival, the veneration of saints includes the memory of founders of the shrine or local paradigmatic figures. The festival is often preceded by a communal pilgrimage to the graves of the priests who worked for the community in the past.

Other important aspects of this solemn mass include: (1) the reading of prayer requests or petitions before the mass;[67] (2) offerings of agrarian products and the likes in the forms of sacred mountain (Jv. *gunungan*);[68] (3) a procession of the Most Blessed Sacrament in the sacred space (Jv. *mandala*) of the temple compound that would include the threefold ritual circumambulation of the temple; (4) the blessings of the holy water (Jv. *perwitasari*).

Another special feature of the mass is the ritual role of a non-presiding priest in charge of the ritual incense; sitting cross-legged right in front of the temple during the whole ritual, this priest in a traditional Javanese outfit is performing a ritual duty that is clearly borrowed from the Javanese ritual world. In general, this festival is imbued with an overwhelming presence of Javanese culture. Its major features are strikingly similar to the royal celebrations (Jv. *garebeg*) at the courts of Yogyakarta and Surakarta (Chapter 2), such as the Javanese outfits worn by all the officials, the offerings in the shape of sacred mountain (Jv. *gunungan*) and the way these offerings are distributed to those present, and the use of the Javanese traditional music (Jv. *gamelan*). The shrine's volunteers at Ganjuran call themselves "*abdi dalem*" (lit. the servants of His Majesty) because they serve Christ the King; but it also shares the same term used to designate those who serve the Sultan, as well as the guardians at Muslim shrines under the patronage of the royal court. The connection to and influence of the Javanese spiritual tradition is also made clearer in the fact that the shrine's volunteers at Ganjuran hold a special prayer session on the eve of Friday *Kliwon*, the most supernaturally potent night

---

[66] In 1935, throughout the month of June, the *Swara-Tama* featured various reports on the processions in Central and East Java that drew many Muslim locals as well.

[67] These prayer requests or intentions are sent to the shrine's committee. Every month, the committee would receive roughly between 800 to 1,000 letters, both via mail or presented in person. The first Friday ritual also features the reading of these petition prayers at the beginning. For these letters come from all over Indonesia, as well as from Indonesian immigrants residing in foreign countries, effecting a certain degree of worldwide communion among devotees.

[68] These offerings would be blessed by the presiding priest and the devotees will compete (Jv. *rebutan*) to grab part of it at the end of the mass, because it is believed to contain God's blessings, a feature reminiscent of the *garebeg* celebration at the court of Yogyakarta.

in Javanese belief. Javanist and Muslim shrines are packed with pilgrims during this night as well.

Highly interesting as well in this regard is the communal meal (Jv. *kenduri* or *slametan*) that is held a day or two prior to the celebration. Staying true to the inclusive spirit of this communal meal, it is attended by peoples of different faiths, which is common in central Java. However, what is more specific here is that the prayers of thanksgiving are offered consecutively by officiants of other faiths too, something that is still rather unusual in Java.[69] During the *kenduri* in 2009 that I attended, which also occurred on the occasion of the anniversary of the parish, the interfaith prayers were offered by Muslim (who prayed in Arabic), Protestant, and Catholic officiants, with a single intention that the church might become a blessing for others. In addition to fostering an interfaith brotherhood, this communal meal was also conceived as an effort to preserve the Javanese culture. More than three hundred people participated in this communal meal, and probably around a hundred of them were Muslims.

During this annual festival, the foundational spirit of the shrine is renewed through the re-consecration of the whole country (I. *Nusantara*) to the protection of the Sacred Heart.[70] The sense of universalism of the festival and the re-consecration becomes apparent in the usage of Indonesian language (instead of Javanese) during some parts of the ceremony as well as in the widespread presence of the members of the Sacred Heart community from all over the country and beyond, including those who send their prayer requests from abroad, such as Europe and North America. The presence of Chinese Catholics is quite striking and the concelebrating priests normally include those from outside Java, as well as foreign missionaries.

Concluding Remarks

In this chapter I have discussed how the three Catholic shrines under study have become privileged sites for the flourishing of the culture of devotion and identity formation of the local Javano-Catholic community, where the hybrid notion of a Javano-Catholic self is continually negotiated by engaging different forms of otherness, mainly the Hindu past and the Muslim present, in diverse ways that

---

[69] In many places throughout Java, this inclusive communal meal is ordinarily led by a religious officiant of the respective religion of the host. Thus what happens at the Ganjuran shrine, where different religious officiants say their prayers consecutively, is rather unique. However, the spirit of such an interfaith prayer is not far from the series of interfaith prayers for peace led by Pope John Paul II at Assisi in 1986, 1993, and 2002.

[70] This feature is also known in other historical contexts, such as the annual re-consecration of the city of Marseille to the Sacred Heart in the eighteenth century, a practice that began following the deadly plague in 1720. Cf. Raymond Jonas, *France and the Cult of the Sacred Heart* (Berkeley, 2000).

incorporate the other into the spatial, architectural, and ritual dimensions of these shrines.

The community seems to be resolute in grounding this negotiation in an ever-widening hermeneutic of openness to and inclusion of the other. In this regard, one can identify the major elements of this hermeneutic by referring to the vision of Josef Schmutzer quoted at the beginning of this chapter. Schmutzer understood the purpose of this vision as the creation of a new hybrid Javano-Catholic culture that would be thriving and rich, something that would serve as a special contribution of the Javanese Catholics to the world. He anchored this whole conception in the basic framework of the clarity of Christian Revelation guided by the Holy Spirit, whom he understood as Love.

For him, however, this vision would only be fruitful if realized through the means of prayers and works, through the spirit of cooperation and hybridity between the science of the Occident and the art of the Orient. In connection with this point, my discussion has shown that the level of interfaith cooperation has recently been increasing at the three shrines. His mention of prayer is also insightful, because it becomes the deepest arena in which the revelatory power of this hybrid culture of the shrine can be experienced.

Thus, through the wider and deeper application of the hermeneutic principle of communion, the traces of the other—especially in architecture and ritual of the shrines—would not be dead traces, but rather a sign of a living embrace that needs to be extended continuously. Within this framework, taking this trace seriously marks the birth of a new and vibrant culture that Schmutzer envisioned. As the contemporary developments in the three shrines have shown, this new culture is marked more and more by cooperation in works, hybridity in arts where Christianity and Javaneseness meet in a new artistic synthesis, openness in rituals, as well as solidarity, generosity, and a wider other-orientedness in prayers. These are among various ways in which the Javano-Catholic community has been trying to understand the meanings of their Catholicism—or what Schmutzer called the framework of "the luminous clarity of Revelation"—and they have come to illustrate the largely creative formation of their identity *vis-à-vis* the other amid the particularities of contemporary Javanese society in south central Java.

Chapter 6
Immersed in the Web of Blessings and Communion

> In times of troubles and humiliations, we become stronger because of Him, despite the frailty of our human nature.
>
> Albertus Soegijapranata, S.J.[1]

During the ceremony of the laying of the first stone of the Sacred Heart shrine at Ganjuran in 1927, a very unusual and surprising scene occurred. A crippled elderly Javanese woman with crutches suddenly emerged from the multitude, then climbed to the platform of the temple, and hobbled to the opening on the ground where the replica of the statue of Christ the King was being placed. Then in earnest she fell to her knees to pay homage (Jv. *sembah*) three times to Christ.[2]

What this episode reveals is not just the intensity and sincerity of a Javanese woman's devotion to the Sacred Heart. For what is more striking is probably the specific and tangible ways in which she expressed her devotion, since her encounter with God (the Sacred Heart of Jesus) in that particular moment took on a distinctive quality. It was a highly personal experience of devotedness to Jesus that was also subject to public gaze. And it was a spiritual moment that was also deeply sensuous and bodily. For her, the statue of Jesus was not just a religious symbol, but acquired a special power and meaning, so much so that she felt the spontaneous urge to rush, kneel down and pay homage, overcoming all the difficulties connected to her disability.

For the spectators, such an episode might have left them not only with wonder but also questions. Father van Rijckevorsel, who was present at the ceremony and wrote a report on the event, remarked that the scene was very unexpected and deeply moving, but did not specify whether the woman was seeking a cure for her disability. If she was not motivated by cure, then what exactly was she looking for? Here, one should not take it for granted that this scene happened at a shrine. Scenes like this do occur so often at pilgrimage sites, and I would argue

---

[1] *ST*, November 1, 1939. This quotation is taken from the homily of Soegijpranata during the celebration at the Ganjuran Sacred Heart Shrine (October 29, 1939). The following year, Soegijapranata was appointed the first native apostolic vicar (bishop) of Semarang, Central Java.

[2] L. van Rijckevorsel, "Eerste Steenlegging van een H. Hart-Monument op Java," *St. Claverbond* (1928): p. 137.

that the logic of this event can be understood more fully only by delving deeper into the experiential world of the pilgrims, their personal experience, as well as their religio-cultural sensibility.

So this chapter is an endeavor to delve deeper into the dynamics of pilgrimage tradition in the three Catholic shrines under study as experienced by pilgrims in the context of Javanese religious and cultural sensibilities. My analysis here will focus on five salient categories or elements of the pilgrimage experience that also define the five main sections of the chapter. These categories include: (1) devotion as connectedness; (2) peacefulness as fundamental blessing; (3) the tangibility of sacramental blessings; (4) communion with self and others, and (5) the question of the pilgrims of other religious traditions.

In the first section my analysis begins with the category of devotion, understood not as a merely sentimental religious habit, but rather as personal connectedness and communion to the Divine in all His manifestations. I take devotion as the most foundational framework of pilgrimage that underlines the personal motivation, and wider inner processes, as well as the outcomes of pilgrimage. In this respect, I argue that pilgrimage is a habit of the heart that contributes to the formation of the pilgrims' identity. This framework also helps us understand the ongoing creation of wider milieus of devotion through the building of new shrines in connection to the old ones. Then, in the second section, I continue with the discussion of the desired "outcome" (blessings) of pilgrimage, centered on the experience of peacefulness as the most common, fundamental, inclusive, and transforming form of pilgrimage blessing. There, I will explore the religio-cultural specificities of the ways in which Javanese pilgrims come to experience peacefulness at the shrine and beyond. The third section deals with another aspect of the blessings of pilgrimage, that is, their tangibility. In this section I will examine the sacramental character of pilgrimage blessings. Often viewed as a distinctive category of Catholic theology, sacramentality or sacramental vision basically points to the presence of God in concrete realities. It draws our attention to the visibility, tangibility, and mediatedness of the invisible grace, God's self-communication. In pilgrimage, sacramentality is intimately connected to the idea of memory through things associated with the pilgrimage journey and shrines, such as holy water, architecture, statuary, souvenirs, and so forth. While this section deals more with the sacramentality of "things" connected to pilgrimage and sacred space, section four of this chapter deals with the communal aspect of this experience of grace, a dynamic that of course involves an engagement with self as well. For pilgrimage often serves as a privileged moment for the unveiling of one's spiritual self that becomes a foundation for a stronger communal sense among pilgrims. Then, in the last section, I will take up a rather crucial aspect of this community, that is, the experience of pilgrims from other religious traditions, mostly Muslims. I will also examine briefly how the pilgrimage experience helps the Javanese Catholic pilgrims deal with the question of alterity, more specifically the presence of pilgrims of other traditions as well as the darker episode in the history of the relationship between the original Catholic mission and the surrounding Muslim community.

Foundational Experience: Devotion as Connectedness

Even to casual visitors, the daily display of devotion among pilgrims at the Sacred Heart shrine at Ganjuran can seem rather unusual. So many pilgrims, young and old, come to the shrine to perform very seriously their personal devotions and prayers. Typically, after washing their hands, feet, and face with the shrine water (Jv. *perwitasari*), they would take this holy water in a bottle and then place it on the terrace of the shrine. They then light the candles in the candle boxes on the edges of the terrace. Many would spend some moment of silent prayers in the courtyard of the shrine before ascending to the terrace (Figure 4.2). During busy hours, they have to form a line there by sitting reverently to get to the inner sanctum where a Hindu-Javanese image of the Sacred Heart of Jesus is enthroned. There in the inner sanctum, either kneeling or sitting cross-legged, they would pray in earnest.

When I asked a group of university students who seemed to be very intense with their prayers at the shrine why they always wanted to go to the inner sanctum, they unanimously replied: "We don't feel spiritually satisfied (Jv. *manteb*) unless we ascend to the sanctuary and pray in front of the statue of Jesus!"[3] This might have been the same motivation of the crippled woman mentioned at the beginning of this chapter. In my view, this heartfelt desire for proximity and the whole scene at the shrine can only be explained in the larger framework of devotion, understood as each pilgrim's most personal connectedness to God. Devotion can also be considered the affective-spiritual side of the larger principle of communion that features prominently in my argument in this book. In general, devotion is of course directed to God and His heavenly court (Mary, the saints, and angels), but as I will demonstrate later, it also has some ramifications on how pilgrims come to consider the earthly realities and symbolisms that are intimately connected to this Divine realm. In this respect, devotion is the inner eye of love that enables the hearts of the pilgrims to see and experience much more.

Along this line, devotion can be viewed as the most personal and deepest dimension of the whole movement of including the other, of creating some space for the other, that happens around the shrines. In Chapters 4 and 5, I have examined several major elements of this communal hermeneutic of including that occurs at the shrines. It was the same devotion that inspired the Schmutzer family to build the shrine in the first place. Theologically, as noted, Josef Schmutzer anchored this dynamism in the centrality of Love in the Christian theology of the Trinity. In this framework, it is the Spirit who stirs the hearts of the pilgrims toward the movement of devotion and toward deeper and wider communion, as it is the Spirit who keeps the heart of Jesus overflowing with unbounded mercy and love.

In light of this pneumatological framework of love, then, pilgrimage is an act of love and devotion of the heart on the part of the pilgrims, as a Javanese writer wrote: "As a sign of true love (Jv. *katresnan sedjatos*), pilgrims are eager to visit

---

[3] Interview, Ganjuran shrine, June 30, 2009.

Our Lady."[4] This writer was deeply moved by the communal display of love and devotion to Mary by Javanese pilgrims, as he was witnessing their procession uphill to the Sendangsono grotto. It was a large group of pilgrims, both old and young, men and women, marching up to the grotto, passing through the rolling hills of Menoreh. The provisions were carried on long poles on the shoulders of the younger members of the group. He concluded in a Javanese rhyme: "true love knows no hardships" (Jv. *katresnan sedjatos sanadjan kanti rekaos, boten dipoenraos*).

In this regard, there is a certain distinctive way in which this understanding of pilgrimage is experienced by Javanese Catholics in south central Java. This distinctiveness stems from the traditional Javanese religio-cultural categories of *sowan* (dutiful and loving visit), *sembah* (paying homage and respect), and *bekti* (loving devotion; from S. *bhakti*) that the pilgrims employ.

It is very common for Javanese Catholics to refer to the pilgrimage to Marian shrine as "*sowan Ibu Maria*," that is, paying a dutiful, reverent, and loving visit to Mary.[5] The term "*sowan*" is a refined Javanese word, typically used to refer to the whole act of paying respectful and dutiful visit by a disciple to his master, or a child to his parents, or a subject to his king. It assumes an unequal relationship, a relationship of dependence or respect. Although it connotes a sense of duty, the religious semantic field of the term *sowan* emphasizes the framework of a loving relationship. The visit is not motivated by sheer duty but rather by affectionate and respectful connectedness or devotedness (Jv. *sembah bekti*).

This sense of devotion, loving relationship, and dutiful respect is rather perfectly expressed in the Javanese translation of the Hail Mary, especially the first line. The Javanese translation of the line "Hail Mary, full of grace" reads as "*sembah bekti kawula Dewi Maria, kekasihing Allah*," which literally means: "O Mary, our reverence and devotion to you; you are the Beloved of God." The Javanese sensibility of this translation is only made clearer when compared with the other alternatives. The Indonesian translation, for instance, is more literally faithful to the biblical version (Luke 1:28). The Javanese apparently opt for a rather different semantic field that is more fitting to their religious sensibility. By using the words *sembah* and *bekti*, they attempt to emphasize their being devoted to Mary in a loving-respectful relationship. In Javanese, the words "*sembah-bekti*" are not words of common greeting among people. The greeting of Gabriel to Mary is not reproduced literally in Javanese probably because it did not express this semantic element of devotedness, love, and filial dependence.

Furthermore, there is surely an echo of the Hindu tradition of *bhakti* in this Javanese use of the word *bekti*; for it is derived from the Sanskrit word *bhakti*, a term that originally means "to share in, to belong to, and to worship." Sometimes it is also used in the sense of respect. In Hinduism, *bhakti* is understood in terms of personal relationship between the devotees and God, an intense feeling of love, that could

---

[4] *ST*, June 15, 1935.

[5] See the various accounts of pilgrims to this shrine in Sindhunata, *Mengasih Maria*, p. 149 and *passim*.

lead up to union with God, albeit through a long and arduous journey of efforts, purification, and so forth; and it always involves the context of worship and rituals.[6]

So in terms of the personal (loving relationship) and ritual aspects of *bhakti*, the depth of the trace of this Hindu other is still very visible in the religious sensibility—as opposed to religious doctrine—of the Javanese Catholic pilgrims when they understand their pilgrimage in terms of *bekti*. The connection to the Hindu tradition is also made more interesting by the appellation of Mary as "*Dewi Maria*" in Javanese. The word "*dewi*" is of course derived from the Sanskrit "*devi*" that refers to the great goddess or simply goddess.[7] As illustrated in Chapter 5, the shrine's iconographic depiction of Mary as the new Prajnaparamita or Laksmi helps to make the association of Mary with the goddess tradition of Hinduism or Buddhism (whatever this may mean) more visible to the eyes of the pilgrims. Although the Javanese Catholics obviously do not consider Mary as a goddess, this appellation and association seem to make it even more proper to approach Mary with such deep reverence and dependence (Jv. *sembah*) and loving-devotion (Jv. *bekti*), as occurs in the Hindu *bhakti* context.

Furthermore, in this framework of *bhakti*, a sense of absolute security, an overwhelming sense of being protected, that results from a loving surrender and taking refuge at the feet of Mary, can also be experienced more deeply.[8] It is precisely this quality that lies at the heart of the most popular Javanese Marian hymn, *Ndherek Dewi Maria* ("In the Protection of Mary"). This hymn extols Mary as the loving and powerful protector against all dangers that are identified mainly in terms of the Evil one. The main message is that all those who surrender to Mary (Jv. *sumarah*) need not worry about these dangers anymore, even at the point when one feels powerless against the Evil one, because Mary will rescue and protect. So it seems that the religious sensibility of Javanese Catholic pilgrims combine aspects of both the Hindu sense of *bhakti* (loving devotedness) and *prapatti* (loving surrender).[9]

In this connection, it should be noted that pilgrimage is often understood in terms of *nyekar*; that is, visiting the shrine or grave of saints and ancestors as a sign

---

[6] Raj Sing, *Bhakti and Philosophy* (Lanham, 2006), p. 1.

[7] In Sanskrit, *devi* means simply a goddess. However, the Hindu tradition also identifies Devi as the great goddess; She is Shiva's consort and the supreme Deity, the source of power of all deities. On major aspects of the portrayal of Devi in Sankara's hymn *Saundarya Lahari*, see Francis Clooney, "Encountering the (Divine) Mother in Hindu and Christian Hymns," *Religion and the Arts*, 12 (2008): pp. 230–43.

[8] As Clooney shows in his study of Vedanta Desika and Francis de Sales, loving surrender and taking refuge (S. *prapatti*) to God can be considered the apex of the dynamic of devotion in Srivaisnava Hinduism and Catholicism. See his *Beyond Compare* (Washington, D.C., 2008).

[9] On the importance of self-surrender to God (through Mary) in the experience of Catholic pilgrims at the Sendangsono grotto, see Sindhunata, *Mengasih Maria*, pp. 62, 106 and *passim*.

of respect, love, and remembrance. In 1926, a Javanese former student of van Lith wrote that he went to the retreat in Muntilan partly because he wanted to pay this *nyekar* visit to the grave of his former teacher.[10] As shown earlier, the community of the Sacred Heart shrine at Ganjuran has a tradition of making pilgrimage to the tombs of their deceased priests. Among Javanese Catholics and Muslims alike, this tomb visitation is rather closely to the wider notion of "*bekti*" (loving devotion and reverence) toward deceased parents or ancestors. There is a widespread Javanese belief that *bekti* towards parents and ancestors is a potent source of blessings.

Pilgrimage as a Habit of the Heart

In the framework of devotion understood as a loving relationship that grows over time, pilgrimage becomes a habit. It is not an isolated activity because it has become a rather crucial part of the religious sensibility of the pilgrims in the continuum of their life journeys. Here pilgrimage becomes a particular religious act that is filled with a sense of personal memory and history. This is because what happened in the previous pilgrimage will affect the next (or *vice versa*), in the sense that the next pilgrimage carries the memory of the previous ones and also deepens one's appreciation of the meaning of these past pilgrimages. Often times the process of spiritual growth or purification occurs precisely when this series of pilgrimage is viewed as a longer unity.

There is a close relationship between pilgrimage as a habit of the heart (memory) and a journey of purification. This point is crucial because among Javanese across religious backgrounds, pilgrimage is always understood in its organic relationship with its ascetic and purifying aspects. As noted, the Javanese understand pilgrimage as *tirakat* and *laku*, two terms that point to the extended and intensive practice of asceticism and spiritual purification, both outward and inward. Many pilgrims reveal that the outward hardship of the journey has helped them to feel inwardly closer to God and Mary. "The experience is so much deeper! (Jv. *luwih rumesep*)," a pilgrim exclaimed, trying to explain the logic of this purifying asceticism in pilgrimage.[11]

Furthermore, the quality of gratitude and devotion often goes hand in hand with the hardship of the journey. A Javanese middle-aged man told me that he could not express his gratitude enough to God and Mary for the blessings he has received unless he walked to the grotto.[12] However, in the case of this man, this type of pilgrimage also has a more personal dimension since it is connected to his earlier personal history with the shrine. For seven years he was visiting the shrine, asking for a child, but to no avail. At some point he gave up the visit and felt terribly upset toward God and Mary for not responding to his reasonable request. "I was really upset with God (Jv. *jengkel*)," he said, for he had been a faithful pilgrim

---

[10] *ST*, April 16, 1926.
[11] Interview, Sendangsono grotto, May 24, 2010.
[12] Interview, Sendangsono grotto, May 24, 2010.

to this shrine since his youth. He even took many Catholic youngsters from his parish in the inner city of Yogyakarta on group pilgrimages, on foot, to this shrine. Looking at how other pilgrims got an easier time with God made him even angrier. However, when he was tired of complaining and feeling bitter about all this, he came to a sense of surrender to God. To his surprise, God responded to his request. So, overwhelmed with enormous gratitude, he decided to respond to this by walking to the shrine again. There was no other way imaginable for him to do the pilgrimage in an appropriately thankful manner, precisely given his own personal history with God and the Sendangsono grotto. It was during this pilgrimage that all kinds of memories of his past pilgrimages came up to him, including his temporary standoff with God. And for him personally, this kind of moment was one that particularly helped him reintegrate his life, due to his personal history.

As a habit of the heart, pilgrimage begins as a habitual desire to be at the shrine. The Sendangsono grotto is probably the most popular destination of this habitual desire for pilgrimage, due to its longtime role in the personal devotion and memory of so many Catholic pilgrims in Java. At this shrine, one would find many elderly pilgrims who come in larger groups. Although they might want to visit other shrines once in a while, this particular shrine still holds a special place in their spiritual life due to the long-term relationship that has been built around it. Many of them actually come from some neighboring areas, but due to their financial situation, physical frailty, as well as other limitations, pilgrimage to this grotto could not always be taken for granted. It means so much for them and that is why they have to make a rather long preparation. Most of the time, they would save the money to visit the shrine during the Marian months of May or October.[13]

Another crucial characteristic of pilgrimage here is its intergenerationality. Most pilgrims would learn the art of making pilgrimage from their parents or grandparents who would regularly take them to certain shrines when they were younger.[14] To a certain degree, pilgrimage of this kind is also related to rites of passage. Javanese Catholic parents would go to a shrine to pray for their children as they are about to embark on a new and crucial phase in their lives, such as going to college, getting a job, getting married, entering religious life, and so forth. In this particular context, visits to the shrine go hand in hand with visits to the family tombs, believing that the heavenly support would also include their ancestors. This point shows how Catholic veneration of saints in Java is organically connected to the framework of relationships with ancestors.

Due to this feature, pilgrimage also becomes inseparable from a memory of the parents, grandparents or other members of the extended family. Pilgrims want to

---

[13] This point is rather well illustrated by a group of elderly pilgrims, mostly women, who traveled to visit the Sendangsono shrine from their hometown of Temanggung, some thirty miles away from the shrine. These simple women said that they had anticipated this May pilgrimage for long; they prepared the journey by saving the money that their grandchildren gave. Interview, Sendangsono shrine, May 24, 2009.

[14] Cf. Sindhunata, *Mengasih Maria*, p. 62.

return to certain shrines because these are places that connect them in a special way to the memory of their family.[15] The personal side of this feature can be seen in the kinds of prayers that many pilgrims leave on the guest books of the shrines. Here one finds the predominance of prayers for family members: parents pray for the wellbeing of the children, while the children for their living or deceased parents. Many parents make a special promise to visit the shrines again as a gratitude for the granted prayers.[16] Thus, as parents bring their children, both physically and spiritually, to the shrine, these children would later bring their parents (as well as their own children) back to the shrine, and this dynamic continues generation after generation.[17] Due to this web of memory and familial connections, pilgrimage often serves as a rare moment when familial relationships take on a deeper quality. All of this reflects the structure of Javanese society in which family is the most immediate and real context of one's life.

The Spread of Devotion: Creation of Daughter Shrines

In the context of pilgrimage culture among Catholics in south central Java, devotion as connectedness has a special characteristic of mimesis and memorialization that becomes evident in phenomenon of building a new grotto or shrine as a "daughter shrine" of the older one. As a tangible memorialization of love and devotion, expectation of miracles would not normally be part of its motivation. But often times, as I will illustrate below, previous miraculous events can serve as a catalyst for building new shrines.

Among Javanese Catholics, this penchant for building new shrines has begun quite early in their identity formation, sparked off by the foundation of the Sendangsono grotto in 1929. In 1935, for example, the *Swara-Tama* wrote on the significance of erecting a Marian grotto:

> The grotto would be a token of our love and devoted reverence to our Lady, our Mother and Queen, our Protector. It is through the building of the grotto that we communally express our love and devotedness to our Mother, as well

---

[15] For some Javanese priests and nuns, pilgrimage to the Sendangsono grotto serves as a powerful memory and reiteration of their religious vocation. For, many pious Javanese Catholic families would still pray for the gift of priestly and religious vocations for their children, and family pilgrimage also serves as a milieu in which this kind of prayer occurs. During their formation, many young seminarians and nuns would also continue to do this pilgrimage. Cf. Wismapranata, *Kenangan*, pp. 41–51; Sindhunata, *Mengasih Maria*, pp. 89–93, 102, and 108.

[16] This feature is of course related to the wider aspects of making vows (Ar. *nazr*) in the pilgrimage culture across religious traditions, including Islam.

[17] Cf. Catrien Notermans, "Connecting the Living and the Dead: Re-membering the Family through Marian Devotion," in Anna-Karina Hermkens, *Moved by Mary*, p. 140.

as our determination to be Her children. The grotto would be a testament to this forever.[18]

As this quotation shows, devotion often leads to the creation of new shrines, a process that at times involves a mimetic element. As noted in Chapter 5 the same logic was behind the initial creations of the Sendangsono grotto (as "the Lourdes of Java") as well as the Ganjuran Sacred Heart shrine. In the case of the latter, it was a personal token of thanksgiving on the part of the Schmutzer family; but it was also an extension of the same pattern of devotion that was popular then among Catholics in the Netherlands or Europe.[19] In a sense, the creation of the shrine was an expression of a desire to unite the land and people of Java (and Indonesia) to the Netherlands on a spiritual plane.[20]

The recent decades have seen the mushrooming of Marian shrines in many places in Java, a sign of the enormous energy of devotion among Catholics in the area. One major shrine begets other foundations with the creation of "daughter shrines" that at times are located in the private homes of devotees. In this regard, the Marian grotto of Marganingsih (in reference to Mary, "the mediator of all grace") near the Muslim shrine of Tembayat is a good example. For this shrine began with the special devotion of a Javanese woman to Mary. In the 1930s she would go on countless pilgrimage trips on foot to the Sendangsono grotto. One of her intentions was to have a child, for she was childless for many years. She vowed that if God granted her prayers, she would offer the child for His cause. As it turned out, God granted her prayers generously. She would have 12 children in all and the eldest would become a prominent Jesuit priest. This was obviously a miracle. Then, as a token of gratitude, she built a small grotto in her home, a replica of the Lourdes shrine of Sendangsono.[21] Overtime, this grotto became known outside of the family, and after her death it turned into a rather important pilgrimage site in south central Java.[22]

---

[18] *ST*, June 5, 1935.

[19] *ST*, February 14, 1930.

[20] In much more dramatic ways, this dynamic of unification or extension occurred in France with the creation of Basilique du Sacré-Cœur at Montmartre (1919), a symbol of national dedication of France to the Sacred Heart. As this basilica expressed, the whole country was united on this spiritual plane after the period of disunity following the Revolution. See Jonas, *France and the Cult of the Sacred Heart*.

[21] This pious woman considered the religious vocation of her eldest son as a sign of further favor of God and Mary to the family, as well as the proper token of gratitude of the family. It was her Jesuit son who developed the shrine further. Interview with the caretaker of the Marganingsih grotto, Tembayat, June 28, 2009.

[22] Another good example would be the Marian grotto of Our Lady of the Rosary in the town of Juwana, in the north central Java. This grotto was built in the late 1990s by a Chinese Catholic family in the backyard of their home, as a token of gratitude to Our Lady of Lourdes whose intercession had cured the matriarch of this family. At first the grotto was

In this phenomenon, one sees a very interesting dynamic of mimesis in pilgrimage culture. For the distant shrine is made closer to home through the creation of its replica, a mimesis and remembrance. Interestingly, this dynamic does not strip pilgrimage of its basic characteristic as a journey. For the journey is now more inwardly conceived, a process of becoming nearer to God and self, almost on a daily basis, rather than a physical travel. The sense of personal commitment to Mary, in the case of Marian grotto, is also strengthened. The devotees feel more personally attached to the shrine without losing their habitual desire to visit far away sites from time to time (including the mother shrine) as well.

This phenomenon of proximity between shrine and home is quite striking. In a sense, the shrine becomes home by proximity or the home becomes a shrine by extension. Brought from a distant place, the shrine is now part of the devotee's intimate home. To a certain degree, this dynamic blurs the boundaries between private and public space. This is so because the shrine becomes a private sacred space of the family. But this privatization often does not last for long, for the "private" shrine can typically develop into public and ecclesial site through the blessing of the bishop as its fame spreads around. Thus, in this sense, the shrine transforms the private space of a home into a public or communal space of devotion.

Peacefulness as Foundational Blessing of Pilgrimage

In the experience of many pilgrims, the quality and depth of devotion is closely related to the experience of being in touch with an overwhelming peacefulness during pilgrimage. To a large degree, this experience of peacefulness constitutes the most foundational blessing of pilgrimage since it gives pilgrims the most solid foundation for appreciating other more specific blessings. Connecting pilgrims to a deeper sense of purpose and meaning, it has the power to help them reintegrate their lives on a more solid foundation and thus assists them in their dealing with smaller questions or problems.

Seeking peacefulness in the simple sense of having peace of mind at the shrine is among the most common direct motives for making a pilgrimage. Of course many of these pilgrims have many troubles or crises in life that contribute to their motivation for doing the pilgrimage. Yet even if their pilgrimage does not result in "magical" solution to these problems, pilgrims do normally experience a profound peace at the shrine that has enduring effects beyond that particular moment. This peacefulness is clearly the result of a profound experience of being in more intense communion with God. At the same time, the make-up of this peacefulness may also involve the right constellation of disparate elements that participate in this moment of communion.

---

private, but with the blessing of the bishop in 2006, it became quite an important pilgrimage site. Interview with Mr. Indro Ludiro, May 15, 2009.

In this regard, many pilgrims come seeking to be in touch with the therapeutic dimensions of the shrine as sacred space. More specifically, they mention its natural beauty, its location and other specificities, its distance from the monotony of daily life, and a stronger sense of divine presence there.[23] In this regard, quite often pilgrims desire to visit distant shrines for this therapy of place, combining religious and recreation purposes.[24]

Many pilgrims speak about this experience of peacefulness in terms of being at home at the shrine. The shrine becomes a "home" because it is the place where one is at peace with his self with a deeper sense of identity. It is at this moment that the pilgrims regain self-confidence and self-integration, coming to a deeper sense of their identity in relation to God. This peacefulness (Jv. *tentrem*) thus stems from the personal realization of being connected to the larger framework of life. This connection is especially crucial to pilgrims whose lives have been plagued by disorientations and confusions. In this regard, peacefulness heals indeed. The healing quality of this peacefulness is probably more obviously appealing to many urban pilgrims who live in cramped housing with a hectic life-style and demanding profession.[25]

In some cases, pilgrims would be made aware of this desire to seek peacefulness only after they got to the shrine. A young pilgrim from the inner city of Yogyakarta wrote in the guestbook of the Ganjuran shrine: "When I decided to visit this shrine, I was not too sure about my real intention; the only thing I know while I am at the shrine is that my mind is opened, cleared up."[26] And at moment, he started realizing his existential condition, made more aware of his sinfulness. This kind of experience raises a crucial point because it shows that pilgrimage is a spiritual practice whose dynamic lies principally, though not solely, in the realm of the spirit. Victor Turner speaks about pilgrimage as an "exteriorized contemplation."

---

[23] One pilgrim explains his experience at the Sendangsono grotto thus: "Upon arriving at the grotto, I was sitting in the shade of the big tree. Here I feel so much at peace. My burdens become lighter and a sense of true happiness overcomes me." See Sindhunata, *Mengasih Maria*, p. 90.

[24] Contemporary scholarship has found that the rigid boundary between pilgrims and tourists is hard to maintain, confirming Victor Turner's saying that "pilgrim is half tourist, while tourist is half pilgrim." This is so because tourists also undergo personal transformation through their encounter with the Sacred in many different ways, especially through their quest of personal meanings of life. Cf. Ellen Badone and Sharon R. Roseman (eds), *Intersecting Journeys: The Anthropology of Pilgrimage and Tourism* (Urbana, 2004).

[25] The Ganjuran shrine attracts many pilgrims of this type. Many of them come originally from central Java but work in Jakarta. They always tend to compare the inhumanly frenzied urban life in Jakarta with the peace, serenity, and naturalness of the shrine. A pilgrim of this category remarked to me that this is the "rational" explanation of the blessing of pilgrimage. This experience of peacefulness makes him function better as a human being in general as well as a professional at his working place. Interview at the Ganjuran shrine, May 25, 2009.

[26] Guestbook, March 18, 2009.

Precisely as a contemplation, its ultimate meanings are largely governed by the dynamics of the spiritual (interior) life of the pilgrims.[27] At any point during the pilgrimage journey, the human spirit can be awakened toward deeper communion with God. This was exactly what happened to Thomas Merton in Rome, a realization that initiated his long conversion into a life of fuller communion with God.[28] Interestingly most pilgrims would define the effect of this communion in terms of peacefulness. The guestbook of the shrine at Ganjuran, for example, is filled with testimonies of such experiences.

Among many Javanese pilgrims, striking is the employment of *rasa*—a rather delicate category in the Javanese culture discussed previously in the context of the experience of Javanese Muslim pilgrims—to express the quality of this peacefulness (Jv. *tentrem*). Andreas Handika, a pilgrim at the Ganjuran shrine, for example, has no other way to describe the pervasive peace that he experiences every time he spends time at this shrine.[29] He belongs to the type of urban pilgrims mentioned before. He would come regularly to the Ganjuran shrine every time he returns from his job in Jakarta to visit his family in Yogyakarta, and would stay overnight at the shrine. Around midnight he would ascend to the inner sanctum of the temple for a session of prayer during which the sense of peace is most overwhelming. "When I come to feel the peace through the *rasa*, I know that I have come to the true quality of peace," he explained. In his case, his particular propensity to talk about his experience in terms of *rasa* might be related to his deeper exposure to some Javanese spiritual and mystical movements (Jv. *kebatinan*) whose doctrine revolves around the presence of the divine spirit in the human person that could be awakened through the cultivation of *rasa* during meditation. In Jakarta, he joins a kind of spiritual conversation held by a circle of Javanese adherents of this kind of spiritual movement.

By using the term *rasa*, Javanese pilgrims like Handika mean something very deep and real (almost immediate), yet hard to describe, precisely because it occurs in the complicated realm of the interaction between the inner and outer worlds. As mentioned a few times earlier (especially Chapter 1), this concept of *rasa* has been used by the Javanese as an important category of the inner life of the human person. The Javanese understand *rasa* to point to "inner sensing" as a spiritual-epistemological category. Paul Stange argues that "*rasa* is at once the substance, vibration, or quality of what is apprehended and the tool or organ which apprehends it."[30] As such, the cultivation of *rasa* connects a person with his world of experience in a deeper, personal, spiritual, and integral way.

In the Javanese practice of mysticism (Jv. *kebatinan*), the ultimate goal of the cultivation of *rasa* is a mystical union with God.[31] Here the Javanese have

---

[27] Victor and Edith Turner, *Image and Pilgrimage in Christian Culture*, p. 33.
[28] Thomas Merton, *Seven Storey Mountain* (New York, 1999), pp. 119–20.
[29] Interview at the Ganjuran shrine, April 20, 2009.
[30] Stange, "The Logic of *Rasa* in Java," p. 119.
[31] Ibid., p. 121.

combined the original Sanskrit meanings of the words *rasa* and *rahasya* (secret or mystery), and then using this connection to translate the Islamic concept of *sirr*.[32] In Ibn al-'Arabī's thought, for example, this concept of *sirr* refers the innermost being of human person where God communicates with the soul in the most intimate way through "immediate spiritual inspirations, as opposed to the more complex processes of ordinary spiritual understanding."[33] This Islamic framework seems to make it possible for the Javanese mystics to identify *rasa* more and more with the innermost core of the human person.[34] For them, anyone who is completely in touch with his *rasa* is in contact with the unmediated presence of God as the Spirit.

With this background in mind, one can better understand the fuller scope of the Javanese Catholic pilgrims' insistence on the primacy of the category of *rasa* in pilgrimage experience. By resorting to this category, they mean that their pilgrimage experience is deep and real, as opposed to banal and illusory, as well as authentic and personal. Sometimes, by using the term *rasa*, they want to say that the experience has reached the deepest layer of their being. For *rasa* is both the instrument of spiritual knowing as well as the milieu of deep communion with God and the whole reality.

However, the cultivation of *rasa* that makes this deep experience of intimate communion with God (that results in peacefulness) possible in the context of pilgrimage could not be separated from two intertwined categories, that is, ascetic purification (Jv. *laku*) and the necessary silence or solitude. In the experience of many pilgrims, true peacefulness (Jv. *tentrem*)—in the deepest sense of harmony and homeostasis both on the level of microcosm and macrocosm, that includes reconciliation with self and surrender to God—is hard to obtain except through inner struggle and spiritual purification that at times requires the help of ascetic practices. Ascetic purification (*via purgativa*) is of course a constant element in the experience of pilgrims in general. However, as I have argued, in the context of Javanese culture, pilgrimage is fundamentally understood as *laku* or *tirakat*, that is, a serious and focused period of spiritual cultivation aided by intensive spiritual as well as ascetic practices (Chapter 3).

Among the three Catholic shrines under study, the shrines at Ganjuran and Sendangsono are more closely associated with pilgrimage as *laku* or *tirakat*. Due to its rather remote and difficult location, the Sendangsono grotto has been traditionally connected to this ascetic purification. Especially at the Ganjuran shrine in the last few years, there is a constant group of pilgrims who would stay overnight or longer at this shrine as part of their *laku*. Compared to its Muslim counterpart, the Catholic tradition of pilgrimage in Java knows very few wandering or ascetic pilgrims. But there have always been some Catholic pilgrims who attempt to incorporate a more intense degree of asceticism in the pilgrimage, through walking on foot, biking to the shrine, and so forth. In some cases, this

---

[32] Ibid., p. 127.
[33] Morris, *The Reflective Heart*, p. 220.
[34] Cf. J. Gonda, *Sanskrit in Indonesia* (New Delhi, 1973), p. 256ff.

practice among Javanese Catholics still retain the rather traditional idea of doing penitential pilgrimage as a fulfillment of a promise to God, Jesus, Mary, and the saints. However, its role in the quest for peacefulness remains central. For by driving away distractions of the mind and the heart, it puts pilgrims to a closer relationship with their selves and God.[35]

This purifying asceticism helps the pilgrim arrive at silence and solitude at the shrine, and without it pilgrims would have a harder time reaching deeper into the depth of their selves, the world of *rasa*, where intimate communion with God occurs. Frederick Wijaya, a Chinese young pilgrim at Ganjuran, remarked that pilgrims often look for God in "buildings" like churches, shrines, and temples, but God resides in the hearts of the faithful and it is there that He could always be encountered.[36] He was thus making the point that unless pilgrims pay attention to this dimension, they would not come to this true experience of encountering God inside.

In this respect, Catholic shrines in Java are places where boisterous feasts and festivals are combined with peaceful serenity and deep solitude. In fact, the former archbishop of Semarang (Mgr. Ignatius Suharyo) has adopted the Javanese philosophy of tranquility, solitude, and total self-awareness as a spiritual framework for another nearby Catholic pilgrimage site. As expressed at the Marian shrine of Jatiningsih, located seven miles to the west of Yogyakarta, this framework is formulated thus: "At this shrine, we compose ourselves through maintaining solitude so that we achieve clarity of mind and conscience and thus come to terms with the core of our being and the spiritual state of our existence" (I. *Di tempat ini kita meneng agar wening dan dunung*)."

This archbishop enumerates the triad of spiritual principles of *meneng*, *wening*, and *dunung*. In the context of Javanese philosophy, the term *meneng* is associated with being in emotional equilibrium, unperturbed by the externals and trivialities in life; it represents the state of a soul purified from the gross temptations and confusions of material and worldly life and so forth. While the concept of *wening* refers to the state of having a clear vision or truth, good conscience, and inner peace (mindfulness) that is a natural result of *meneng*. In turn, the exercise of these two principles will result in the achievement of *hanung*, namely, the state of knowing the deepest core of one's being and personal mission in life. In the traditional rendering of it, these three principles will bring human beings to true victory (Jv. *menang*), which is nothing other than overcoming the lower, illusionary or egotistical self, the *nafs* in the Islamic spiritual anthropology. These four principles are normally abbreviated as *neng-ning-nung-nang*, a combination of the last syllables of the four Javanese words.[37] In the Archbishop's message,

---

[35] Sindhunata, *Mengasih Maria*, pp. 89, 109–11; also Obed Asmoditomo and Agust Sunarto, *Hati Kudus Tuhan Yesus dari Ganjuran* (Yogyakarta, 2001), p. 42.

[36] Interview at the Ganjuran shrine, May 22, 2009.

[37] These four principles have been taken up by Ki Hajar Dewantara (d. 1959), an important Javanese thinker whose cultural and educational vision shares some affinity to

the *hanung* is defined as *dunung* that refers to the process of coming to terms with one's true place and mission in the world and one's spiritual state, and it ultimately points to the existential challenge to act out this awareness in daily life.

In my view, all the elements of this whole dynamic constitute the experiential side of the *mandala* framework at Ganjuran (Chapter 5). For, at least in its Buddhist context, the *mandala* functions, among other things, as an inner map for attaining peacefulness that comes from reintegration. On this point, Kate O'Brien writes: "As a devotee meditates on a *sadhana* [sacred designs and figures of divinities], the *mandala* becomes his map for reintegrating the various components of his currently turbulent and misguided psyche back to its primordial state of serene 'oneness,' i.e. its original divinity."[38]

Understood in this framework, the shrine becomes a true *mandala* in both physical and spiritual senses. It is a space in which the pilgrims find the right physical atmosphere and spatial context to reintegrate pieces of their lives, especially in the cases of pilgrims with real "broken" lives, generating an inner sense of peacefulness. This experience of peacefulness and integration, as well as the transforming power that comes with it, is one of the ways in which God is experienced as the source of power for pilgrims, recalling the words of Soegijapranata cited at the beginning of this chapter: "In times of troubles and humiliations, we become stronger because of Him despite the frailty of our human nature."

Indeed the words of Soegijapranata still ring true today as they did in 1939 when he uttered them. Many pilgrims today come to shrines driven by a sense of crisis, a sense of being helpless and so forth, and look for different kinds of favors and healings. However, even if their "problems" do not find immediate solutions during pilgrimage, many of them would come to a greater clarity about not only the nature of their problems but also what these problems reveal in terms of the larger context and direction of their lives. The experience of peacefulness during pilgrimage seems to put the pilgrims in a better term with their lives and to be more attuned to their inner or spiritual condition.[39] This way, they indeed become stronger.

The Tangibility of "Sacramental" Blessings

As I have argued, pilgrimage tradition among Catholics in south central Java is governed by a framework of devotion that makes the pilgrimage experience deeply spiritual yet also very sensuous and tangible. So, the spiritual blessing of

---

that of Fr. van Lith, as the core for the indigenous educational system that he founded in 1922 in Yogyakarta, the Taman Siswa. See Ki Priyo Dwiarso, "Problem Solving ala Ki Hadjar Dewantara," *Kedaulatan Rakyat Daily*, April 3, 2008.

[38] O'Brien, *Sutasoma*, pp. 160–70.

[39] Cf. Sindhunata, *Mengasih Maria*, pp. 61, 80, 86, 89, etc.; Asmoditomo and Sunarto, *Hati Kudus*, pp. 43–5.

peacefulness is also related to the physical or material specificities of the shrines and the journey of pilgrimage. In fact, this is one of the most distinctive traits of pilgrimage and saints veneration in general. In the Sendangsono grotto and the Ganjuran shrine, for example, those pilgrims who prize the conduciveness of the shrine in terms of helping them cultivate their interior life to achieve peacefulness through silent prayers and meditations would still assign much meaning to the tangible things considered sacred in the shrines, such as the water, the flower petals, the vestments of the priest during procession, the statue of Christ the King, and so forth (see my description at the beginning of this chapter). During certain nights in the Ganjuran shrine, many pilgrims including young people would spend hours in spiritual exercises until the time comes for them to undertake the bath, believing that this brings the blessing of God. Curiously some Protestant pilgrims do all these things as well.

During the procession of the Holy Sacrament, toward the end of the first Friday Eucharistic celebration that includes a complete Sacred Heart ritual (Chapter 5), many pilgrims would try to touch the vestments worn by the presiding priest who holds the monstrance as he circumambulates the shrine-temple. So, in this ritual, the spiritual blessing is sought in ways that are sensory as well. Pilgrims jostled one another as they tried to get some share in the material or sensory embodiment of the blessing, as in the forms of flowers that have been blessed in the rituals through the sprinkling of the sacred water, the *perwitasari*.

In the case of the Sendangsono grotto and the Ganjuran shrine, the sacredness of the water has been part of the identity formation of the shrine. At Sendangsono, from the very beginning, the water from the shrine spring has been perceived to have healing powers; and at times, this cure would lead people to the Church.[40] The spring at the Ganjuran shrine was discovered with the revival of the shrine in the late 1990s and has contributed to its renewed popularity, including among Muslim pilgrims. The custom of ritual bathing is a rather common feature at Islamic shrines in Java.[41] Catholic pilgrims also bring this water to their interested Muslim friends and neighbors. Stories about the cures of Muslims through this water circulate rather widely among pilgrims at the Ganjuran shrine and the Sendangsono grotto.

Without being associated with any miraculous or healing power, the hybrid Javano-Catholic architecture and statuaries of the Ganjuran shrine also hold a particular appeal, mainly for certain type of pilgrims who have more exposure to, or admiration for, the Hindu past of Java. For these pilgrims, apart from its aesthetic

---

[40] Fr. Prennthaler reported that a certain Javanese woman by the name of *Mbok* Kramadimeja was totally healed from her putrid mouth due to the powers of the water of the grotto. She had vowed that if she were cured, she would seek baptism. She indeed did this shortly after the healing. See his letter of March 9, 1930; *Brieven*, p. 185.

[41] For example, the bathing rite at the shrine of Sunan Gunung Jati in Cirebon. See Inajati Romli et al., *Jejak Para Wali dan Ziarah Spiritual*, pp. 127–44. Night bathing is also an important part of the popular ritual at the royal mausoleum of Kotagedhe in Yogyakarta where two natural springs are found.

particularities, this architecture exudes a distinctive spiritual aura and serenity to the whole space, thus helping create the sense of sacredness of the space. Here, pilgrims use two important concepts to describe this quality, namely beauty and uniqueness. Quite a number of pilgrims at Ganjuran wrote on the guestbook that they were impressed by the particularity of the Ganjuran shrine's architectural style, something that can be expected from pilgrims who are also connoisseurs of Javanese culture. One of them, an expert in Javanese architecture, clearly assigned the "home"-like qualities of the shrine to its Hindu-Javanese architectural style.[42]

The Ganjuran shrine also attracts Hindu Balinese who come both because of the sacredness connected to the water and because of its Hindu-Javanese architecture.[43] These pilgrims consider their visit to this shrine as part of their *tirtha yatra*, a pilgrimage in quest for the holy water. They asked the Catholic priest of the shrine whether it was allowed for them to visit Jesus. In recognition of the shrine's sanctity but also to make it "their own," these Hindu pilgrims donated a yellow cloth that they normally use to mark their sacred temple to be placed around this Catholic shrine.[44] These two cases are quite natural. However, it is rather striking that some non-Javanese or non-Balinese pilgrims are also taken by the beauty and uniqueness of the architecture.[45]

Mainly due to its unique and beautiful architecture, the local government now promotes the Ganjuran shrine as a site of tourism. As I have argued, the hybrid architecture and religious arts at this shrine are not a bastardization of the originals, mainly since its religious character is retained. Here again, the quality of arts should be understood mainly in the framework of the religious categories of devotion, connectedness and communion between the pilgrims and the shrine. For this reason, the beauty of the shrine and its statuary becomes distinctively deeper. A pilgrim describes his experience with the image of Our Lady of Lourdes at the Sendangsono grotto thus: "I was so mesmerized by this tall statue of Mary. Her countenance is filled with beauty, while her eyes exude an aura of peace and surrender. I was so exuberant and taken by all this and brought to my knees."[46] Another pilgrim at the Sendangsono grotto remarks on the statue: "I was staring intently at the statue of Our Lady. She was smiling at me and I responded

---

[42] Interview, Ganjuran shrine, May 25, 2009.

[43] It is common among Hindu Balinese to visit Hindu pilgrimage sites in Java, such as Tengger, the Cetho temple, the Prambanan temple, and so forth. To a certain degree, Balinese Hinduism still considers Javanese Hinduism as its ancestry.

[44] Interview with Fr. Gregorius Utomo, the Ganjuran shrine, June 8, 2009.

[45] I was struck by a group of Bataknese pilgrims from North Sumatra at the Ganjuran shrine who said they were so taken by the architecture of the shrine (Interview June 10, 2009). However, this Hindu-Javanese style also poses a kind of otherness. For instance, a number of young pilgrims had a hard time understanding why Jesus looked like a Hindu-Javanese king at the Ganjuran shrine. Ironically, one of these pilgrims was a Balinese Catholic. Interview at the Ganjuran shrine, June 15, 2009.

[46] Sindhunata, *Mengasih Maria*, p. 150.

accordingly, smiling back at her. Then I murmured a prayer: 'Mother, You are the anchor of my life; You listen to me and understand me.' Then, I took the holy water of the grotto and felt the freshness of the water all over my body like a new force of life."[47] Thus, for these pilgrims, the meanings of religious arts are to be found mainly in the dynamics of relationship between these arts and their personal and spiritual lives.

Unveiling of Self and Community

A crucial wider aspect of pilgrimage is the creation of community marked by communion with fellow pilgrims, with the Divine, and the cosmos as well. In the previous chapter, I have shown how a sense of wider community is created through the rituals of the Sacred Heart; a sense of communion with the cosmos through prayers of healing is also effected. Now, I delve into another aspect of this communion and community, namely the creation of a special bond between pilgrims as a result of the unveiling of self among them during pilgrimage.

At the Ganjuran shrine, this dynamic of unveiling of self and communal bonding would normally happen among pilgrims who stay overnight at the shrine on a regular basis, for example after the monthly mass of the first Friday. Many pilgrims of this type would know each other quite well due to frequent encounters, although other pilgrims would join as well. The topics of conversation range from mundane affairs to deep spiritual experiences. For instance, during a conversation with a group of pilgrims at this shrine, while we were enjoying the snacks after a rather long celebration of the Eucharist, suddenly a pilgrim exclaimed in Javanese: "*Gusti Yesus kuwi konsekuen, yen dhawuhi mlaku mesti yo maringi sangu!*" (The Lord Jesus is dependable; for, when he invites us to do the pilgrimage, he gives us the means to do it).

This man was a middle-aged Javanese pilgrim by the name of Pak Andi. Since the year 2000, he has fostered a personal habit of making a pilgrimage to this shrine every first Friday of the month from his hometown of Pati on the north coast of Java, roughly a hundred miles away. Pak Andi is a poor pilgrim with no permanent job, due to his partial disability from an accident. So many times he could not secure any financial provision two or three days before his monthly pilgrimage. However, it has happened many times as well that he would get the needed money just one day prior to the trip. This is why he could say that true pilgrimage is God's invitation and it is also He who makes it happen. He then shared his life struggle as well as his experience of coming to know the shrine to the whole group. His period of struggle began with his messy divorce. He also lost his job, but he was lucky when his brother took him in. Then he had an accident that makes it even harder for him to find a job. He fell down from a mango tree in a very mysterious way. For, instead of falling down directly on the ground below the tree, he was

---

[47] Ibid., p. 91.

brought to the side, to the softer ground. His hip was injured quite severely, but he was thankful he did not die. He was sure that it was Jesus who saved him. When he decided to visit the Ganjuran shrine for healing, a miraculous thing did happen. For he did not feel the pain at all during the long (six hours) and rather gruesome bus trip from his hometown to the shrine. He took it as a providential sign from God. However, when he got off the bus at the last intersection leading to the shrine, he was too proud and sure of himself that God taught him a lesson. He became paralyzed and could not even get to the motorbike of a young man who offered him a ride to the shrine. He got the lesson, and he keeps coming to the shrine every month. Ever since he started coming to this shrine, the healing process has been steady. He is healed step by step, and has abandoned all medical treatment. When shared, stories like this would of course make the bonding between pilgrims stronger. It is a sign of a sincere self-unveiling. It could also deepen the pilgrimage experience of fellow pilgrims because it could well serve as an avenue of God's communication.

In connection to this creation of a sense of community, shrines like Sendangsono and Ganjuran are favorite places among Catholic youth for building up a deeper sense of friendship and group-identity. Typically, they would come as a group, and their pilgrimage consists of a combination of traditional features of Catholic pilgrimage such as praying the Stations of the Cross and the rosary and more contemporary group-oriented activities such as simple games, faith sharing, conversations about their associations, and so forth. In this sense, shrines help create communities because the pilgrimage strengthens the bonds between the group members or pilgrims. Thus the sense of community being forged here is very much group oriented, though not necessarily in the Turnerian sense of *communitas* that is liminal in nature and assumes some suspension of larger societal structures.[48]

This feature is also revealing of the pattern of pilgrimage among the youth. Although many of them would have learned the art of making pilgrimage the first time through their parents, networks of close friends are also instrumental in the maintenance of this tradition. Young pilgrims learn about certain shrines from their friends and would then visit those shrines together. Yogyakarta is the largest college town in Indonesia, and many students from other cities and islands flock to this town to get their education. A good number of Catholic students from other provinces would then learn about various pilgrimage sites in this area through networks of friends. Many Catholic students of Chinese descent from Borneo, for example, would also learn the specificities of the Javano-Catholic culture of devotion and come to be part of this culture during their studies. The same is true with regard to Catholic students from other ethnic groups.

In general, the bonds among these young pilgrims do indeed get strengthened during pilgrimage. This kind of pilgrimage also becomes distinctive because it is situated in the day-to-day dynamics of their lives as a group. Common experience in terms of grappling with the various challenges of being students as well as

---

[48] Victor and Edith Turner, *Image and Pilgrimage in Christian Culture*, p. 250.

trying to chart their futures beyond college put them in a similar situation. So it is natural that they come up with similar ways to deal with these common challenges. Pilgrimage is one of these ways. In some cases, Protestant students would also join their Catholic friends on their pilgrimage due to the power of this bonding and networks of friends. Furthermore, youth activities in the shrine often feature close collaboration with Muslim students.

Pilgrimage Experience and the Question of the "Other"

What all of the four previous sections of this chapter have demonstrated, among others, is that pilgrimage among Catholics in south central Java makes a rich tapestry of personal and communal devotion. It is indeed very alive and thriving, attracting more and more pilgrims from all walks of life. Thus one can understand why the practice of pilgrimage could well serve as an important milieu for the identity formation of the pilgrims and their communities. In what follows I will discuss how a particular question of alterity occurs in the pilgrimage practice at these shrines, such as how Catholic pilgrims regard the religious "other" at the shrine and beyond, and how the pilgrims of other religious traditions experience their own pilgrimages at these Catholic shrines.

The first thing to note here is that for Javanese Catholic pilgrims today, pilgrimage tends to be understood simply as part of their identity and practice as Catholics, not in comparison with or opposition to other Christians. It is extremely rare that Catholic pilgrims in Java would be motivated by religious debate about the veneration of saints or Marian veneration with local Protestants or Muslims.[49] They would just do it because it is the habit of devotion that has become an essential part of what makes them truly Catholic. This is why they would say there would be something missing and regretful when they failed to do that periodically, especially during the Marian months of May and October. This way, pilgrimage is intimately connected to religious identity, although not always in a conscious manner. Here, the logic is not so much that they come to terms specifically with their Catholic identity during pilgrimage, but rather it is their Catholic identity—built through this habit of devotion from generation to generation and personal participation in that tradition—that leads them to do the pilgrimage.

More than an absence of religious rivalry, a rather conscious spirit of openness and inclusion of the other has become part of the self-understanding of the Catholic shrines in south central Java. I have demonstrated how this element is

---

[49] Occasional and minor conflicts did occur between a Marian shrine and its Muslim neighbors, for example at the Marian grotto of Marganingsih in Tembayat. The shrine is located in a very close proximity to the tomb of Sunan Pandanarang. During its initial stages, tension with the Muslim neighbors flared up and the statues of Mary kept being stolen from the shrine. However, there was no sign that Catholic pilgrimage at this shrine was motivated by this conflict.

at work in terms of history, architecture, and rituals of the shrines in the previous chapters. With regard to the presence of pilgrims of other faiths, the same pattern occurs. The following story is a rather moving account of a Muslim woman who was touched by the Divine grace at the Sacred Heart shrine of Ganjuran. Mgr. Pujasumarta, the then vicar general of the Archdiocese of Semarang, told this story to thousands of Catholic pilgrims at the annual festival of the Sacred Heart of Jesus in 2007.[50] The point he was trying to get across was the universality and inclusiveness of the grace of the Sacred Heart.

The story itself runs as follows. Deeply afflicted by the fact that her husband just took a second wife, a certain Muslim woman was thinking of taking her own life by jumping off a bridge into the Progo River, a few miles away from the shrine of Ganjuran. She did not execute her suicidal thought only on account of her love for her son, who she felt was calling her home all the time. Although she was a Muslim, this woman has heard about the Sacred Heart shrine from her friends. And then, moved by an inner inspiration, she came to pay a visit to this shrine and felt something different, some kind of peacefulness and assurance. She took the water from the temple, lingered for a while in the temple premises, and came into contact with the priest who was ready to offer help. Eventually the priest helped her to acquire a sewing machine. For her and her son, this sewing machine became a source of new life. The fact that such a story was told at the annual festival of the Sacred Heart reveals that the presence of the "other" has been embraced as a significant part of the identity of the shrine and its community.

Like their Catholic counterparts, non-Catholic pilgrims come to these shrines for diverse reasons. Various elements such as personal devotion and faith (in the sense of personal history of connectedness to God that might or might not include Jesus or Mary), the search for peacefulness and particular blessings, networks of friends and family members and so forth, might be involved in a constellation that is subject to change and would differ from pilgrim to pilgrim. In this regard, a few examples might be in order.

Mbah Iman Suwongso, for example, is a simple and elderly Javanese food peddler who used to go to the Sendangsono grotto every month. She is a Muslim, albeit perhaps nominally, and frames her habit of pilgrimage in terms of *nyekar*, namely, visiting the tombs of deceased ancestors and paradigmatic figures. As mentioned earlier, this framework is rather common among the older generation of Javanese across religious boundaries. But her neighbors accused her of looking for a talismanic source (Jv. *cekelan*) for the success of her business. However she herself understands the practice and the whole experience in terms of peacefulness (I. *ketenangan hidup*) that came from surrendering (Jv. *pasrah*) all the struggle and suffering of life to God through Mary. She explained her conviction in simple terms thus: "With *Dewi Maria* [Mary], I come to experience true peace and calmness; so, what is the point of messing around with your life?" Furthermore, she also

---

[50] After briefly serving as the bishop of the diocese of Bandung, West Java, in 2009, Mgr. Pujasumarta was appointed Archbishop of Semarang in 2010.

anchored her practice in the conviction of the universality of God's blessing for those who are sincere: "I believe that God, the Author of life, is always pleased with those who are sincere and well-meaning."[51] As a Javanese Muslim, she would pray her own way at the shrine. She believes in the relative sacredness of holy things associated with Mary, such as the water, rosary, statues, and so forth. So, this elderly woman has a very personal and rather complex reasoning for her habit of making pilgrimage to a Marian shrine, a reasoning that involves devotion, personal faith conviction with regard to the nature of God and His mercy, as well as personal experience in terms of the propriety of her visit to Mary in relation to her own life.

Other cases would highlight other dimensions. A Muslim pilgrim who also has a personal habit of visiting the tombs of the Muslim saints in Java (the *Wali Songo*) would visit the Sendangsono shrine rather regularly, at times triggered by inner stirrings (Jv. *wisik*) that his wife received. Thus his visit has nothing to do with a sense of desperation for help. He said he liked visiting sacred places that would enhance his spiritual life. Interestingly, he called Mary "*Eyang Putri Maria*" (literally means Mary, the Grandmother), implying that Mary belongs to the category of pious ancestor. He kept his Muslim canonical prayers during his visit. Ironically, during one of his pilgrimages to this shrine, his wife received an inner omen that his Catholic sister should not come directly to the grotto due to her improper spiritual state, while he and his wife (both Muslim) were allowed to come closer.[52] The whole visit was so memorable because he experienced a profound peace and gratitude. In fact his prayers in the grotto were those of gratitude to God, not to Mary although he was aware of her presence and role. He argued that true pilgrimage to Mary has to be based on sincerity and purity of intention (Ar. *ikhlas*). Thus, like the elderly woman above, this pilgrim emphasizes peacefulness as a foundational blessing of pilgrimage as well as the role of spiritual sincerity. As a Javanese, he also seems to understand his pilgrimage to Mary in terms of *nyekar*. The element of family network in his case is also apparent. In many other cases, it is at times hard to really pinpoint the exact motivation of these pilgrims, for example a group of Muslims who visited a Marian shrine of Kerep, Ambarawa, north central Java, upon their arrival from their canonical pilgrimage to Mecca.

In general, the search for peacefulness and blessings seems to be one of the major motivations of the non-Catholic pilgrims, due to its theological neutrality. A Mennonite-Protestant university student, for example, would go up with so much ease to the inner chamber of the Ganjuran temple and prayed there in front of the Hindu-Javanese styled statue of the Sacred Heart of Jesus. She did not have any problem with the appearance of the statue, knowing that it was Jesus, and she experienced so much peace there. Framing her pilgrimage as a prayerful and meditative moment (I. *renungan*), she prized the serenity and solitude at this

---

[51] Sindhunata, *Mengasih Maria*, p. 80.
[52] Ibid., pp. 117–19.

shrine. This same pattern seems to be at work among Protestant pilgrims at the shrine of Our Lady of Annai Velankanni, in the outskirt of Medan, north Sumatra.[53]

In terms of rituals, these pilgrims of other faiths are given freedom to do their own during their visits to these Catholic shrines. At Ganjuran, some Chinese Buddhists or Confucians would perform their distinctive ritual gestures of homage in front of the temple without inhibition. While refraining from going into the inner sanctum of the shrine, Muslim pilgrims would go to the water area to do a kind of ablution and then take some water with them as they move to the courtyard of the shrine for personal prayers. In general, this atmosphere is in line with the principle adopted by the shrine: while every pilgrim is entitled to express his personal relationship with God in ways that he deems appropriate, mutual respect and sensitivity should be kept in mind.[54]

This institutional openness on the part of the shrine toward the other is without doubt an expression of the same standpoint on the part of most of the Catholic pilgrims themselves. The long history of peaceful interaction between different religious communities in south central Java might have served as a crucial factor while the role of the Javanese culture as a unifying factor should not be overlooked either. For, as I have shown in many instances throughout this book, Javaneseness becomes an important layer of common identity among Javanese Muslims as well as Javanese Catholics. The Javanese cultural emphases on communal, cosmic and personal harmony, moral refinement, cultivation of inner spirituality, asceticism, and so forth have definitely helped lay the ground for more meaningful engagement with all forms of otherness, religious and otherwise. This being said, I would also argue that in the context of pilgrimage experience, the overwhelming sense of peacefulness and integration that I have discussed in the previous sections plays its role as well in the formation of a favorable inner disposition of the pilgrims *vis-à-vis* the religious other.

An interesting case in point is the Mausoleum of Muntilan where the memory of the slain priest, Fr. Sanjaya, is pivotal. As discussed earlier, Fr. Sanjaya was murdered by a Muslim mob during the tumultuous period of confrontation between the Indonesian nationalist forces and the Dutch military (1948) following the independence of the Indonesian Republic. Thus, to a certain degree, this shrine commemorates a darker period in the relationship between the local Catholic community and its Muslim neighbors. However, there is a remarkable absence of bitterness or hard feelings on the part of Catholic pilgrims at this shrine toward the Muslims. "God has a unique plan for every one of us; it was ultimately God who was behind what Father Sanjaya had to endure," explained Mr. Hardono (45 years old),

---

[53] North Sumatra is a rather heavily Protestant area. Thus, it is not surprising that this major Marian shrine in the Catholic Archdiocese of Medan is frequented by many Protestant pilgrims, mostly students. As reflected in the contents and styles of their prayers that they left at the shrine, they would seek special blessings from God through Jesus, without having to mention the role of Mary in this economy of Divine grace.

[54] See the shrine's brochure on rituals, *Doa-doa untuk Ziarah di Ganjuran*, p. 12.

an avid pilgrim to the mausoleum of Muntilan. That is why he never harbored any hard feeling against the Muslims. He even refused to specifically mention that it was a Muslim mob that killed Fr. Sanjaya, saying only that there was a little segment in the neighborhood who did not like the Church.[55] Mr. Subandi (50 years old), another Javanese pilgrim, said he was well aware that Fr. Sanjaya was murdered by a Muslim mob, but he forgave them for their violence. "They did not exactly know what they did, and they are God's children too," he explained his reasoning with much confidence. Furthermore, he added, the motive might have been political, although he was sure that they also hated the Catholic mission there for religious reasons.[56]

The way these two Javanese pilgrims make sense of history is rather interesting, for they put it in the framework of the mystery or otherness of God. As noted earlier, surrender to the mystery of God's will is a common spiritual experience during pilgrimage. In the same framework, the question of the existence of different religions could be engaged as well. The difference that pilgrimage experience makes in this regard is that this popular theology of religions is ultimately placed within the pilgrims' own struggle in understanding their own lives, finding the directions, meanings, and integration in a long process of discernment that involves God in different forms and degrees, in the continuum of their lives. Furthermore, in light of the exclusive elements in the foundational stories of the Catholic shrines under study, this absence of triumphalism and bitterness on the part of the present day Javano-Catholic community can be striking.

Concluding Remarks

During the liturgy of the consecration of the Sacred Heart shrine at Ganjuran in 1930, the Jesuit Father Henricus van Driessche led a prayer that still seems quite insightful. The final part of his consecration prayer runs as follows:

> God, we pray that You deign to pour your love and grace to all of us, those of us who have faith in You and those who have not come to the faith (Jv. *kapir*), so that eventually all the people of Java would belong to the same stall (Jv. *sakandang*), joyfully praising You, the mighty King Jesus Christ, the Lord of all nations, and the eternal Protector of the Java mission. Amen.[57]

In light of the ways in which this shrine has been developing in the last decade or so, one might pose a question as to whether this prayer has already been granted. In many ways, it surely has. For, the temple-shrine of Ganjuran has become one "stable" (Jv. *kandhang*) where all sorts of sheep are gathered. In their own ways,

---

[55] Interview, Muntilan mausoleum, May 29, 2009.
[56] Interview, Ganjuran shrine, May 25, 2009.
[57] *ST*, February 14, 1930; also Steenbrink, *Catholics in Indonesia*, vol. 2, p. 494.

the pilgrims of other faiths also praise God in response to their encounter with Him at the shrine. In certain cases, this experience possesses some Christian overtone in the inclusion of Jesus and Mary, although it very rarely results in baptism.[58] In the manners that are particularly appealing to the religio-cultural sensibilities of the current Javano-Catholic community in south central Java, the kingship of Christ is becoming a reality at the shrine of Ganjuran, most obviously through the outpouring mercy of the Sacred Heart. This development can be taken as the realization of the foundational message of the shrine as a vehicle of God's blessing to all.[59]

Thus one might even suggest that the prayer of consecration has been granted in all the Catholic shrines in south central Java, not just the Sacred Heart shrine. What is crucial to note here is the continuous communal discernment and hermeneutics of the community, their tireless effort to understand their identity and mission for all their contemporaries. In the spirit of *resourcement* and creative fidelity, they have tried to design effective solutions to the tensions embedded in the foundations of these shrines. This is the hermeneutic of communion that enables them to negotiate their Javano-Catholic identity in a way that takes seriously not only the trace but also the continued presence and significance of the other. And, as this chapter has shown, the fruitfulness of this hermeneutic is confirmed as well by the actual experience of pilgrims from other religious traditions.

Due to its intensity, liveliness and popular participation, this hermeneutic of communion results in the creation of a rather distinctive "culture" around the shrines. Reporting on the consecration of the Ganjuran shrine, the Javanese Catholic newspaper *Swara-Tama* prophetically wrote that this shrine would serve as a symbol of a distinctive "Christian culture" (D. *Christelijk beschaving*).[60] In this respect, the development of the shrines discussed previously represents the birth of this distinctive culture, a Christian culture that is also truly Javanese (or Indonesian) because of its response to the real needs and spiritual aspirations of the Javanese or Indonesian society.

---

[58] A telling example here is the experience of a Muslim woman who claimed to have a series of encounters with Jesus in the context of pilgrimage to this shrine and beyond. She said that Jesus wanted her to remain a Muslim with a special devotedness to him. Interview, June 6, 2009.

[59] *ST*, February 14, 1930.

[60] *ST*, February 14, 1930.

PART III
Comparative Perspective

Chapter 7
A Double Visiting: Comparative Insights on Muslim and Catholic Pilgrimage Practices in Java

> If we are to read the texts together, our reading has to take on the characteristics of an agile dance, as the texts are made to defer to one another, each read for a moment before the other steps again into the foreground.
>
> Francis X. Clooney, *Beyond Compare*[1]

This chapter is entitled "a double visiting" for two reasons. Firstly, it is reflective of the essence as well as the method of my comparative theological framework in this book, in which I move back and forth between my own tradition of Catholic Christianity and the tradition I visit, Islam. In line with the nature of the new comparative theology as a theological learning process done through a close study of the religious other, this dynamic of double visiting turns into a real religious pilgrimage to God and His saints where on various levels I learn more about God, my own self, and my religious tradition, from the richness of the Muslim tradition as it is found in the pilgrimage practice in Java. My pilgrimage as a movement of double visiting has provided me with these dynamics of multi-layered learning through what is familiar (identity) and what is other (alterity), as well as the deeper connections between the two.

Secondly, since this book is conceived as a very modest experiment in the new comparative theology, I intentionally use the term "double visiting" also as a way to situate this book within the discourse of this discipline of new comparative theology as proposed by Francis Clooney, James Fredericks, and others.[2] I find this comparative theological framework highly appropriate to shed light on the major dynamics of the Catholic and Muslim pilgrimage traditions precisely because of its attentiveness to the properly religious and theological dimensions of the subject matter. It strives to illuminate theological dimensions of one's home tradition through comparative journey to other religious tradition(s). In this process, the comparativist-cum-pilgrim pays extended and multiple visits to the religious world of the other and then returns home more refreshed both in terms of spiritual

---

[1] Francis Clooney, *Beyond Compare*, pp. 26–7.
[2] See especially Francis Clooney, *Comparative Theology* (2010) and *Beyond Compare* (2009); Fredericks, *Buddhists and Christians* (2004).

affect and theological understanding.[3] In this respect, Clooney's image of agile dance (quoted above) is particularly insightful. In a way, this is a highly particular example of my argument on the propriety of pilgrimage as a remarkably fruitful metaphor for comparative theology that I have made elsewhere.[4]

In the context of the new comparative theology, this double reading and visiting is also intentionally embraced as a milieu for a cross-fertilization by which a comparative theology deeply rooted in one tradition becomes a theology indebted to one or more other theologies as well.[5] As an experiment in comparative theology, this book is aimed at bringing together the Javano-Muslim (Part I) and Javano-Catholic (Part II) pilgrimage practices, understood as a particular mode of piety and devotion founded on the larger framework of the Catholic and Islamic traditions.

So, in what follows I will pursue a properly comparative act, namely, identifying the similarities—and to a lesser degree, differences—between the Muslim and Catholic traditions of pilgrimage as it is practiced in south central Java. These similarities constitute the major ways in which the Islamic and Catholic pilgrimage traditions in south central Java intersect, coalesce, and illuminate each other. One can say that these two pilgrimage traditions have been involved in an agile dance together. Through these similarities the various forms and structures of interplays between these two traditions are represented. So my analysis will be focused on identifying the shared religious, cultural, and theological structures and logic of these pilgrimage traditions, including their role in the identity formation of the respective community, as well as the contents, such as the religious experience of the pilgrims.[6]

To serve this purpose, this chapter is divided into five sections. I will begin by making some observation on the existence and role of a shared spiritual milieu and a common culture of devotion in south central Java (1), as well as the particular role of the Javanese culture as the common bond (2) in these dynamics of shared life and blessings. I consider this reality of shared life as foundational because it serves as the cultural and existential context and basis for the different forms of intersections between Muslim and Catholic pilgrimage practices. By the same dynamic, I shall show as well how the two communities have come to embrace similar frameworks in appropriating the Javanese culture into their religious sensibility and traditions. I will then discuss three major points of similarity between the two pilgrimage traditions, namely, the role of saints and paradigmatic figures as ancestors (3), the nature of pilgrimage as an occasion for spiritual renewal (4), and the deeply sacramental worldview that lies at the heart of these pilgrimage traditions (5).

---

[3] Clooney, *Beyond Compare*, p. 186; also Fredericks, *Buddhist and Christians*, p. 95.

[4] See my chapter "Comparative Theology: Between Identity and Alterity," in Francis Clooney (ed.), *The New Comparative Theology*, pp. 1–20.

[5] Clooney, *Comparative Theology*, p. 38.

[6] Cf. Clooney, *Hindu God, Christian God* (Oxford, 2001), p. 167.

Shared Spiritual Milieu, Common Culture of Devotion

The first thing to notice about Muslim and Catholic pilgrimage practices in south central Java is the more fundamental framework of communion between the two communities. Due to the presence and proximities of its multitude of sacred shrines, including the ones under study here, south central Java forms a sacred space filled with spiritual energies emanating from the constancy of the prayers, the devotions, and the sacred rituals of the people and pilgrims. On a certain level, what is born in this milieu of communion is an inclusive *mandala*, understood simply as a space, both internal and external, of complex encounters with God, self, and the other. Even before looking more closely into the more direct interactions and encounters between the two pilgrimage practices, the level of energy that is there in this *mandala* is rather remarkable. It is mostly on Thursday night (the eve of Friday) that this energy of devotion can be seen in its most remarkable manifestation (Chapters 3 and 6). For during this night, shrines of all kinds in this area are packed with pilgrims, many of whom would stay well until the wee hours at the shrines. It is the night of devotion for all, a night filled with *berkah* (Ar. *baraka*), the blessings of God for all.

As Map 3 shows, many of these shrines are located outside the two major royal cities in the area, Yogyakarta and Surakarta. However, during this night, these shrines turn into small "cities" that shine in the darkness, cities that break the silence of the night by their unending praises and songs to God. Even on rainy and cold nights, pilgrims still flock to these shrines. This geographical or physical proximity of these diverse shrines should be taken into account in a comparative theological study like this one. For, in different ways and on various levels, that proximity can serve as a deeper foundation for more explicit encounters between pilgrims of different faith traditions. In the case of south central Java, it is definitely not a mere coincidence that almost each major Marian shrine has its Muslim counterpart nearby, and *vice versa*.[7] The history behind this proximity has not always been marked by amicable intention and friendly interactions, as the foundational narrative of the Marian shrine of Sendangsono reveals (Chapter 4). However, generally speaking, this spatial proximity of Muslim and Catholic shrines comes to be seen as a sign of mutual respect, and at times it even makes possible a closer collaboration between the two communities. Through long-term communal discernment and dynamics, the communities are

---

[7] As Map 3 shows, the Sendangsono Marian shrine and the mausoleum of Muntilan share physical proximity with the Muslim shrine of Raden Santri at Gunungpring; while the Sacred Heart shrine of Ganjuran is not far from the tomb of Mawlana Maghribi and other Javanist sacred sites in the Parangtritis area, the south coast of Yogyakarta. The shrine of Tembayat is just a few hundred meters away from the Marian shrine of Marganingsih. In the north of Yogyakarta, the origin of the Marian grotto of Our Lady of Perpetual Sorrow (Jv. *Ibu Risang Sungkawa*) in Pakem is related also to the shrine of Jumadil al-Kubra on the hill of Turgo.

able to reinterpret these tensions and ambiguities through a complex and more inclusive framework of religio-cultural hermeneutics. For one thing, the fact that the respective communities decided not to put a physical and institutional barrier between these diverse shrines reveals their real and enduring quality as a common and inclusive space of encounter.

In this regard, it is insightful to examine the significance of the designation of this space in south central Java as a *mandala*. As examined in Chapter 1, the framework of *mandala* is used as the sacred cosmology of the Mataram court, the common ancestral kingdom of the present day sultanates of Yogyakarta and Surakarta. In this context, *mandala* is a sacred space marked by sacred poles and figures.[8] In turn, this sacred cosmology has a profound impact on the placement of the pilgrimage sites. That is why most of these shrines are clustered in the center (the city of Yogyakarta), in the north pole of Mount Merapi, as well as in the southern pole of the Parangtritis coast (Map 3). For many traditional Javanese pilgrims, these sacred figures and the locations of the shrines naturally bring about a stronger sense of supernatural presence, precisely because they turn this area into a highly charged milieu.

As discussed in Chapter 6, the community of the Sacred Heart Shrine at Ganjuran also intentionally employs this language of inclusive sacred milieu of *mandala* to capture the complex spatial and spiritual dynamics of the encounters between pilgrims and God. Here the framework of *mandala* is used as a particular way of envisioning the complex spiritual import of a place due to the presence of God, the blessings and memory of the righteous and paradigmatic figures or saints, as well as the spiritual effects of the continuing encounters between pilgrims and God in the site. In the story of the Sacred Heart shrine at Ganjuran, the idea of placing the shrine in the sacred cosmology of the Javano-Islamic kingdom of Mataram is quite foundational. It is intimately connected as well to the idea of Josef Schmutzer, the shrine's founder, to revivify the sacredness of the area through Christian spiritual presence (Chapter 5). Revivication is of course qualitatively different from replacement. For in this framework, instead of simply replacing the other completely, Christianity revivifies the *mandala* through its spiritual presence, a long and complex religio-cultural process made possible through different ways, such as the celebrations of the sacraments, individual and communal prayer sessions, spiritual devotion, the intentions and experience of the pilgrims, both Catholics and others, discernments of the community, reception by the wider Javanese community, and so forth.

Highly crucial in this regard as well is the idea of history as collective memorialization of the sacred past that includes paradigmatic (founding) figures, events, and places. In the case of south central Java, the role of sacred history of the community in the making of sacred sites could not be overemphasized. In many cases among both Javanese Muslims and Catholics, a particular space becomes sacred because it corresponds intimately to the sacred history of the

---

[8] Woodward, *Islam in Java*, p. 199.

community. In this framework, the significance of such a space surpasses its mere physicality since it has accumulated so much communal religio-cultural meaning. For it has become an important means for the wellbeing of the whole community. In this dynamic, pilgrimage is basically an act of making present the sacred history of the community. As examined in Chapters 1 and 4, pilgrimage among Muslims and Catholics in south central Java is practiced as a personal and communal participation in this dynamic of sacred space and sacred history as memory. And since the two communities share some common history by virtue of their Javanese identity, there is a natural predisposition toward shared shrines, or simply toward understanding their land as a very special place, a spiritual milieu, a *mandala*.

The accumulation of spiritual energy in the sacred places is, in my view, significant in terms of the cosmic framework of pilgrimage experience. Many pilgrims testify that they are in heightened contact with the concentration of cosmic energy and the energy of Love at the shrine during their pilgrimages (Chapters 3 and 6). This kind of spatial openness to one another that effects greater spiritual presence can be especially appreciated when compared to the exact opposite, something that could well happen, as contemporary cases in the Holy Land testify.

In this respect, the case of the pilgrimage traditions among Muslims and Catholics in south central Java presents itself as a rather specific case of an overwhelming sense of spiritual and religio-cultural unity, given the mutual sharing and communion in all these diverse movements of devotion in different shrines or sacred spaces. Equipped with the right ears, as many pilgrims are, one can listen to these diverse movements forming a beautiful symphony. Beneath all the differences that are still clearly visible and intentionally maintained to be so, there is a lead melody of praise to the same God, of sincere devotion, of the underlying desire for communion and blessings that at times take on a cosmic characteristic.

To a certain degree and on a deeper level, these prayers and devotions intersect in ways pilgrims themselves do not always know or anticipate. This is not only because they pray at exactly the same time, but also because they might end up praying for one another, due to the intersecting webs of familial relationships as well as the overlapping networks of friendships that they share. Thus, the divine blessings that these pilgrims receive might have rippling effects on the larger society, well beyond the formal boundaries of any religious communities.

Javanese Culture as the Common Bond

In Parts I and II, I have shown how pilgrimage tradition as a whole—the shrines, the saints, the rituals, communal activities, and so forth—has become a privileged milieu in which a distinctively hybrid religio-cultural identity formation and negotiation is forged among Javanese Muslims and Catholics. In this dynamic, Javanese culture has served as an important unifying force between the two communities. Thus, what these Muslim and Catholic shrines and the pilgrimage practices reflect is the particular dynamics of Islamization and the formation of

Catholic community in south central Java. Throughout this book, I present this identity formation as complex religio-cultural negotiations and interactions between different entities such as Islam and Christianity together with the cultures and societies of those who bring these religions to Java on the one hand, and the religio-cultural realities and peoples of Java, on the other. In both Islamic and Catholic contexts, this process is far more complex than simply a transplantation of foreign religious practices and ideas. Furthermore, it is crucial to note that this process has been guided largely by the principle of communion and continuity. However, both communities apply this principle rather selectively through complex cultural and communal discernment over a long period of time.

Again, Javanese culture has played a crucial role in these identity formations around shrines and pilgrimage traditions. Due to the influence of the Javanese culture, Muslims and Catholics in south central Java come to have many things in common that render various forms of encounters at the shrines not only possible, but also natural, desirable, and more intimate. Precisely in this kind of context, one can see the role of the Javanese culture as a *mandala*, as a unifying religio-cultural force and a common religio-cultural milieu for mutual engagement between the two religious communities. In light of the sacred geography of south central Java mentioned earlier, this category of cultural *mandala* explains how this common vision of sacred geography comes to be concretely interpreted and enacted through a particular localized understanding of history, rituals, architecture, and so forth. In particular, this religio-cultural *mandala* provides a common framework for the hybrid Javano-Islamic and Javano-Catholic identity formations among pilgrims and their communities.

Along this line of thought, I have attempted to illustrate in different ways how Javanese, Indic, Arab/Persianate, and European religio-cultural traditions—which sometimes come to be associated more closely with the idea of indigenousness, Hinduism, Islam, and Christianity respectively—have encountered one another in the context of pilgrimage traditions and beyond. In the case of both the Muslim and Catholic communities in Java, the dynamics of encounter have been governed by the principle of appropriating the local Javanese culture, and this process occurs in all its ambiguities and complexities, especially in the earlier stage. For example, the early attempt of the Dutch Jesuit missionaries to embrace the so-called "Javanese culture," for all its noble effort at appropriating the culture of the natives, still smacked of a colonial project of "othering" or minimizing the Islamic presence; while the determination of the first Javanese Catholic intellectuals to forge a hybrid identity—that is, to become truly Javanese and truly Catholic—was not completely freed from ambiguity either (Chapter 4). For one thing, they were faced with a delicate and complex task of navigating their way into the intricate connections between religion and culture amid ongoing nationalistic political struggles. While they readily celebrated the hybridity of Javanese and Western cultures, they needed much more time to work out the proper relationship between their Catholicism and the traditional Javanese religious or spiritual traditions that have been under the influence of Hinduism, Buddhism, and Islam. On the Islamic side, the *wali*s and the Javano-Islamic courts of Yogyakarta and Surakarta in preceding centuries had been negotiating the same process of appropriation that was also marked by tensions over much longer historical continuum.

However, the transformation effected by this religio-cultural process is quite real, despite or precisely due to these complex ambiguities and tensions. It is obvious that all parties involved have undergone a certain degree of transformation. The exact degree of this transformation might run the whole gamut and varies greatly from period to period, and is always open to further questions or negotiations. But, as the previous chapters have hopefully demonstrated, one can say that just as the practice of Islam in south central Java has been "Javanized" in a complex and subtle manner, so has the practice of Catholicism. It is based on this reality of transformation that one can talk about the realities of "Javano-Islamic" and "Javano-Catholic" identities. As I have attempted to show, these Javanese are arguably authentic Muslims and Catholics. However, they practice Islam and Catholicism respectively, to a large degree, through the lens of a shared Javanese religio-cultural sensibility, a rather deep layer in their selves.

In the context of south central Java, this religio-cultural framework is highly influenced and perpetuated by the Mataram court, represented at present mainly by the sultanates of Yogyakarta and Surakarta, particularly in terms of traditional rituals and symbolism. And, in many respects, this practice of Islam is in line with the spirit of the traditionalist Nahdlatul Ulama, especially in terms of the paradigmatic role of the *wali*s or saints, the master-student relationship, the practice of mysticism, the devotional and ritual treatment of the dead, and so forth. One of my principal arguments throughout this book is that the presence of the Javanese culture has become particularly and dramatically visible in the whole pilgrimage tradition, including its religio-spiritual framework, its symbolic and material culture (distinctive rituals and architectures), and its communal significance.

On the fundamental level of spiritual experience, the Javanese category of *rasa* comes to be crucial in the ways in which many Javanese pilgrims of all religious persuasions come to cultivate their spiritual life. As illustrated earlier, *rasa* is the inner compass that many Javanese pilgrims naturally use to gauge the quality of the presence of God and the saints, the deeper reality of divine blessings, as well as the corresponding discernment that ensues from this experience (Chapters 3 and 6). In other words, *rasa* is an inner instrument and realm of communion; it is an experience of a deep and personal communion of the heart with its Lord. More importantly perhaps, *rasa* has served as a marker for a distinctively Javanese way of communing with God and the true self. Due to its crucial role, *rasa* is also used in the ongoing discernment to obtain the true blessings of pilgrimage, namely fundamental peacefulness (Jv. *tentrem*) and integral wellbeing (Jv. *slamet*).

Furthermore, in order to obtain peacefulness and wellbeing, pilgrimage in the two traditions comes to be understood and practiced in the Javanese framework of *laku* or *tirakat*, that is, an intense period of spiritual cultivation and discernment, done in tandem with the necessary process of ascetic purification of the self. In this regard, the category of *rasa* presents itself as a profoundly inclusive vision, due to its experiential and foundational character. Through the cultivation of *rasa*, Javanese pilgrims come to be in touch with the Divine in many sacred sites across religious boundaries. In this respect, the exclusive dimension of religious identity has to be confronted with a more pervasive reality of common spiritual experience and communion. This results in not only a vision of inclusivity but also an experience of communing with God through diverse means and in different locations that might include the religious other. The cultivation of *rasa* is foundational because it deepens the spiritual experience of Javanese Muslim and Catholics as they do their respective traditional spiritual practices that, at least on the surface, are not affected by Javanese culture, such as the *tahajjud*, the *munājāt*, various forms of meditation, rosary, prayers of the Stations of the Cross, and so forth. This is because what is emphasized in the framework of *rasa* is the deeper, non-discursive mode of experiencing the Divine. It is about the experience of communion, its depth and subtleties.

In the realm of rituals, the pilgrimage traditions in both communities also come to be intimately related to the pan-Javanese ritual of communal meal (Jv. *slametan*), both as a communal ritual as well as a ritual related specifically to the remembrance of paradigmatic ancestors and founders ("saints") of the community. Under the influence of court culture, pilgrimage tradition also incorporates a certain degree of public veneration of the saints' relics (Jv. *pusaka*), especially among Javanese Muslims (Chapters 2 and 5).

So it has become clear that certain distinctive, common facets of Javanese culture play an important role in shaping the Muslim and Catholic pilgrimage traditions in Java. However, in the same dynamics, I have also argued that the so-called "Javanese culture"—as it concretely comes to be understood by these Muslim and Catholic Javanese pilgrims—also undergoes certain degrees of transformation along the way. In the context of pilgrimage tradition, the degree and forms of this transformation are visible in these Muslim and Catholic shrines. Under the influence of the wider Islamic tradition, for instance, Javanese Muslims utter a direct salutation for the dead when visiting their tombs. The Islamic *tahlīl* prayers that represent the monotheistic theological framework of *tawḥīd* are also incorporated into the Javanese communal meal (Jv. *slametan*), while this same ritual incorporates Muslim figures and saints in the list of the prophets, saints, and ancestors of the community.

On the Catholic side, one can argue that the Catholic pilgrimage culture in south central Java has introduced the figure of Mary in a rather distinctive way. With regard to the figure of Prajnaparamita Mary at Ganjuran, the Virgin is visually represented as a distinctively hybrid Javano-Christian figure, of course not identical with the Buddhist figure of Prajnaparamita, but similar enough. Furthermore, especially among Javanese Muslim pilgrims to the grotto of Sendangsono, the Qur'ānic figure of Maryam comes to be spiritually experienced partly through the encounter with the symbols and presence of Mary in the Catholic tradition (Chapter 6). In this respect, due to the inclusive role of *rasa* as a spiritual intuition and tasting, Muslim pilgrims are able to experience the deeper spiritual presence and significance of Mary in this context of a different tradition. This kind of encounter would also enable Javanese Muslim pilgrims to understand the deeper significance of Catholic symbolisms of Mary in the shrine mainly by way of spiritual experience with Mary, something that is possible in the Muslim tradition.

In the larger context beyond the pilgrimage tradition, this process of acceptance of Catholicism into the religio-spiritual fabric of Javanese society could be seen as rather dramatic, given the rejection of Catholicism (as a "foreign" tradition) among a large segment in the Javanese society at the beginning of the twentieth century. The question of double alterity, namely, the image of Christianity as colonial and anti-Islamic, was so real then and at times seemed to be overwhelming (Chapter 4). So the fact that the Catholic pilgrimage culture in south central Java has now drawn a rather significant participation of some segments in the (Muslim) Javanese society should not be taken for granted. Again, the religio-cultural strategy of the first Javanese Catholic intellectuals to foster a hybrid Javano-Catholic identity—that is, embracing Catholicism while clinging rather stubbornly to the Javanese identity—proved to be quite creative, timely, and fruitful. This complex and long process of religio-cultural encounters has presented the richness of Catholicism, including its spiritual treasure, to the Javanese in ways that are not intrusive, largely because they have invited spiritual tasting and participation, not coercion. In this process the deeper and more inclusive meaning of the "catholic" character of the Catholic tradition was taken as a principle of enrichment through engagements with local culture and reality (Chapter 4). It is in this framework of catholicity that one can understand the deepest inspiration behind Josef Schmutzer's idea of the Christian revivification of Javanese culture. This language might have begun primarily as a Christian project of turning the other into the self, but as it turns out, at the end of the day the "self" is also deeply transformed.

The principle of catholicity has indeed been rather pivotal in the formation of the hybrid Javano-Catholic identity. However, this principle, as it was put forward by early Javanese Catholic intellectuals, had one rather serious lacuna, since it ignored the crucial role of Islam in the formation of the Javanese culture. Under the tutelage of the Dutch Jesuit missionaries who in turn were influenced by Orientalism under late colonial conditions, a large part of these Javanese Catholic intellectuals' religio-cultural vision was to revivify the past glory and goodness of the Javanese culture—identified rather exclusively in terms of the Hindu-Buddhist legacy—through Christian values, based on the openness and universalism of both religio-cultural systems. However, this discourse on Javanese culture failed to take into account the complex role of Islam. Against this background, the more Islam-friendly culture of the contemporary Catholic pilgrimage tradition in south central Java presents itself as an antidote: it is a creative and timely response on the part of the contemporary Javanese Catholic community *vis-à-vis* the tensions and ambiguities embedded in the earlier interpretation of the hybrid Javano-Catholic identity.

In light of this rather interesting dynamic among Javanese Catholics, it is interesting to observe how Islam in Java, especially through the traditionalist

Nahdlatul Ulama, has also been negotiating its role and vision *vis-à-vis* the formation of the Javanese culture and the possible ways of appropriating this culture into its self-understanding and practice, roughly from the same time period as the Javanese Catholic intellectuals (ca. 1920s).[9] For the purpose of my discussion here, it is important to see that the traditionalist Nahdlatul Ulama has always been understood by its members and scholars primarily as a religio-cultural identity, anchored in the idea of a "tradition" that consists of a creative synthesis between Islamic principles and a certain degree of appropriation of local culture and customs (Ar. ʿādāt), founded on the principles of tolerance (Ar. *tasāmuḥ*) and moderation (Ar. *tawassuṭ*) that include both the ideas of equity or harmony (Ar. *iʿtidāl*) and balance (Ar. *tawāzun*).[10] On this point, the remarks by Achmad Siddiq (d. 1991), a prominent Javanese Muslim scholar and former chairman of the Nahdlatul Ulama, are highly insightful:

> *At-tawassuth* (including *al-iʿtidal* and *at-tawazun*) or moderation does not mean complete compromise and does not mean the blending together of a range of elements (syncretism). Nor is it a matter of excluding oneself from rejecting certain combination of elements. The characteristics of *at-tawassuth* begin with the fact that *God placed within Islam all manner of good things*, and it is definitely the case that all those good things are to be found between the two limits of *tatharruf*, or the tendency to go to extremes. ... Consequently, it is logical that Islam acknowledges that positive values can be found to have already developed in individuals, or groups of people, prior to their accepting the teaching of Islam. *Islam does not adopt an attitude of rejecting, destroying, or eliminating, a priori, these 'old' values, but rather seeks to accommodate them, in a selective and balanced fashion.*[11] (emphases added)

As this text reveals, a crucial framework for Achmad Siddiq's vision is the notion of Islam as God's blessings for the entire universe (Ar. *raḥmatan lil-ʿālamin*).[12]

---

[9] The Nahdlatul Ulama (the NU) is the biggest traditionalist Muslim organization in Indonesia. Founded in 1926 largely as a reaction to the rise of the modernist Muhammadiyah (founded in 1912 in Yogyakarta) with its reformist agenda, the demise of the Ottoman Empire after World War I, and the takeover of the Hejaz by the Wahhabis in 1924, the NU claims to have more than sixty millions followers. Most pilgrims in south central Java are associated in some ways with this group, albeit only culturally at times. However, some of them identify themselves rather surprisingly as the followers of the modernist Muhammadiyah organization that in general tends to dismiss the practice of pilgrimage to sacred tombs as a "dangerous innovation."

[10] Van Bruinessen, "Traditions for the Future," in Barton and Fealy, *Nahdlatul Ulama*, pp. 163–89.

[11] Greg Barton, "Islam, Pancasila and the Middle Path of *Tawassuth*: The Thought of Achmad Siddiq," in Barton and Fealy, *Nahdlatul Ulama*, p. 118.

[12] Barton, "Islam, Pancasila and the Middle Path of *Tawassuth*," p. 118.

This theological perspective places the whole identity and *raison d'être* of Islam on the cosmic level. Within this framework, the practice of pilgrimage to the tombs of the saints and the ancestors that traditionally marks the socio-religious identity of traditionalist Muslims in Java, then takes on a deeply cosmic dimension.[13] This principle of adaptation to, or appropriation of, local culture is also regarded as one of the most distinctive elements in the legacy of the saints of Islam in Java (Jv. *Wali Songo*), in whose image the Nahdlatul Ulama understands itself.[14]

At this point one should recall the paradigmatic role of Sunan Kalijaga, who as the *wali* par excellence was able to align the recalcitrant Mosque of Java in Demak to the Ka'ba in Mecca, symbolizing the foundation of a distinctive Javano-Islamic identity, an authentic practice of Islam that is deeply grounded in the particularities of Javanese society and culture (Chapter 1). Quite foundational as well in this regard is the story of Sunan Kalijaga asking his protégé, Sunan Pandanarang, the saint of Tembayat, to remove his mosque from the top of the hill to lower ground, signifying the need for a humble posture of Islam as a new religious force and its immersion into local reality in Java (Chapter 1). This pattern of religio-cultural accommodation has of course helped overcome the binary opposition between the center and periphery. Thus, in this framework, for the traditionalist Javanese Muslims, Islamic identity is in principle bound to local realities, under the overarching theological principle of spreading God's undiscriminating mercy (Ar. *raḥma*) to the whole creation.

At this point, it is crucial to note these similar patterns of how these two communities, the traditionalist Javanese Muslims and Catholics, have negotiated their identity *vis-à-vis* the Javanese culture as the intimate other. For, in light of this comparative insight, one can speak of a shared or common paradigm of inculturation or appropriation of local culture, expressed in the arts, architectures, rituals, and festivals of the shrines. What one sees here are the many ways in which the principle of communion and continuity has been continually at work in both communities in their respective identity formation. A crucial element of this socio-religious hermeneutic of the self is the reconstruction or re-imagination of the personalities and roles of the saints or paradigmatic figures of the respective communities—Sunan Kalijaga, Sunan Pandanarang, Father Frans van Lith, the Schmutzers, Father Sanjaya, and so forth—as well as their founding moments.

As I have just mentioned, Sunan Kalijaga has been hailed as the Javanese *wali par excellence*, especially due to his overall religious sensibility and religio-cultural role. Particularly important in the context of the formation of Javano-Islamic identity in south central Java is his role as the spiritual advisor to the founders and early monarchs of the Mataram dynasty. As examined in Chapter 1,

---

[13] Fattah, *Tradisi Orang-Orang NU*, pp. xii, xix.

[14] In this respect, Alwi Shihab goes even further by saying that due to the work of the early *wali*s in Java, Islam was able to assimilate itself to the Javanese reality to such a degree that its Arab identity became invisible (his *Islam Sufistik: "Islam Pertama" and Pengaruhnya Hingga Kini di Indonesia* [Bandung, 2001], p. 24).

all the Muslim saints whose cults are popular in south central Java were related to the Mataram dynasty—thus to Kalijaga as well—and to the Hindu-Javanese kingdom of Majapahit. In south central Java, this model of creative and hybrid religio-cultural identity formation continues up to the present.

On the Catholic side, the Dutch Jesuit missionary, Father Frans van Lith, has been portrayed not only as the "founder of the Java mission," but more specifically and affectionately as the "father of the Javanese Catholics." This is because he was a Dutch missionary who, almost miraculously, had become thoroughly "Javanese." The same pattern occurs with regard to the stature of the Schmutzers in the movement of Catholic appropriation of Javanese culture in the post-van Lith era. Among Javanese Catholics in south central Java, inculturation of the Catholic faith in Javanese soil has also been conceived as one of the most distinctive legacies of the Schmutzers, due to their various crucial roles in this realm (Chapters 5 and 6).

Communion with Saints as Ancestors

As the preceding chapters (Parts I and II) have all made clear, keeping the memory of the community's founders as ancestors has served as a larger context for the pilgrimage tradition in both Muslim and Catholic communities in south central Java. In fact it is one of the most salient and important similarities between the two. Along this line, what I have attempted to show as well is the shared nexus between culture and religion. As examined in Chapter 1, Javanese culture considers the sacred past as having a real authority and bearing over the present, and the ancestors belong to this category of sacred and authoritative past. In this framework, one can understand the importance of memory and history among the Javanese as fundamentally a category of presence and communion. History is by no means a matter of collective nostalgia of the past, but rather a communal habit of keeping the memory of the sacred past alive, celebrating the presence of and connection with this sacred past—which includes paradigmatic figures, ancestors, and founders as well as founding events—in various festivals, rituals, communal meals, grave visitation, and so forth.

A crucial element in this framework is the inclusivity of the category of ancestors. In general, the Javanese understand their ancestors not individually, but rather as an inclusive company of paradigmatic figures. In this framework, the idea of sainthood takes on a deeply communal character in the sense that these saints and paradigmatic figures achieve their "sainthood," so to speak, due to their role and location in the history of the community, that is, in the very process of the becoming of the community. Here sainthood is not solely a matter of personal piety and moral excellence. The piety and excellence of the saints are of course still quite crucial, but the more important criterion is whether these moral and spiritual categories play a concrete role in the wellbeing of the community. Such an organic relationship between sainthood and community helps explain the characteristic of sainthood and saint as a living reality and figure in the community, as well as the need of this community to keep the memory of these founding and paradigmatic figures alive.

There are principal ways in which the category of respecting and keeping memory of the saint-ancestors has continued to play a crucial role in the pilgrimage traditions both among Muslims and Catholics in south central Java. On the Islamic side, it has to be mentioned that respectful devotion (Jv. *bekti*) to the dead ancestors is an important part of the traditional Muslim piety in Java—represented largely, but not exclusively, by the traditionalist Nahdlatul Ulama—through the tradition of the *tahlīl* prayers as well as the ritual communal meal (Jv. *kenduri*).[15] This explains the prevalence of these rituals in Muslim shrines such as at the grave of Tembayat where the buried saint, Sunan Pandanarang, is considered the founding ancestor (Jv. *pundhen*) of the local community (Chapter 3). Many Javanese Muslim pilgrims to this shrine understand their pilgrimage as a respectful visit to their own ancestor (Jv. *nyekar*, *sowan*). During this visit, pilgrims combine the traditional Javanese etiquette of tomb visitation—such as putting a certain kind of flowers on the gravestone and holding a communal ritual meal—with the Islamic etiquette of visiting sacred tombs that includes specific prayers and vows related to the saint.

In this regard, it is important to see the larger relationship between the *tahlīl* prayers for the dead and the spirit of the ritual communal meal. Among traditionalist Muslims in Java, the *tahlīl* prayer is considered as a special prayer for the dead and it basically consists of chanting a combination of certain *sūras* of the Qur'ān and some *dhikr* formulas, especially the formula "There is no god but God" (Ar. *lā ilāha illā Allāh*). It typically begins with the opening chapter of the Qur'ān (Ar. *al-Fātiḥa*) and closes with the declaration of the intention (Ar. *du'ā*). It is crucial to note that this prayer is directed not only for certain dead members of the host family, but rather for all the (Muslim) dead and ancestors. In most cases, this *tahlīl* prayer is part of the communal meal (Jv. *slametan*) where food is shared after being blessed. In fact, this Islamized ritual-communal meal is also popularly called *tahlilan*, and the sharing of food is also considered a sharing of God's blessings.[16] Muslims consider the food to be shared during this communal meal as voluntary alms (Ar. *ṣadaqa*), a means of fostering brotherhood and solidarity.[17]

---

[15] These practices are still considered religio-cultural markers of traditional Islam in Java, as has been made clear by the recent defense of the practices among the traditionalist Muslim scholars. See, for instance, Anies, *Tahlil dan Kenduri*; Fattah, *Tradisi Orang-Orang NU*.

[16] The various *ḥadīth*s that become the foundation of this practice revolve around the idea of the relationship between communal sharing of food and the blessing of God. It is also crucial to see that the idea of doing the *ṣadaqa* for the dead is part of the foundation of the communal ritual meal (Jv. *slametan*) among traditionalist Muslims in Java. See Anies, *Tahlil dan Kenduri*, p. 5; also Fattah, *Tradisi Orang-Orang NU*, pp. 232–4; Bambang Pranowo, *Memahami Islam Jawa*, pp. 286–90.

[17] Anies, *Tahlil dan Kenduri*, p. 5.

As has been shown, many traditionalist Muslims in Java would also go to certain shrines and holy tombs to do these prayers for the deceased family members at least on the anniversary of their deaths. Most prevalent in this regard is holding prayers for them in the shrines of the saints. This is why one finds in many sacred tombs or shrines abundant copies of prayer booklets composed in commemoration of the dead, especially deceased parents. Among Javanese Muslims, devotion to the parents is spoken of as *bekti*, to translate the Arabic expression of filial piety (Ar. *birr al-wālidain*).[18] In this dynamic, one sees an expansion of the circle of communion in the community of Muslims. For the dead members of the family are placed in the secure protection of God and His company of the righteous dead, the *walis*, who are also considered the community's paradigmatic ancestors. This feature is also organically related to the deeply communal characteristic of saint and sainthood discussed earlier in this chapter.

The remarkable sense of communion with the entire community that includes not only the living and the dead members (ancestors) but also the future members is also expressed in the ritual etiquette of tomb visitation, especially in the greeting to the dead: "May God bless our predecessors as well as those who come after us; and God willing, we will join you in the intermediate world (Ar. *barzakh*)."[19] Thus, there is the sense that the living members of the Muslim community are not only praying for the dead, but also for the new generation of Muslims. Furthermore, the communion between the living and the dead is greatly enhanced by the realization that the pilgrims will eventually be joining the community of the dead as well. In all this, the intergenerational aspect of communion is quite remarkable, as well as its universalism or inclusivity. For while special categories of the dead are also acknowledged such as particular saints and one's parents, all the dead (Muslim) are also addressed.[20]

In the preceding paragraph, I have attempted to show how in the context of pilgrimage to shrines of the saints and the tombs of the ancestors and family members, certain Islamic practices and rituals around the dead have been combined with the Javanese framework of respecting the ancestors and keeping their memory alive. In this regard, there is another important feature of the Islamic tradition that is quite pivotal in this dynamic. It is the notion of *isnād* or *silsila*, that is, the chain of relationship between teachers and students. In the early Islamic tradition, the *isnād* is of course crucial to the legitimacy of the *ḥadīth* transmission. However, the *isnād* also functions as a means of placing oneself in the dynamic continuity of Islam as a prophetic tradition.[21] Furthermore, it is also understood as

---

[18] Ibid., pp. 96–7.

[19] Based on a *ḥadīth* on the authority of 'A'isha; in *Saḥīḥ Muslim*, I/388.

[20] Anies, *Tahlil dan Kenduri*, pp. 96–7.

[21] Cf. Jonathan A.C. Brown, *Hadith: Muhammad's Legacy in the Medieval and Modern World* (Oxford, 2009), p. 46.

a medium of special blessings precisely because it brings the person to a closer connection with or proximity to the Prophet, great teachers, and saints.[22]

Among the traditionalist Muslims in Java, this concept of *isnād* and *silsila* refers to the relationship between a master and a student that goes beyond the technical sense of knowledge transmission. For this relationship is highly personal as well as intergenerational. It is personal because the students would keep the spiritual remembrance of the teacher(s) throughout their lives. These teachers have become their ancestors in faith. In a real sense, their relationship with the teachers defines their religious identity. To a certain degree, they are also known by others in the community in terms of their association with these teachers. This relationship also places them in the wider networks of relationships with other masters and students. Thus, they also regard the teachers of their teacher as their own teachers, and the other students of their master as their brothers, and so forth. This way, the *isnād* or *silsila* relationship becomes wider and deeply intergenerational. This explains the popular phenomenon of pilgrimage done by the *pesantren* students to the tombs of their former teachers and other tombs and sacred sites associated with their teachers, as happens at the Gunungpring shrine where the students of Gus Miek regularly visit the tomb of *Mbah* Dalhar, their former teacher's master (Chapters 1 and 3). Again, this phenomenon reveals one of the distinctive characteristics of pilgrimage culture as a culture of communion with an ever widening dynamic.

It is interesting to see that among Catholics in Java the same logic is also at work, as shown in Part II of this book. For instance, the tomb of Fr. van Lith in Muntilan continues to be a favorite place of pilgrimage among his former students and their families. To a certain degree, this is a Catholic version of the Muslim *isnād* relationship. Although the great majority of Javanese Catholics would feel connected to Fr. van Lith as the founder of their community, this *isnād* relationship was particularly strong among Javanese Catholics who went to the mission school of Fr. van Lith, something that to a certain extent gets passed on to their children. Students from the adjacent Catholic High School named after this great missionary also pay regular visits. In the same line, one also notices that other great missionaries receive the same affective treatment, such as Fr. Prennthaler (Chapter 5). This affection for former teachers in the faith becomes much more widespread in the community precisely because they have become the founders, the ancestors of the whole community.[23]

In many different ways, this feature is at work in all the three Catholic shrines under study (Chapter 5). The identity of the Marian shrine of Sendangsono would never be separated from the memory of Father van Lith and Father Prennthaler,

---

[22] Ibid., pp. 49, 273.

[23] In this framework, the mausoleum of Muntilan becomes a focal point of pilgrimage for Catholics in south central Java precisely because it houses the tombs of many paradigmatic figures of the community, from the earliest time to the most recent one (Chapter 5).

as well as Barnabas Sarikrama. In the same way, the mausoleum of Muntilan has become so significant for the entire community, not only due to the memory of Father van Lith and Father Sanjaya, the martyr, but also due to the memory of other founders and ancestors of the community who are buried here. It has also been shown how the memory of the Schmutzer family features rather prominently in the Sacred Heart prayer session at the Sacred Heart shrine of Ganjuran.

This intergenerational dynamic of the *isnād* relationship, to a lesser degree, has also been at work in the mushrooming spread of Marian shrines (Chapter 6). In this dynamic, a particular shrine is connected to its mother shrine through its "founder," i.e., the pilgrim who built it, and who in turn passes it on to his or her children and the larger local community. Thus this kind of shrine becomes a complex memory of founders or ancestors, both communal and familial. In all these, one sees how the *isnād* type of relationship, so to speak, becomes an important pillar in the Javano-Catholic identity.

Earlier in this chapter I have discussed the role of the ritual-communal meal of *slametan* among traditional Muslims in Java in relation to the role of saints as the community's paradigmatic ancestors. Along the same line, through the practice of *slametan*, Javanese Catholics also appropriate this larger framework of connection with the ancestors as understood in the Javanese culture. As mentioned, the *slametan* is held regularly in both Islamic and Catholic shrines (Chapters 2 and 5). This should be not be surprising given the role of the *slametan* as a pan-Javanese ritual that lies at the heart of Javanese religion.[24] Due to this kind of common practice, the two communities get closer to each other, and this practice also reveals the adaptation of similar religio-cultural strategies to respond to the need of the contemporary Javanese society.

To conclude, in this section I have shown how the category of ancestral memory that is prominent in the Javanese culture connects the Muslim and Catholic communities with their paradigmatic figures in some distinctive ways;[25] and how through the framework of ancestral relationship, sainthood and the pilgrimage tradition take on a strongly communal and intergenerational character. This way, pilgrimage is an expression of a deep sense of belonging to the community with

---

[24] Affirming what Geertz has argued a few decades ago, Beatty remarks on the *slametan*: "As a ritual frame adaptable to diverse faiths and ideologies *it remains at the heart of Javanese religion*. As an example of religious syncretism, it shows how—and with what inventive grace—people can come to terms with their differences." Beatty, "Adam and Eve and Vishnu," p. 286.

[25] In this respect, it is interesting to see a similar phenomenon in Egypt where the prevalence of the cult of saints among Coptic Christians and Muslims is also based on certain features of the ancient Egyptian belief with regard to the dead and their interaction with the living. For instance, the popularity of the tradition of writing letters addressed to the Muslim jurist al-Shāfi'ī (d. 820) at his tomb in the famous al-Qarafa cemetery in Cairo, is actually an Islamic borrowing from the ancient Egyptian custom of writing letters to the dead. See Hoffman, *Sufism, Mystics, and Saints in Modern Egypt*, p. 354.

its sacred history. In both communities, this process results in the stronger sense of communal identity that never becomes exclusive, precisely because of the shared Javanese cultural symbols and sensibilities as well as more direct encounters between the two communities in this framework of ancestral relationship. They foster respect, in various ways and degrees, for Javanese paradigmatic figures of the past.[26]

Pilgrimage as Devotion and Spiritual Quest for Peace and Wellbeing

As illustrated in Chapters 3 and 6, the desire to achieve integral wellbeing and peacefulness is among the most common motivational frameworks for both Muslim and Catholic pilgrims. I have shown how the category of *tentrem*—the Javanese understanding of peacefulness in its most fundamental and comprehensive sense—is also understood as the true blessings of God by Javanese Muslim pilgrims (Chapter 3).

This phenomenon is, in my view, highly revealing in terms of the Javanese spiritual sensibility, expressing a deepest longing for the full flourishing of life marked by depth, balance, and integration. It is in this larger framework of searching for the true meaning of life that Muslim pilgrims at the Tembayat shrine make the distinction between worldly and ambiguous boon (Jv. *perolehan*) and true blessings of God (Jv. *berkah*). For crisis-ridden pilgrims, both Muslim and Catholic, this search for true peace might take a more arduous path. Many of them would stay for a longer period in the shrine, or do the visits repeatedly, to go through a rather intense process of self-questioning and soul-searching in the larger context of their relationship to God so that they are able to come to terms with the particular "problematic" aspects of their own lives. Among Muslim ascetic wandering pilgrims, this search of true peace takes the form of an even longer and more arduous journey, moving from one shrine to the next during a more extended period of time (Chapter 3). In this highly personal context of pilgrimage, true peace could not be achieved without purification of the heart.

Among Javanese Catholic pilgrims, this framework of peacefulness is also remarkable, serving as the framework for understanding other more specific blessings of pilgrimage. Even among young pilgrims, the search for peace is quite striking. In this regard, it is also crucial to see how the Javanese spiritual method of attaining deep peace (the *ning-nang-nung* philosophy) is appropriated by Javanese

---

[26] Although this respect is expressed differently, many Javanese across religious affiliations would have respect for paradigmatic figures such as Panembahan Senapati (r. 1588–1601), the legendary founder of the Mataram dynasty, Sultan Agung (r. 1613–46), the greatest monarch of this dynasty, Prince Dipanagara (1785–1855), the Sufi prince who fought against the Dutch in the Java War (1825–30), Ranggawarsita (1802–73), the Sufi poet of the Surakarta court, and so forth. Pilgrimage as *laku* or *tirakat* is part of the communal remembrance of these figures in sacred sites associated with them.

Catholics precisely because it has been the traditional Javanese way of achieving a deeper sense of peacefulness that results from getting in touch with one's true self—that is, purifying the self or the heart from all sorts of distractions caused by egoism, narrow-mindedness, and other distorted desires—as well as communing with God through spiritual practices (Chapter 6).

The core of this philosophy of life is still quite prevalent among Javanese in general, to such a degree that it serves as a common framework to describe the dynamics of pilgrimage as an intense period of purification of the heart (Jv. *laku, tirakat*). Although no Muslim shrine in south central Java formally adopts this philosophy, the spirit of this practice lies at the heart of many Muslim pilgrims' spiritual experience during pilgrimage. For, as I have pointed out throughout this book, crucial in the practice of pilgrimage among many Javanese Muslims is the process of purifying the lower self (Ar. *nafs*) and spiritual intentions through ascetic and spiritual practices, in order to achieve the true *baraka* of peacefulness and wellbeing (Jv. *tentrem, slamet*).

In all this, one sees how the spiritual means employed might be specific to Islam and Catholicism (such as the *dhikr*, the *munājāt*, the Station of the Cross etc.) as well as Javanese spirituality (meditation, fasting, the spiritual practices of *ning nang nung*, and so forth). However, the underlying framework remains the same, namely, cultivating the spiritual self in order to achieve a deeper sense of communion and harmony with God, the self, the other, and the surroundings, both social and cosmic.

For so many Muslim and Catholic pilgrims, this experience of peacefulness serves as the deepest, most personal, and long lasting blessing and fruit of pilgrimage. This is so because this experience involves a deeply personal and spiritual process of discernment, openness, clarity, and balance in communing with the Divine presence. On the personal level, this search for peacefulness makes the relationship between pilgrimage and the "self" overwhelmingly evident. I have argued that this feature is intimately related to the general notion of devotion in pilgrimage as deeper and dynamic connectedness to God and His spiritual company of saints. This devotion is highly personal and it develops over time. It is also intergenerational in the way it gets passed on from generation to generation. That is why I argue that devotion and the search for true peace and wellbeing should be taken as a more fundamental factor in the pilgrimage experience understood in its experiential and contextual complexities, rather than short-term quests for some worldly boon.

Many pilgrims also employ the inner experience of peacefulness as an important criterion to gauge the deeper and personal meanings of the shrines, i.e., whether the shrine is filled with God's presence. Due to this characteristic, peacefulness is an inclusive experience and criterion in the context of pilgrimage among Muslims and Catholics in south central Java. The fact that peacefulness (Jv. *tentrem, slamet*) is at the heart of Javanese philosophy of life is of course crucial with regard to its inclusiveness. In the framework of the *ning-nang-nung* philosophy discussed earlier, this inclusiveness stems also from its basic spiritual dynamism toward *hanung* and *dunung* (Chapter 6). These two Javanese words are normally employed to explain the last part of the philosophy (the *nung* part). The semantic field of these Javanese words includes magnanimity, generosity, wisdom, loving-kindness, balance, open-mindedness, forgiveness, freedom from fanaticism or extremism, and so forth.[27] In the Javanese concept of *dunung*, there is a dynamic of knowing the existential state of the self in relation to the whole reality. Thus it involves the process of coming to deeper terms with one's true self, the true nature of reality and life, and then acting accordingly. At the end of the day, one would obtain a spiritual mastery over the self (Jv. *wenang*, being in control of one's self) that amounts to true wisdom.[28] As noted earlier, this very dynamic is pivotal in the Javanese understanding of pilgrimage as *laku* and *tirakat*. This is why, for instance, the custodian of the Tembayat shrine remarks that life without *laku*, including *ziarah*, will be very hard; for, it is extremely difficult to achieve the state of peace and surrender (Jv. *tentrem*, *sumeleh*) without this practice.[29]

As I have tried to demonstrate as well, the dynamism of devotion among both Muslim and Catholic pilgrims leads to more fundamental and longer lasting peacefulness, a deeper sense of integration with the whole reality, God, the self, and the other. Furthermore, true peacefulness includes and is manifested in the dynamism toward an act of loving surrender to God. The Javanese word for this stage is *sumeleh*, as opposed to the rather fatalistic sense of *pasrah*. In the experience of many pilgrims, the movement from resigning to a difficult reality or crisis in life (Jv. *pasrah*) to true comprehensive self-surrender to God (Jv. *sumeleh*) is never easy and it takes an arduous path. However, as many pilgrims would testify, it is this very process—namely, realizing the crisis, struggling to understand its major factors and directions, then finding the deeper meanings and educational purposes of the crisis through an act of faith in the providential care of God—that forms the core of spiritual renewal. Again, one can say that the peak of the process is attainment of the spiritual virtue of *sumeleh*, surrendering one's whole self to God. This virtue is deeply related to the Javanese ideal of serenity, as well as to Islamic spirituality's notion of the culminating spiritual station of the soul at peace with God (Ar. *nafs al-muṭmàinna*, Qurʾān 89: 27). In *Serat Cabolèk*, a Javano-Islamic mystical treatise from the eighteenth century, this idea is described in terms of a profound experience of peace that occurs when the seeker, the Mahabharata hero Bhima, enters into the womb of Dewaruci, the spiritual figure that represents both his master and his true self. The text says: "Bhima's heart is now peaceful and tranquil, in complete surrender, no longer troubled by anything."[30]

---

[27] See Ki Priyo Dwiarso, "Problem Solving a la Ki Hadjar Dewantara," The *Kedaulatan Rakyat Daily*, April 3, 2008.

[28] Another possibility suggested by the word *nang* here is "me-*nang*," which means victory, understood more spiritually or internally in this context, like the key Qurʾānic terms *fatḥ/futāḥ* and *naṣr* in Arabic.

[29] Interview, May 18, 2009.

[30] *Serat Cabolèk*, Canto VIII. 53.40; Soebardi, *The Book of Cabolèk*, p. 126.

The Sacredness of Space, Things, and Time (Sacramentality)

Earlier in this chapter, I have discussed the *mandala* as a cosmic framework for sacred space, that is, as a space of supernatural presence and communion. In the context of south central Java, this framework is Javano-Muslim, used by the Sultanate of Yogyakarta to understand its geographical territory as supernaturally charged. However, the Catholic shrine of the Sacred Heart at Ganjuran takes up the *mandala* symbolism to also emphasize the inner or deeper aspect of the encounter between pilgrims and God in the spatial context of the shrine. Both Catholic and Muslim pilgrims find the geographical or "cosmic" location of the shrines very instrumental in rendering these shrines special as a space for encountering and communing with the Divine. To a certain degree, both Catholic and Muslim pilgrims see this sacred cosmic dimension of the shrines in deeply "sacramental" terms because in many different ways it conveys the presence of God and it helps them commune with this presence.

In a nutshell, I understand the sacramentality as a vision that basically understands the dynamics of our deeper communion with God as always occurring in the larger context of God's presence and manifestation in the world, both the natural and social worlds. Thus, I do not understand the word "sacramental" in its specific relation to the institution of the Church as a mediation of this sacramental encounter with God, as Avery Dulles seems to emphasize.[31] My understanding and emphasis are related to the more fundamental sense of "catholicity" of the grace of God and the nature of the Church, that is, the universality of God's grace, providence, and presence in the whole created reality, making it sacramentally instrumental in the communion between humans and God.[32]

At the heart of this distinctive Catholic theological category is the theological vision of earthly realities as capable of carrying, mediating, embodying, and revealing the supernatural, universal, and absolute reality.[33] In other words, implicit in this sacramental vision is the refusal to see the whole created reality as "homogenous," that is, as empty and isolated. Rather, sacramental vision is a vision of communion, relationship, and presence. Within this vision, nothing stands on its own in isolation. In this theological language, the meaningfulness and significance of each particular reality should be found in its capability to make present and real the universality of God's self-communication and grace. In the sacramental worldview, "the created things are a visible 'sign' which both bears

---

[31] See his *The Catholicity of the Church* (Oxford, 1985), chapter 6.

[32] I draw fundamental insights from the "sacramental ontology" developed by various Catholic theologians in the so-called *nouvelle théologie* school, such as Henri de Lubac, Marie-Dominique Chenu, Yves Congar, Hans Urs von Balthasar, and others. See Hans Boersma, *Nouvelle Théologie and Sacramental Ontology: A Return to Mystery* (Oxford, 2009).

[33] Roberto Goizueta, *Caminemos Con Jesus* (Maryknoll, 2005), p. 48.

within itself and simultaneously points beyond itself to an invisible 'reality,' which is, in the final analysis, the Creator."[34]

However, over against the danger of losing sight of the meaning of the particularity of each reality in this sacramental worldview, Roberto Goizueta argues:

> Implicit in the definition of sacrament is the presupposition that the concrete, particular object or entity that embodies the universal reality is in fact historically concrete and particular. Consequently, an indispensable prerequisite of any sacramental relationship with a particular entity, i.e., a relationship in which the supernatural Absolute is revealed, is that one affirms both the particularity and the historical concreteness of that particular entity.[35]

In terms of sacramental vision, one sees an overwhelming similarity between Javanese Muslim and Catholic pilgrimage practices. For, while the more spiritual or inner meaning or blessing of pilgrimage as a journey of self to God through purification becomes more and more crucial for pilgrims in the continuum of their spiritual journey, this overarching spiritual framework also translates into a myriad of more tangible ways in which communion with God is concretely experienced, and then reflected in the pilgrim's life. It is this distinctive aspect of pilgrimage that renders it appealing to pilgrims, serving as a rich and integral framework for their religious formation.

So, in what follows I will reiterate the many tangible ways of communion with God, self, and others, that happen in the Muslim and Catholic pilgrimage traditions and experience. In this respect, the structure of my presentation of this comparative theological study is actually governed by the breadth of the sacramental vision as a vision of communion. This is why the structure of this book on the dynamics of communion with God in pilgrimage revolves around three major elements, namely history (1); sacred space, arts, architecture, and rituals (2); and the experiential world of the pilgrims (3). Since I have just discussed the third element in the preceding section, the rest of this section will be devoted to the discussion on how a sacramental logic works in the context of the first two elements.

Within this sacramental view of reality, history is understood as a sacred past that has become a pivotal instrument of God's providential care for the community. In this particular understanding of history, the memory of the founding moment of the community, as well as the role of the saints as the founding figures, become distinctively crucial. As pointed out earlier in this chapter, the Javanese Muslim

---

[34] Schloesser, *Jazz Age Catholicism* (Toronto, 2005), p. 6.

[35] Roberto Goizueta, *Caminemos Con Jesus*, p. 48. Along the same line, Philip Sheldrake argues that the Incarnation requires the view that God is committed to particularities. But this commitment to particularities is accompanied by a sense that God is not bound or limited by such particularities. Sheldrake, *Spaces for the Sacred*, p. 30; also Peter Scott, "A Theology of Eucharistic Place: Pilgrimage as Sacramental," in Bartholomew and Hughes, *Explorations in a Christian Theology of Pilgrimage*, pp. 152–3.

saint Sunan Kalijaga and the Dutch Jesuit missionary Father Frans van Lith are considered important religiously for the Javanese Muslim and Javanese Catholic communities respectively, not only because of their spiritual virtues, feats, and miracles, but also because of their special location in the community's sacred history. In this regard, as I have argued, pilgrimage is also driven by a desire to commune with the sacred past, something that plays an ongoing role in the identity formation of the community. In this sense, identity formation is deeply religious in the sacramental sense as understood here. Or, stated differently, sacramental vision of the past—that is, the ability to see the past as sacred, as revealing the very particularity of God's loving providence and care for the community—becomes one of the concrete ways in which complex identities such as Javano-Islamic and Javano-Catholic are negotiated. This is the religious logic underlying what I call "the principle of continuity with the past" that has been embraced by both communities in south central Java in their hybrid identity formation. As illustrated in different places in this book, both communities always strive to not sever their connection with the past, a shared characteristic that is noticeable in their aversion to the notion of rupture or radical break. For instance, this principle is at work in the conversion story of the Muslim saint, Sunan Kalijaga, as well as in the foundational story of the Sendangsono Marian shrine.[36]

The second major aspect in this sacramental vision has to do with its more concrete spatial, artistic, architectural, and ritual dimensions. In the context of pilgrimage, the continuing presence of God, the sacred past, the collective identity of the community, as well as the discernment of the current community in negotiating this complex identity are also understood as intimately related in different ways to the sacred spaces such as shrines and tombs of the saints, together with their distinctive architectural features and rituals. Again, in this context, spiritual experience has a deeply sensuous aspect to it.

In terms of architectural styles, I have demonstrated the distinctive way that the particular stylistic forms of the Grand Mosque of Java (the Demak Mosque) and the shrine of Tembayat were governed by a principle of respecting local reality, the Javanese culture. Quite memorable in this respect is the story of Kalijaga's feat in negotiating the ongoing place of the Javanese culture in the formation of the Muslim community in Java (Chapter 1). In this regard, sacramental vision is a vision of respecting particular realities including local culture as ultimately related to the concreteness of God's communication and grace to the people. By the same token, the formation of a hybrid identity, such as Javano-Islamic identity, could also be understood in this dynamic of respecting local reality that has become part and parcel of the collective self-identity of the people themselves. As has been examined, this is the religio-cultural vision embraced by the traditionalist

---

[36] In particular, note the smooth replacement (from within) of the local guardian spirits by the Christian figures of Mary and Jesus in the founding narratives of this Marian grotto (Chapter 5).

Nahdlatul Ulama, whose wide and deep-rooted presence in rural Java has helped shape the distinctive Javano-Islamic pilgrimage culture.

In terms of architecture and rituals, this sacramental principle of communion has enabled the Javano-Islamic community to embrace the religious "other," not only in terms of its outward forms, whether ritual, architectural or artistic, but also its deeper significance. The process has of course been selective, but it is crucial to see this selectiveness as a concrete expression of a broader communal discernment, a religio-cultural hermeneutic on identity formation *vis-à-vis* forms of alterity. At this point there is no need to reiterate the various Hindu-Javanese artistic symbolisms that have been embraced by different Islamic shrines and their communities in Java (Chapters 2). In general, this inclusion of the other signals an acknowledgement of the continuing validity of the older legacy, a crucial point whose meanings could only be identified through a complex religio-cultural process that includes the corresponding religious and spiritual experience of the community itself. This appropriation of "the other" has turned these sacred spaces into more inclusive sites, but it also requires an ongoing discernment that can be complex and fragile. I have attempted to offer in Chapter 2 some pertinent interpretation on the possible meanings of Javano-Islamic hybrid art in the Tembayat shrine.[37] However, this kind of interpretation is only plausible and makes sense if it is placed within the larger framework of pilgrimage as an integral practice where pilgrims themselves are made to realize and undergo the purification of intentions in their unending process of making sense of the whole experience (Chapters 3 and 6).

On the Catholic side, this complex discernment is well illustrated in Josef Schmutzer's agenda of inculturating the universality of Christian faith in the particularities of Javanese people and culture. For Schmutzer, the founder of the Sacred Heart shrine at Ganjuran, the particular Hindu-Javanese style of the shrine was instrumental in expressing the concreteness of God's love in Christ and the work of the Holy Spirit for the Javanese people. The universality of God's love needs to be made concrete and particular, also in terms of artistic and architectural symbolism. In his Catholic imagination, the universal divine Love—which he always understood in terms of Christ's outpouring of mercy and the Spirit's work—meant profound respect for the particularities of local realities and peoples (Chapters 4 and 5). In this framework, while Christianity was initially conceived of as a reviver of the Javanese culture, as it turns out in the process, Christianity itself is revivified and reinvigorated by the particularities of the Javanese reality and culture, especially through the participation of the Javanese people, including the non-Catholics, who are the living embodiment of the culture.

---

[37] For example, the deeper meanings of the various images of meditating Buddhas, Hindu temples or Hindu-Javanese crown (flanked by lions, crocodiles etc.) in the shrine of Tembayat might have to be put in the framework of the corresponding experience of pilgrimage as a journey of self-purification (Chapter 2).

In the context of pilgrimage, any discourse on sacramentality of course has to take into account the nature of sacred things or items used in the rituals or otherwise connected to the shrines and their saints. Again, pilgrimage is at its foundation a habit of the heart, but it is also a very tangible experience, involving a rich material culture and driven by the principle of finding concrete ways to obtain the blessings of God. Among the most tangible manifestation of God's blessing is the holy water that is very popular in Catholic shrines, but also not completely absent in the Muslim shrines. In this regard, the blessings that the holy water contains also unite Muslims and Catholics, as the case of the Sacred Heart shrine at Ganjuran shows (Chapter 6). Here it is very interesting to see the development in the discernment of the Javanese Catholic community on the sacramental principle of communion with regard to the holy water of the Marian shrine at Sendangsono. For this water with a healing power was used first as a sign of superiority of Christianity over paganism and Islam, but it is now taken as truly sacramental sign of God's grace that brings about an ever widening communion between people across religious traditions (Chapter 5).

Muslim and Catholic pilgrims in Java also share a similar understanding of the sacramentality of time. Influenced by a constellation of their respective religious tradition and common Javanese culture, they have come to regard certain times as more propitious for shrine visitation. For example, Thursday night (Friday eve) in general is considered to be propitious, most likely due to the influence of the Islamic tradition. However, the Javanese also consider the eve of the Friday *Kliwon* that occurs every 35 days in the hybrid lunar Javano-Islamic calendar particularly propitious, unmistakably showing the influence of the Javanese local culture. On the Catholic devotional side, the popularity of Friday largely stems from the tradition that the first Friday is devoted to the Sacred Heart of Jesus. However, the influence of the Javanese culture can be seen in the fact that it is the eve of Friday (as opposed to the day of Friday) that is particularly viewed as favourable. For as a comparison, it is the day (instead of the eve) of Friday that is considered propitious both by Muslims and Christians in many Middle Eastern countries.[38] Furthermore, due to a common Javanese culture, the eves of Tuesday and Friday *Kliwon* are considered particularly favorable among Javanese Muslims and Catholics, despite the absence of scriptural or more widespread traditional bases in their respective traditions. In my view, what this similarity achieves or signifies is the creation of

---

[38] In Syria, many Muslim families foster a habit of doing the tomb visitation on Friday morning. Typically they would visit the cemetery, cleaning the graves and then reading Qur'ānic verses and offering prayers for the deceased family members. They also visit shrines of the saints, such as the shrines of Shaykh Arslan and various Muslim figures in the Bab al-Saghir cemetery in Damascus. Curiously, the Christians have a similar habit of visiting various shrines on Friday morning, such as the shrines of Our Lady of Seidnayya and St. Thecla in Ma'alula that also attract Muslim pilgrims. During my stay in Syria in 2008, I divided my Fridays between Muslim cemeteries and Christian shrines, a dynamic of double visiting that I discussed earlier in this chapter.

a dramatic moment of common devotion. For this common sacred time creates a shared framework of sacramental time. During this sacred moment, the two traditions merge on a uniquely spiritual level, together emanating that common energy of devotion that I described at the beginning of this chapter.

By way of conclusion, let me reiterate that one of the basic theological arguments in this comparative study is that the whole practice of saint veneration in Islam and Catholic Christianity presupposes a sacramental worldview. Stated broadly, this sacramental worldview holds that God's presence can be encountered in the very reality of our personal, interpersonal, natural (material, cosmic) and social world; that this reality has the capability of becoming the vessel of the manifestation of God's glory, wisdom and grace, and thus becoming sacred by participating in the dynamics of God's involvement with the world; that our world and community are connected to God in various ways, including through paradigmatic figures, saints, and founders of the community. I argue that the spirit of integral and comprehensive communion with God in the sacramental worldview and traditional cosmology—such as found among traditional Javanese today—lies at the very foundation of the understanding and practice of sainthood and saint veneration in both traditions.

Observable Particularities

So far the focus of my comparative analysis is on the overwhelming similarities, the meeting points between Muslim and Catholic pilgrimage traditions as they are practiced in south central Java. Of course, this preferred way of proceeding does not mean that particularities or differences among the two are non-existent. For, even the points of similarities that I have identified so far occur in the context of particularities. In different ways and to various degrees, I have also tried to make this aspect rather clear in my discussion. For example, while the blessing of peace is strikingly common to both Muslim and Catholic pilgrims, and is often understood and achieved in and through shared Javanese cultural framework, it is still to a large degree connected to the specificities of Islam and Catholic traditions. In the religious sensibility of most Catholic pilgrims, the grace of this peace is ultimately bestowed by God through Christ, while the experience of praising and being in spiritual communion with the Prophet Muḥammad could not be separated from the pilgrimage ritual and experience of many Muslim pilgrims. Many traditional Muslims strongly believe that *salawāt*, the special prayers for the Prophet that have become part of the standard ritual etiquette of Muslim tomb visitation, bring God's abundant blessings to them, including peacefulness in the heart. One can also say that the role of Mary in this dynamic of communion and blessing is in general much more central and affectionate among Catholic pilgrims, compared to Muslim pilgrims, although they might visit the same Marian shrine.

Here I can only briefly identify two most important and observable differences in these Muslim and Catholic pilgrimage traditions, particularly with regard to the profile of the venerated paradigmatic saintly figures as well as the nature of the spread of the shrines. In this regard, as shown, Islamic pilgrimage sites in Java are originated in historical and "local" saintly persons, that is, the *wali* or the charismatic religious leaders who lived or are buried there. This fact reveals that Islam has over time been rooted more deeply in the history and fabric of Javanese society. While none of the Muslim saints under study here is widely known beyond Southeast Asia, this fact of regionalism might point to the different notion of oikumene in Islam. In a rather stark contrast to Roman Catholicism, Sunni Islam has no official list of saints (Ar. *awliyā'*) to be venerated worldwide, thus providing a spacious room for the inclusion of local paradigmatic and saintly figures.[39] In fact, the inclusion of local paradigmatic figures or saints has been one of the distinctively local characteristics of Islam in Java that ultimately contributes to the richness of universal Islam.

As I have argued throughout this book, the practice of Catholic Christianity in south central Java has taken a distinctively local flavor, but combined with its connection to international network and symbolism. This feature is visible in the profiles of its shrines. To commemorate the founding of the local Catholic community, the Sendangsono Marian shrine is intentionally modeled after the famous mother shrine of Lourdes in France; while the provenance of the Sacred Heart shrine at Ganjuran that marked the coming of age of this local Catholic community could not be separated from the popularity of that devotion in Europe and the Netherlands since the nineteenth century. This combination of local history and international connection has without doubt played a major role in the popular appeal of these shrines. Apart from its more obvious connection to Catholic internationalism and relative uniformity of saint veneration, this fact is no doubt related as well to the comparatively recent historical presence of the Catholic Church in Java. This explains why the list of the paradigmatic figures or founders of this community is still predominantly European. However, in this regard, the figure of the martyred priest, Fr. Sanjaya, represents the presence of a thoroughly local saintly figure in Roman Catholicism in Java.

Also worth noting here is the related pattern of the creation of daughter-shrines among Catholics in south central Java. As shown in Chapter 6, the mushrooming of Marian pilgrimage sites in this area reflects the pattern of building a daughter shrine in memory of the mother shrine. This pattern is born out of devotion and particular experience with the mother shrine. In some cases, it is also an expression of the deeply intergenerational character of pilgrimage tradition, that is, when children decide to build a Marian shrine in memory of their deceased parents with

---

[39] This does not mean that no "international" Muslim saints are known in Java where 'Abd al-Qādir al-Jīlānī is still the most popular transregional saint. His life story or deeds (Ar. *manāqib*) is well known in Java, and the ritual of *manakiban*, a gathering in praise and commemoration of al-Jīlānī based on his *manāqib*, is rather widespread among traditionalist Muslims. See Lukens-Bull, *Peaceful Jihad* (New York, 2005), pp. 75–7; Julian Millie, *Splashed by the Saint*.

their particular devotion to Mary and in gratitude for the blessings of God given to them through pilgrimage. In most cases, one sees a movement from Marian shrine as a private sacred space at home to a sacred space open to the local community and beyond.

To a certain degree this feature is a rather distinctive feature of Catholic pilgrimage culture that is largely unknown in the Muslim context. However, the movement from private to public also occurs in the Muslim pilgrimage tradition as the tombs of prominent local charismatic Muslim leaders (Jv. *kyai*) that begin mostly as a private or family place turn into popular pilgrimage sites. Here, an excellent example is the grave of Kyai Haji Hasyim Asyari (1875–1947), the founding father of the Nahdlatul Ulama, in the compound of the Tebu Ireng *Pesantren* (Islamic boarding school) in Jombang, East Java, which has become a major pilgrimage site.[40] As happens throughout the Islamic world, Muslim sacred tombs do not normally require the sanction from an institution to become public. At this initial stage the process largely depends on the stature and spiritual presence of the saintly persons being buried there, as well as their networks of families, former students, and so forth. This is of course rather different from the Catholic case in which a shrine typically requires some form of local ecclesial approval to become a public space of veneration and worship.

Concluding Remarks

I began this comparative chapter by talking about "double visiting" that has enabled me to learn more about God, my own self, and my religious tradition, from the richness, complexities as well as particularities of the Muslim tradition. In comparative theology, this back-and-forth visiting is an agile dance between two traditions that eventually result in an extended form of encounters marked by depth and beauty. In my experience, the dynamics and fruits of this double visiting were made smoother and richer by the similar structures between the Muslim and Catholic pilgrimage practices that I examined in this chapter. During these back-and-forth visits, I feel I was already living in a comparative theological context, so to speak, where a common language is in place, and where encounters and conversations between peoples of different religions can occur using a third language that does not obliterate these traditions, but rather enriches

---

[40] Due to his prominence among traditionalist Muslims in Indonesia, Hasyim Asyari is called the "*hadrat al-shaikh*." His grandson, the late Abdurrahman Wahid, not only was the president of Indonesia (1999–2001), but is also considered to be a *wali*. About 80 percent of the total visitors to this famous school came for religious visit to the tomb of Hasyim Asyari (and also to that of Abdurrahman Wahid). In a typical month, an average of 3,000 pilgrims is recorded, while during the month of Muharram, the figure reaches over 3,000 pilgrims per day. See Lukens-Bull, *A Peaceful Jihad*, p. 28.

them on many different levels, including the level of affective connections.[41] In a way, this common language points to comparative learning where Muslims and Catholics find a concrete common ground to talk about their spiritual practices and theological underpinnings.

---

[41] Cf. Clooney, *Comparative Theology*, p. 86.

Conclusion
Going Home and Setting Off Again

> The world changed, as he returned to the one he knew.
> *Serat Cabolèk*[1]

In every pilgrimage the return journey is no less important than the preparation, the journey to the shrine, and the actual time spent there. For pilgrims return to their quotidian and ordinary life with a certain degree of newness. In the words of the *Serat Cabolèk* quoted above, one can say that pilgrims return to a changed world, even though its familiarity might still be overwhelming. In the same spirit and to conclude this book, I am going to identify some of the most crucial insights of this study.

As I see it, there are five most important comparative insights that can be drawn from this study. The first has to do with the crucial and complex role played by pilgrimage and the larger tradition of saint veneration in the formation of the distinctive and hybrid identity of the Muslim and Catholic communities in south central Java. As I have shown in both Muslim and Catholic cases, these hybrid identities become quite distinctive in their richness, with the potential to contribute to their larger traditions of Islam and Catholic Christianity. Perhaps more importantly, these identities each constitute robust and authentic religious traditions that not only have survived the storms of changing times, but have also resulted in quite remarkable and dynamic religious communities. For, in both cases, this hybrid identity is marked by creativity and inclusivity that stems, to a large extent, from its rootedness in the common local Javanese culture that continues to enable both to interact fruitfully on many different levels.

The significance of this phenomenon should not be taken for granted, and it serves as a crucial comparative fruit of this study. For as shown in the Introduction, the nature, propriety, and role of pilgrimage (shrine visitation) or saint veneration in general in both Christian and Muslim traditions was disputed in certain historical periods in the past, and still is in some circles in both traditions. So, although these practices are grounded in theology and continue to inspire robust theological reflections, they are not traditionally associated with areas in which fundamental theological reflection occurs in either religious tradition. Against this background, this book shows how pilgrimage traditions turn out to be crucial in the actual identity formation of the Muslim and Catholic communities

---

[1] Canto VIII, 54:41. In the original Javanese: "*Wus salin alamipun, angulihi alamé lami*"; Soebardi, *The Book of Serat Cabolèk*, p. 126.

in south central Java. The practice is embedded quite deeply in the communal structure and shared habits of their piety and religious lives, a fact that in turns invites deeper theological reflection.

Viewed from the Catholic perspective, this finding might not appear to be particularly novel, since pilgrimage has been one of the most distinctive hallmarks of Catholicism.[2] However, given the background of the more recent fading away of the phenomenon in much of the Western world, this finding could still be crucial. My argument in this respect is that if the principles of sacramentality (finding God in all things), mediation (the always specifically, concretely mediated nature of God's grace), and communion (that Christian faith is always communal or ecclesial) constitute the truly distinctive pillars of the Catholic theological vision as many theologians have argued, then the entire pilgrimage tradition can serve as a natural milieu for an integral realization of this expansive and deep Catholic vision.[3] This is so precisely because all these aspects—namely, sacramentality, mediation, and communion—are at the heart of the Catholic practice of pilgrimage and saint veneration. In addition, pilgrimage and saint veneration has the capability to anchor these aspects in highly personal and lastingly influential spiritual experience.

This first insight gives rise to the second one, regarding pilgrimage tradition or saint veneration as a communal practice that is popularly associated—in Java and elsewhere—equally with Catholicism and Islam. My comparative finding has showed that pilgrimage practice or saint veneration is by no means uniquely Catholic, given the abundant similarities that one finds in the Muslim tradition. Or, stated more positively, the Catholic saint veneration as it has been practiced at least in south central Java is not an isolated Catholic phenomenon. In this regard, I want to argue further that the larger spirit, practice, and understanding of the deeply sacramental doctrine of *communio sanctorum* (communion with God and the Holy, including the saints) could also be found within the Islamic tradition. Here, one need to recall that the Islamic tradition of pilgrimage and the larger tradition of saint veneration, are surprisingly crucial—indeed, almost universal—in the real lives of many Muslim believers and their communities throughout history, despite the absence of an explicit doctrinal formalization of those practices in the creedal formulae of the *mutakallimūn* or Kalam theologians.

It is in light of this fact that the practice of saint veneration could well be a rich locus for Muslim-Catholic encounters. As I have attempted to show in the context of south central Java, the common dimensions of these practices among Muslims and Catholics, helped considerably by the shared Javanese culture, have been quite instrumental not only in supporting the preservation and flourishing of pilgrimage practices in both traditions but also in enabling deeper and closer encounters with each other. In this respect, the encounters between the two religious traditions on the experiential level—that in the case of this study include

---

[2] Hence the statement of Avery Dulles: "Hardly any practice is so distinctively Catholic as the cult of the saints." Dulles, *The Catholicity of the Church*, p. 85.

[3] Richard P. McBrien, *Catholicism* (San Francisco, 1994), pp. 9–14, 1196–200.

religio-cultural frameworks of a particular society—could well be the basis for a distinctive comparative theology that owes its life and crucial insights not only to both traditions *qua* religious tradition, but also to their concrete historical and cultural interactions.

In this regard, this comparative study has hopefully shown the deeper theological reasons for this dynamic of mutual openness, such as the similarities in the religious and theological dimensions involved between the two communities with regard to pilgrimage practice. I have attempted to show that this vision of deep and expansive inclusivity could be based comparatively on the two traditions' insistence on the theological notion of the universality of God's grace, its sacramentality, the role of God's Friends (saints) in this dynamic of the outpouring of divine grace, and so forth.

My third comparative insight concerns the underlying role of a culture such as the Javanese in the flourishing of the pilgrimage practice in both traditions, as well as in the encounters between the Muslim and Catholic pilgrimage traditions. In broad strokes, I argue that Javanese culture is extremely conducive in the flourishing of the pilgrimage culture in both religious traditions, not least due to the nature of this culture as a living representation of the traditional cosmological synthesis where God, human beings, and the cosmos are related to each other in an organic whole. In particular, one can identify certain salient features of the Javanese culture that have lent themselves to the flourishing of the pilgrimage culture in both Muslim and Catholic traditions. The first of these features is a shared understanding of history as participatory memory of the sacred past, and the conception of the past as having an authority over the present, including but not exclusively, through the role and continued presence of paradigmatic saintly figures of the ancestors. Secondly, they have in common a profoundly communal understanding of the individual self. And third, they share a theological anthropology that understands the human journey as a pilgrimage to God and the true self through a process that includes cultivation of spiritual and purifying practices which can typically occur in the context of pilgrimage or visiting to sacred places and spiritual figures deeply connected with the sacred past of the community.

Of course, there are different ways of interpreting the significance of this phenomenon. However, it is interesting to see the promise of this whole phenomenon over against the breakdown, at least in the modern West, of the traditional cosmological synthesis in which the three components (God, the cosmos, and the humans) used to be understood in an integral whole. As Louis Dupré has argued, the breakdown of this synthesis since the high Middle Ages, initiated by nominalist philosophy, has led to the development of a "modern" worldview in which the three components are detached from each other—God is detached from nature, while humans become independent subjects with a tendency to exploit nature as an empty object (disenchantment of the world).[4] Over against

---

[4] Louis Dupré, *Passage to Modernity: An Essay in the Hermeneutics of Nature and Culture* (New Haven, 1993).

this background, the whole phenomenon of the flourishing of pilgrimage and saint veneration does offer a promising avenue toward a re-enchantment of the world.

The fourth fruitful insight pursues this idea of cosmological synthesis further in the context of the method of the emerging discipline of the new comparative theology. For in both Islamic and Catholic traditions, pilgrimage has many characteristics—such as personal, inclusive, cosmic, intergenerational, and so forth—that can be summed up under the governing principle of communion. Based on my comparative study as well as personal experience as "comparative pilgrim," I argue that the fuller and deeper scope and richness of this pilgrimage tradition as a complex practice of communion would only become more real and personally transforming if one actually does the back-and-forth visiting between the two traditions, which also means immersing ourselves into the sensory and experiential world of the other.[5] Thus arises the need for a comparative act and reflection to deepen our experience and knowledge with regard to the fuller scope, premises, and deeper consequences of this pilgrimage tradition.

Learning from my own experience, this process would hopefully bring pilgrims to the different yet familiar territory of the other, a step that means being inundated by both new and familiar images at the same time.[6] As a Javanese native from south central Java, I can say I was quite familiar with the figure of Sunan Kalijaga since childhood, for example, since he is the most popular Muslim saint in the area. However, my deeper appropriation of this figure and his role in the formation of Javano-Islamic identity became much more appealing to me as a Javanese Catholic only as I immersed myself deeper into the real dynamics of the Javano-Muslim community whose life has been inspired by this saint in the ways in which he has been "imagined" in that community. This is the case because only then could I recognize the real impact of the "catholicity" of this saint, namely, his religio-cultural vision of universalism, appropriating everything good in the other. In my back-and-forth visits, this sense of catholicity was transformed from vague abstraction into a very sensory experience. My Catholic prayers of devotion became diversified and richer—thus, becoming more "catholic"—due to my transfigured religious sensibility as a result of these double visits. The scope of my communion with God, the saints, the community, and so forth does not stay the same because of the qualitative presence of the Muslim saints and their communities in my transfigured religious sensibility.

At this point, I need to emphasize the sensory experience of being in the vicinity of the other precisely because of its power to make us not only open but also vulnerable to the world of the other, not primarily on the level of religious language, but rather on deeper experiential level. I am referring here to the more concrete step in this dynamic movement of comparative theology, that is, the stage when one actually "senses" the other. For the power of sensory experience in forging a religious identity could not be overestimated. In late antiquity, for

---

[5] Cf. Clooney, *Comparative Theology*, p. 126.
[6] Cf. Clooney, *Beyond Compare*, p. 141.

instance, the Church prohibited mixed marriage between Christian wife and pagan husband for similar reasons, i.e., to ensure that the Christian wife's religious identity was not diluted by the exposure to the pagan religion through sensory experiences in daily life through rituals.[7]

In the flowering of pilgrimage or saint veneration in general, the undeniable power of this sensory exposure to the other seems to be quite real, as I have illustrated in many ways throughout this book. My experience in going back-and-forth between Catholic and Muslim sites both confirms and defies this kind of fear. This exposure definitely opened up the reality of the world of the other to me, a delicate process that has eventually led me to understand and to perceive my identity rather differently. But this transformation of my understanding of my own identity does not blur my sense of solid identity, but rather deepens it in a real and remarkable sense. For in this very process I have come to understand better both the Javanese and Catholic elements of my personal identity, the wideness and depth of both elements, as well as the particularity of the Islamic tradition that has become an inherent part of the Javanese culture to which I belong.

This fourth insight leads directly to the fifth insight regarding the kind of contemporary religio-cultural reality that grounds comparative theology's non-effacing language. As I have shown in this book, there is a degree to which Islamic and Catholic traditions of pilgrimage have come together to form a religio-cultural common field of practice under the influence or in the larger context of the ambient Javanese culture. In my view, this common practice and its logic could be called "the third pilgrimage tradition."[8] What I mean by this common field is the kind of religio-cultural practice whose very logic, structures, and contents, if pursued further, lend themselves to a vast array of comparative theological reflections. For, due to the existence of this "third pilgrimage tradition," Islam and Christianity as distinctive religious traditions do not obliterate each other. In the context of this book, my argument is that this sort of comparative theological logic has already been found in the dynamics of common understanding and practice among Muslim and Catholic pilgrims, especially in terms of the understanding of sacred history with its paradigmatic figures and saints, the spatial, architectural and ritual expressions of religiosity, as well as the structure and contents of pilgrimage as a spiritual experience. This dynamic toward forming a "third pilgrimage tradition"

---

[7] Susan Ashbrok-Harvey, "Locating the Sensing Body: Perception and Religious Identity in Late Antiquity," in David Brakke et al. (eds), *Religion and the Self in Antiquity* (Bloomington, 2005), pp. 140–62.

[8] By stating this, I am aware of the complexities surrounding the question of "the originality" of each of the parties involved here ("Javaneseness," "Islam," and "Catholicism"). As I have stated earlier, all the parties get transformed in the process of encounters, so it is even harder to pinpoint the original starting point of each before the encounter. But, on the other hand, it is also clear that just as Islam brings its distinctive (and more universal) concepts to the table, so does Catholicism. Thus, one can of course talk about the birth of a new reality out of these encounters.

can become more explicit and deeper when pilgrims visit the shrine of the other, or when pilgrims of one faith encounter pilgrims of other faiths in their own shrines.

In this dynamic, then, the role of comparative theology is precisely to bring these common expressions, understanding, and experience into the realm of a proper theological reflection. In this particular case, comparative theology is at its core an enterprise of retrieval and systematization that owes its life to more than one theological tradition. However, as I argue and attempt to exemplify (in a very limited sense) in this book, it should ideally have a constructive aspect as well, that is, identifying some new theological meanings that the reality of these commonalities and multilevel encounters might point to. Working from a Catholic perspective, I can identify the comparative enrichment of the Catholic theology of *communio sanctorum* ("communion with God and the Holy") as a theologically constructive framework that these commonalities point to.[9] However, due to the limited space in this book, I will not flesh this insight out in a full-fledged comparative theological construction of the Catholic theology of *communio sanctorum*. This kind of work should naturally follow this present book.[10] At this point, it suffices to say that this comparative theological construction should be based on the already existing dynamics of common understanding—cultural, spiritual and theological—and experience. Hopefully, this theological grounding, once it becomes more widespread, could help the communities understand each other better on a spiritual and theological level, as well as socio-cultural level, thus creating a deeper mutual understanding that would prevent the sense of narrow rivalry that at times could still happen in this type of communal interactions under certain circumstances as the case in the Holy Lands and others have testified.

Lastly, and in connection with the problem of rivalry and tensions, let me emphasize once more that Muslim and Catholic pilgrimage practices in south central Java have served as a privileged milieu in which the pilgrims and their respective local communities continue to negotiate their religio-cultural identity in ways that are creative, authentic, and historically sustainable. This process is creative because it opens up new avenues for the growth of self-understanding, on both the individual and communal levels. It is authentic because despite occasional ambiguities, pilgrimage typically helps pilgrims strengthen their religious identity from within, in terms of the personal dimension of their lives and in the context of their respective religious traditions. For their respective religious community, this process of identity formation in the context of pilgrimage occurs to such a degree that this often creative and hybrid identity becomes a concrete historical embodiment of the wider framework of their religious tradition, in this case, Catholic Christianity or Islam. And this identity formation is also historically

---

[9] For a new understanding of this doctrine, see Elizabeth Johnson, *Friends of God and Prophets*.

[10] I have developed this kind of comparative theological renewal of *communio sanctorum* in my original Ph.D. dissertation, *Journeying to God in Communion with the Other* (Boston College, Mass., 2011), Chapter 9.

sustainable due to the fact that pilgrimage tradition has become a collective religio-cultural phenomenon of inclusive communal encounter that draws persons of all walks of life and faiths for centuries, a process that has been able to help pilgrims and their communities navigate their complex and intersecting journeys in many fruitful ways.

Glossary

Adab al-ziyāra (Ar.): Islamic ritual etiquette to be followed during pious visitation to tombs.

Sultan Agung (r. 1624–45): the greatest monarch of the Mataram dynasty, often portrayed as a Sufi-type of Muslim.

Babad: sacred historical account or chronicles produced in Javanese courts.

Berkah (Jv; Ar. *baraka*): God's blessings obtained through various means and in various forms.

Bhima (Dewaruci): a central figure in the Mahabharata epic; in Java, his mystical journey becomes a symbol for Kalijaga's initiation to sainthood.

Brawijaya V (ca. late fifteenth–early sixteenth century): the last monarch of the Javano-Hindu Majapahit kingdom in East Java.

Mbah **Dalhar** (d. 1959): a prominent Muslim saint in south central Java, buried in the Gunungpring shrine; a distant descendant of a Mataram king, Amangkurat III (d. 1734), he was mainly associated with the Darussalam Islamic boarding school (*pesantren*) near Gunungpring, Muntilan.

Garebeg (Sekaten): large public festivals held annually in the courts of Yogyakarta and Surakarta for the celebrations of major Islamic feasts; an important part of court culture, elements of *garebeg*s are featured in the pilgrimage culture in various Muslim and Catholic shrines.

Sunan Kalijaga (late fifteenth–sixteenth century): a Javanese Muslim saint, most popular in south central Java where he is considered a personification of a Javano-Islamic identity.

Kraton: court of the sultans with all its power, prestige, and distinctive religio-cultural traditions. In south central Java, the *kraton* culture is associated with the Javano-Muslim Sultanates of Yogyakarta and Surakarta.

Laku: purifying practices of prayers, meditation, and asceticism, associated with the practice of pilgrimage (see *tirakat*).

Franciscus van Lith (1863–1926): Dutch Jesuit missionary, founder of the Catholic mission in central Java.

Majapahit (1294–1478): the last Hindu kingdom on Java, which extended its control to southern Philippines, the Malaka straits, and the Malayan peninsula; succeeded by the Demak Sultanate (first Islamic kingdom on the north coast of Java).

Mataram: a Javano-Muslim dynasty; founded in the late sixteenth century by Panembahan Senapati in south central Java, it claims a lineage to Majapahit; this dynasty is now represented mainly by the courts of Yogyakarta and Surakarta.

Masjid Demak (Demak Mosque): the oldest congregational mosque on Java; founded by the *wali*s (early sixteenth century).
Muhammadiyah: the largest reformist Muslim organization in Indonesia; founded in 1912 in Yogyakarta by Achmad Dahlan.
Nahdlatul Ulama (the NU): the biggest traditionalist Muslim organization in Indonesia, founded in 1926. The NU has a large network of *pesantren*, and it is associated traditionally with the practice of traditional Islam such as mysticism, saint veneration, pilgrimage culture, and so forth.
Nyekar (Jv.): pious and respectful visitation to the tombs of ancestors that includes putting the flowers on the graves.
Sunan Pandanarang (ca. sixteenth century): a prominent Javanese Muslim saint in central Java; one of the prominent students of Sunan Kalijaga; buried in the Tembayat shrine.
Henri Maclaine Pont (1884–1971): Dutch Catholic architect, pioneer of indigenous architecture in the Dutch East Indies; also involved in the archeological excavations of Java's Hindu-Buddhist sites.
Panembahan Senapati (r. 1582–1601): founder of the Mataram dynasty.
Pesantren: Belonging to one of the central pillars of Islamic Java (especially among traditionalist Muslims in the Nahdlatul Ulama organization), the *pesantren*s are Islamic religious schools that also become, in most cases, centers of mystical learning and practice, associated with local and international mystical orders (Ar. *ṭarīqa*).
Prajnaparamita: a goddess figure associated with wisdom in Buddhism; taken up as an image of Mary at the Sacred Heart shrine and parish in Ganjuran.
Johannes Prennthaler (1885–1946): Austrian-born Jesuit missionary who worked in the Sendangsono area for many years (1921–36; 1942–46), under whose initiative and leadership the Marian grotto of Sendangsono came into being in 1929.
Rasa (S.): the inner or spiritual realm in the human constitution, as well as the means to get to touch with this realm; the deepest spiritual experience or knowledge that could not be acquired or explained through discursive reasoning or concepts; also related to the Islamic concept of *sirr*, the most subtle and hidden recess in the human heart where God and the soul are intimately in contact.
Father Sanjaya (d. 1948): a Javanese priest slain by an Islamic militia group in the mission town of Muntilan during a conflict between the Dutch and Indonesian forces in the period following the independence of Indonesia in 1948; popularly considered as a "martyr" of the faith by Javanese Catholics in central Java.
Raden Santri (Pangeran Singasari; ca. late sixteenth–seventeenth century): a Javanese Muslim saint of the Mataram dynasty (the brother of Panembahan Senapati), buried in the shrine of Gunungpring, Muntilan.
Barnabas Sarikrama (1874–1940): a Javanese Catholic catechist, the right hand man of Father van Lith in the formation of the newly baptized Catholics in the Sendangsono area, south central Java.

Josef Schmutzer (1882–1946) and **Julius Schmutzer** (1884–1954): two prominent brothers of the Schmutzer family, the founders of the Sacred Heart Shrine in Ganjuran, Yogyakarta. Josef was also a pioneer of Javano-Catholic arts; while Julius is remembered especially for his service in the Catholic mission's social welfare program for the Javanese natives.

Slamet (Jv., from Ar. *salāma*): Javanese holistic notion of well-being that is personal, communal and cosmic (see *tentrem*).

Slametan (Jv.): the pan-Javanese ritual communal meal offered to God, the prophets, saints and ancestors, for thanksgiving (or for the wellbeing of the community).

Tentrem (Jv.): profound, true and integral peace.

Tirakat*:* vigil, or pilgrimage as an intentional and intensive period of purification involving a series of ascetic practices such as fasting, prolonged meditation and so forth at the shrines (see *laku*).

Wali (Ar. *walī*, pl. *awliyā'*): friend of God or saints in Islam.

Wayang (Jv.): popular shadow theatre performance in Java, taking up the stories from the Mahabharata and the Ramayana epics and combining them with Islamic themes.

Wilāya/Walāya (Ar.): Islamic conception of "sainthood," emphasizing spiritual proximity or intimate friendship with God that also results in the bestowal of authority.

Ziarah (Jv; Ar. *ziyāra*): pious visit to shrines or tombs.

Bibliography

Archival Sources

Brieven van Pater J.B. Prennthaler aan Pater Directeur van de St Claverbond (1922–1937). Archive, the Jesuit Provincial Office, Semarang, Indonesia.
Voorzetting van het "Chronologisch Overzicht" van de werkzaamheid der Jesuieten in de Missio Bataviensis, 9 Juli 1934–12 Maart 1956. Archive, the Jesuit Provincial Office, Semarang, Indonesia.

Periodicals and Newspapers

Berichten Uit Java. Dutch Jesuit Missionary Journal. 1947–54.
The Jakarta Post
Kedaulatan Rakyat
Kompas
Missienieuws: Tijdschrift der Paters Jezuieten. Nijmegen. 1955–67.
St. Claverbond. Dutch Jesuit Missionary Journal. ca. 1889–1941.
Suara Merdeka
Swara-Tama. Javanese Newspaper. 1921–40s.

Shrine Brochures

Doa-doa untuk Ziarah di Ganjuran: Mohon Berkat Menjadi Berkat. Ganjuran shrine's brochure on rituals. No Date.
Gereja Hati Kudus Tuhan Yesus Ganjuran: Rahmat Yang Menjadi Berkat. The official Brochure of the Sacred Heart shrine, Ganjuran, Yogyakarta. 2008.
Silsilah Kyai Raden Santri (Eyang Pangeran Singasari) Puroloyo Gunungpring Muntilan. Published by Paguyuban Abdi Dalem Kraton Ngayogyakarta Hadiningrat. Ca. 2004.

Websites and Video Recordings

al-Hasani, Muhammad Wafa. "Waliyullah Mbah Kyai Dalhar Watucongol." http://al-kahfi.net/tarikh-watsaqafah/waliyullah-mbah-kyai-dalhar-watucongol/ (accessed September 2009).

Edi Psw Blog. "Ziarah Wali Songo 2008" (an entry on a Pilgrimage to the Nine Saints of Java). www.edipsw.com/opini/ziarah-wali-songo-2008/ (accessed July 2010).

Komunitas Tusing Kandha. *Candi Hati Kudus Yesus Ganjuran: Tanah Para Terjanji.* Yogyakarta, 2005 (Video Program).

S.A.V. Puskat, *Sendangsono: Mata Air Penyejuk Iman di Kaki Sang Ibu.* Yogyakarta, 2004 (Video Program).

Printed Matter

Ahearne, Jeremy. *Michel de Certeau: Interpretation and Its Other.* Stanford: Stanford University Press, 1995.

Albera, Dionigi. "Pelerinages mixtes et sanctuaries 'ambigus' en Méditerranée." In *Les pèlerinages au Maghreb et au Moyen-Orient: espaces publics, espaces du public.* Edited by Sylvia Chiffoleau and Anna Madoeuf, 347–78. Damas: Institut français du Proche-Orient, 2005.

Ali, Zakaria. *Islamic Art in Southeast Asia 830 A.D.–1570 A.D.* Kuala Lumpur: Dewan Bahasa and Pustaka, 1994.

Anies, H.M. Madchan. *Tahlil dan Kenduri: Tradisi Santri dan Kiai.* Yogyakarta: Pustaka Pesantren, 2009.

Aritonang, Jan Sihar, and Karel Steenbrink, eds. *A History of Christianity in Indonesia.* Leiden: Brill, 2008.

Ashbrok-Harvey, Susan. "Locating the Sensing Body: Perception and Religious Identity in Late Antiquity." In *Religion and the Self in Antiquity.* Edited by David Brakke et al., 140–62. Bloomington: Indiana University Press, 2005.

Asmoditomo, Obed, and Agust Sunarto. *Hati Kudus Tuhan Yesus dari Ganjuran.* Yogyakarta: Yayasan Pustaka Nusatama, 2001.

Badone, Ellen, and Sharon R. Roseman, eds. *Intersecting Journeys: The Anthropology of Pilgrimage and Tourism.* Urbana: University of Illinois Press, 2004.

Bailey, Gauvin. *Art on the Jesuit Missions in Asia and Latin America 1542–1773.* Toronto: University of Toronto Press, 2001.

Bartholomew, Craig, and Fred Hughes, eds. *Explorations in a Christian Theology of Pilgrimage.* Aldershot: Ashgate, 2004.

Barton, Greg. "Islam, *Pancasila* and the Middle Path of *Tawassuth*: the Thought of Achmad Siddiq." In *Nahdlatul Ulama, Traditional Islam and Modernity in Indonesia.* Edited by Greg Barton and Greg Fealy. Clayton: Monash Asia Institute, 1996.

Beatty, Andrew. "Adam and Eve and Vishnu: Syncretism in the Javanese Slametan." *The Journal of the Royal Anthropological Institute*, 2 (1996): 271–88.

Ben Ami, Issachar. *Saint Veneration among the Jews in Morocco.* Detroit: Wayne State University Press, 1998.

Bennet, James. *Crescent Moon: Islamic Art and Civilization in Southeast Asia.* Adelaide and Canberra: Art Gallery of South Australia and National Gallery of Australia, 2005.

Bitton-Ashkelony, Bruria. *Encountering the Sacred: The Debate on Christian Pilgrimage in Late Antiquity.* Berkeley: University of California Press, 2005.

Bizawie, Zainul Milal. "The Thoughts and Religious Understanding of Shaikh Ahmad al-Mutamakkin: The Struggle of Javanese Islam 1645–1740." *Studia Islamika*, 9 (2002): 27–62.

Bloembergen, Marieke. *Colonial Spectacles: The Netherlands and the Dutch East Indies at the World Exhibitions, 1880–1931.* Translated by Beverley Jackson. Singapore: Singapore University Press, 2006.

Boersma, Hans. *Nouvelle Théologie and Sacramental Ontology: A Return to Mystery.* Oxford: Oxford University Press, 2009.

Bonneff, Marcel. *Pérégrinations javanaises: les voyages de R.M.A. Purwa Lelana: une vision de Java au XIXe siècle (c. 1860–1875).* Paris: Editions de la Maison des Sciences de l'Homme, 1986.

Boss, Sarah Jane. *Mary.* New York: Continuum, 2003.

Brauen, Martin. *The Mandala: Sacred Circle in Tibetan Buddhism.* Boston: Shambala, 1998.

Brenner, Suzanne. *The Domestication of Desire: Women, Wealth, and Modernity in Java.* Princeton: Princeton University Press, 1998.

Brown, David. *God and Enchantment of Place: Reclaiming Human Experience.* Oxford: Oxford University Press, 2006.

Brown, Jonathan A.C. *Hadith: Muhammad's Legacy in the Medieval and Modern World.* Oxford: Oneworld, 2009.

Brown, Peter. *The Cult of Saints: Its Rise and Function in Latin Christianity.* Chicago: University of Chicago Press, 1981.

van Bruinessen, Martin. "Najmuddin al-Kubra, Jumadil Kubra and Jamaluddin al-Akbar: Traces of Kubrawiyya influence in early Indonesian Islam." *BKI*, 150 (1994): 305–29.

Bühnemann, Gudrun. *Mandalas and Yantras in the Hindu Traditions.* Leiden: Brill, 2003.

Burckhardt, Titus. *Art of Islam: Language and Meaning.* Commemorative edition. Bloomington: World Wisdom, 2009.

Cammann, Schuyler V.R. "Religious Symbolism in Persian Art." *History of Religions*, 15 (1976): 193–208.

Carey, Peter. *The Power of Prophecy: Prince Dipanagara and the End of an Old Order in Java, 1785–1855.* Leiden: KITLV, 2008.

Chambert-Loir, Henri, and Claude Guillot. *Le culte des saints dans le monde musulman.* Paris: École française d'Extrême-Orient, 1995.

Chambert-Loir, Henri, and Anthony Reid, eds. *The Potent Dead: Ancestors, Saints, and Heroes in Contemporary Indonesia.* Honolulu: University of Hawai'i Press, 2002.

Chodkiewicz, Michel. *The Seal of the Saints: Prophethood and Sainthood in the Doctrine of Ibn 'Arabi.* Cambridge: The Islamic Texts Society, 1993.

Clooney, Francis X., ed. *The New Comparative Theology: Interreligious Insights from the Next Generation.* New York: T&T Clark, 2010.

Clooney, Francis X. *Comparative Theology: Deep Learning across Religious Borders.* Chichester: Willey-Blackwell, 2010.

———. *Beyond Compare: St. Francis De Sales and Vedanta Desika on Loving Surrender to God.* Washington, D.C.: Georgetown University Press, 2009.

———. "Encountering the (Divine) Mother in Hindu and Christian Hymns," *Religion and the Arts*, 12 (2008): 230–43.

———. *Divine Mother, Blessed Mother: Hindu Goddesses and the Virgin Mary.* Oxford: Oxford University Press, 2005.

Cornell, Vincent J. *Realm of the Saint: Power and Authority in Moroccan Sufism.* Austin: University of Texas Press, 1998.

Courtens, Ien. "Mary, Mother of All: Finding Faith at the Sacred Source of Sendangsono, Indonesia." In *Moved by Mary: The Power of Pilgrimage in the Modern World.* Edited by Anna-Karina Hermkens et al., 101–16. Aldershot: Ashgate, 2009.

Cuffel, Alexandra. "From Practice to Polemic: shared saints and festivals as 'women's religion' in the medieval Mediterranean." *The Bulletin of the School of Oriental and African Studies*, 68 (2005): 401–19.

Dahles, Heidi. *Tourism, Heritage and National Culture in Java: Dilemmas of a Local Community.* New York: Routledge, 2001.

Daneshvari, Abbas. "The Iconography of the Dragon in the Cult of the Saints of Islam." In *Manifestations of Sainthood in Islam.* Edited by Grace Martin Smith and Carl W. Ernst, 16–25. Istanbul: The Isis Press, 1993.

Daniels, Timothy. *Islamic Spectrum in Java.* Aldershot: Ashgate, 2009.

van der Deijl, S.J. "Geloof en Wetenschap." *St. Claverbond* (1930): 150–58.

Dempsey, Corrine. *Kerala Christian Sainthood: Collisions of Culture and Worldview in South India.* Oxford: Oxford University Press, 2001.

van Dijk, Kees. "Dakwah and Indigenous Culture: the Dissemination of Islam." *BKI*, 154 (1998): 218–35.

Dirks, F., S.J. "'N Christen onder Mohammedanen." *St. Claverbond* (1937): 60–63.

Dodds, Jerrylynn D., et al. *The Arts of Intimacy: Christians, Jews and Muslims in the Making of Castilian Culture.* New Haven: Yale University Press, 2008.

van Dorn-Harder, Nelly, and Kees de Jong. "The Pilgrimage to Tembayat: Tradition and Revival in Indonesian Islam." *The Muslim World*, 91 (2001): 325–54.

Dowling, Nancy. "The Javanization of Indian Art." *Indonesia*, 54 (1992): 117–38.

Drewes, G.W.J., ed. and trans. *An Early Javanese Code of Muslim Ethics.* The Hague: Martinus Nijhoff, 1978.

———. "The Struggle between Javanism and Islam as Illustrated by the *Serat Dermagandul*." *BKI*, 122 (1966): 309–65.

Dubisch, Jill. *In a Different Place: Pilgrimage, Gender and Politics of a Greek Island Shrine.* Princeton: Princeton University Press, 1995.

Dulles, Avery. *The Catholicity of the Church.* Oxford: Clarendon Press, 1985.
Dumarcay, Jacques. *Borobudur.* Oxford: Oxford University Press, 1992.
Dupré, Louis. *Passage to Modernity: An Essay in the Hermeneutics of Nature and Culture.* New Haven: Yale University Press, 1993.
Dwiarso, Ki Priyo. "Problem Solving ala Ki Hadjar Dewantara." *Kedaulatan Rakyat Daily*, April 3, 2008.
Dwidjasoesanta, P.C. "Rama Sanjaya zijn levensschets en roemvol einde: Het martelaarschap van de eerste Javaanse seculiere priester." *Berichten uit Java* (1949): 54–8.
Eliade, Mircea. *The Myth of the Eternal Return: Cosmos and History.* Princeton: Princeton University Press, 2005. First edn 1949.
Elmore, Gerald T. *Islamic Sainthood in the Fullness of Time: Ibn al-ʿArabī's Book of the Fabulous Gryphon.* Leiden: Brill, 1999.
Esack, Farid. *Qur'an, Liberation and Pluralism: An Islamic Perspective of Interreligious Solidarity Against Oppression.* Oxford: Oneworld, 1997.
Fattah, H. Munawir Abdul. *Tradisi Orang-Orang NU.* Yogyakarta: Pusaka Pesantren, 2006.
Fehérvári, Géza. "Islamic Incense-burners and the Influence of Buddhist Art." In *The Iconography of Islamic Art.* Edited by Bernard O'Kane, 127–41. Edinburgh: Edinburgh University Press, 2008.
Florida, Nancy K. *Writing the Past, Inscribing the Future: History as Prophecy in Colonial Java.* Durham: Duke University Press, 1995.
———. *Javanese Literature in Surakarta Manuscripts.* 2 Vols. Ithaca: Southeast Asia Program, Cornell University, 1993, 2000.
———. "Reading the Unread in Traditional Javanese Literature." *Indonesia*, 44 (1987): 1–15.
Fox, James J. "Sunan Kalijaga and the Rise of Mataram: A Reading of the *Babad Tanah Jawi* as a Genealogical Narrative." In *Islam: Essays on Scripture, Thought and Society.* Edited by Peter G. Riddell and Tony Street, 187–218. Leiden: Brill, 1997.
———. "Ziarah Visits to the Tombs of the *Wali*, the Founders of Islam on Java." In *Islam in the Indonesian Social Context.* Edited by M.C. Ricklefs, 19–36. Victoria: Centre of Southeast Asian Studies, Monash University, 1991.
Frank, Georgia. *Memory of the Eyes: Pilgrims to Living Saints in Christian Late Antiquity.* Berkeley: University of California Press, 2000.
Fraser-Lu, Sylvia. *Indonesian Batik: Processes, Patterns and Places.* New York: Oxford University Press, 1986.
Fredericks, James. *Buddhists and Christians: Through Comparative Theology to Solidarity.* Maryknoll: Orbis Books, 2004.
Fuhrmann, Klaus. *Formen der javanischen Pilgerschaft zu Heiligenschreinen.* Ph.D. Dissertation. Albert-Ludwigs-Universität, Freiburg im Breisgau, 2000.
Geertz, Clifford. *Islam Observed: Religious Development in Morocco and Indonesia.* Chicago: University of Chicago Press, 1968.

———. "The Javanese Kijaji: The Changing Role of a Cultural Broker," *Comparative Studies in Society and History*, 2 (1960): 228–49.

———. *The Religion of Java.* Chicago: University of Chicago Press, 1976. First edn 1960.

Gifford, Julie. *Buddhist Practice and Visual Culture: The Visual Rhetoric of Borobudur.* New York: Routledge, 2011.

Gitsels, Jos, S.J. "'N Eeenzaam Afsterven." *St. Claverbond* (1923): 271–4.

Goizueta, Roberto. *Caminemos con Jesus: Toward a Hispanic/Latino Theology of Accompaniment.* Maryknoll: Orbis Books, 2005.

Goldziher, Ignaz. "The Veneration of Saints in Islam." *Muslim Studies*, 2 (1971): 255–341.

Gonda, J. *Sanskrit in Indonesia.* New Delhi: International Academy of Indian Culture, 1973.

de Graaf, H.J. *Awal Kebangkitan Mataram: Masa Pemerintahan Senapati.* Jakarta: Grafiti Press and KITLV, 1985.

———. *De regeering van Panembahan Sénapati Ingalaga.* 's Gravenhage: Martinus Nijhoff, 1954.

de Graaf, H.J., and Th. G. Pigeaud. *De Eerste Moslimse Vorstendommen op Java, Studiën over de Staatkundige Geschiedenis van de 15de en 16de Eeuw.* Leiden: KITLV, 1974.

Grabar, Oleg. *Islamic Art and Beyond: Constructing the Study of Islamic Art.* Vol. 3. Aldershot: Ashgate, 2006.

———. *Early Islamic Art, 650–1100: Constructing the Study of Islamic Art.* Vol. 1. Aldershot: Ashgate, 2005.

von Grunebaum, G.E. *Muhammadan Festivals.* London and Totowa: Curzon Press and Rowman and Littlefield, 1976. First edn 1951.

Hadiwikarta, J., Pr., ed. *Mengenal dan Mengenang Rama R. Sanjaya Pr.* Jakarta: Obor, 1984.

Hamengkubuwono X. *Kraton Jogja: The History and Cultural Heritage.* Yogyakarta: Karaton Ngayogyakarta Hadiningrat, 2002.

al-Harawī, ʿAlī ibn Abī Bakr. *A Lonely Wayfarer's Guide to Pilgrimage.* Translated by Josef W. Meri. Princeton: Darwin Press, 2004.

Hardawiryana, Robert. *Romo J.B. Prennthaler, S.J.: Perintis Misi di Perbukitan Menoreh.* Yogyakarta, 2002.

Harnish, David D. *Bridges to the Ancestors: Music, Myth, and Cultural Politics at an Indonesian Festival.* Honolulu: University of Hawai'i Press, 2006.

Haryadi, Sugeng. *Sejarah Berdirinya Masjid Agung Demak dan Grebeg Besar.* Jakarta: CV Mega Berlian, 2003.

Hermkens, Anna-Karina, et al., eds. *Moved by Mary: The Power of Pilgrimage in the Modern World.* Aldershot: Ashgate, 2009.

Hoffman, Valerie. *Sufism, Mystics and Saints in Modern Egypt.* Columbia: University of South Carolina Press, 1995.

Ibad, Muhamad Nurul. *Perjalanan dan Ajaran Gus Miek.* Yogyakarta: Pustaka Pesantren, 2007.

Inge, John. *A Christian Theology of Place.* Aldershot: Ashgate, 2003.
Izutsu, Toshihiko. *Sufism and Taoism: A Comparative Study of Key Philosophical Concepts.* Berkeley: University of California Press, 1983.
———. *The Concept of Belief in Islamic Theology: A Semantic Analysis of Īmān and Islām.* Tokyo: The Keio Institute of Cultural and Linguistic Studies, 1965.
Jaiz, Hartono Ahmad. *Tarekat, Tasawuf, Tahlilan, Mawlidan.* Solo: Wacana Ilmiah Press, 2006.
———. *Mendudukkan Tasawuf: Gus Dur Wali?* Jakarta: Darul Falah, 1999.
Jamhari. "The Meaning Interpreted: The Concept of *Barakah* in *Ziarah.*" *Studia Islamika*, 8 (2001): 87–128.
———. "In the Center of Meaning: Ziarah Tradition in Java." *Studia Islamika*, 7 (2000): 51–90.
Jaques, R. Kevin. "Sajarah Leluhur: Hindu Cosmology and the Construction of Javanese Muslim Genealogical Authority." *Journal of Islamic Studies*, 17 (2006): 129–57.
Java-Instituut. *Verslagen der Javaansche Cultuurcongressen 1918–1921.* Weltevreden: Uitgave van het Java-Instituut, ca. 1922.
Jessup, Helen. "Dutch Architectural Visions of the Indonesian Tradition." *Muqarnas*, 3 (1985): 138–61.
Johns, Anthony H. "From Buddhism to Islam: An Interpretation of the Javanese Literature of the Transition." *Comparative Studies in Society and History*, 9 (1966): 40–50.
Johnson, Elizabeth. *Friends of God and Prophets: A Feminist Theological Reading of the Communion of Saints.* New York: Continuum, 2005.
Jonas, Raymond. *France and the Cult of the Sacred Heart: An Epic Tale for Modern Times.* Berkeley: University of California Press, 2000.
de Jonge, Huub. "Heiligen, middelen en doel: ontwikkeling en betekenis van twee islamitische bedevaartsoorten op Java." In *Islamische Pelgrimstochten.* Edited by Willy Jansen and H de Jonge, 89–95. Muiderberg: Coutinho, 1991.
van Kalken, S.J. "Hunne Werken Immers Volgen Hen." *St. Claverbond* (1930): 142–9.
Kerkeling, Hape. *I'm Off Then: Losing and Finding Myself on the Camino de Santiago.* New York: Free Press, 2009.
Kieser, Bernhard, S.J. "Maria, Siapa Punya? Orang Kristiani dan Orang Muslim Menghormati Maria." In *Mengasih Maria: 100 Tahun Sendangsono.* Edited by Sindhunata, 189–204. Yogyakarta: Kanisius, 2004.
Kimmenade-Beekmans, J.M. v.d. *De Missie van de Jezuiten op Midden-Java tijdens het Interbellum.* Tilburg: Katholieke Leergangen Tilburg, 1987.
Kinney, Ann R., et al. *Worshiping Siva and Buddha: The Temple Art of East Java.* Honolulu: The University of Hawaii Press, 2003.
van Klinken, Gerry. "Power, symbol and the Catholic mission in Java: The Biography of Frans van Lith, S.J." *Documentieblad voor de Geschiedenis van de Nederlandse Zending en Overzeese Kerken*, 1 (1997): 43–59.

Knooren, F., S.J. "Bijzonderheden over den Dood van Pater Prennthaler S.J. – RIP." *St. Claverbond* (1946): 93–6.

Kumar, Ann. *Java and Modern Europe: Ambiguous Encounters*. Richmond: Curzon Press, 1997.

———. *The Diary of a Javanese Muslim: Politics and the Pesantren 1883–1886*. Canberra: Australian National University, 1985.

Kusno, Abidin. *Behind the Postcolonial: Architecture, Urban Space and Political Cultures in Indonesia*. New York: Routledge, 2000.

Labib, M.Z. *Tuntunan Ziarah Walisongo*. Surabaya: Bintang Usaha Jaya, 2000.

Laksana, Albertus Bagus. "Perjumpaan Yang Tak Biasa: Tradisi Wali Pitu di Pulau Dewata." *Basis*, 11–12 (2012): 32–8.

———. "Comparative Theology: Between Identity and Alterity." In *New Comparative Theology: Interreligious Insights from the Next Generation*. Edited by Francis X. Clooney, 1–20. New York: T & T Clark, 2010.

———. "Ziarah Kasiyo Sarkub." *Basis*, 56 (2007): 14–19.

———. *The Spirit at Work: Asian Pneumatology from Below and the Problem of Religious Pluralism*. Licentiate Thesis. Weston Jesuit School of Theology, Cambridge, Massachusetts. 2005.

van Leerdam, Ben F. *Architect Henri Maclaine Pont: Een speurtocht naar het wezenlijke van de Javaanse architectuur*. Den Haag: CIP-Gegevens Koninklijke Bibliotheek, 1995.

Levtzion, N. and J.F.P. Hopkins, eds. *Corpus of Early Arabic Sources for West African History*. Princeton: Markus Wiener Publishers, 2000.

Lincoln, Andrew T. "Pilgrimage and the New Testament." In *Explorations in a Christian Theology of Pilgrimage*. Edited by Craig Bartholomew and Fred Hughes, 29–49. Aldershot: Ashgate, 2004.

van Lith, Franciscus. "Raden Larang en Raden Sumana." *Tijdschrift voor 'Indische taal-, land- en volkenkunde*, 66 (1926): 435–46.

———. "Het gebed van Ardjoena tot Ciwa." *Studiën*, 56/101 (1924): 362–75.

———. *De Politiek van Nederland ten opzichte van Nederlandsch-Indie*. 's-Hertogenbosch, Antwerpen, 1922.

———. "De Godsdienst der Javanen." *St. Claverbond* (1922): 193–201.

———. *Kjahi Sadrach: Eene les voor ons uit de Protestantsche zending van Midden-Java*. Manuscript. ca. 1922.

———. "De Javaansche grammatica op Javaanschen grondslag." In *Handelingen van het Eerste Congres voor de Taal-, Land- en Volkenkunde van Java, Solo, 25 en 26, 1919*. Weltevreden: Albrecht, 1921, pp. 273–85.

Lukens-Bull, Ronald. *A Peaceful Jihad: Negotiating Identity and Modernity in Muslim Java*. New York: Palgrave Macmillan, 2005.

Mabbett, I.W. "The Symbolism of Mount Meru." *History of Religions*, 23 (1983): 64–83.

McAullife, J.D., ed. *Encyclopedia of the Qur'an*. Vol. 3. Leiden: Brill, 2003.

McBrien, Richard P. *Catholicism*. San Francisco: HarperSanFrancisco, 1994.

Madjid, Nurcholish. *Islam Doktrin and Peradaban*. Jakarta: Paramadina, 1992.

Magnis-Suseno, Franz. *Pijar-Pijar Filsafat.* Yogyakarta: Kanisius, 2005.
Makdisi, George. "Ibn Taimīya: A Ṣūfi of the Qādiriya Order." *American Journal of Arabic Studies*, 1 (1973): 118–29.
Masuzawa, Tomoko. *The Invention of World Religions: Or, How European Universalism Was Preserved in the Language of Pluralism.* Chicago: The University of Chicago Press, 2005.
Meibohm, Margaret. *Cultural Complexity in South India: Hindu and Catholic in Marian Pilgrimage.* Ph.D. Dissertation. University of Pennsylvania, 2004.
Memon, Muhammad Umar. *Ibn Taimiya's Struggle Against Popular Religion.* The Hague: Mouton, 1973.
Meri, Josef W. *The Cult of Saints among Muslims and Jews in Medieval Syria.* Oxford: Oxford University Press, 2002.
Merton, Thomas. *Seven Storey Mountain: An Autobiography of Faith.* New York: Harcourt Brace and Co., 1999.
Miksic, John. "The Art of Cirebon and the Image of the Ascetic in Early Javanese Islam." In *Crescent Moon: Islamic Art and Civilisation in Southeast Asia.* Edited by James Bennett, 120–38. Adelaide: Art Gallery of South Australia and National Gallery of Australia, 2007.
Millie, Julian Patrick. *Splashed by the Saint: Ritual Reading and Islamic Sanctity in West Java.* Leiden: KITLV, 2009.
Milner, A.C. "Islam and the Muslim State." In *Islam in South-East Asia.* Edited by M. Hooker, 23–49. Leiden: Brill, 1983.
Moertono, Soemarsaid. *State and Statecraft in Old Java: A Study of the Later Mataram Period, 16th to 19th Centuries.* Ithaca: Cornell University, 1968.
Morris, James W. *The Reflective Heart: Discovering Spiritual Intelligence in Ibn 'Arabī's "Meccan Illuminations."* Louisville: Fons Vitae, 2005.
———. "Remembrance and Repetition: Spiritual Foundations of Islamic Art." *Sufi*, 47 (2000): 15–23.
———. "Situating Islamic 'Mysticism': Between Written Traditions and Popular Spirituality." In *Mystics of the Book: Themes, Topics, and Typologies.* Edited by R. Herrera, 293–334. New York: Peter Lang, 1993.
———. "Reading 'Aṭṭār's *Conference of the Birds.*" In *Approaches to the Asian Classics.* Edited by Wm. Theodore de Bary and Irene Bloom, 77–85. New York: Columbia University Press, 1990.
Motyer, Steve. "Paul and Pilgrimage." In *Explorations in a Christian Theology of Pilgrimage.* Edited by Craig Bartholomew and Fred Hughes, 50–69. Aldershot: Ashgate, 2004.
Mulkhan, Abdul Munir. *Islam Murni dalam Masyarakat Petani.* Yogyakarta: Bentang Budaya, 2000.
Nijs, W., S.J. "Moentilan." *St. Claverbond* (1946): 52–78.
Norris, H.T. *Popular Sufism in Eastern Europe: Sufi Brotherhoods and the Dialogue with Christianity and "Heterodoxy."* New York: Routledge, 2006.
Notermans, Catrien. "Connecting the Living and the Dead: Re-membering the Family through Marian Devotion." In *Moved by Mary: The Power*

of Pilgrimage in the Modern World. Edited by Anna-Karina Hermkens et al., 135–48. Aldershot: Ashgate, 2009.
O'Brien, Kate. Trans. *Sutasoma: The Ancient Tale of a Buddha-Prince from 14th century Java by the Poet Mpu Tantular.* Bangkok: Orchid Press, 2008.
Pakubuwana XII. *Karaton Surakarta: A Look into the Court of Surakarta Hadiningrat, Central Java.* Singapore: Marshall Cavendish, 2006.
Pemberton, John. *On the Subject of "Java."* Ithaca: Cornell University Press, 1994.
Pigeaud, Th. *Literature of Java.* Vol. 2. The Hague: Martinus Nyhoff, 1968.
Pranowo, Bambang M. *Memahami Islam Jawa.* Ciputat: Pustaka Alvabet and Indonesian Institute for Society Empowerment (INSEP), 2009.
———. "Traditional Islam in Contemporary Rural Java: The Case of Tegal Rejo Pesantren." In *Islam in the Indonesian Social Context.* Edited by M.C. Ricklefs, 39–55. Victoria: Centre of Southeast Asian Studies, Monash University, 1991.
———. "Islam Faktual: Antara Tradisi dan Relasi Kuasa." Adicita Karya Nusa, No Date.
Prennthaler, J. "Het Testament van Pater Prennthaler." *St. Claverbond* (1946): 203–5.
———. "Open Brief van Pater J. Prennthaler, S.J." *St. Claverbond* (1935): 169–72.
Quinn, George. "Local Pilgrimage in Java and Madura: Why is it booming?" *IIAS Newsletter*, 35 (2004): 16.
Ras, J. "The genesis of the *Babad Tanah Jawi*: Origin and function of the Javanese court chronicle." *BKI*, 143 (1987): 343–56.
Reichle, Natasha. *Violence and Serenity: Late Buddhist Sculpture from Indonesia.* Honolulu: University of Hawai'i Press, 2007.
Renard, John. *Friends of God: Islamic Images of Piety, Commitment, and Servanthood.* Berkeley: University of California, 2008.
Ricklefs, M.C. *A History of Modern Indonesia since c. 1200.* Stanford: Stanford University Press, 2008.
———. *Polarizing Javanese Society: Islamic and Other Visions (c. 1830–1930).* Honolulu: University of Hawai'i Press, 2007.
———. *Mystic Synthesis in Java: A History of Islamization from the Fourteenth to the Early Nineteenth Centuries.* Norwalk: EastBridge, 2006.
———. *The Seen and Unseen Worlds in Java: History, Literature and Islam in the Court of Pakubuwana II, 1726–1749.* Honolulu: University of Hawai'i Press, 1998.
———. "Dipanagara's Early Inspirational Experience." *BKI*, 130 (1974): 227–58.
van Rijckevorsel, L. "Eerste Steenlegging van een H. Hart-Monument op Java." *St. Claverbond* (1928): 129–37.
Rinkes, D.A. *The Nine Saints of Java.* Translated by H.M. Froger. Kuala Lumpur: Malaysian Sociological Research Institute, 1996.
Robson, Stuart. "Kjahi Raden Santri." *BKI*, 121 (1965): 259–64.
Robson, Stuart, and Singgih Wibisono. *Javanese-English Dictionary.* Singapore: Periplus, 2002.

Romli, Inajati A., et al., eds. *Jejak Para Wali dan Ziarah Spiritual.* Jakarta: Penerbit Kompas, 2006.

van Roojen, Pepin. *Batik Design.* Boston: Shambhala, 1997.

Rosariyanto, Hasto. *Father Franciscus van Lith, S.J.: Turning Point of the Catholic Church's Approach in the Pluralistic Indonesian Society.* Doctoral Dissertation. Gregorian University, Rome, 1997.

Santoso, Soewito, trans. and ed. *The Centhini Story: The Javanese Journey of Life.* Singapore: Marshal Cavendish International, 2006.

Schimmel, Annemarie. *Deciphering the Signs of God: A Phenomenological Approach to Islam.* Albany: SUNY, 1994.

———. *And Muhammad Is His Messenger.* Chapel Hill: University of North Carolina Press, 1985.

———. *Mystical Dimensions of Islam.* Chapel Hill: University of North Carolina Press, 1975.

Schloesser, Stephen. *Jazz Age Catholicism: Mystic Modernism in Postwar Paris, 1919–1933.* Toronto: University of Toronto Press, 2005.

Schmutzer, Eduard J.M. *Dutch Colonial Policy and the Search for Identity in Indonesia 1920–1931.* Leiden: E.J. Brill, 1977.

Schmutzer, Josef. "Het Apostolaat der Kunst." *St. Claverbond* (1935): 53–68

———. "Javaansche Madonna's." *St. Claverbond* (1935): 214–22

———. "Irene Peltenburg en de Aangepaast Missiekunst." *St. Claverbond* (1934): 65–8.

———. "Het Algemeen Regeeringsbeleid en het Arbeidsvraagstuk in den Volksraad." In *Publikatie der Indische Katholieke Partij (1929).* Vol. 1.

———. *Un Art Javanais Chrétien.* Paris and Louvain: A Giraudon and De Vlaamsche Drukkerij, ca. 1929.

———. "Bezieling en Arbeid." In *Eerste Internationaal Missiecongres in Nederland.* Utrecht, September 25–9, 1922, pp. 193–208.

———. *Solidarisme in Indië.* Leiden, 1922.

———. "Leekenarbeid in het Indische Missiegebied." In *Eerste Nederlandsche Missiecongres.* Leiden: Ars Catholica, 1921.

Schmutzer, Josef, and J.J. Ten Berge, S.J. *Europeanisme ou Catholicisme?* Paris: A Giraudon, 1929.

Schots, J.A.C. S.J. "Eerstelingen te Ambarawa!" *St. Claverbond* (1923): 289–97.

Scott, Peter. "A Theology of Eucharistic Place: Pilgrimage as Sacramental." In *Explorations in a Christian Theology of Pilgrimage.* Edited by Craig Bartholomew and Fred Hughes, 151–69. Aldershot: Ashgate, 2004.

Sears, Laurie. *Shadows of Empire: Colonial Discourse and Javanese Tales.* Durham: Duke University Press, 1996.

Shahid, Irfan. "Arab Christian Pilgrimages in the Proto-Byzantine Period (V–VII Centuries)." In *Pilgrimage and Holy Space in Late Antique Egypt.* Edited by David Frankfurter, 373–92. Leiden: Brill, 1998.

Sheldrake, Philip. *Spaces for the Sacred: Place, Memory and Identity.* London: SCM Press, 2001.

Shihab, Alwi. *Islam Sufistik: "Islam Pertama" and Pengaruhnya Hingga Kini di Indonesia.* Bandung: Mizan, 2001.

———. *The Muhammadiyah Movement and Its Controversy with Christian Mission in Indonesia.* Ph.D. Dissertation, Temple University, 1995.

Shiraishi, Takashi. *An Age in Motion: Popular Radicalism in Java 1912–1926.* Ithaca: Cornell University Press, 1990.

Sidel, John T. *Riots Pogroms Jihad: Religious Violence in Indonesia.* Ithaca: Cornell University Press, 2006.

Simon, Hasanu. *Misteri Syekh Siti Jenar.* Yogyakarta: Pustaka Pelajar, 2008.

Sindhunata, ed. *Mengasih Maria: 100 Tahun Sendangsono.* Yogyakarta: Kanisius, 2004.

Sing, Raj. *Bhakti and Philosophy.* Lanham: Lexington Books, 2006.

Soebardi. *The Book of Cabolèk.* The Hague: Martinus Nijhoff, 1975.

Soegijapranata, Alb., "Pastoor van Lith als onze opvoeder." *Berichten uit Java* (1952): 101–5.

Soekmono, R. "Notes on the Monuments of Ancient Indonesia." In *Ancient Indonesian Art of the Central and Eastern Javanese Periods.* Edited by Jan Fontein et al., 13–17. New York: The Asia Society Inc., 1971.

Soeratno, Siti Chamamah. "Tokoh Khidlir dan Tradisinya pada Masyarakat Jawa: Tinjauan atas Dampak Penyebaran Islam di Jawa." Balai Kajian Sejarah dan Nilai Tradisional Yogyakarta, Museum Benteng Yogyakarta, November 9, 1995.

Stange, Paul. "The Logic of *Rasa* in Java." *Indonesia*, 38 (1984): 113–34.

Steenbrink, Karel. *Catholics in Indonesia*, 2 Vols. Leiden: KITLV, 2003, 2007.

Stirrat, R.L. "Demonic Possession in Roman Catholic Sri Lanka." *Journal of Anthropological Research*, 33 (1977): 133–57.

Stutterheim, W.F. "Note on Saktism in Java." *Acta Orientalia*, 17 (1938): 144–52.

———. "The Meaning of the Hindu-Javanese Candi." *Journal of the American Oriental Society*, 51 (1931): 1–15.

Sumarsam. *Gamelan: Cultural Interaction and Musical Development in Central Java.* Chicago: University of Chicago Press, 1992.

Tartono, St. *Barnabas Sarikrama.* Museum Misi Muntilan, 2005.

Taylor, Christopher S. *In the Vicinity of the Righteous: Ziyara and the Veneration of Muslim Saints in Late Medieval Egypt.* Leiden: Brill, 1999.

Thoyibi, M. et al., *Sinergi Agama dan Budaya Lokal: Dialektika Muhammadiyah dan Budaya Lokal.* Surakarta: Muhammadiyah University Press, 2003.

Turner, Victor and Edith. *Image and Pilgrimage in Christian Culture.* New York: Columbia University Press, 1978.

Vriens, G., S.J. *Seratus Tahun Misi.* Yogyakarta: Kanisius, 1959.

———. "De Javanen-Missie der Jezuieten in de Republiek." *Missiewerk*, ca. 1950: 1–22.

Walker, Peter. "Pilgrimage in the Early Church." In *Explorations in a Christian Theology of Pilgrimage.* Edited by Craig Bartholomew and Fred Hughes, 73–91. Aldershot: Ashgate, 2004.

Webb, Diana. *Medieval European Pilgrimage, c. 700–1500.* Oxford: Palgrave Macmillan, 2000.

———. *Pilgrims and Pilgrimage in the Medieval West.* London: I.B. Tauris, 1999.

Wehr, Hans. *Arabic-English Dictionary.* Edited by Milton Cowan. 4th edition. Spoken Language Services, 1994

Wheeler, Brannon. *Mecca and Eden: Ritual, Relics, and Territory in Islam.* Chicago: University of Chicago Press, 2006.

Wieringa, Edwin. "An Old Text Brought to Life Again: A Reconsideration of the 'Final Version' of the *Babad Tanah Jawi.*" *BKI*, 155 (1999): 244–63.

———. "The Mystical Figure of Haji Ahmad Mutamakin from the Village of Cabolèk." *Studia Islamika*, 5 (1998): 25–40.

Wilson, Chris. *Ethno-religious Violence in Indonesia: From Soil To God.* New York: Routledge, 2008.

Wismapranata, et al. *Kenangan atas 100 Tahun Sendangsono: Syukur atas Kurnia Iman.* Yogyakarta, 2004.

Wood, Michael. *Official History in Modern Indonesia: New Order Perceptions and Counterviews.* Leiden: Brill, 2005.

Woodward, Mark. *Java, Indonesia and Islam.* New York: Springer, 2010.

———. "Resisting Wahhabi Colonialism in Yogyakarta." *COMPS Journal* (2008): 1–8.

———. *Islam in Java: Normative Piety and Mysticism in the Sultanate of Yogyakarta.* Tucson: University of Arizona Press, 1989.

———. "The 'Slametan': Textual Knowledge and Ritual Performance in Central Javanese Islam." *History of Religions*, 28 (1988): 54–89.

Zoetmulder, P.J. *Pantheism and Monism in Javanese Suluk Literature: Islamic and Indian Mysticism in an Indonesian Setting.* Leiden: KITLV Press, 1995.

Index

adab al-ziyāra 28, 63, 65, 69, 227
Adam 29, 68, 70, 206, 232
adaptation 101, 201, 206
aesthetic 146, 151, 153–4, 178
ahl al-qubr 66, 69
Allah 38, 54, 166, 203
alterity 53, 73, 88, 117, 126–7, 182, 191, 213, 238; *see also* otherness
  double alterity 105, 199
ambiguity 2, 20, 30–31, 42, 53, 62, 73, 75, 109, 134, 136, 141, 194, 196–7, 199, 224
ancestor(s) 2, 7, 24–5, 29, 45, 47, 63–70, 89, 100, 117–18, 134, 139, 156, 167–9, 198, 201–6, 228–9, 236; *see also* founders
  pious 184
  remembrance of 68–70, 82, 158
  saintly and paradigmatic 75, 198, 204, 206
  tomb of 69, 167, 204, 228
angelus 120, 156
aniconic 53, 55
Annai Vellankanni 11, 185
anthropology 17, 91
  Islamic theological (mystical/spiritual) 31, 40–41, 58, 176
  Javano-Islamic spiritual (mystical) 34, 41
Aquinas, Thomas 124
architectures 9, 19, 54, 56, 59, 61–2, 74, 111, 126, 142–3, 146, 152–4, 161, 164, 179, 183, 196, 201, 211, 213, 228
  Javano-Catholic 138–9, 141, 178
  Javano-Islamic 55
arts 59–61, 73–4, 124, 138, 140, 143–7, 153, 161, 179–80, 201, 211
  Javano-Catholic 139, 151, 154, 229
  Javano-Islamic 54

ascent 58–61, 66, 75
  to God and the true self 57, 61
  to sainthood 42, 57
ascetic 32, 34, 36, 56, 86, 89–90, 92, 94, 100, 117, 168, 175, 208, 229, 239
  ascetic and soul-searching pilgrims 79, 90
  ascetic-wandering pilgrims 91, 207
  Hindu 44
  Muslim 48
  pilgrimage 25, 77, 88, 95–6, 137
asceticism 61, 88–90, 92–3, 100, 114, 175
  purifying asceticism 168, 176, 227
Astasahasrika Prajnaparamita 151
ʿAṭṭār, Farīd al-Dīn 57, 59
  Manṭiq al-ṭayr (Conference of the Birds) 57, 239

Babad literature 29–30, 36, 227
  Babad Cirebon 38
  Babad Jaka Tingkir 43, 51
  Babad Tanah Jawi 35, 46, 235
  Babad Tembayat, Serat 42–3
Bailey, Gauvin 154, 232
Bali 31, 93, 158
baraka (blessing) 2, 43, 64, 67–8, 86–8, 98–9, 193, 208, 227, 237
al-Barzanjī 71
bastardization 153–4, 179
batik 55, 147–8, 153
Beatty, Andrew 68, 206, 232
beauty 35, 91, 150, 179, 217
bekti 82, 166–8, 203–4; *see also* "*bhakti*"
Bèla-Bèlu, Sèh 47, 95
berkah 68, 87, 207, 227
Bethlehem of Java 127
bhakti 166–7; *see also* "*bekti*"
Bhima 34–5, 77, 209, 227
Bhimasuci 34
Bloembergen, Marieke 140, 152–3, 251

Bondan Kejawan, Raden 46, 48
Borobudur 7–8, 25, 58, 110–11, 115, 117–18, 236
Bouwens, Herman 127, 129, 130
Brawijaya V (King of Majapahit) 31–2, 39–43, 45–8, 227
brokers, religio-cultural 19, 73–5
van Bruinessen, Martin 45–6, 233
Buddha 58, 139, 144, 151, 157
Buddhism 7, 35, 54, 74, 135, 137, 144, 167, 237
　Mahayana 149
　Tantric 137
Bühnemann, Gudrun 137–8, 233
Burckhardt, Titus 61–2, 251

Cabolèk, Serat 34–5, 44, 219, 242–3
candi 53, 137, 139, 242
Candi Sari 141
Carita Iskandar 23, 29, 45
Catholicism 6–7, 106–7, 109, 115, 118, 122, 125, 139–40, 161, 167, 196–7, 199, 208, 211, 216, 220, 223, 241
catholicity 106, 199, 210, 240
Centhini, Serat 2, 23–4, 51, 93, 154
Chambert-Loir, Henri 17, 52, 233
Chinese 46, 56, 97, 106–7
　Catholic pilgrims 9, 160, 171, 176, 181
　pilgrims 8, 65, 88, 185
Christianity 9–11, 105, 118, 129–30, 135–6, 145–6, 151, 161, 191, 196, 199, 213, 215–16, 219, 224
　encounter with Islam 119, 223
christology 164
Chudlori, Kyai 48, 77–8
circumambulation 158–9
Clooney, Francis 18, 151, 167, 191–2, 234, 238
colonialism 6, 105, 124–5, 129, 131, 243
communio sanctorum 133, 220, 224
communion 2, 12, 19–20, 26, 28–30, 50–51, 77–8, 85, 89, 94, 99, 101, 109, 115, 121–2, 127–8, 133–4, 136, 138, 156–9, 163–4, 172, 174–6, 180, 187, 193, 195, 197–8, 202, 204–5, 210–11, 215, 220
　with the dead 13, 29
　with God, the self, and other 3, 101

the principle of 25, 62, 74, 78, 107, 109, 117, 121, 126, 131, 161, 165, 196, 201, 213–14, 222, 224
communitas 93, 181
comparative 17–18, 20, 201, 215, 219
　phenomenological 2
　theology (new) 3, 18, 20, 151, 191–3, 211, 221–4
contemplation 61, 147, 174
　exteriorized contemplation 173
continuity 25, 31, 41, 43, 45, 49, 101, 137, 204, 217–18
　communion and 26, 50
　cultural 4, 39, 42
　principle of 39, 41, 51, 53, 62, 74, 107, 117, 196, 201, 212, 217
conversion 47, 90, 174, 212
　of Brawijaya V 31–2, 41
　to Catholicism 109, 113, 120
　of Pandanarang (Sunan Tembayat) 43–4, 93
Cordova 61
cosmology 16, 29, 31, 40, 215, 237
　sacred 47, 194
Courtens, Ien 155, 234

Dahles, Heidi 3, 234
Dalhar, *Mbah* 7, 48–9, 100, 205, 227, 231
Damascus 11–12, 214
Daneshvari, Abbas 59, 234
Darmojuwono, Cardinal 127, 130, 132
Darussalam, *Pesantren* 48, 227
De Certeau, Michel 52–3, 232
Demak
　Islamic polity of 43
　Mosque (Grand Mosque of Java) 23, 36–8, 152, 201–2, 228
Den Baguse Samijo 115, 117–18
devotion 12–13, 16, 19, 23, 25, 64, 67–8, 70, 77–85, 88, 100, 132, 156, 163–72, 177, 179, 181–4, 192–5, 203–4, 207–9, 215–17
　milieu of 7, 164
　pilgrims of 79, 90
Déwaruci 34–5, 41, 227
Dewi Lantamsari 117–18
Dewi Maria 166–7, 183
dhikr 23, 67, 71, 92, 100, 154, 203, 208

Dipanagara, Prince 8, 37, 47, 97, 137, 240
disenchantment of the world 221
dragon 53–5, 58–60, 64, 234
Drajad, Sunan 98
Dulles, Avery 210, 220, 235
Dupré, Louis 221, 235
Dutch 3, 5, 8, 38, 44, 106–8, 110, 116–17, 122–30, 141–3, 146, 152, 185, 207, 228, 237, 241
    anti-Dutch 128–9
    Catholic Party in the Indies 124
    colonialism 105
    East Indies 121, 228
    Jesuit mission (missionaries) 5–6, 126–8, 135, 140, 196, 202, 212, 227, 231

Egypt 119, 158, 206
Eliade, Mircea 29
    The Myth of Eternal Return 29, 235
enlightenment 32, 34–5, 58, 151–2, 157
eucharist 158, 180
excavations 141
    of Hindu-Buddhist antiquity in Java 140–41, 228

FABC (Federation of Asian Bishops' Conferences) 146
fasting 92, 94, 96, 208–9
Ferrara Manuscript 46
festival 6, 9, 14, 30, 63, 70–71, 73, 79, 86, 120, 154, 176, 227, 234
    haul 69, 71
    of the Sacred Heart 156–60, 183, 201–2
Florida, Nancy K. 5, 28, 33–4, 36–8, 40, 43, 45, 51, 235
founders 19, 31, 114–15, 118, 122–3, 125, 133–4, 201, 229
    and ancestors of the community 17, 25, 29, 100, 139, 156, 158, 198, 202, 205–6, 216
    of Islam in Java 8, 32, 235
    of the Java mission 127
    memory of 117, 159
    saint and 75, 78, 198
Fredericks, James 18, 191–2, 235

friendship 13, 31, 77, 83–6, 108, 141, 143, 181, 195
    with God 16, 57, 81, 229; *see also* *"walāya"*

Gagang Dami Aking, Sèh 47
gamelan 38, 154, 159
Ganjuran 122–7, 136, 138–9, 141, 142, 146–54, 157–9, 173, 178–81, 183–7, 228, 231
    Prajnaparamita Mary of 150–51
    Sacred Heart Shrine of 8, 109–11, 121, 134, 137, 156, 163, 165, 168, 171, 193–4, 206, 210, 213–14, 216, 229
garebeg 63, 70, 73, 159, 227
Geertz, Clifford 32, 36, 74, 96, 235
genealogy 29, 32, 39, 45–6, 48, 70
Geseng, Sunan 94–5
Giri Prapen, Sunan 23, 32, 45–6
goddess 145, 149, 151, 167
    of the Southern Sea 8, 30, 36–7, 47, 73
Goizueta, Roberto 211, 236
Grabar, Oleg 61–2, 236
grace 17, 35, 82, 87, 98, 125, 134, 147, 164, 183, 185–6, 210, 212, 214–15, 220–21
    mediator of all 171
    Uncreated Grace 145
Gresik 46, 55
Gujarat 46
gunungan 58, 70, 159
Gunungjati, Sunan 79
Gunungpring 7–9, 25, 43, 47–9, 71, 78, 80, 83, 91–2, 94, 99, 112, 193, 205, 227–8
Gus Miek (Kyai Haji Hamim Djazuli) 48–9, 94, 205

habit 77, 83, 90, 132, 164, 168, 180, 183–4, 202, 220
    of devotion 68, 182
    of the heart 80, 94, 168–9, 214
Hamengkubuwono IX 3
Hamengkubuwono X 4, 39, 54, 236
al-Harawī, Alī ibn Abī Bakr 77, 91
Hasyim Asyari, Kyai Haji 217
heirloom 29, 36, 38, 63, 71–2, 96

Hejaz 100, 200
hermeneutic 20, 122, 133, 194, 213
　of communion 131, 134, 136, 187
　of openness and inclusion 156, 161, 165
　of self and otherness 122, 201
Hindu-Buddhist 3, 8, 26, 39, 41–2, 97, 108, 111, 135, 140–41, 143, 228
Hinduism 7, 11, 41, 54–5, 74, 135, 144, 166–7, 179, 196
Hindu-Javanese 5, 26, 29–32, 38–9, 45, 51, 53–8, 61, 70, 139–41, 143–4, 147–9, 151–3, 165, 179, 184, 202, 213, 242
history 3–4, 6, 9, 10, 17, 23, 26, 28, 31, 36–9, 44, 47, 51–2, 97, 115, 119, 129, 147, 149, 164, 168–9, 183, 185, 187, 193, 196, 207, 212, 216
　as communion with the past 19, 202, 221
　of Islamization in Java 38, 51, 97, 154
　of Javano-Catholic community 105, 113, 121, 123, 126
　as memory (memorialization) 19, 25, 29–30, 49, 194–5, 211
　of shrine and saint 19, 105, 109, 118, 134, 136
Hizbullah militia 129
hospitality 51, 78, 120
Hud, Prophet 94
hybridity 1, 19, 55, 73, 106, 109, 138, 143, 161, 196

Ibn al-ʿArabī 1, 33, 175
Ibn Qayyim al-Jawziyya 13
Ibn Taimiyya 11–14, 16
identity 4–5, 11, 15, 17, 19, 24, 26, 28–30, 32, 43–4, 47, 53, 56, 63, 72–3, 77–8, 88, 93, 96, 98, 113–14, 117, 120, 123–4, 131–2, 136, 138–41, 143, 152–3, 156, 164, 173, 185, 191, 195, 198, 200–202, 205, 207, 223, 232, 238, 241
　formation 1–3, 6, 10, 18–9, 28, 43, 50, 52, 62, 74, 79, 105–6, 111, 115, 120–21, 126–7, 133, 140, 161, 170, 178, 182, 192, 196, 212–13, 219, 224
　hermeneutics of 20, 213
　hybrid 20, 24, 42, 107, 128, 212, 219, 224
　Javano-Catholic 105, 109, 122, 128, 134–7, 187, 196, 199, 206
　Javano-Islamic (Muslim) 7, 23–5, 31–2, 37, 39, 44, 50–52, 55–6, 61, 68, 73, 77–8, 154, 196, 222, 227
imagination 46, 201, 213
Imogiri, Royal Mausoleum of 47, 53, 81, 95
incarnational 142, 150
inclusivity 29, 42, 45, 56, 61, 66, 70, 73, 101, 106, 198, 202, 204, 219, 221
inculturation
　of Catholic faith 8, 111, 115, 121, 122, 125, 134, 138, 141–3, 146–7, 150, 156, 201, 202
　of Islam 39
indigenization 142
intellectuals
　Javanese Catholic 106, 109, 122, 124, 139, 199, 200
intention 13, 63–4, 67, 77, 80, 82, 85, 87–8, 135, 171, 173, 184, 193, 203, 208
intercessors 16, 100
intergenerational 82, 204–6, 208, 216, 222
Islamization 37–8, 51, 154

Jabal al-Qāf 56–60
Jabalkat 43, 54, 56–7, 63, 66
Jamhari 43, 64, 67, 87, 98, 237
jatimurti 40
Jatiningsih Marian Shrine 176
Java Instituut 108, 140–41, 237
Jayengresmi, Raden 23–4, 51
Jesuit 8, 106, 115–16, 120, 127, 129, 130, 135, 146, 154, 171, 186, 231, 238
　mission in Java 110, 124
　missionaries 5–6, 109, 114, 116, 126, 196, 202, 212, 227–8
Jesus 120, 153–4, 163, 165, 179–81, 183–7, 210–11; *see also* Sacred Heart of Jesus
al-Jīlānī, ʿAbd al-Qādir 33, 45, 66, 216

Kadilangu 36
Kalam 220
Kalijaga, Sunan 7, 19, 25, 31–40, 42, 43–6, 48, 50, 52, 55–7, 61–2, 73–4, 89, 201–2, 212, 222, 227–8, 235
    and Javano-Islamic identity 25, 39
    and Mataram 31–7
    mystical initiation 33, 35
Kebatinan 40, 97, 174
kenduri 160, 203; *see also* "*slametan*"
Kerkeling, Hape 1, 237
kesawaban 86
al-Khaḍir 33–5, 40, 48
Kieser, Bernhard 120
Kitab Usulbiyah 29, 39, 41
Kotagedhe 53, 80, 91, 95, 178
kraton 4, 152, 227, 231
Kubra, Jumadil 8, 45–7, 94, 193, 233
Kudus, Sunan 32, 71

Laksmi 147, 149, 167
laku 32, 57, 61, 88–9, 92, 100, 168, 175, 197, 209, 227, 229; *see also* "*tirakat*"
Lipura 47, 136–7
Lombok (island of) 31, 93
Lourdes 8, 118, 157, 216
    of Java 110, 112, 171
    Our Lady of 117, 121, 179
Love 57, 59, 65, 98, 100, 124, 143, 146–7, 161, 165–6, 168, 170, 183, 186, 195, 213
    Uncreated 145
Loyola, Ignatius 1
lumen gentium 135

Maclaine Pont, Henri 141–3, 228
Madjid, Nurcholish 5
Magelang 48, 77, 94–5, 98, 127, 129
Mahabharata 34, 77, 209, 229
Majapahit 5, 24, 30–32, 35–6, 39, 42–3, 45–6, 51, 53, 55, 139, 141, 148, 202, 227
Malaya, Sèh 33, 35, 41; *see also* Kalijaga, Sunan
mandala 47, 137–8, 177, 193–6, 210
    of the Sacred Heart 137, 159
Marganingsih Marian shrine 171, 182, 193

mariology 120
martyrdom 126–8, 130–31, 133–4
Mary 109, 114–15, 118–20, 147–52, 154–5, 157–8, 165–8, 170–72, 183–5, 187, 198–9, 215, 217, 228, 234
Mataram 3, 8, 11, 23, 25–6, 30–31, 35, 37, 39, 44–7, 49, 53, 56, 81, 95, 137, 194, 201–2, 207, 227–8, 235
Mawlana Ishaq 46
Mawlana Maghribi 45–8
    shrine of 7, 26–7, 45, 52, 63, 71, 81, 84–5, 90–92, 95, 97–8, 193
Mawlana Malik Ibrahim 46
mawlid 71–2
Mecca 11, 37–8, 72, 83, 131, 184
Medina 71, 94
Memon, Muhammad 14, 239
memory 10, 25, 29, 30–31, 39, 45, 49, 56, 63, 67, 72, 74–5, 77–8, 114, 116–17, 125, 133, 137, 139, 158–9, 164, 168–70, 185, 195, 202–6, 211, 216, 221, 235
    identity as 105
    of the other 156
    of pilgrimage blessings 86
Merapi, Mount 7, 46–7, 94, 194
Mertens, Father 127, 131
Merton, Thomas 174, 239
Meru, Mount 57–8, 139, 238
mimetic 193, 155–6, 171
minbar 55
miracles 98, 121, 170, 212
mission 25, 108, 115, 120–21, 126, 129, 131, 134, 146, 151–2, 158, 176–7, 187, 205
    Catholic mission 6, 106–7, 118, 125, 139, 153, 164, 186, 227, 229
    Java mission 110, 113, 116, 127, 131, 202
    Jesuit 6, 124, 154
    Muntilan Museum of 133, 155
    Protestant 6–7
moksa 39–43
Morris, James W. 57, 60, 239
motivation 38, 80, 85–6, 91, 94–5, 164–5, 170, 172, 184, 207
Muḥammad, the Prophet 65, 71, 105

Muhammadiyah 15, 80, 117, 120, 200, 228
Muntilan 6–7, 25, 48, 106, 108, 112–13, 128–33, 168, 205, 227–8, 231, 242
  Mausoleum of 8, 109, 111–12, 126–7, 133–4, 136, 155, 185–6, 206
musafir 92, 94–5
Mutamakin, Ahmad 55, 243
mystical 24, 29–41, 46, 48, 58–9, 68, 75, 77, 90, 93–4, 174, 209
mysticism 16, 35, 43, 58, 96, 197, 228, 239, 241, 243
mystic(s) 1, 37, 175; *see also* mystic synthesis

nafs 57, 59–60, 88, 176, 208
Nahdlatul Ulama 14–15, 74, 80–81, 197, 200–201, 203, 213, 217, 228; *see also* traditionalist
nationalism 3, 125
The Netherlands 6, 117, 123–5, 140–41, 158, 171, 216
New Order 3–4, 30, 79
Nine Saints (of Java) 32, 42–3, 45–6, 81, 86, 94, 232; *see also* Wali Songo
nyekar 64, 82, 167–8, 183, 203, 228; *see also* sowan

O'Brien, Kate 177, 240
Orientalism 199
Orientalist 5, 108, 143, 152
  vision of Javanese culture 140, 142
Other, The 3, 18–19, 26, 42, 49, 51, 53, 58, 60–61, 63, 74, 87, 97, 114, 120, 122, 131, 137–8, 140–41, 150, 152, 154–6, 161, 164–5, 182–3, 185, 191, 193, 199, 201, 208–9, 213, 222–4
  religious 19, 15, 118–19, 126, 133–6, 144, 154, 182, 191, 198, 213
  trace of 52–3, 78, 135–6, 140, 161, 167
  visit to 150
otherness 2, 20, 52–3, 84, 88, 117, 122, 130, 133–4, 139, 140, 156, 160, 179, 185–6; *see also* alterity

Pakubuwana I 36
Pakubuwana XII 4, 240

Pancasila 9, 79, 232
  shrine 88
  tourism 3–4, 79
Pandanarang, Sunan 7, 19, 25–6, 42–4, 50, 57, 65, 69, 72, 74, 89, 182, 201, 203, 228
Parangtritis 7–8, 25, 27, 36, 46–7, 73, 95, 110, 193–4
peacefulness 87, 152, 164, 172–8, 183–5, 197, 207–9, 215; *see also tentrem*
Pemberton, John 4, 44, 240
perolehan (boon) 87, 207, 208
pesantren 77, 217, 228, 240
piety 11, 13, 81, 100, 134, 192, 202–3, 220, 243
Pigeaud, Th. 23, 33, 45–6, 236, 240
pneumatology 146
Prajnaparamita 147–9, 151, 167
  Mary of Ganjuran 150–51
prapatti 167
prayer 12, 16, 23, 36, 43, 49, 52, 54, 61, 63–7, 71, 84–5, 91–2, 95–7, 99, 116, 120, 125, 132, 135, 161, 165, 170–71, 174, 178, 180, 184–7, 194–5, 198, 203–4, 215, 222, 227
  intercessory 94
  interfaith 160
  of the Sacred Heart 125, 156–7, 159, 206
Prennthaler, Johannes 105, 109, 114–20, 134, 154, 156, 205, 228, 238, 240
protector 31, 100, 151, 170, 186
  The Protector of all (God) 16, 81
  Protectorship (of the saints) 16, 70, 81, 83
Protestant 6–7, 10–11, 160
  pilgrims 178, 182, 184–5
proximity 8, 35, 25, 31, 47, 83, 86, 111–12, 136, 165, 172, 182, 193, 205
  to God 57, 60, 81, 84, 91, 95, 98, 100, 229
  of the saints/righteous dead 12, 16
  spatial and cultural 7
Puhsarang 141
Pujasumarta, Mgr. 183

Qādirīya 11
qurbā 12

Rahmat, Raden 32
raḥmatan lil-'ālamin 14, 62, 200
rasa 40–41, 54, 95, 97, 100, 174–6, 197–8
resourcement 109, 114, 126, 133, 187
revivification 147, 194
Ricklefs, M.C. 8, 23, 29–32, 36–7, 41, 45, 47, 70, 77, 96, 235, 240, 228
Rinkes, D.A. 38, 41–2, 94, 240
rites of passage 68, 155, 169
rituals 6, 9, 19, 30, 51, 63, 65, 71, 85–8, 154, 158, 161, 185, 193, 195–8, 201–4, 211–14, 223
    of Sacred Heart 125–6, 180
    of the shrine 73, 156, 183
Robson, Stuart 48, 240
ruwahan 69–70

sacramentality 164, 210, 214, 220–21
Sacred Heart of Jesus 122, 125, 139, 145–8, 152, 156–60, 163, 165, 171, 180, 183–4, 187
    Sacred Heart Shrine 8, 47, 109–11, 121, 134, 136–7, 139, 153, 156, 163, 165, 168, 171, 183, 186–7, 193–4, 206, 210, 213–14, 216, 228–9; *see also* Ganjuran
sainthood 30–31, 42–4, 57, 59, 70–73, 82, 95, 202–4, 206, 215, 227, 229
    Christian 11, 234
    Muslim (Islamic) 15–17, 31, 59, 81, 83
saints 1, 10, 12, 19–20, 23, 25, 30, 36, 42, 52–3, 55–75, 78, 80–91, 93–5, 98–100, 10, 132–3, 159, 165, 167, 191–2, 194–5, 197–8, 201, 203–6, 208, 214, 221, 234–5
    Christian/Catholic 1, 116, 157, 176
    Muslim 7, 16–17, 24, 31–2, 38, 43–50, 184, 202, 212, 216, 222, 227–9
        Javanese Muslim 7, 19, 39, 154
    relics of 72, 75, 132, 198
Samarqand 62
sangkan paran 40–41, 59
Sanjaya, Richardus 8, 112, 126–7, 129–34, 185–6, 201, 206, 228, 235
Santiago de Compostella 19
santri 69, 100, 155, 232
    santri-type pilgrims 90, 92–4, 96–9

Santri, Raden (Pangeran Singasari) 7, 25, 47–9, 83, 193, 228, 231, 240
Sarikrama, Barnabas 114–16, 118, 206, 228, 242
Sasana Sunu, Serat 89
Schmutzer, Eduard J.M. 142, 241
The Schmutzers 8, 110, 121–3, 125–6, 138, 140, 143, 158, 165, 171, 201–2, 206
    Josef Schmutzer 124, 125, 135–7, 141–7, 149–51, 153–4, 161, 165, 194, 199, 213, 229, 241
    Julius Schmutzer 124, 125, 229
Semarang 42–3, 57, 65, 72, 130
    archbishop of 120, 132, 176
    archdiocese of 112, 163, 183
    Jesuit Provincial Office xi, 130, 231
sembah 64, 163, 166–7
Senapati, Panembahan 8, 36, 47–8, 137, 207, 227–8, 236
Sendang Dhuwur Mosque 55–6
Sendangsono Grotto ix, xiii, 8, 25, 109–21, 127, 132, 134, 136, 154–6, 166–73, 175, 178–9, 181–4, 193, 198, 205, 212, 214, 216, 228, 232, 234, 237, 242–3
Shādhiliyya 48–9
Shalawat Katolik 155
Siddiq, Achmad 200, 232
silsila 100, 204–5
Sīmurgh 57, 59
sirr 41, 175, 228
slamet 87, 100, 197, 208, 229
    Kyai Slamet 96
slametan 63, 66–70, 73–4, 88, 94, 160, 198, 203, 206, 229, 232, 243
Soegijapranata, Mgr. 106, 128, 163, 177, 242
Southeast Asia 216
sowan 81–2, 166, 203; *see also nyekar*
space 9, 85, 90–91, 100, 105, 138, 154, 159, 164–5, 172, 179, 193, 194–5, 210–13, 217
    in-between 74
    liminal 57, 60
Spirit, The 10, 146–7, 158, 161, 175
    guardian/tutelary spirits 69, 117–18
Stange, Paul 40, 174, 242
stranger 44, 85, 92
al-Subkī, Taqī al-Dīn 12, 15

Suharyo, Mgr. Ignatius 113, 120, 176
Sultan Agung (of Mataram) 23, 36, 45–8, 53, 207, 227
Suluk Déwaruci 34
Sumatra 11, 94, 185
sunna 11, 13
Surabaya 23, 79, 91, 97
Surakarta, Royal House of 3–5, 8, 24–6, 28, 30, 34, 39, 45, 54, 56, 62, 67, 70–71, 75, 93, 148, 194, 197, 227, 240
al-Suyūti 14
Swara-Tama 106, 123, 130, 159, 170, 187
synthesis 19, 74–5, 77, 161, 200, 221–2
  mystic synthesis 5, 29–31, 34, 36–7, 39, 45, 53, 70, 90, 96–7, 108; *see also* mystic
Syria 116, 214

tahlilan 203
Tales of the Prophets 39
tasbīḥ 65
tawakkul 94
tawassul 65–6, 71, 84, 94
Taylor, Christopher 11–14, 17, 69, 88, 242
Tebu Ireng, Pesantren 217
Tegalrejo Islamic School (Pesantren) 48, 77
Tembayat 7, 9, 23, 25–6, 42–5, 52–4, 56–60, 63, 65–7, 69, 71, 79–81, 87–8, 91, 98, 171, 182, 193, 203, 207, 209, 212–13, 228, 234
  saint of 57, 61, 72, 201
  Sunan 43, 63–4, 93
tentrem 87, 100, 173–5, 197, 208–9, 229; *see also* "*slamet*"
  Nyai Tentrem 96
terbangan 71, 133, 154–6
theology 17, 124, 142, 146, 150–51, 155, 164, 192, 211, 219, 224, 241; *see also* comparative theology of religions 186
tirakat 36, 67, 77, 89, 95, 137, 158
  pilgrimage as 57, 61, 88, 100, 168, 175, 197, 207–9, 229; *see also* "*laku*"
tirtha yatra 179
traditionalist (Muslims) 14–15, 68, 74, 81, 84, 197, 199–201, 203–5, 212, 216, 228; *see also* Nahdlatul Ulama

Trinity, The 144–5, 165
Trowulan 141
Turner, Victor 173, 181, 242

unveiling of self 82, 85, 164, 180–81
Utomo, Gregorius 126, 152, 156

van Driessche, Henricus 186
van Lith, Franciscus 5–6, 8, 106–10, 112–14, 116, 118, 127, 131, 133–4, 140–41, 168, 177, 201–2, 205–6, 212, 227–8, 237–8, 242
van Rijckevorsel, L. 163, 240
veneration of saints 9, 11, 63, 68–72, 75, 139, 156–7, 159, 169, 178, 182, 198, 215–17, 219–20, 222, 228
Virgin, The 105, 109, 148, 150
Vishnu 68, 70, 73, 144, 149, 206, 232
Volksraad 123–4, 241

Wahid, Abdurrahman 80–81, 217
walāya 15, 31, 81, 83, 95, 229
wali-ship 43; *see also* sainthood
Wali Songo 7, 25, 32, 43, 89, 184, 201, 232; *see also* Nine Saints
  pilgrimage tradition to 25, 86
wayang 38, 58, 71, 144, 229
wening 176
Wheeler, Brannon 72, 243
Woodward, Mark 2, 5, 37, 39, 67–8, 243
World Exhibition 140, 152–3

Xavier College 106, 113
Xavier, Francis 6, 158

Yemen 94
Yogyakarta 3–5, 8, 25, 27, 46, 79–80, 94–5, 98, 106, 108, 110, 116, 120–21, 127, 129, 169, 173–4, 176–8, 181, 200
  royal house/sultanate of 3, 6, 8, 26, 28, 30, 47–8, 54, 56, 62, 70–71, 74–5, 148, 152, 159, 193–4, 197, 210, 227–9

ziarah 2, 32, 45, 64, 67, 72, 77, 80–81, 89, 98, 229, 232, 235, 237–8